THEY COULDN'T FIX A SHOE LIKE THIS.

久保帯人

FULL Color!!!
The hellish full-color
section comes to you
in its full of hell form!
Now! Enjoy a hell of a
taste!

My favorite shoe broke.
I'm looking for a
shoe-repair master.
-Tite Kubo

Note: pages 67-86 were full color in the Japanese graphic novel.

BLEACH is author Tite Kubo's second title. Kubo made his debut with *ZOMBIEPOWDER.*, a four-volume series for *WEEKLY SHONEN JUMP.* To date, *BLEACH* has been translated into numerous languages and has also inspired an animated TV series that began airing in the U.S. in 2006. Beginning its serialization in 2001, *BLEACH* is still a mainstay in the pages of *WEEKLY SHONEN JUMP.* In 2005, *BLEACH* was awarded the prestigious Shogakukan Manga Award in the *shonen* (boys) category.

BLEACH
Vol. 19: The Black Moon Rising
The SHONEN JUMP Manga Edition

STORY AND ART BY
TITE KUBO

English Adaptation/Lance Caselman
Translation/Joe Yamazaki
Touch-Up Art & Lettering/Mark McMurray
Design/Sean Lee
Editors/Yuki Takagaki & Pancha Diaz

Editor in Chief, Books/Alvin Lu
Editor in Chief, Magazines/Marc Weidenbaum
VP of Publishing Licensing/Rika Inouye
VP of Sales/Gonzalo Ferreyra
Sr. VP of Marketing/Liza Coppola
Publisher/Hyoe Narita

Printed in the U.S.A.

Published by VIZ Media, LLC
P.O. Box 77010
San Francisco, CA 94107

SHONEN JUMP Manga Edition
10 9 8 7 6 5
First printing, June 2007
Fifth printing, May 2008

www.viz.com

THE WORLD'S
MOST POPULAR MANGA

SHONEN JUMP

www.shonenjump.com

No, nothing can change my world.

BLEACH19 THE BLACK MOON RISING

Shonen Jump Manga

STARS AND

Orihime Inoue

Byakuya Kuchiki

Ichigo Kurosaki

井上織姫

黒崎一護

plot

In the aftermath of Rukia's last-minute rescue, Yoruichi faces her former subordinate Soi Fon in mortal combat, while the 13 Court Guard Companies teeter on the brink of civil war. Meanwhile, Ichigo and Byakuya Kuchiki square off in the final bloody duel that will decide Rukia's fate—and their own!

BLEACH ALL

日番谷冬獅郎
Tôshirô Hitsugaya

四楓院夜一
Yoruichi Shihôin

Soi Fon

砕蜂

STORIES

BLEACH 19

THE BLACK MOON RISING

Contents

159. LONG WAY TO SAY GOODBYE

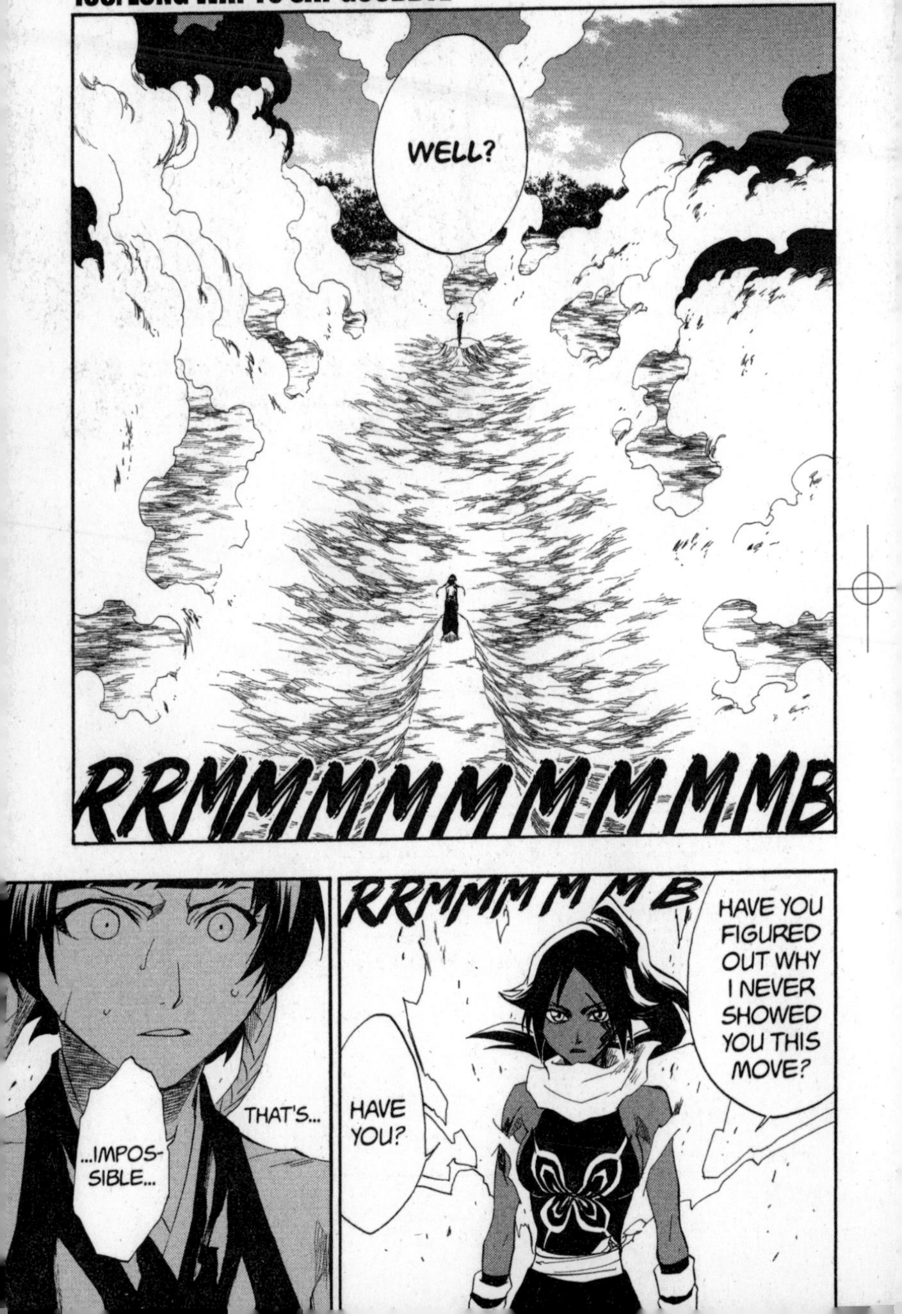

WELL?
RRMMMMMMMMMMB
RRMMMMMMB
HAVE YOU FIGURED OUT WHY I NEVER SHOWED YOU THIS MOVE?
HAVE YOU?
THAT'S...
...IMPOS-SIBLE...

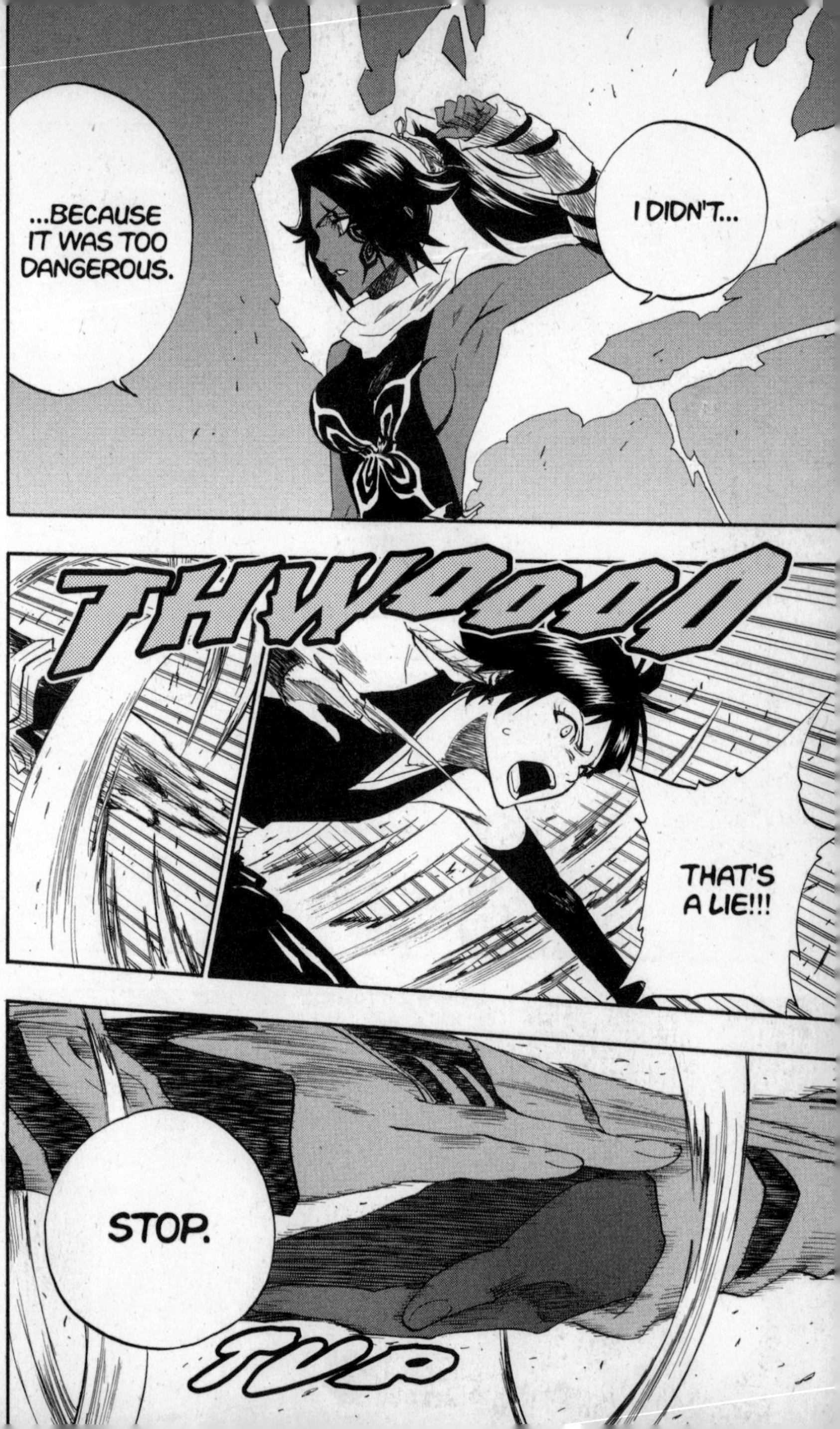
I DIDN'T...
...BECAUSE IT WAS TOO DANGEROUS.
THWOOOD
THAT'S A LIE!!!
STOP.
TUP

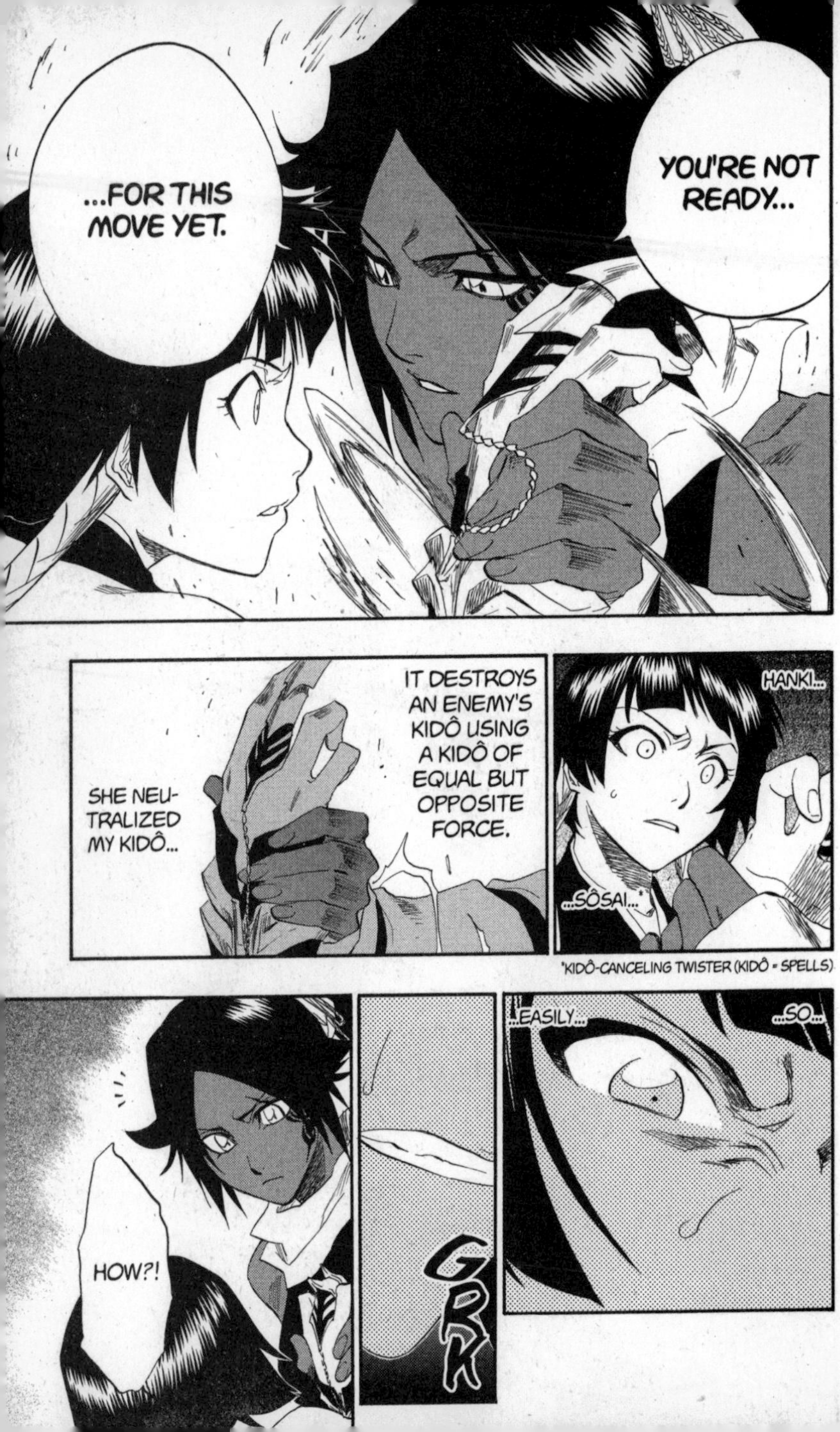
YOU'RE NOT READY...
...FOR THIS MOVE YET.
HANKI...
...SÔSAI...*
IT DESTROYS AN ENEMY'S KIDÔ USING A KIDÔ OF EQUAL BUT OPPOSITE FORCE.
SHE NEU-TRALIZED MY KIDÔ...
...SO...
...EASILY...
GRK
HOW?!

*KIDÔ-CANCELING TWISTER (KIDÔ = SPELLS).

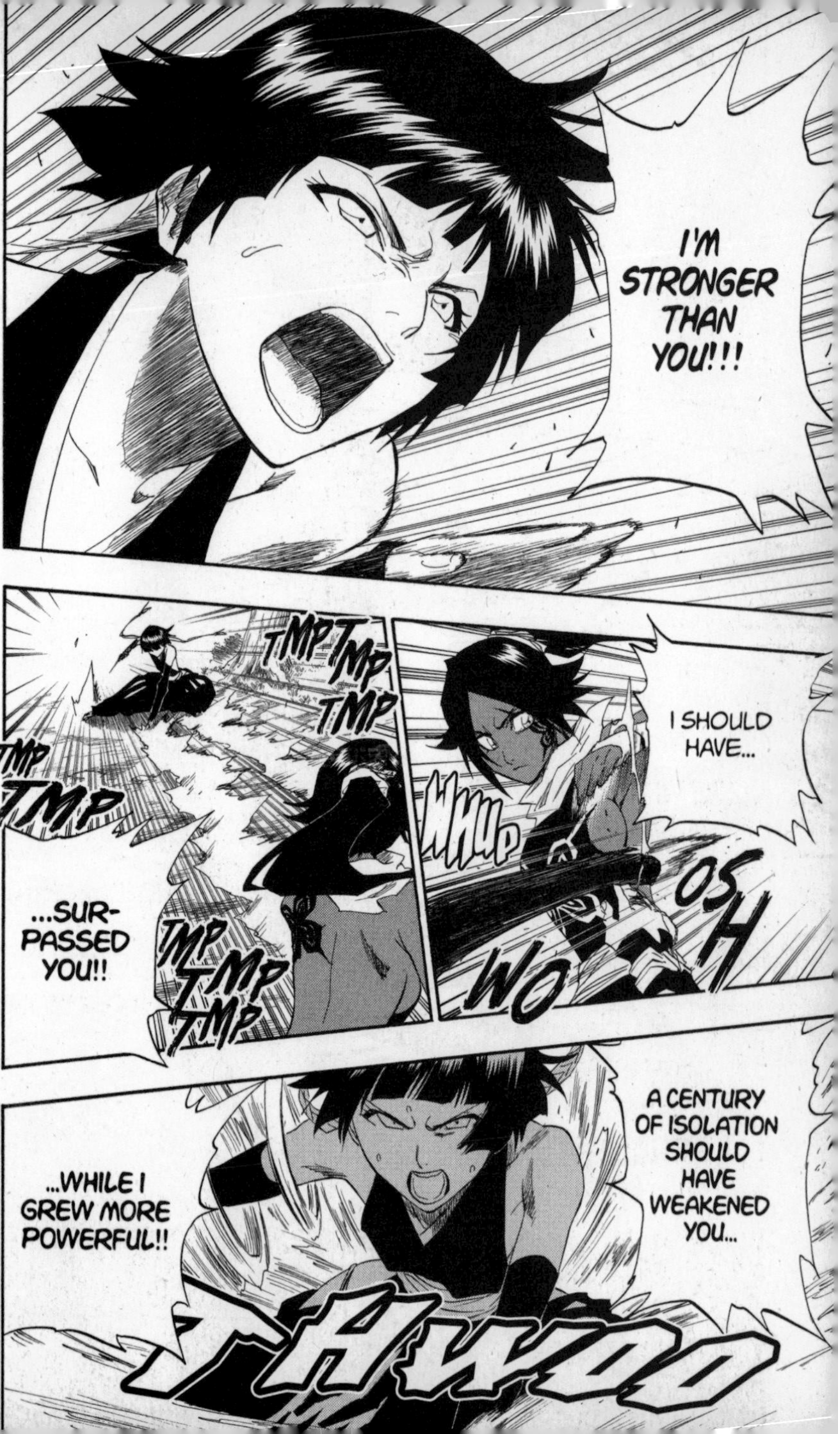
I'M STRONGER THAN YOU!!!
I SHOULD HAVE...
WHUP
WOOSH
TMP TMP TMP
TMP TMP
...SUR-PASSED YOU!!
TMP TMP TMP TMP
A CENTURY OF ISOLATION SHOULD HAVE WEAKENED YOU...
...WHILE I GREW MORE POWERFUL!!
THWOO

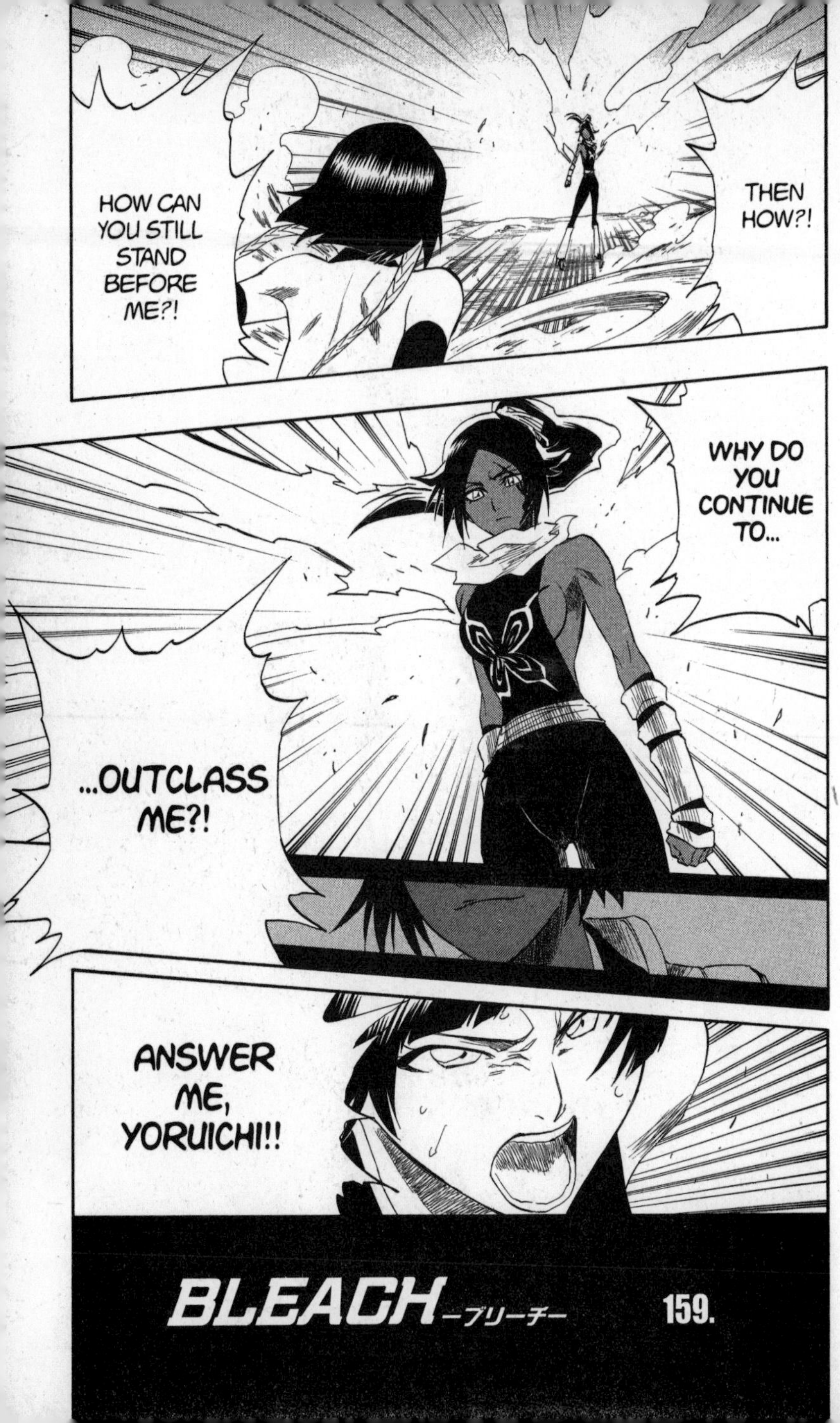
THEN HOW?!
HOW CAN YOU STILL STAND BEFORE ME?!
WHY DO YOU CONTINUE TO...
...OUTCLASS ME?!
ANSWER ME, YORUICHI!!

BLEACH —ブリーチ— 159.

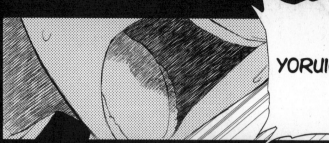

YORUICHI!!!

LONG WAY TO
SAY GOODBYE

...SHAOLIN?

DO YOU
SEE...

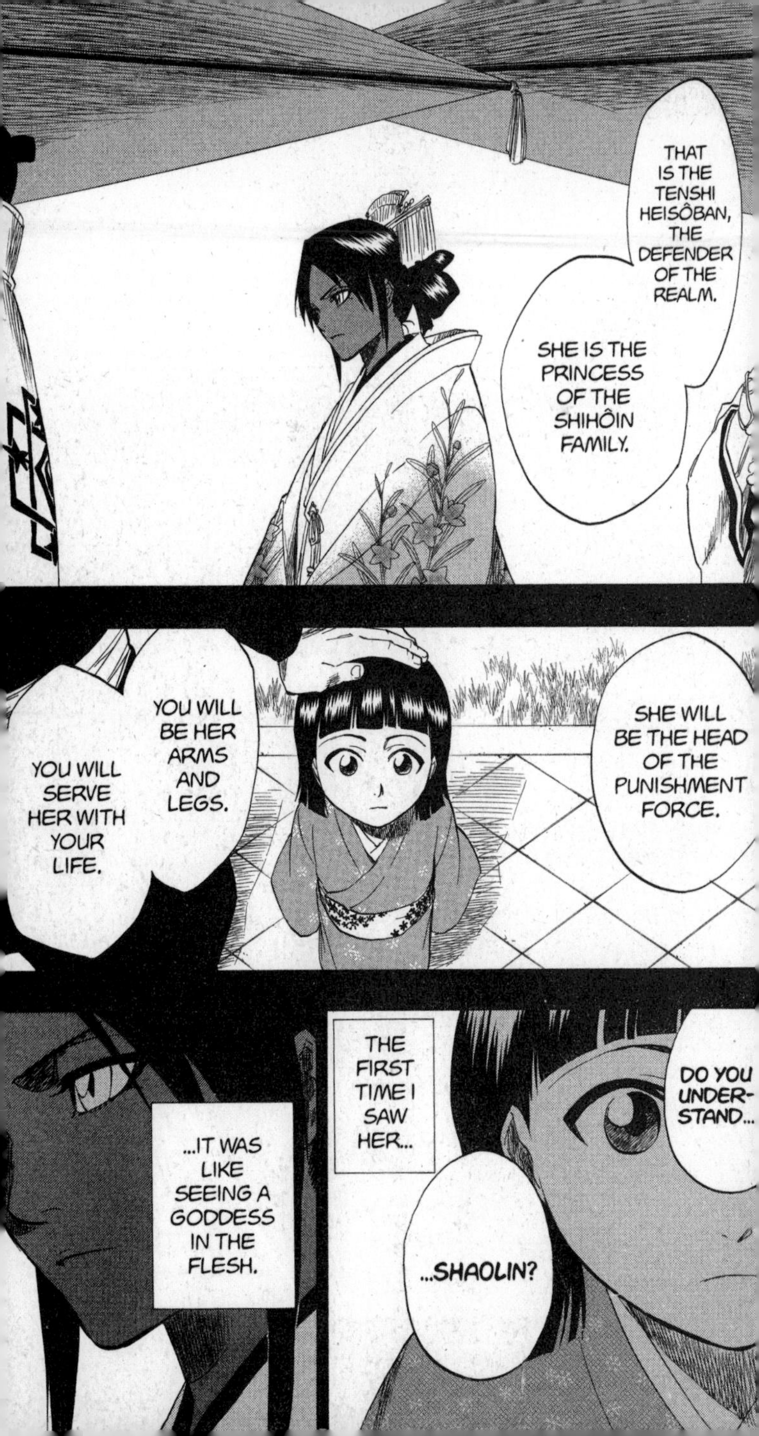
THAT IS THE TENSHI HEISÔBAN, THE DEFENDER OF THE REALM.
SHE IS THE PRINCESS OF THE SHIHÔIN FAMILY.
SHE WILL BE THE HEAD OF THE PUNISHMENT FORCE.
YOU WILL BE HER ARMS AND LEGS.
YOU WILL SERVE HER WITH YOUR LIFE.
DO YOU UNDER-STAND...
...SHAOLIN?
THE FIRST TIME I SAW HER...
...IT WAS LIKE SEEING A GODDESS IN THE FLESH.

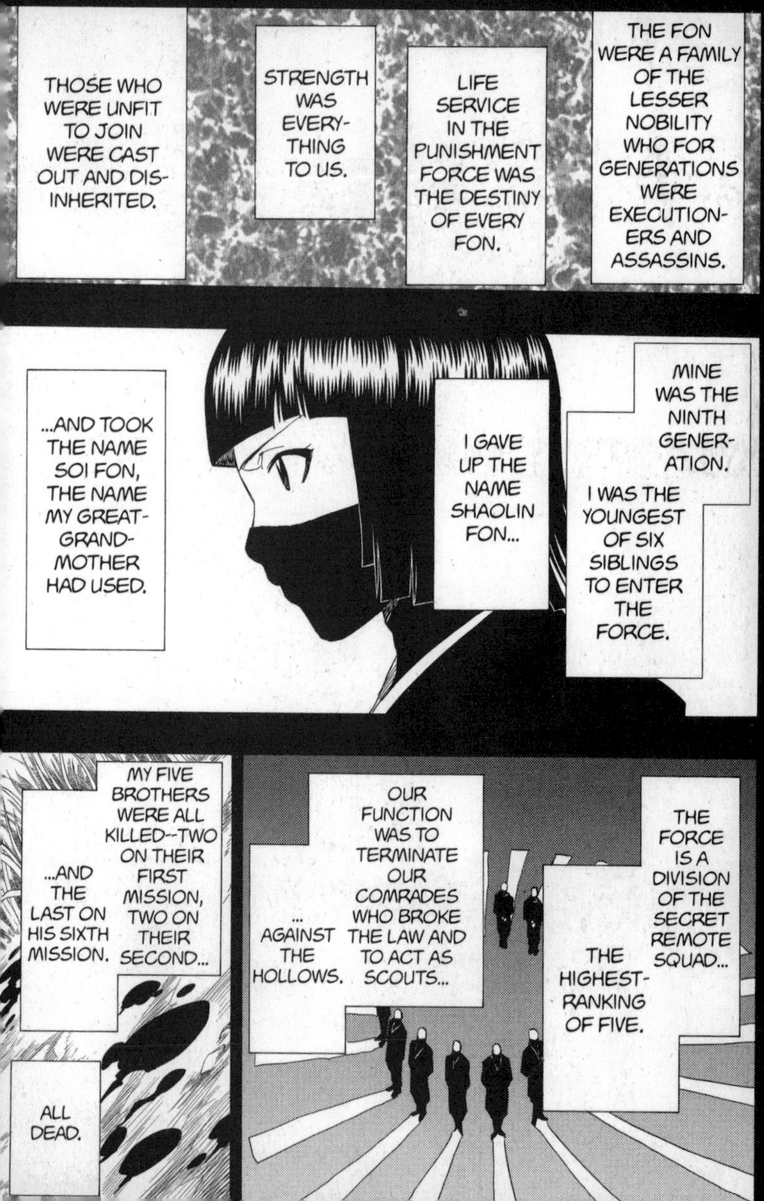
THE FON WERE A FAMILY OF THE LESSER NOBILITY WHO FOR GENERATIONS WERE EXECUTIONERS AND ASSASSINS.
LIFE SERVICE IN THE PUNISHMENT FORCE WAS THE DESTINY OF EVERY FON.
STRENGTH WAS EVERYTHING TO US.
THOSE WHO WERE UNFIT TO JOIN WERE CAST OUT AND DISINHERITED.
MINE WAS THE NINTH GENERATION.
I WAS THE YOUNGEST OF SIX SIBLINGS TO ENTER THE FORCE.
I GAVE UP THE NAME SHAOLIN FON...
...AND TOOK THE NAME SOI FON, THE NAME MY GREAT-GRANDMOTHER HAD USED.
THE FORCE IS A DIVISION OF THE SECRET REMOTE SQUAD...
THE HIGHEST-RANKING OF FIVE.
OUR FUNCTION WAS TO TERMINATE OUR COMRADES WHO BROKE THE LAW AND TO ACT AS SCOUTS...
...AGAINST THE HOLLOWS.
MY FIVE BROTHERS WERE ALL KILLED--TWO ON THEIR FIRST MISSION, TWO ON THEIR SECOND...
...AND THE LAST ON HIS SIXTH MISSION.
ALL DEAD.

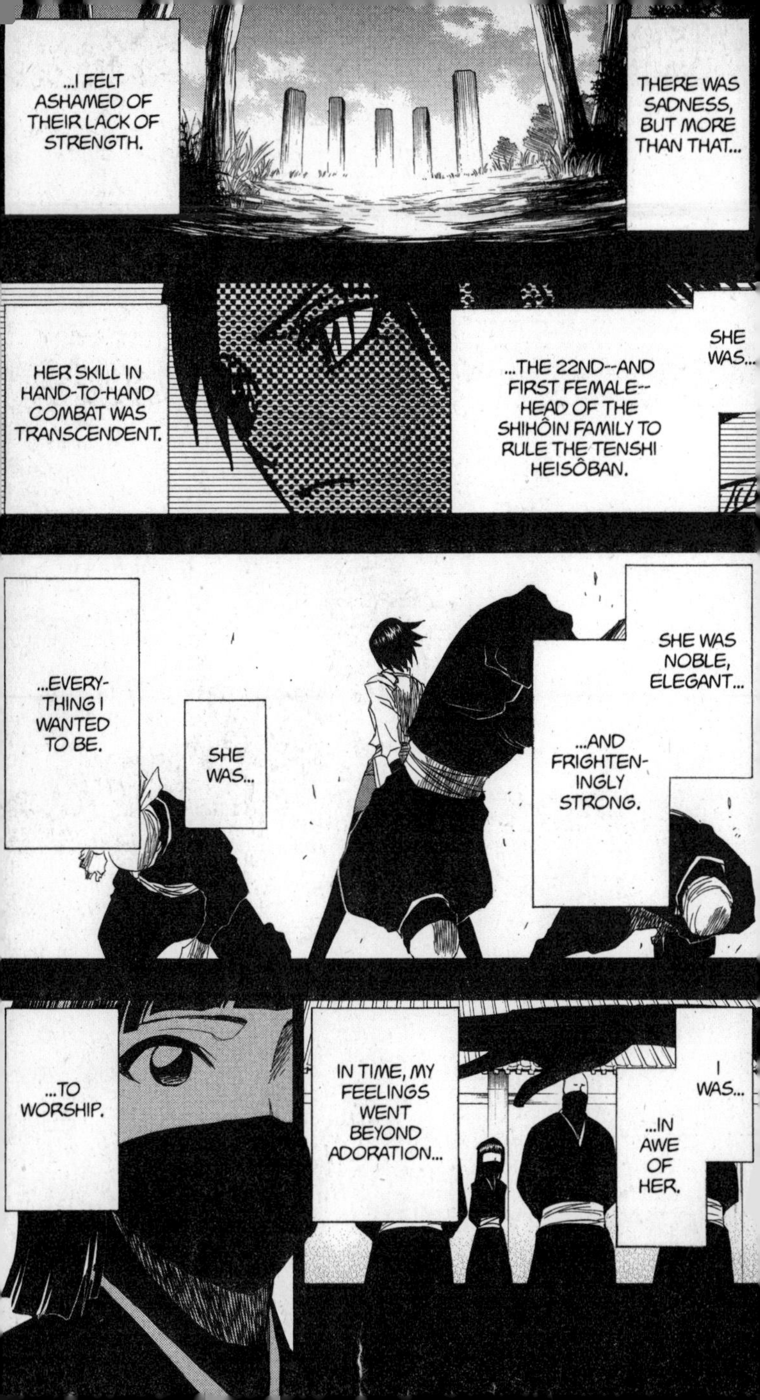
THERE WAS SADNESS, BUT MORE THAN THAT...
...I FELT ASHAMED OF THEIR LACK OF STRENGTH.
SHE WAS...
...THE 22ND--AND FIRST FEMALE--HEAD OF THE SHIHÔIN FAMILY TO RULE THE TENSHI HEISÔBAN.
HER SKILL IN HAND-TO-HAND COMBAT WAS TRANSCENDENT.
SHE WAS NOBLE, ELEGANT...
...AND FRIGHTEN-INGLY STRONG.
SHE WAS...
...EVERY-THING I WANTED TO BE.
I WAS...
...IN AWE OF HER.
IN TIME, MY FEELINGS WENT BEYOND ADORATION...
...TO WORSHIP.

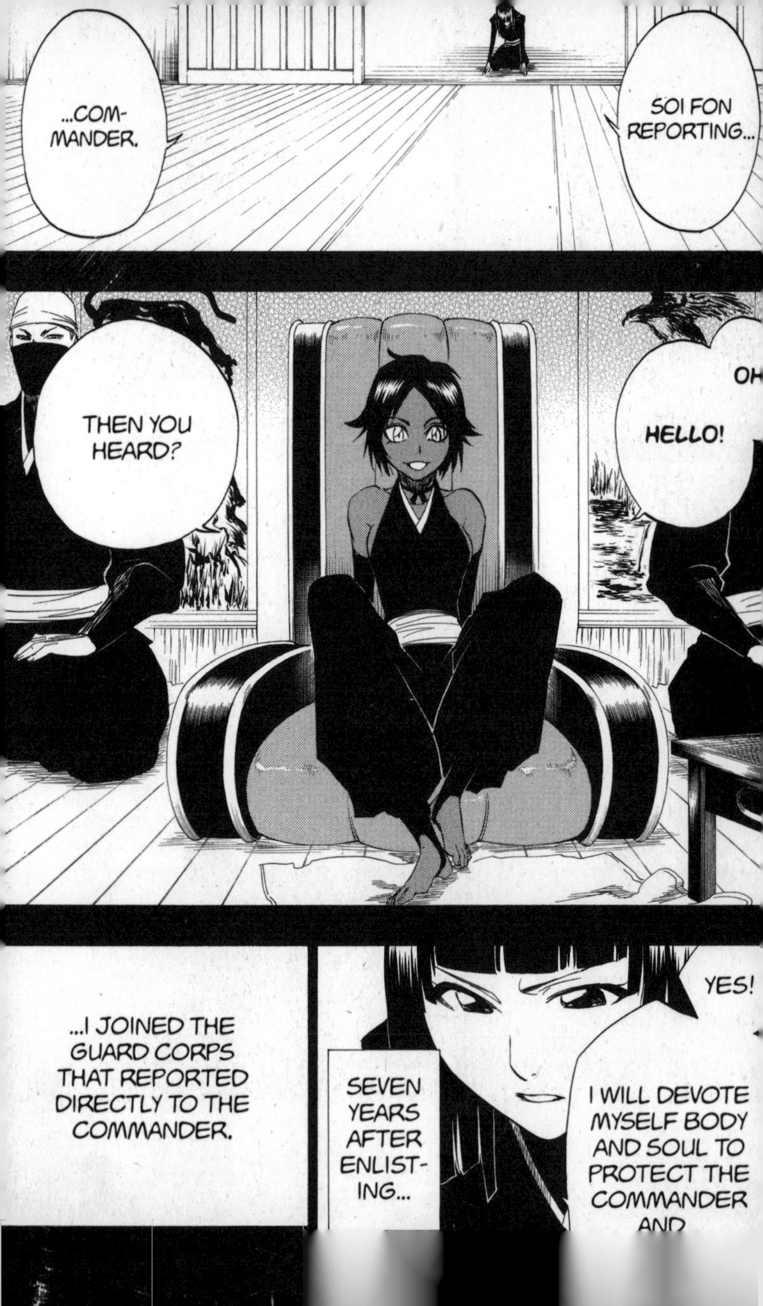
SOI FON REPORTING...
...COM-MANDER.
OH
HELLO!
THEN YOU HEARD?
YES!
I WILL DEVOTE MYSELF BODY AND SOUL TO PROTECT THE COMMANDER AND
SEVEN YEARS AFTER ENLIST-ING...
...I JOINED THE GUARD CORPS THAT REPORTED DIRECTLY TO THE COMMANDER.

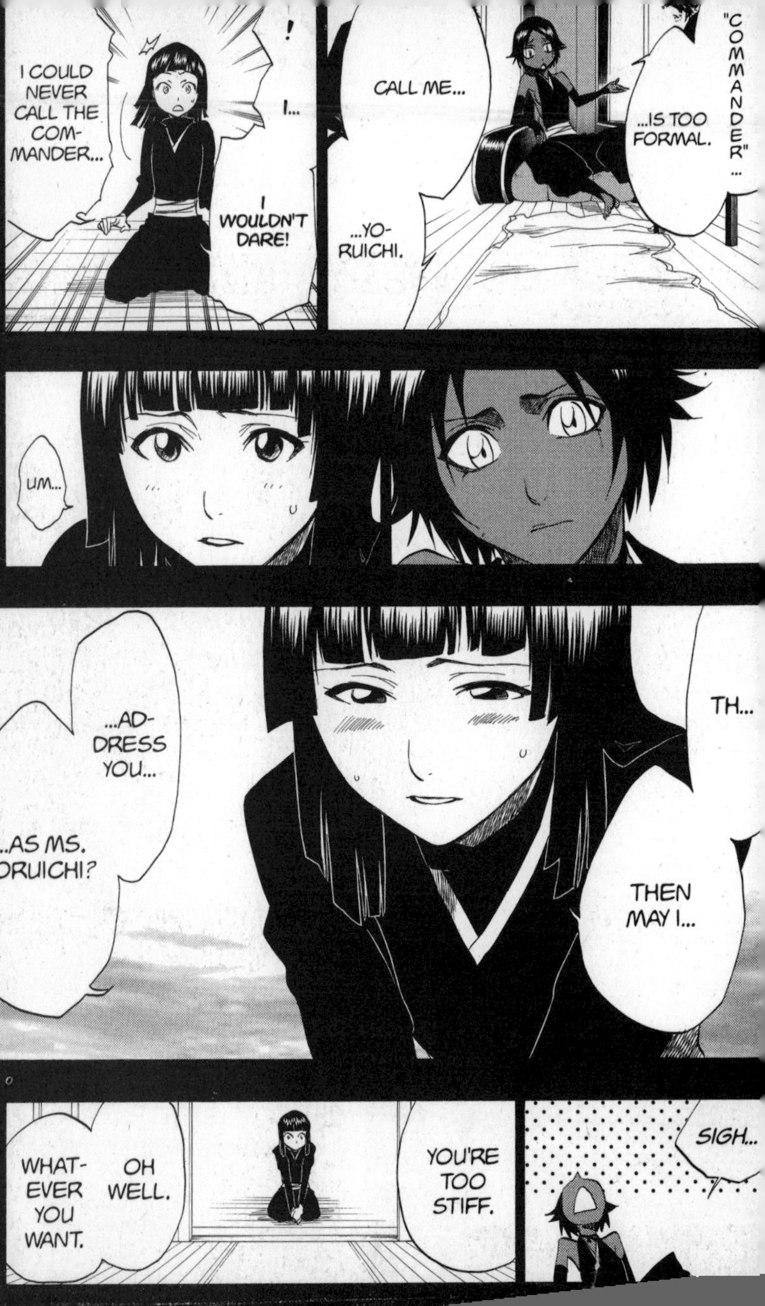
"COMMANDER" ...
...IS TOO FORMAL.
CALL ME...
...YO-RUICHI.
!
I...
I WOULDN'T DARE!
I COULD NEVER CALL THE COM-MANDER...
UM...
TH...
THEN MAY I...
...AD-DRESS YOU...
...AS MS. YORUICHI?
SIGH...
YOU'RE TOO STIFF.
OH WELL.
WHAT-EVER YOU WANT.

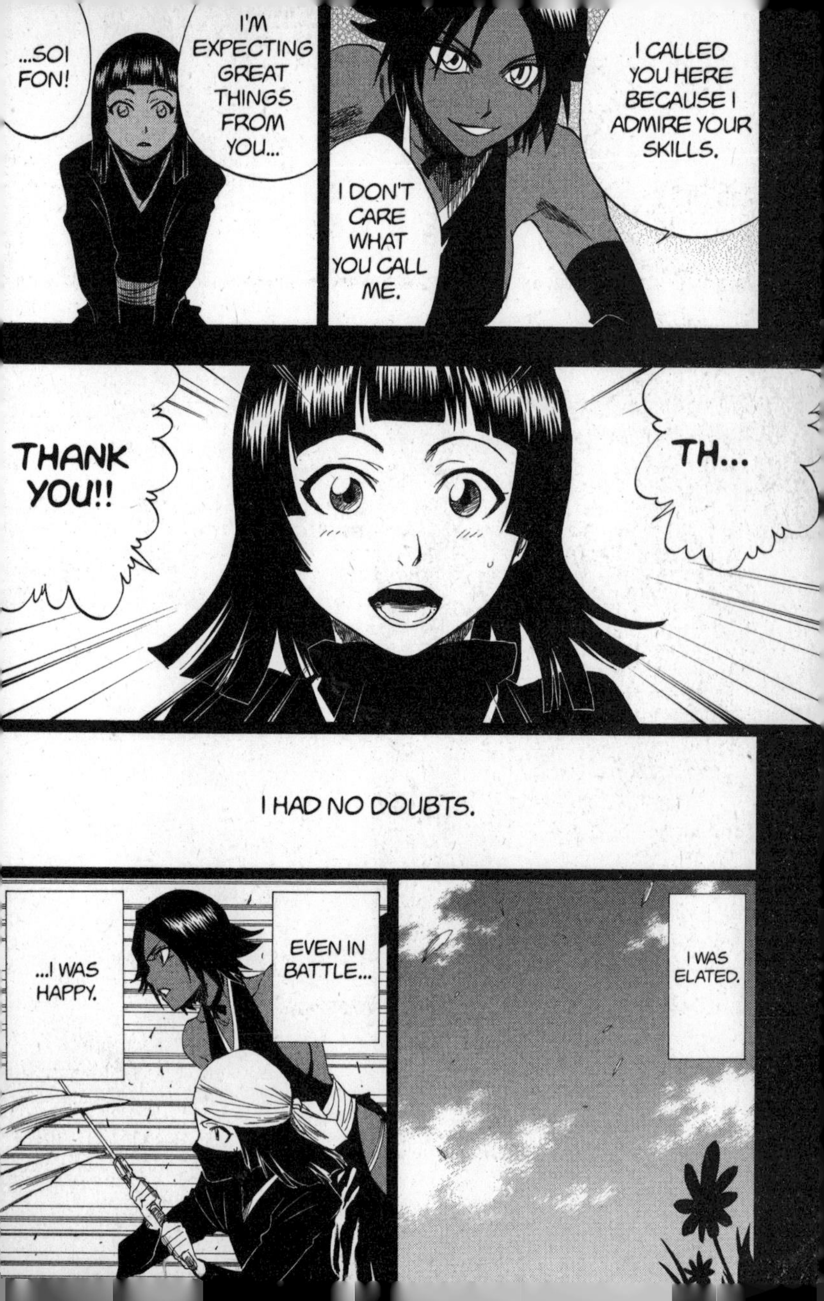
I CALLED YOU HERE BECAUSE I ADMIRE YOUR SKILLS.
I DON'T CARE WHAT YOU CALL ME.
I'M EXPECTING GREAT THINGS FROM YOU...
...SOI FON!
TH...
THANK YOU!!
I HAD NO DOUBTS.
I WAS ELATED.
EVEN IN BATTLE...
...I WAS HAPPY.

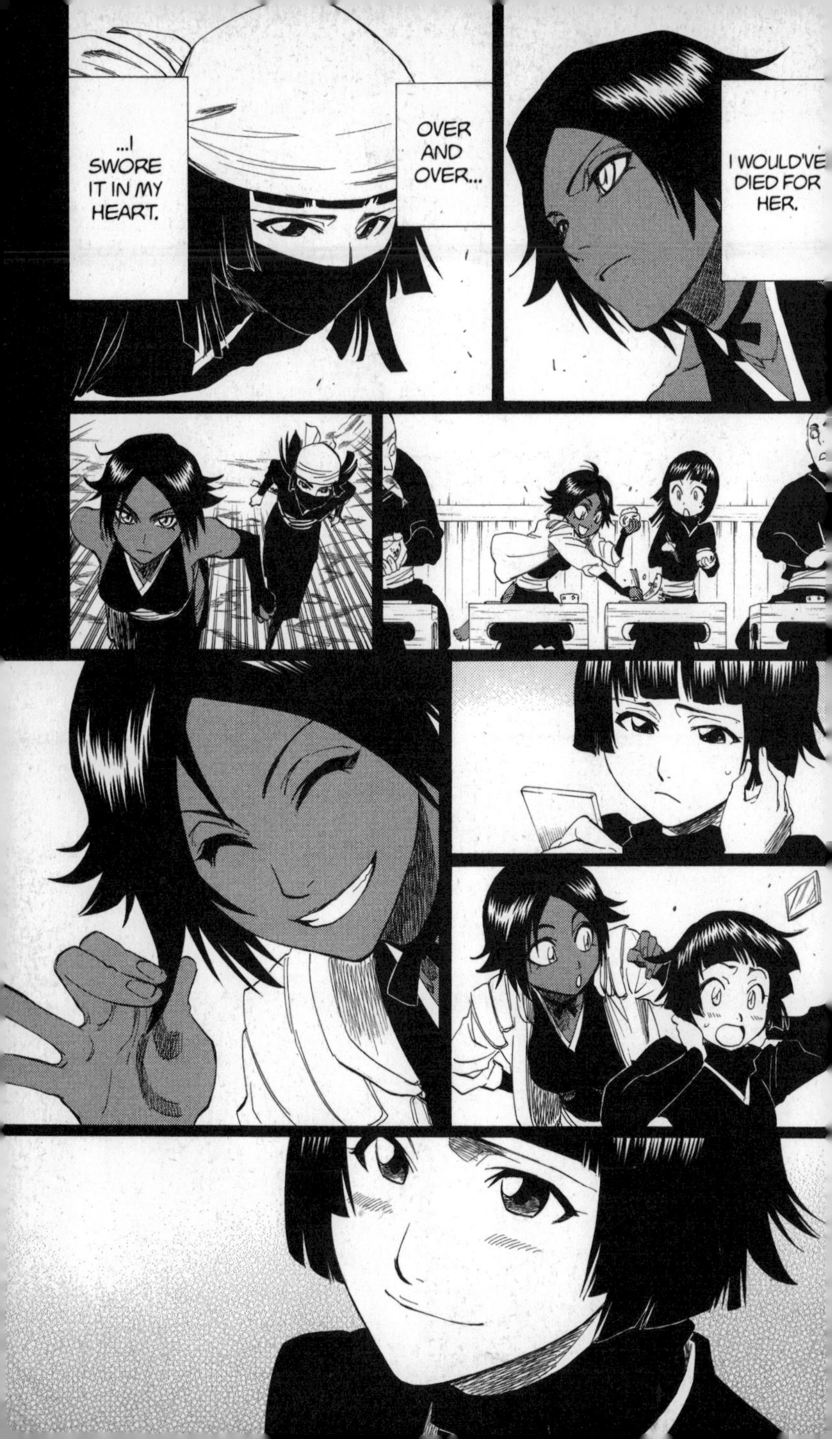
I WOULD'VE DIED FOR HER.
OVER AND OVER...
...I SWORE IT IN MY HEART.

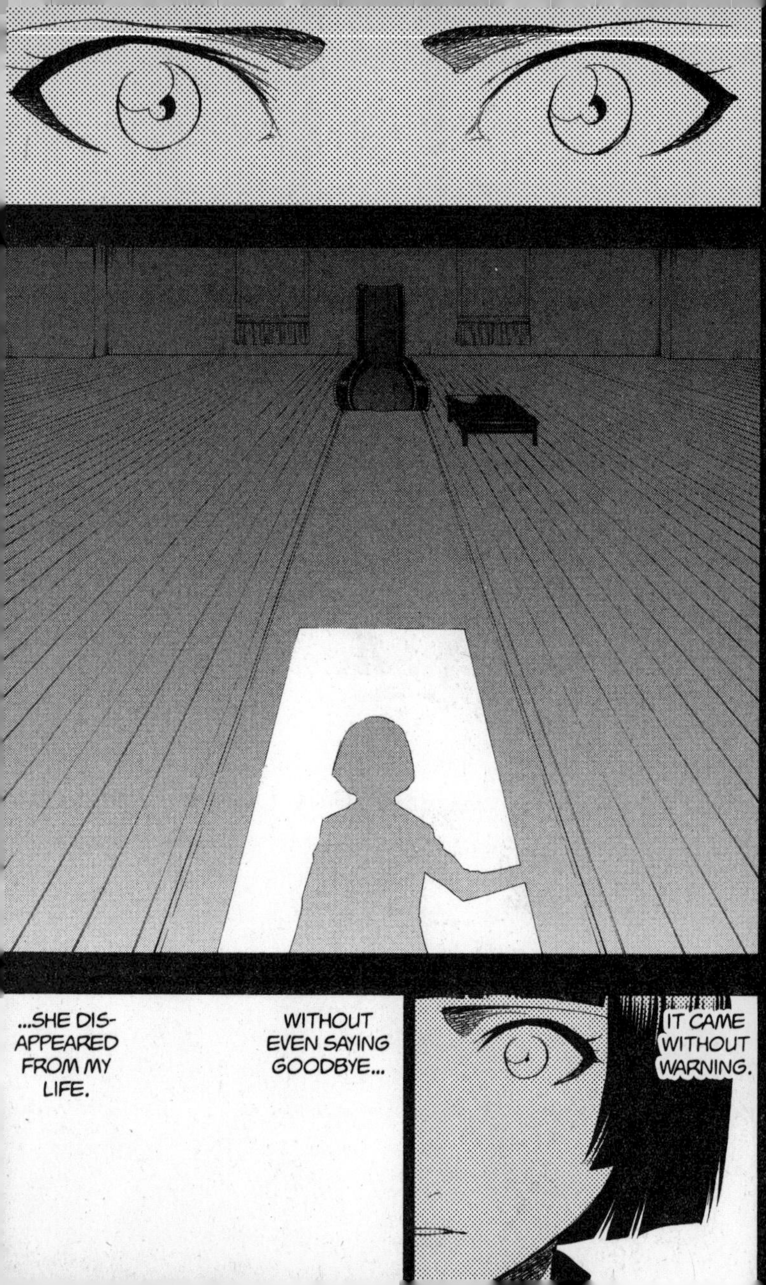
IT CAME WITHOUT WARNING.
WITHOUT EVEN SAYING GOODBYE...
...SHE DIS-APPEARED FROM MY LIFE.

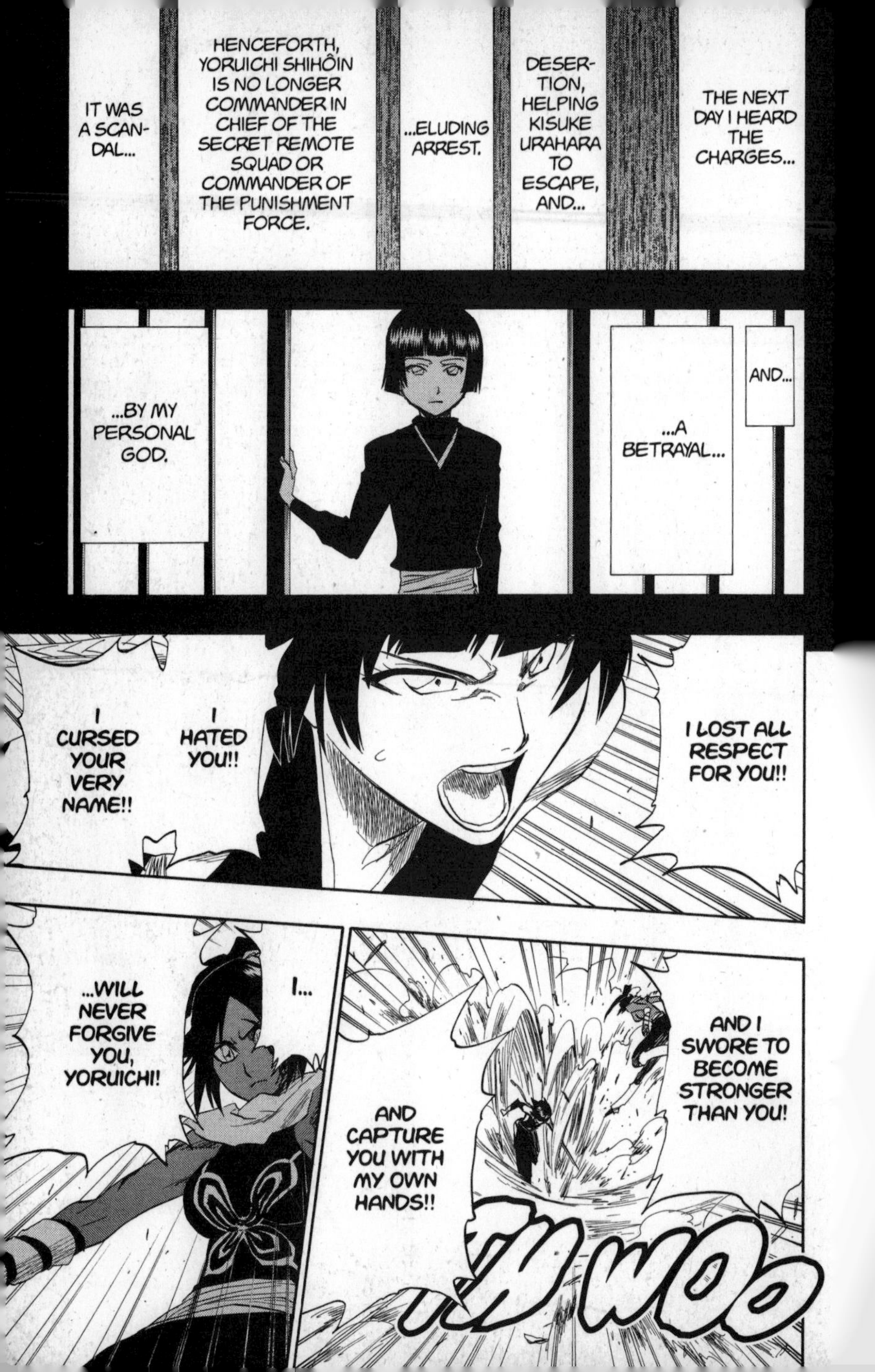
THE NEXT DAY I HEARD THE CHARGES...
DESER-TION, HELPING KISUKE URAHARA TO ESCAPE, AND...
...ELUDING ARREST.
HENCEFORTH, YORUICHI SHIHÔIN IS NO LONGER COMMANDER IN CHIEF OF THE SECRET REMOTE SQUAD OR COMMANDER OF THE PUNISHMENT FORCE.
IT WAS A SCAN-DAL...
AND...
...A BETRAYAL...
...BY MY PERSONAL GOD.
I LOST ALL RESPECT FOR YOU!!
I HATED YOU!!
I CURSED YOUR VERY NAME!!
AND I SWORE TO BECOME STRONGER THAN YOU!
AND CAPTURE YOU WITH MY OWN HANDS!!
I...
...WILL NEVER FORGIVE YOU, YORUICHI!

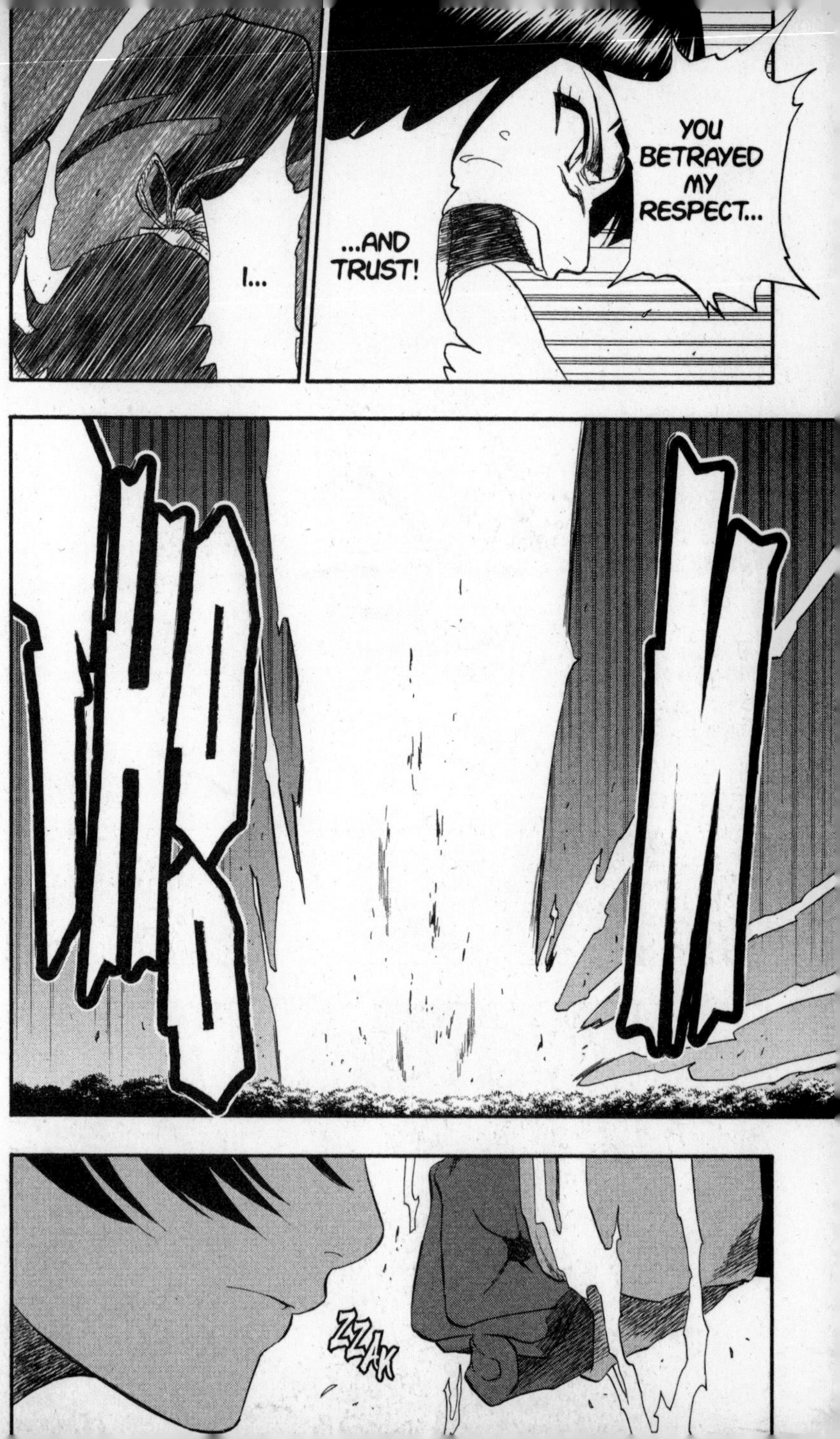
YOU BETRAYED MY RESPECT...
...AND TRUST!
I...
ZZAK

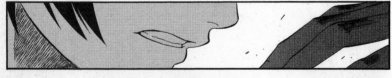

WHY?

WHY?!

KRK

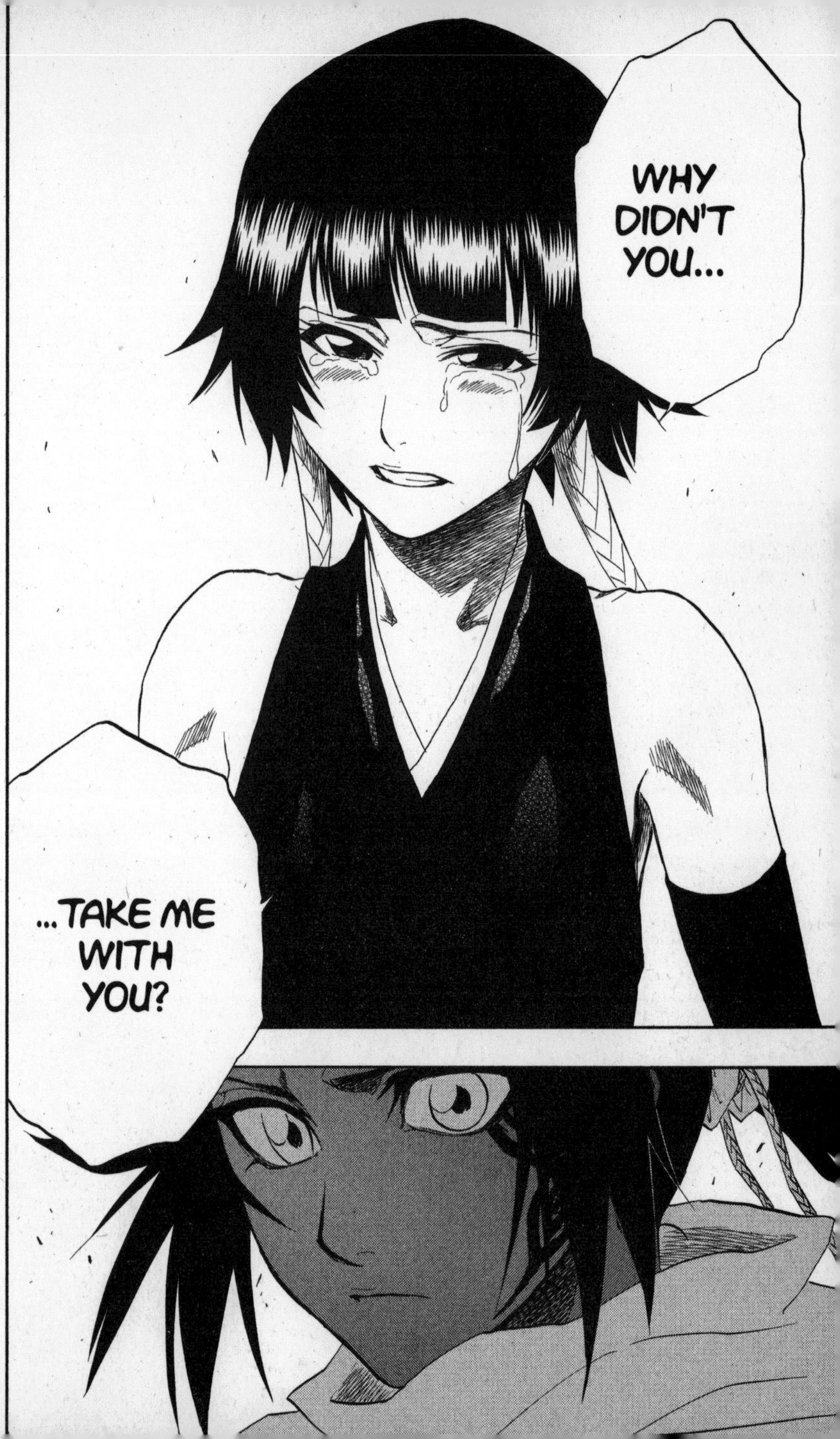
WHY DIDN'T YOU...
...TAKE ME WITH YOU?

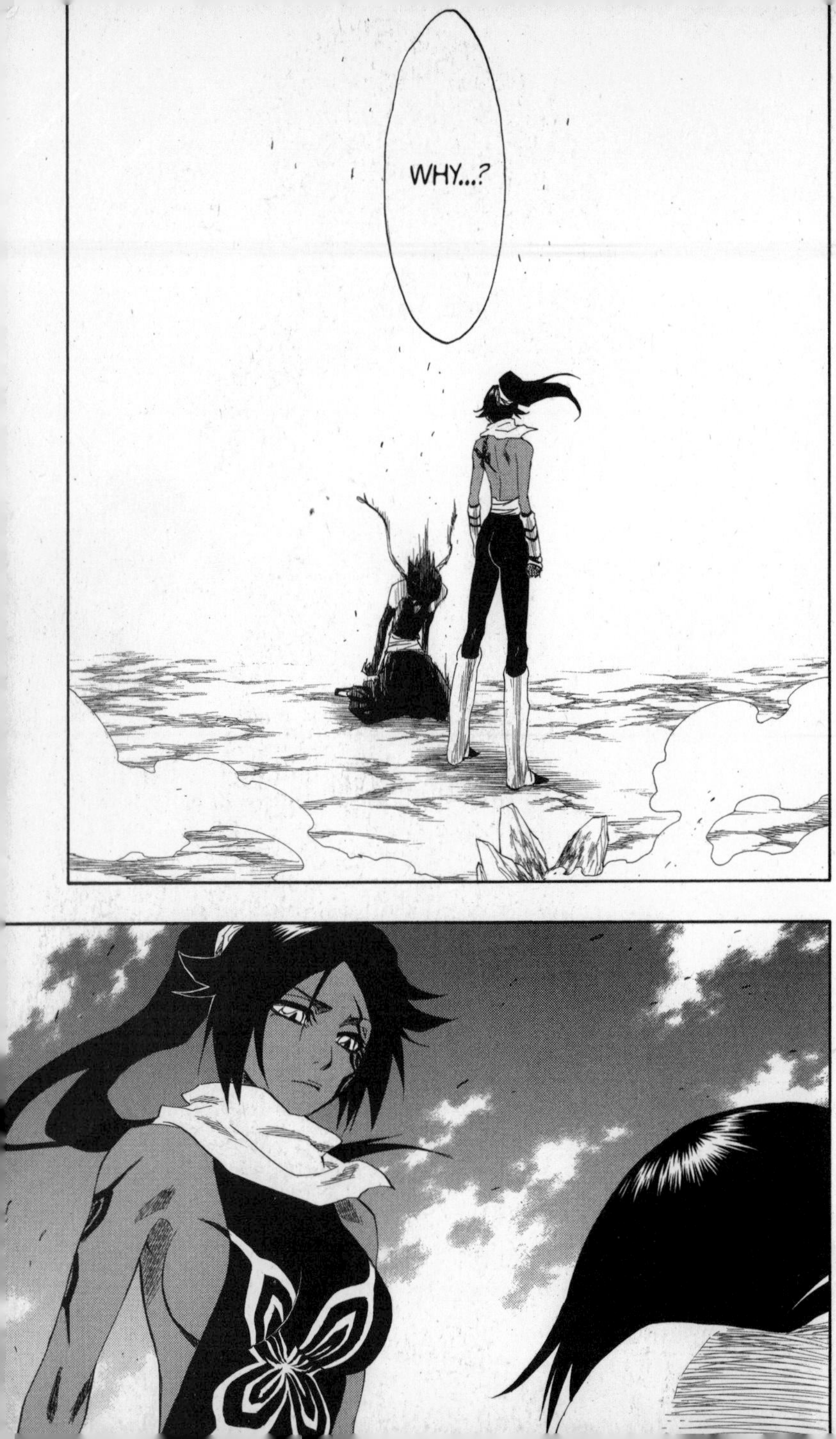
WHY...?

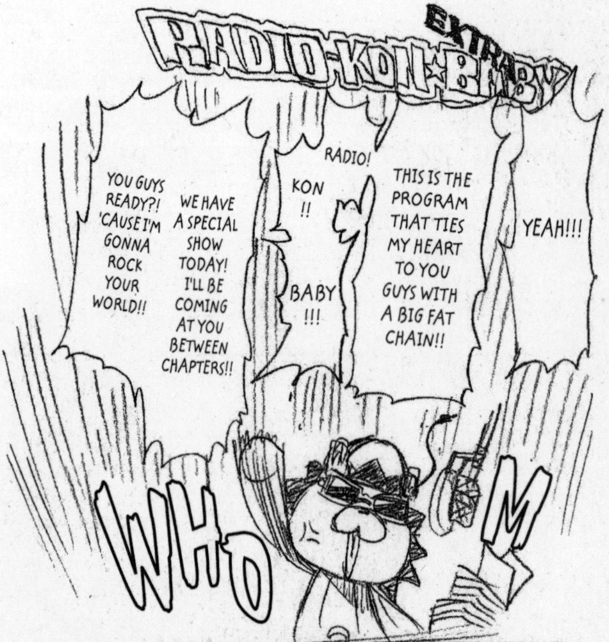
EXTRA
RADIO-KON★BABY
YEAH!!!
THIS IS THE PROGRAM THAT TIES MY HEART TO YOU GUYS WITH A BIG FAT CHAIN!!
RADIO!
KON!!
BABY!!!
WE HAVE A SPECIAL SHOW TODAY! I'LL BE COMING AT YOU BETWEEN CHAPTERS!!
YOU GUYS READY?! 'CAUSE I'M GONNA ROCK YOUR WORLD!!
WHOOM

160. Battle on Guillotine Hill

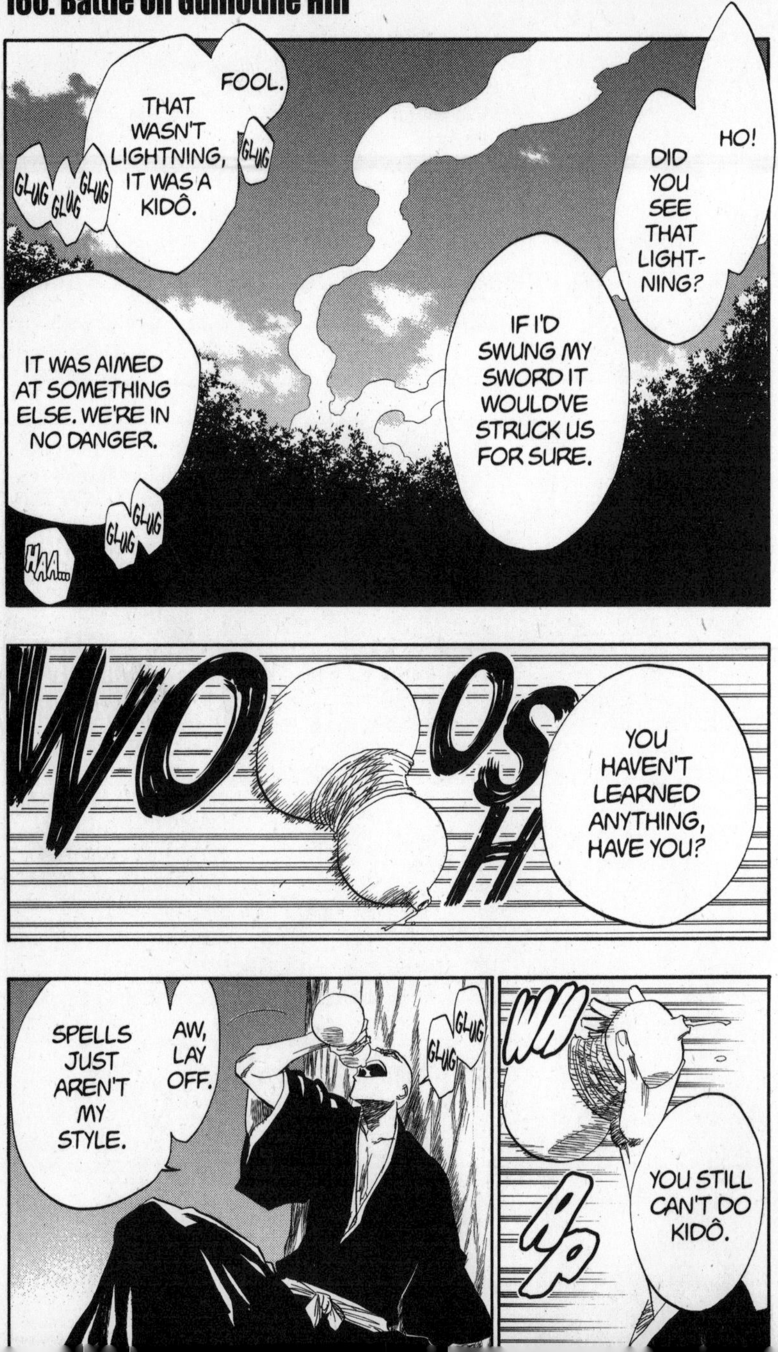
HO! DID YOU SEE THAT LIGHTNING?
IF I'D SWUNG MY SWORD IT WOULD'VE STRUCK US FOR SURE.
FOOL.
THAT WASN'T LIGHTNING, IT WAS A KIDÔ.
GLUG
GLUG GLUG GLUG
IT WAS AIMED AT SOMETHING ELSE. WE'RE IN NO DANGER.
GLUG GLUG
HAA...
WOOOSH
YOU HAVEN'T LEARNED ANYTHING, HAVE YOU?
WHAP
YOU STILL CAN'T DO KIDÔ.
GLUG GLUG
AW, LAY OFF.
SPELLS JUST AREN'T MY STYLE.

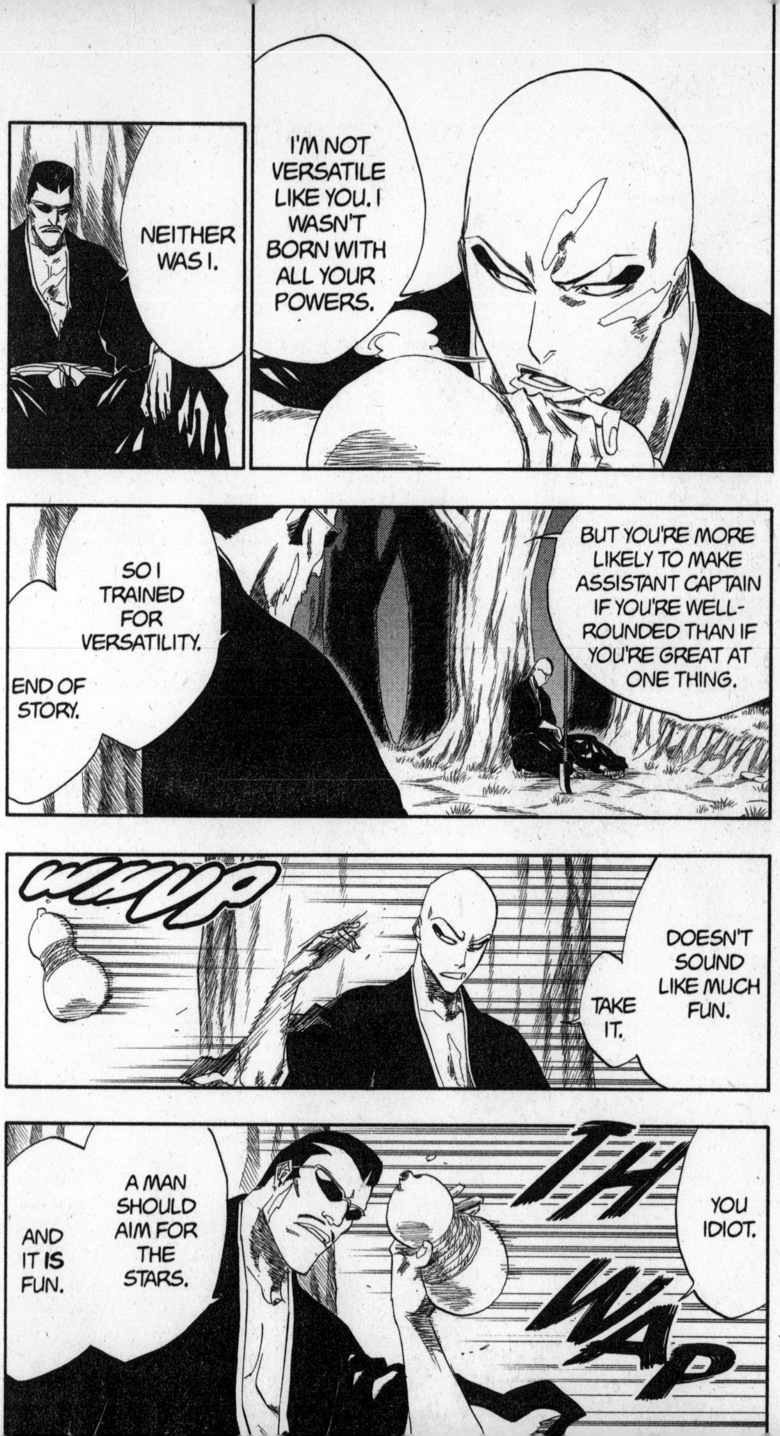
I'M NOT VERSATILE LIKE YOU. I WASN'T BORN WITH ALL YOUR POWERS.
NEITHER WAS I.
BUT YOU'RE MORE LIKELY TO MAKE ASSISTANT CAPTAIN IF YOU'RE WELL-ROUNDED THAN IF YOU'RE GREAT AT ONE THING.
SO I TRAINED FOR VERSATILITY.
END OF STORY.
DOESN'T SOUND LIKE MUCH FUN.
TAKE IT.
WHUP
THWAP
YOU IDIOT.
A MAN SHOULD AIM FOR THE STARS.
AND IT IS FUN.

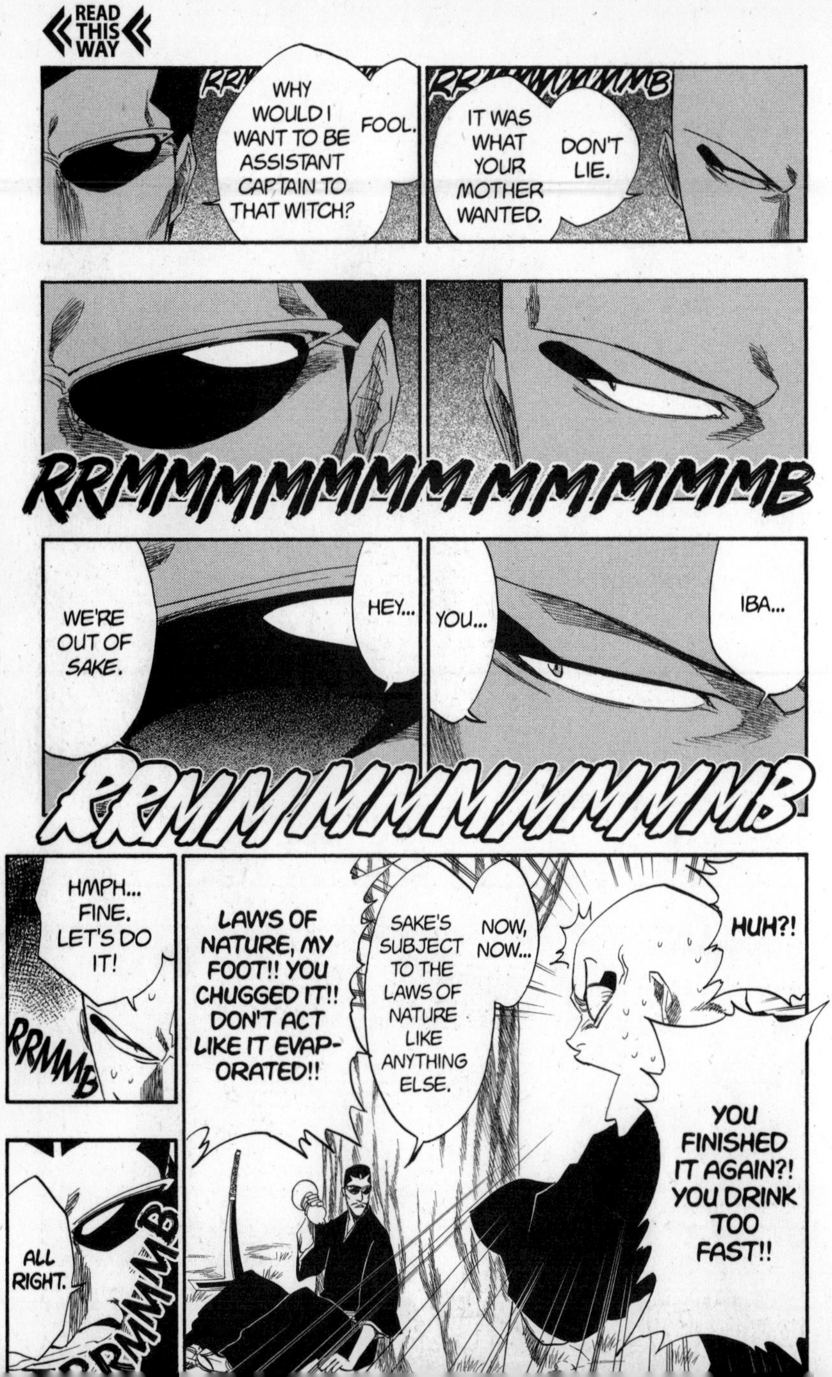
READ THIS WAY
DON'T LIE.
IT WAS WHAT YOUR MOTHER WANTED.
FOOL.
WHY WOULD I WANT TO BE ASSISTANT CAPTAIN TO THAT WITCH?
RRMMMMMMMMMM MMMMMMB
IBA...
YOU...
HEY...
WE'RE OUT OF SAKE.
RRMMMMMMMMMMMB
HUH?!
YOU FINISHED IT AGAIN?! YOU DRINK TOO FAST!!
NOW, NOW...
SAKE'S SUBJECT TO THE LAWS OF NATURE LIKE ANYTHING ELSE.
LAWS OF NATURE, MY FOOT!! YOU CHUGGED IT!! DON'T ACT LIKE IT EVAPORATED!!
HMPH... FINE. LET'S DO IT!
RRMMMB
ALL RIGHT.
RRMMMB

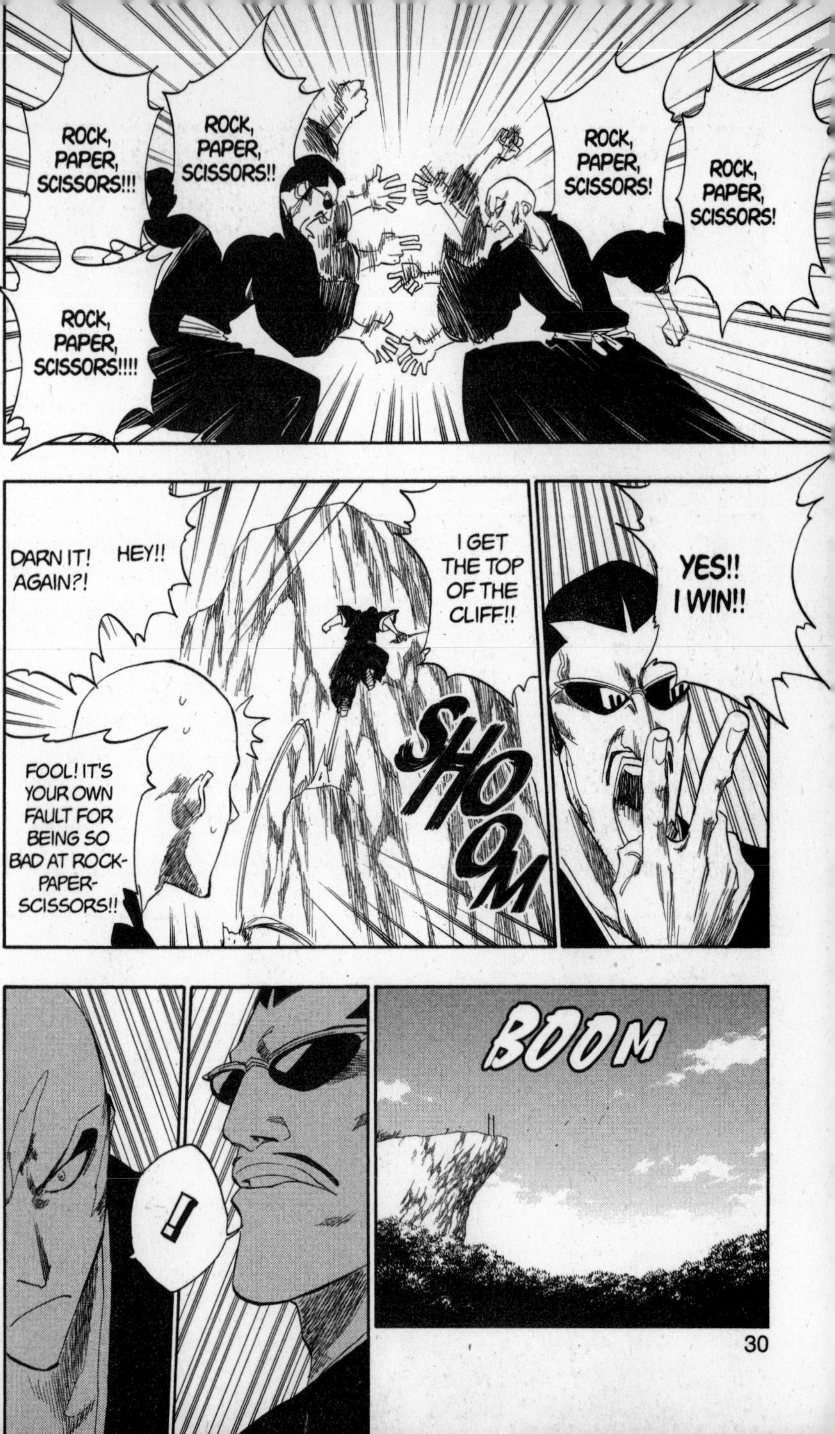
ROCK, PAPER, SCISSORS!
ROCK, PAPER, SCISSORS!
ROCK, PAPER, SCISSORS!!
ROCK, PAPER, SCISSORS!!!
ROCK, PAPER, SCISSORS!!!!
YES!! I WIN!!
I GET THE TOP OF THE CLIFF!!
SHOOM
HEY!!
DARN IT! AGAIN?!
FOOL! IT'S YOUR OWN FAULT FOR BEING SO BAD AT ROCK-PAPER-SCISSORS!!
BOOM
!

READ THIS WAY

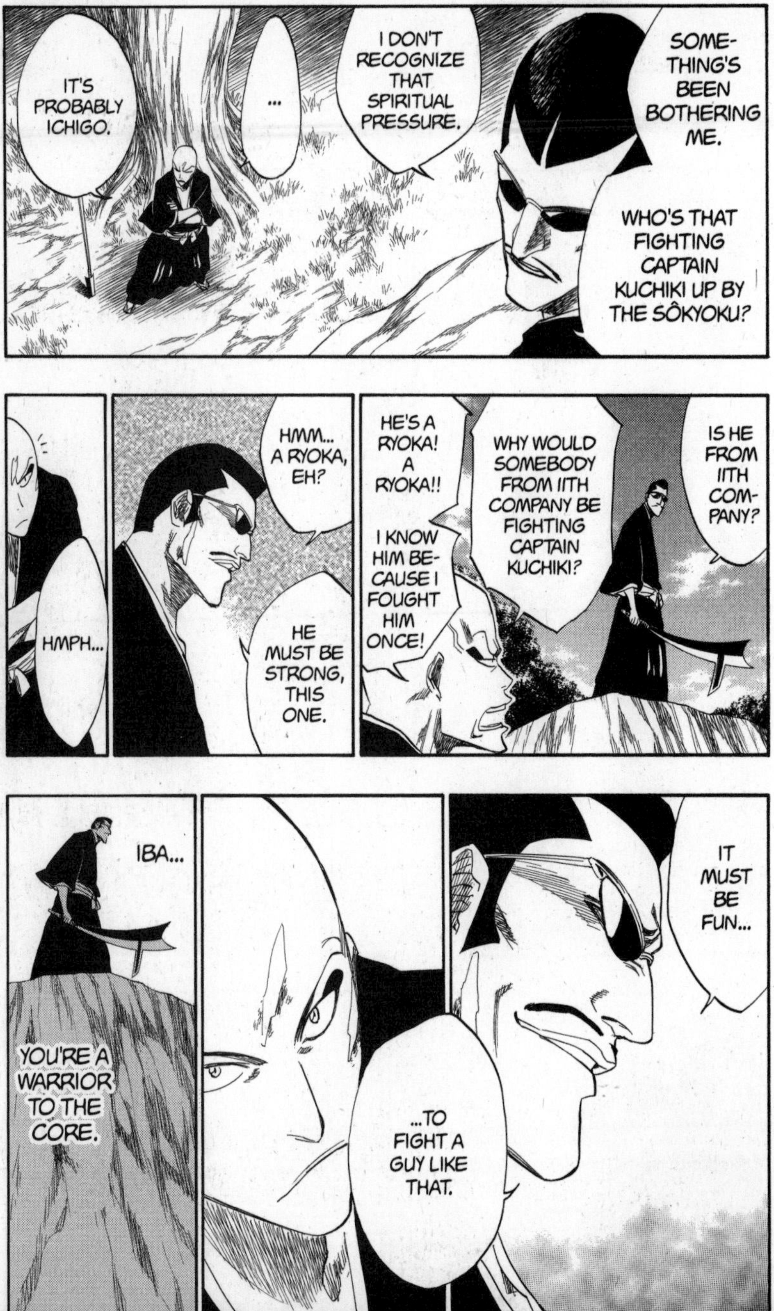
SOME-THING'S BEEN BOTHERING ME.
WHO'S THAT FIGHTING CAPTAIN KUCHIKI UP BY THE SÔKYOKU?
I DON'T RECOGNIZE THAT SPIRITUAL PRESSURE.
...
IT'S PROBABLY ICHIGO.
IS HE FROM 11TH COMPANY?
WHY WOULD SOMEBODY FROM 11TH COMPANY BE FIGHTING CAPTAIN KUCHIKI?
HE'S A RYOKA! A RYOKA!!
I KNOW HIM BE-CAUSE I FOUGHT HIM ONCE!
HMM... A RYOKA, EH?
HE MUST BE STRONG, THIS ONE.
HMPH...
IT MUST BE FUN...
...TO FIGHT A GUY LIKE THAT.
IBA...
YOU'RE A WARRIOR TO THE CORE.

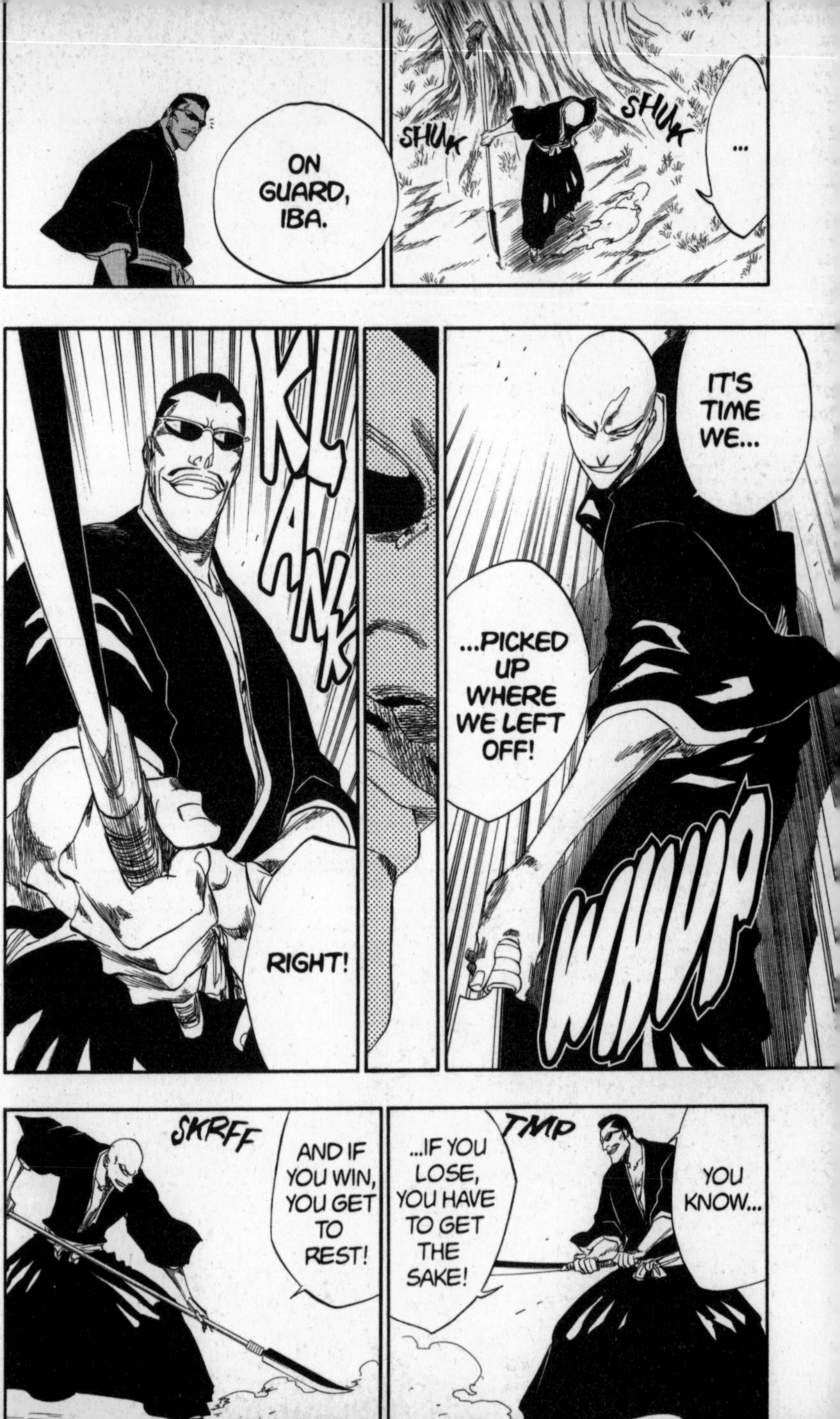
SHUNK
SHUNK
...
ON GUARD, IBA.
IT'S TIME WE...
...PICKED UP WHERE WE LEFT OFF!
WHUP
KLANK
RIGHT!
YOU KNOW...
TMP
...IF YOU LOSE, YOU HAVE TO GET THE SAKE!
AND IF YOU WIN, YOU GET TO REST!
SKRFF

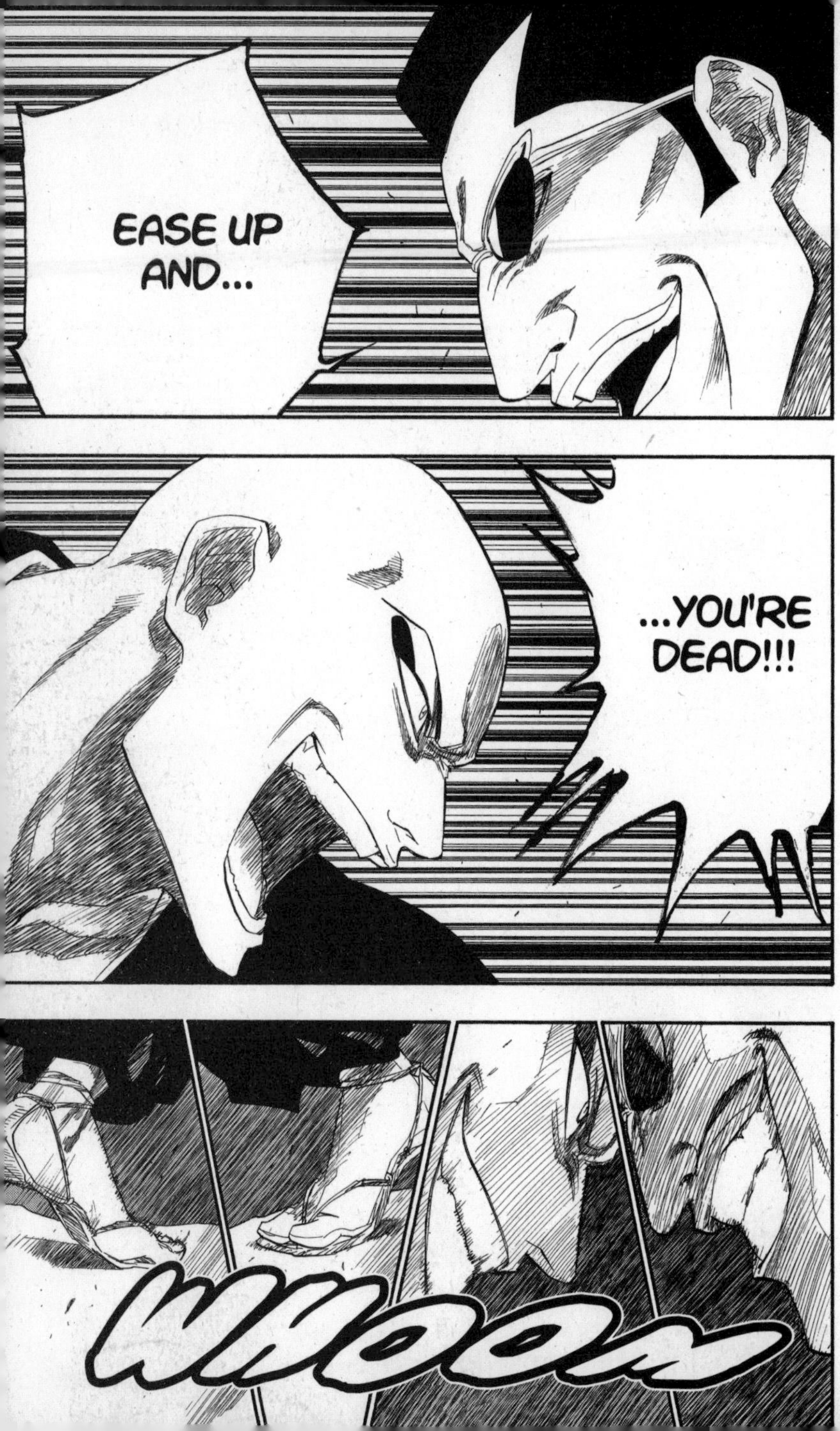
EASE UP AND...
...YOU'RE DEAD!!!
WHOOM

160. Battle on Guillotine Hill

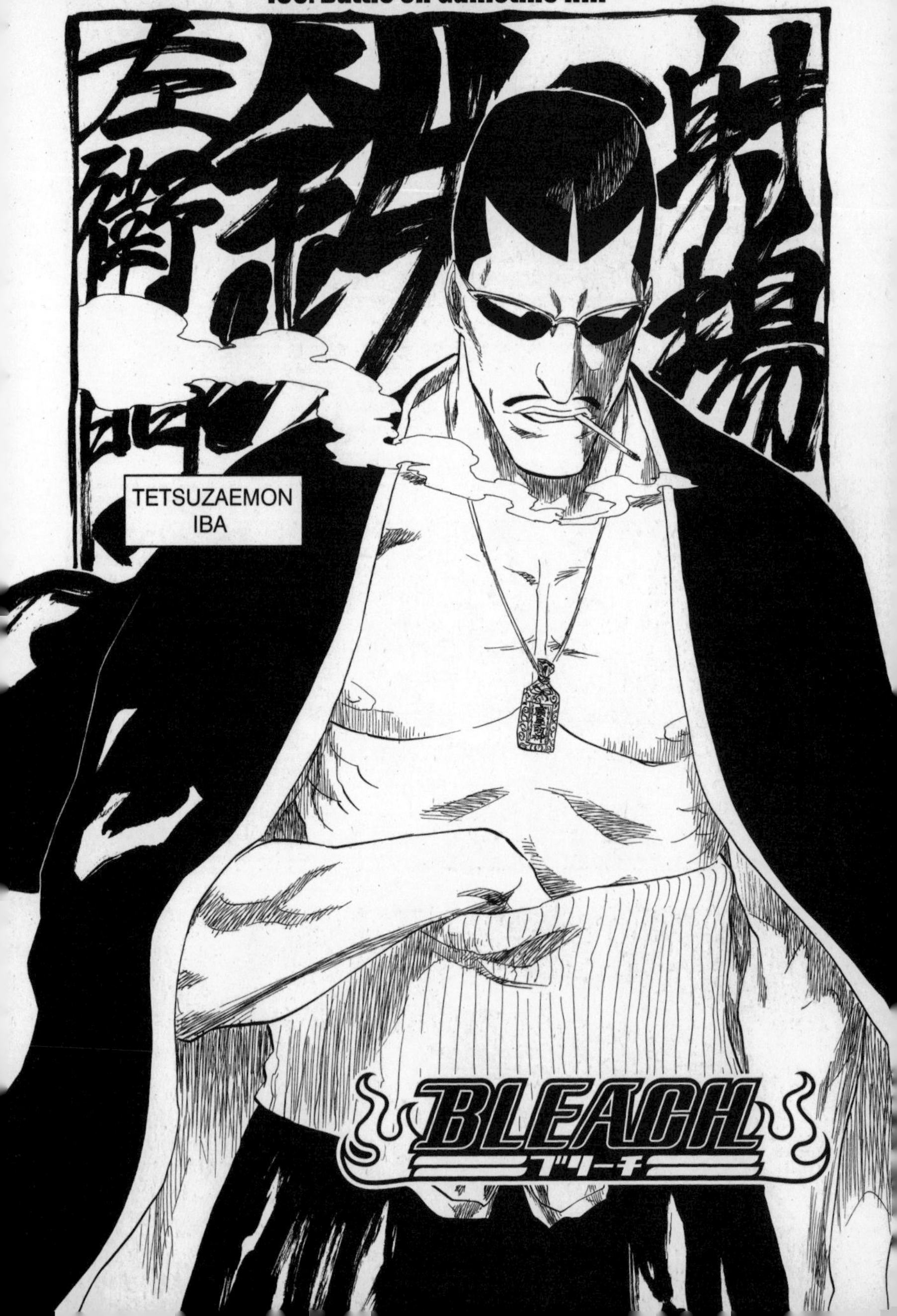
TETSUZAEMON
IBA
BLEACH
ブリーチ

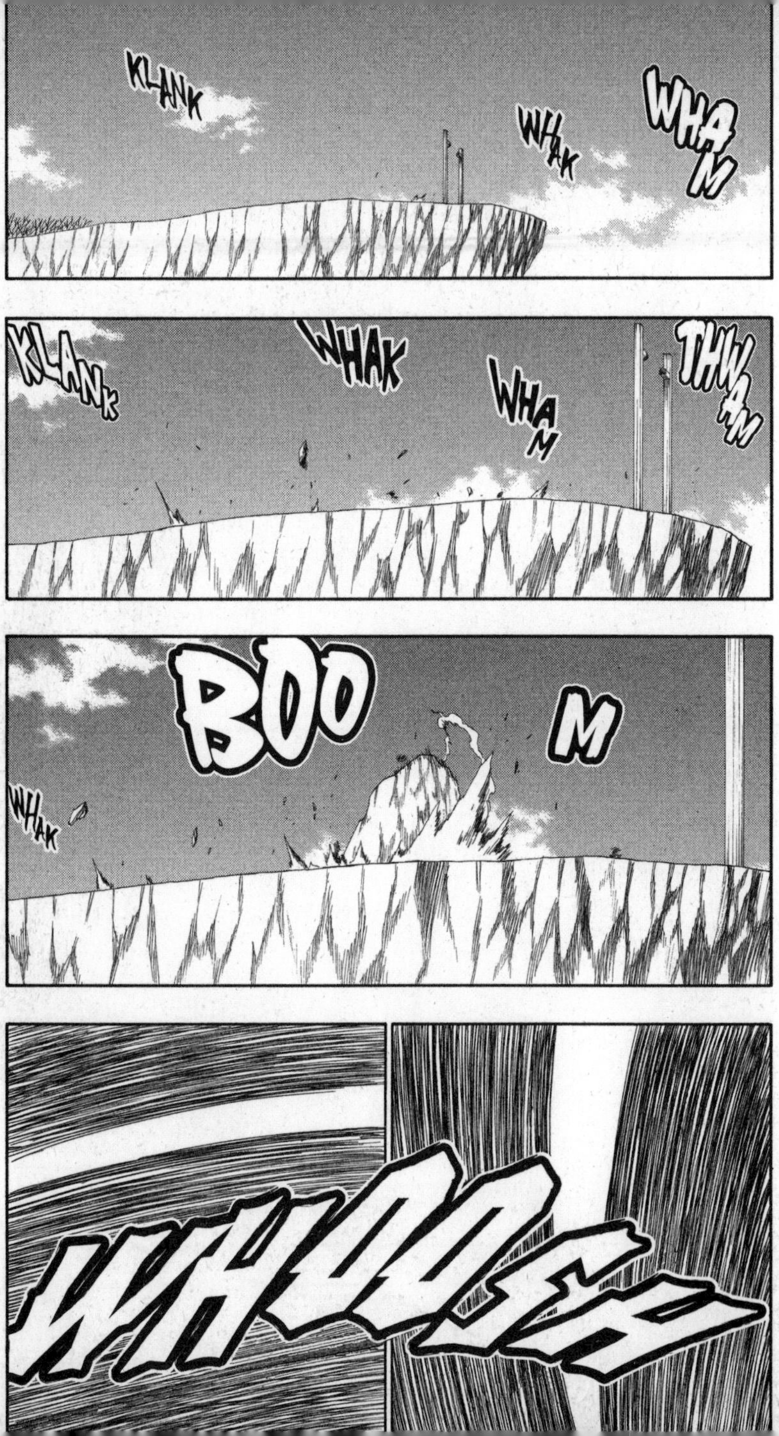
WHAM
WHAK
KLANK
THWAM
WHAM
WHAK
KLANK
BOOM
WHAK
WHOOSH

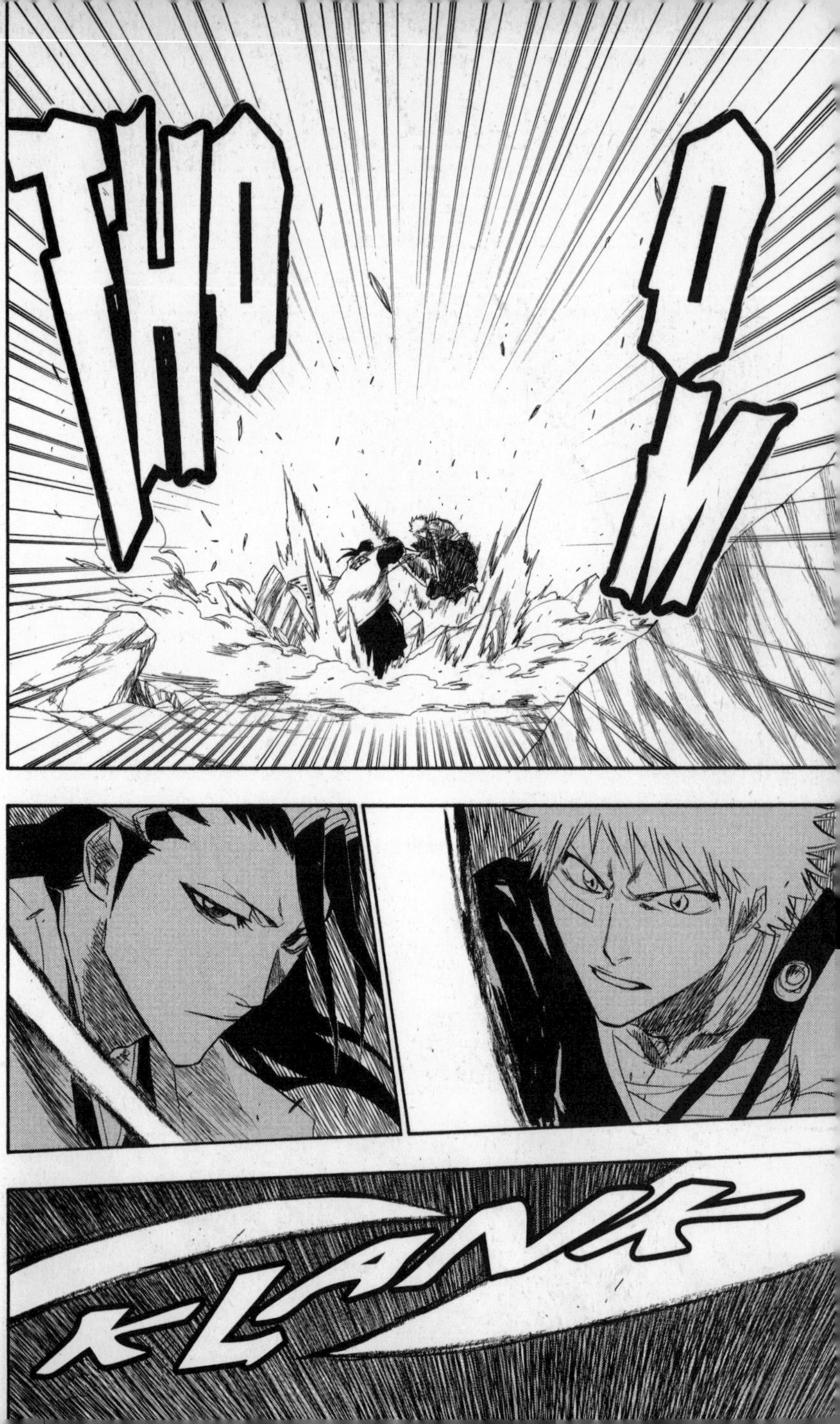
THOOM
KLANK

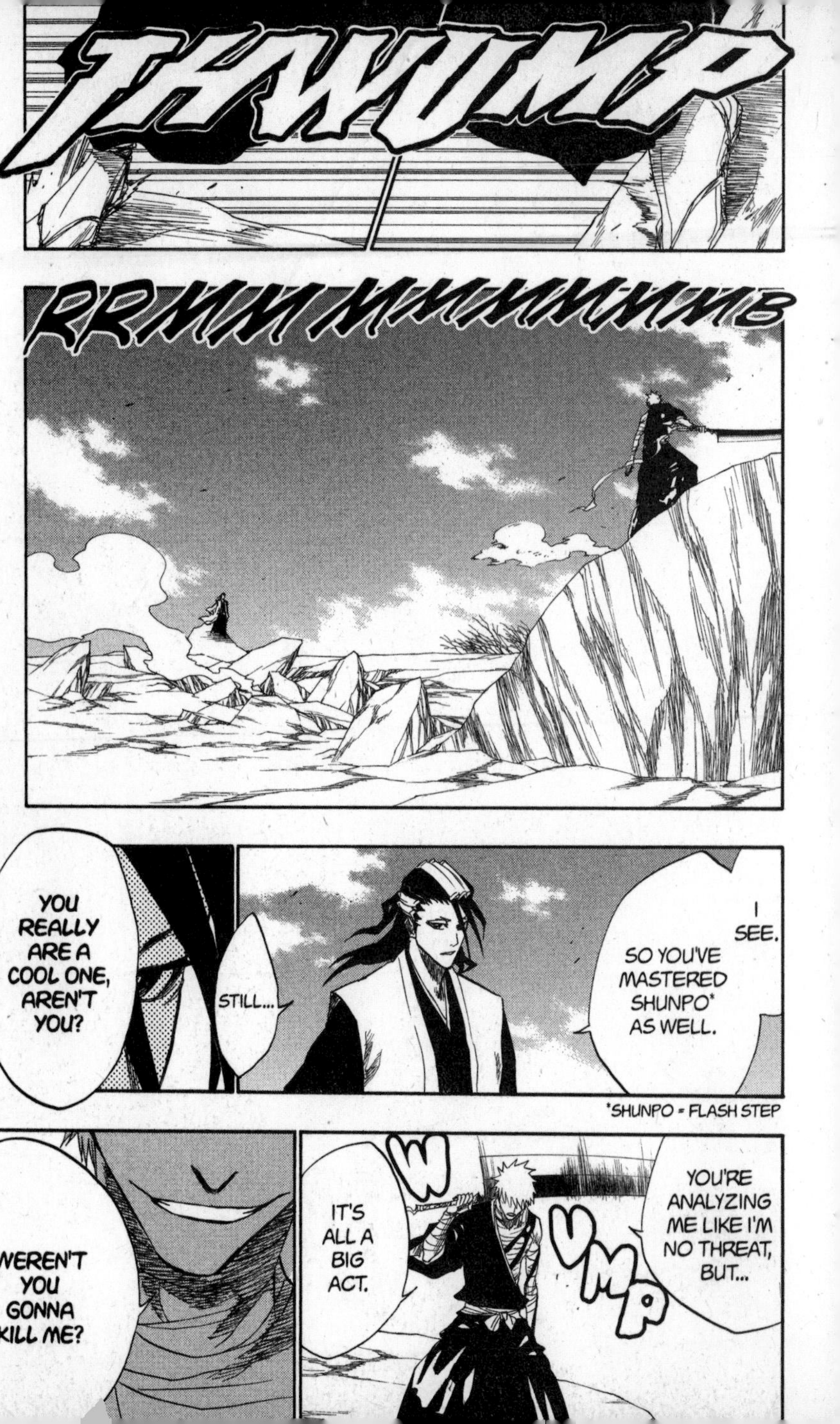
THWUMP
RRMMMMMMMMMMB
I SEE.
SO YOU'VE MASTERED SHUNPO* AS WELL.
STILL...
YOU REALLY ARE A COOL ONE, AREN'T YOU?
*SHUNPO = FLASH STEP
YOU'RE ANALYZING ME LIKE I'M NO THREAT, BUT...
WUMP
IT'S ALL A BIG ACT.
WEREN'T YOU GONNA KILL ME?

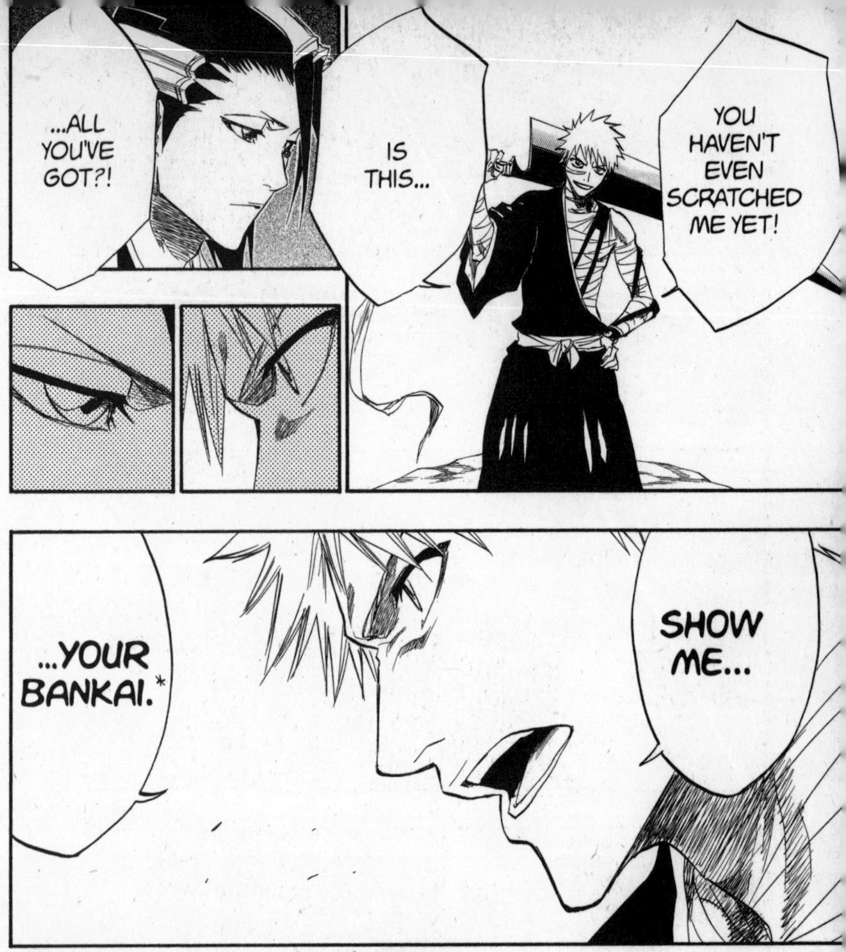
YOU HAVEN'T EVEN SCRATCHED ME YET!
IS THIS...
...ALL YOU'VE GOT?!
SHOW ME...
...YOUR BANKAI.*

*THIS TECHNIQUE RELEASES A ZANPAKU-TÔ'S ULTIMATE POWER.

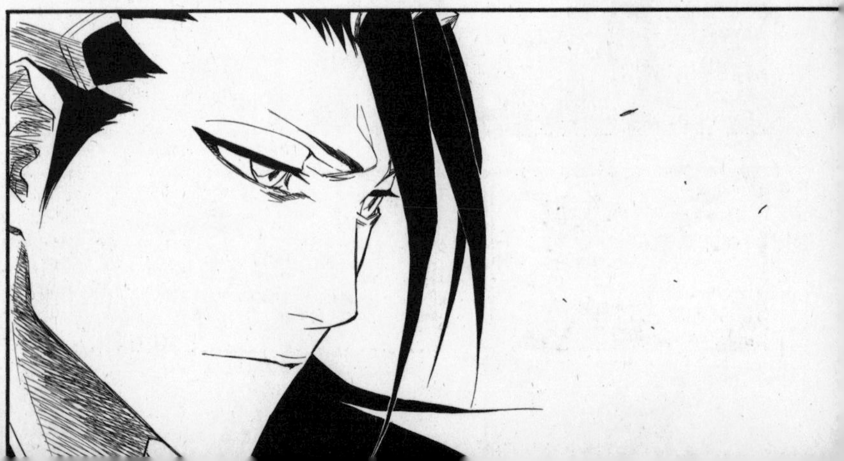

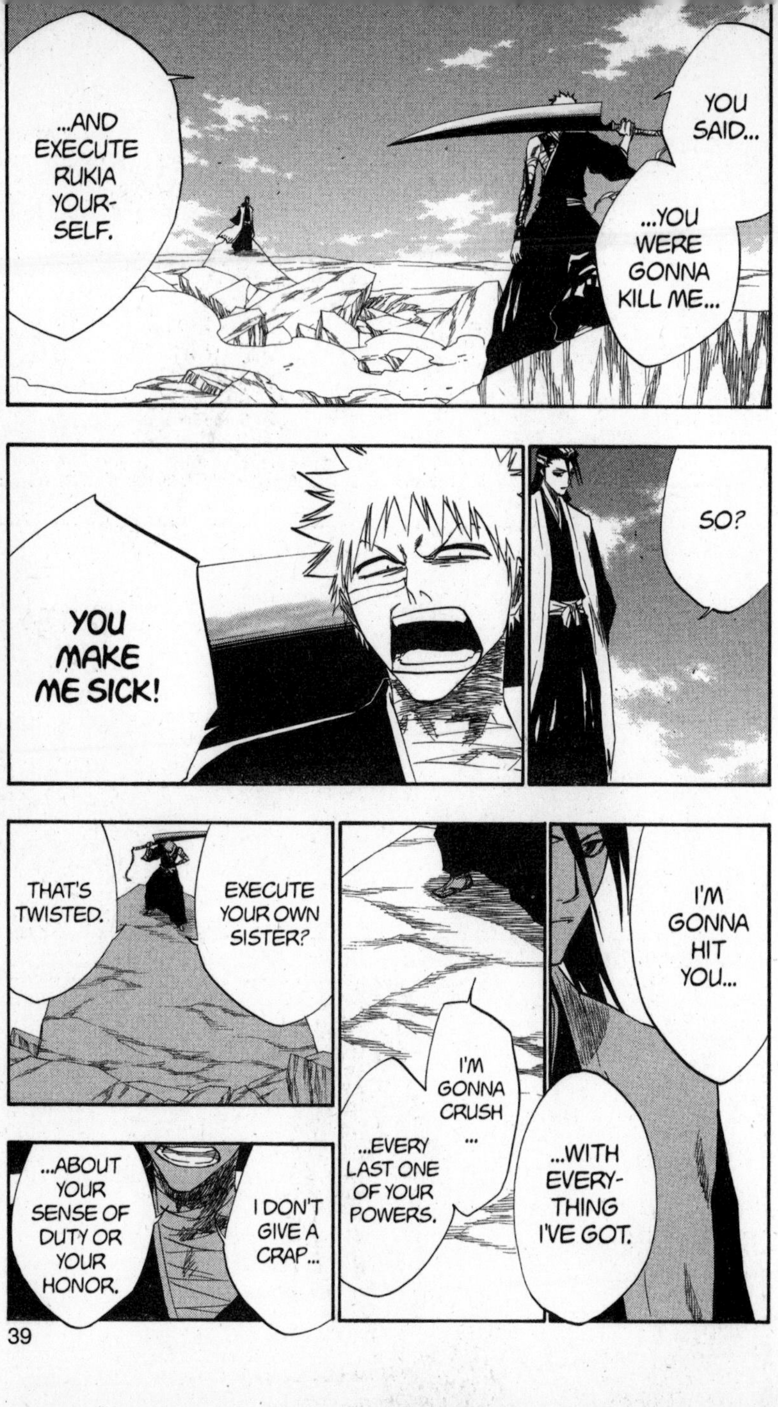
YOU SAID...
...YOU WERE GONNA KILL ME...
...AND EXECUTE RUKIA YOURSELF.
SO?
YOU MAKE ME SICK!
I'M GONNA HIT YOU...
...WITH EVERYTHING I'VE GOT.
I'M GONNA CRUSH...
...EVERY LAST ONE OF YOUR POWERS.
EXECUTE YOUR OWN SISTER?
THAT'S TWISTED.
I DON'T GIVE A CRAP...
...ABOUT YOUR SENSE OF DUTY OR YOUR HONOR.

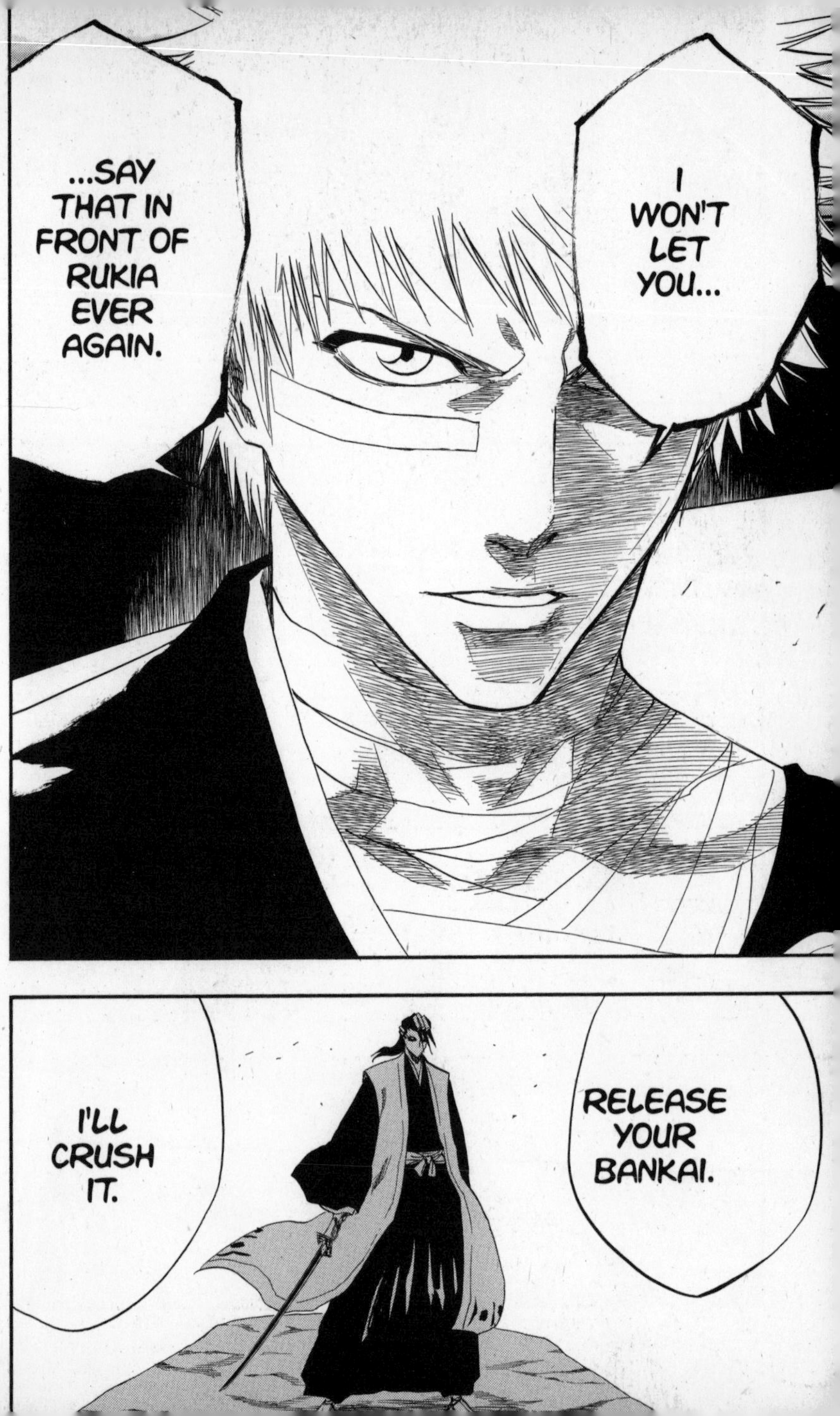
I WON'T LET YOU...
...SAY THAT IN FRONT OF RUKIA EVER AGAIN.
RELEASE YOUR BANKAI.
I'LL CRUSH IT.

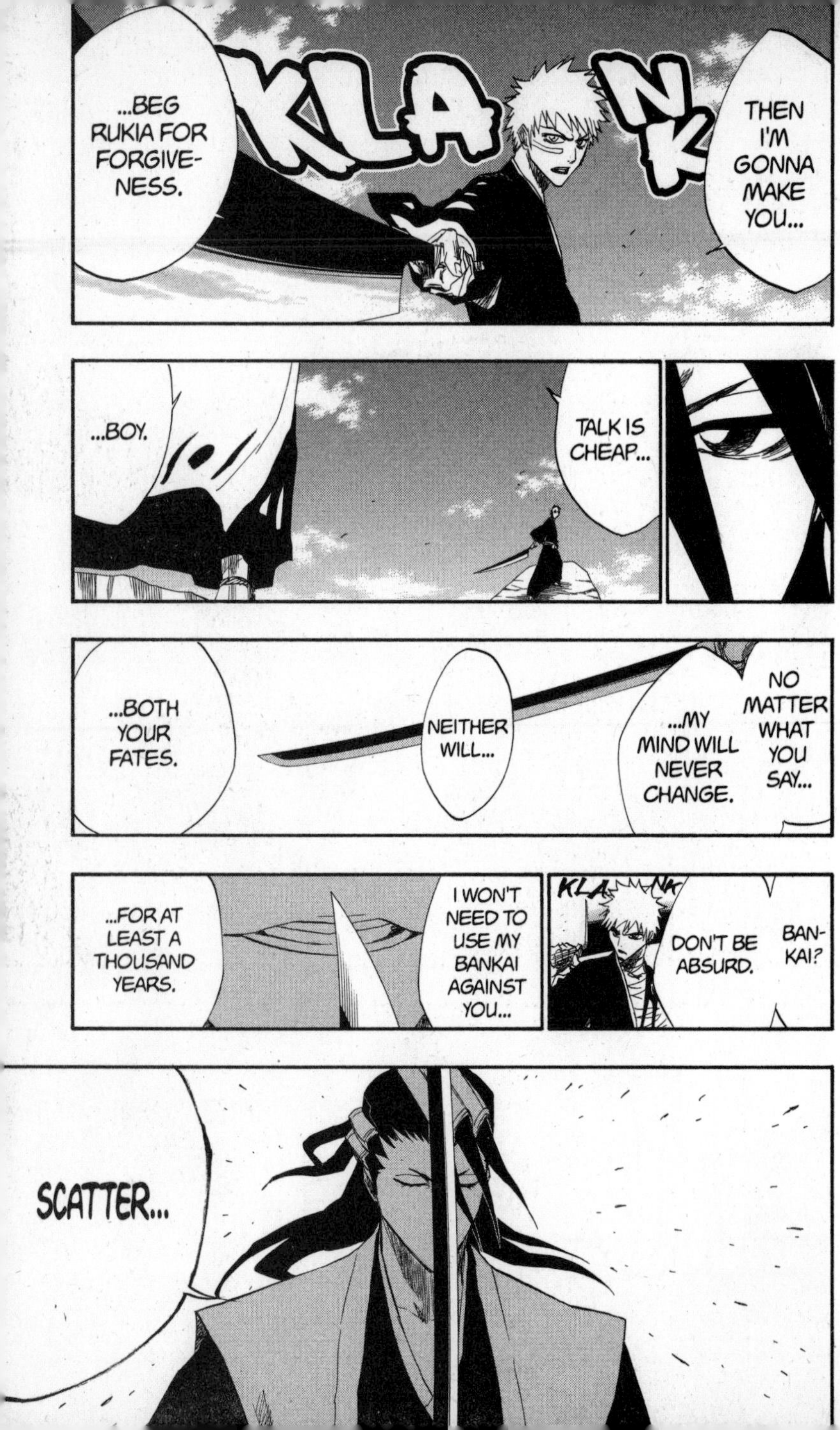

THEN I'M GONNA MAKE YOU...
KLANK
...BEG RUKIA FOR FORGIVE-NESS.
TALK IS CHEAP...
...BOY.
NO MATTER WHAT YOU SAY...
...MY MIND WILL NEVER CHANGE.
NEITHER WILL...
...BOTH YOUR FATES.
BAN-KAI?
KLANK
DON'T BE ABSURD.
I WON'T NEED TO USE MY BANKAI AGAINST YOU...
...FOR AT LEAST A THOUSAND YEARS.
SCATTER...

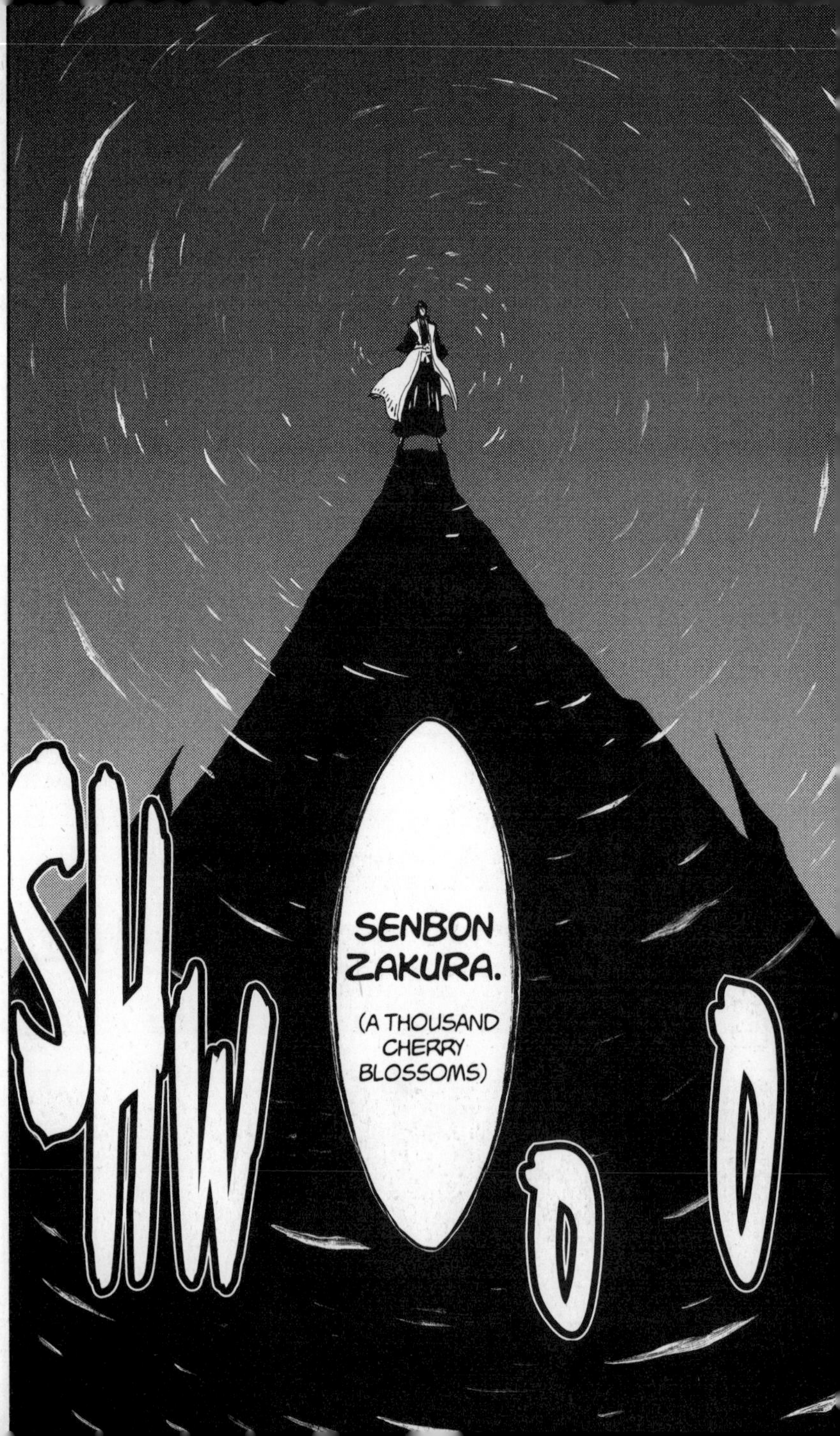
SENBON ZAKURA.
(A THOUSAND CHERRY BLOSSOMS)
SHWOO

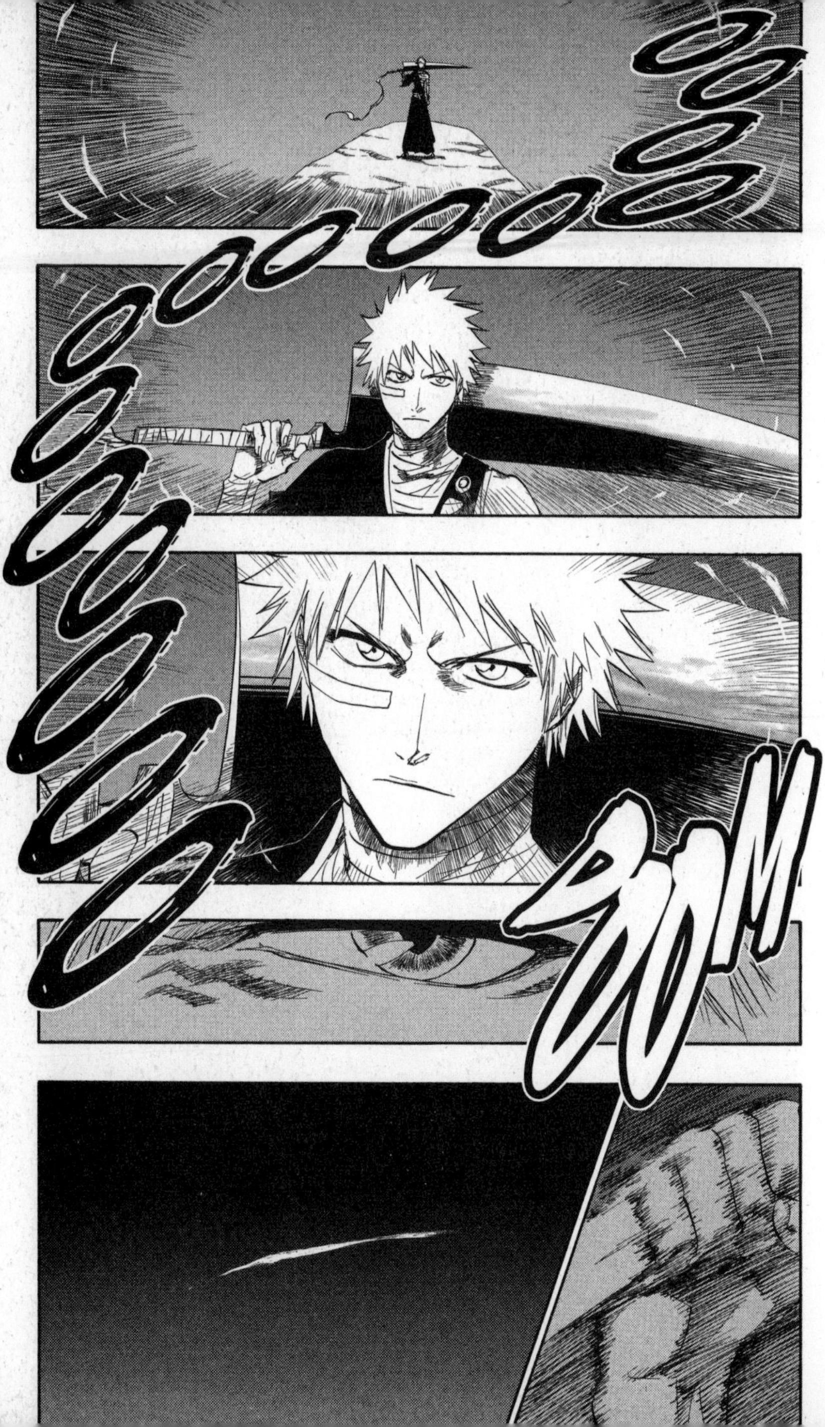
OOOOOOOOOOOOOOOOOOO
BOOM

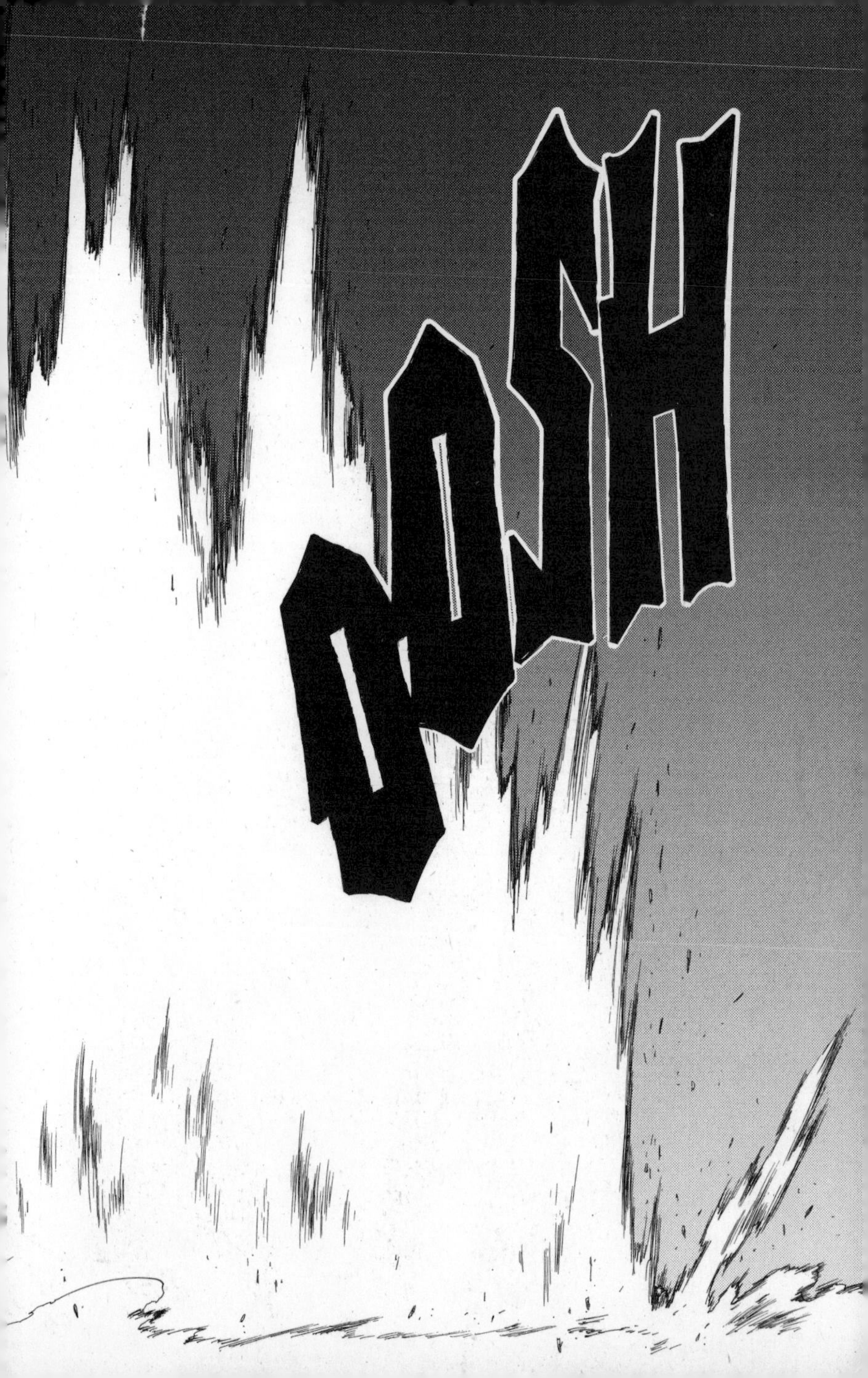
DOSH

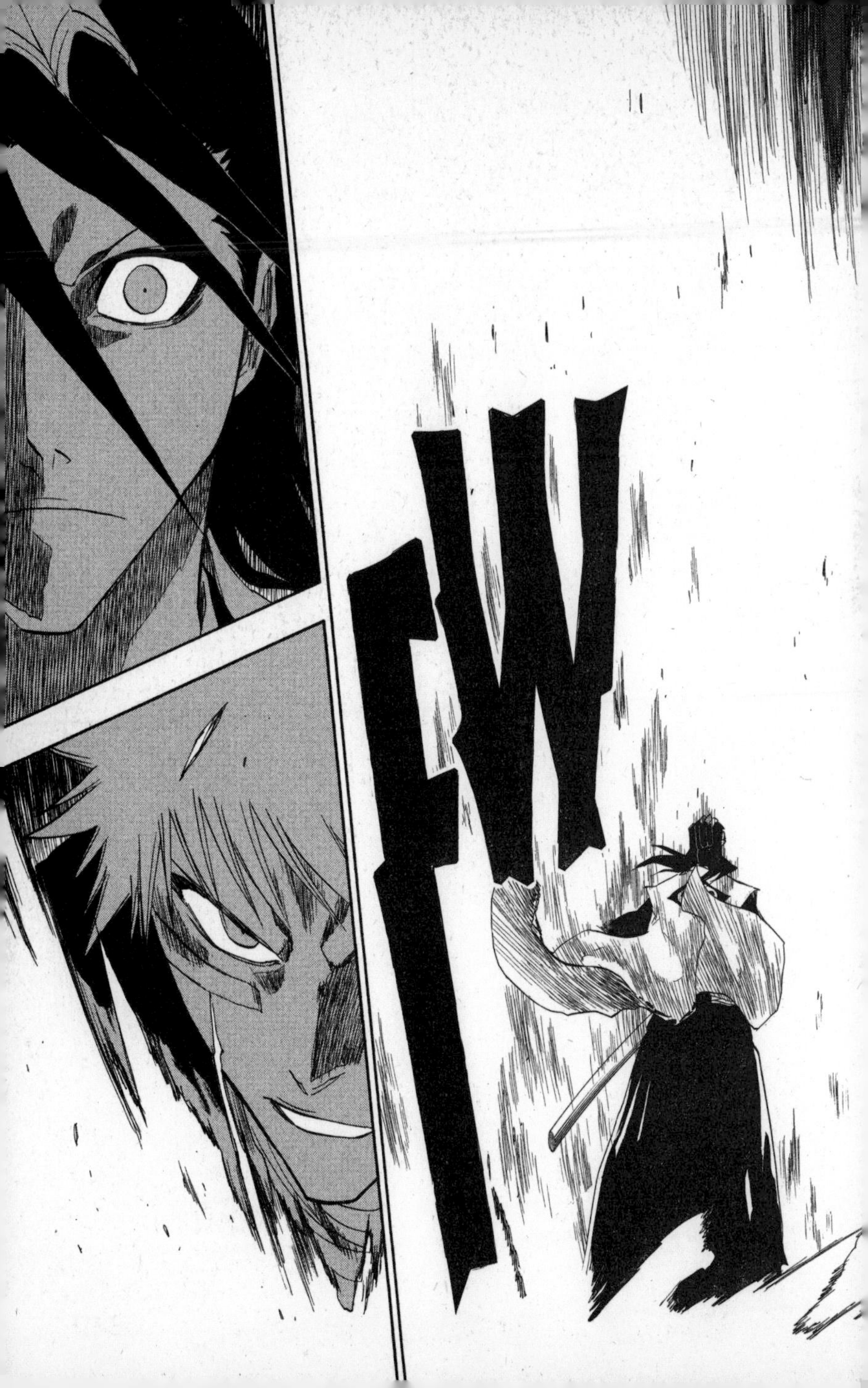
FW

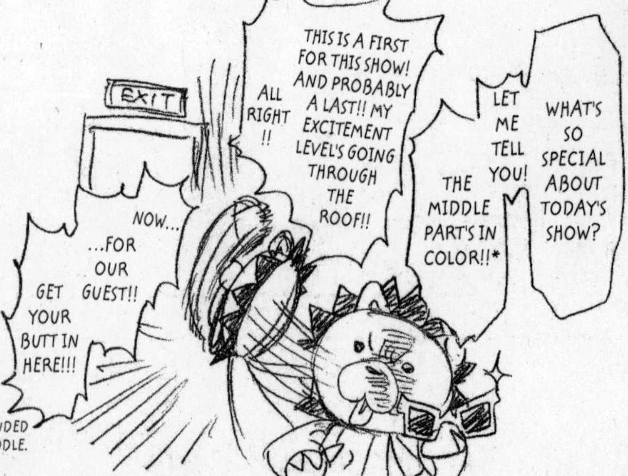
WHAT'S SO SPECIAL ABOUT TODAY'S SHOW?
LET ME TELL YOU!
THE MIDDLE PART'S IN COLOR!!*
THIS IS A FIRST FOR THIS SHOW! AND PROBABLY A LAST!! MY EXCITEMENT LEVEL'S GOING THROUGH THE ROOF!!
ALL RIGHT!!
EXIT
NOW...
...FOR OUR GUEST!!
GET YOUR BUTT IN HERE!!!

*THE JAPANESE EDITION INCLUDED A COLOR SECTION IN THE MIDDLE.

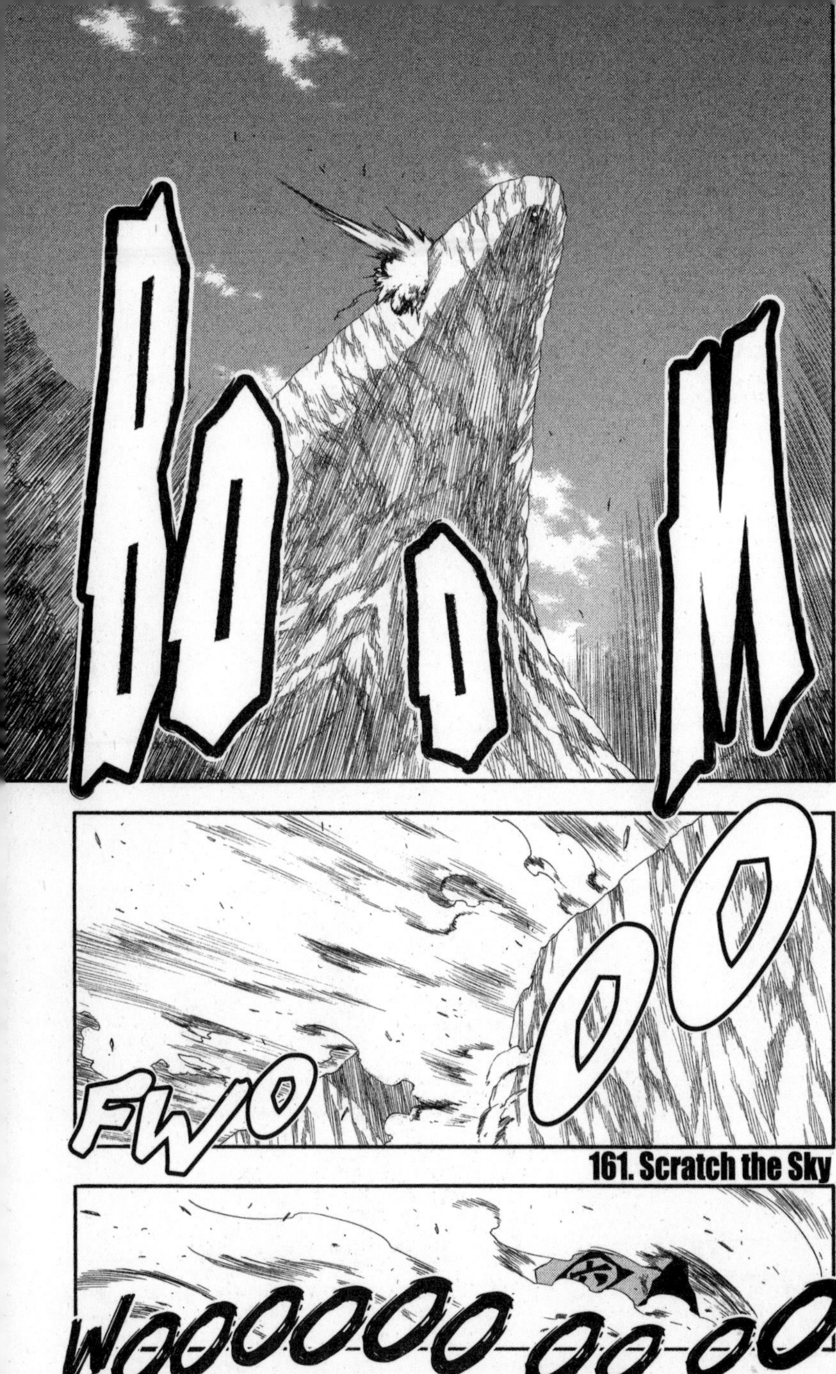
BOOM
FWOOOO
WOOOOOO-OO-OO

161. Scratch the Sky

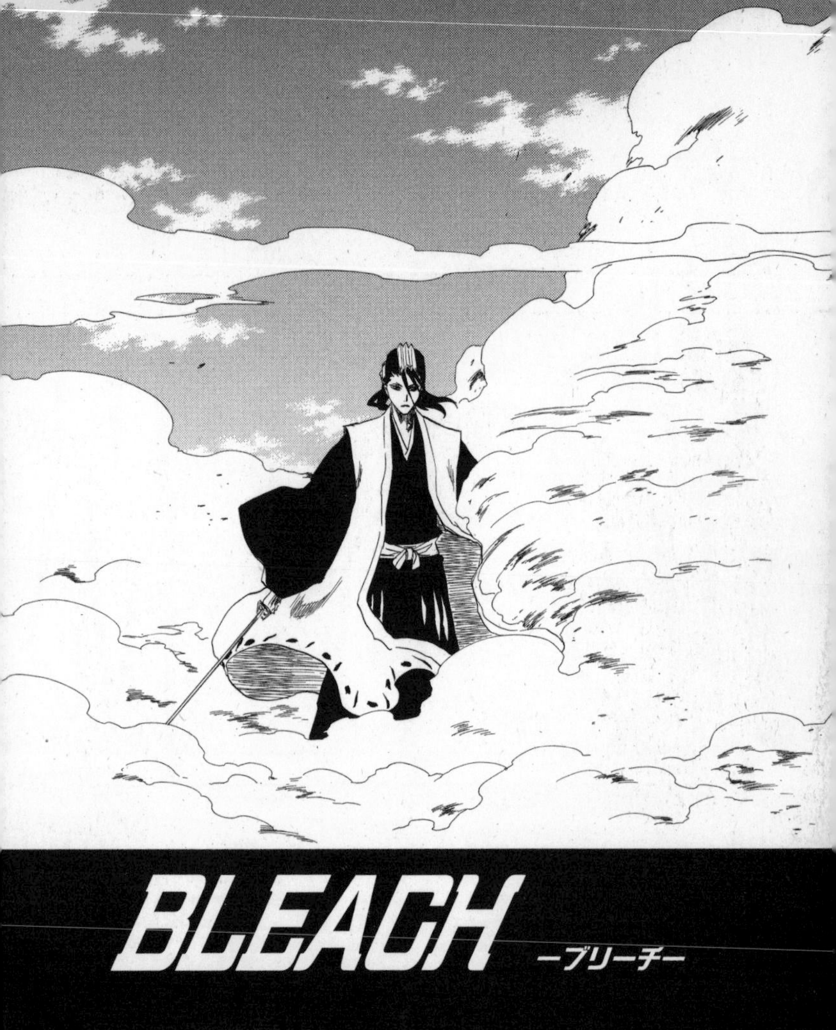

BLEACH

—ブリーチ—

161. Scratch the Sky

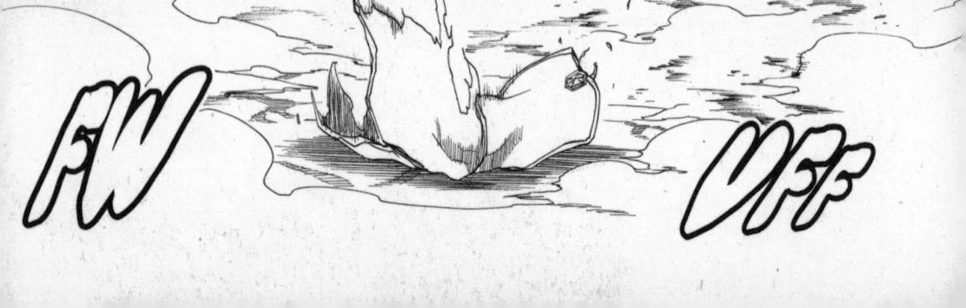
VFF
FW

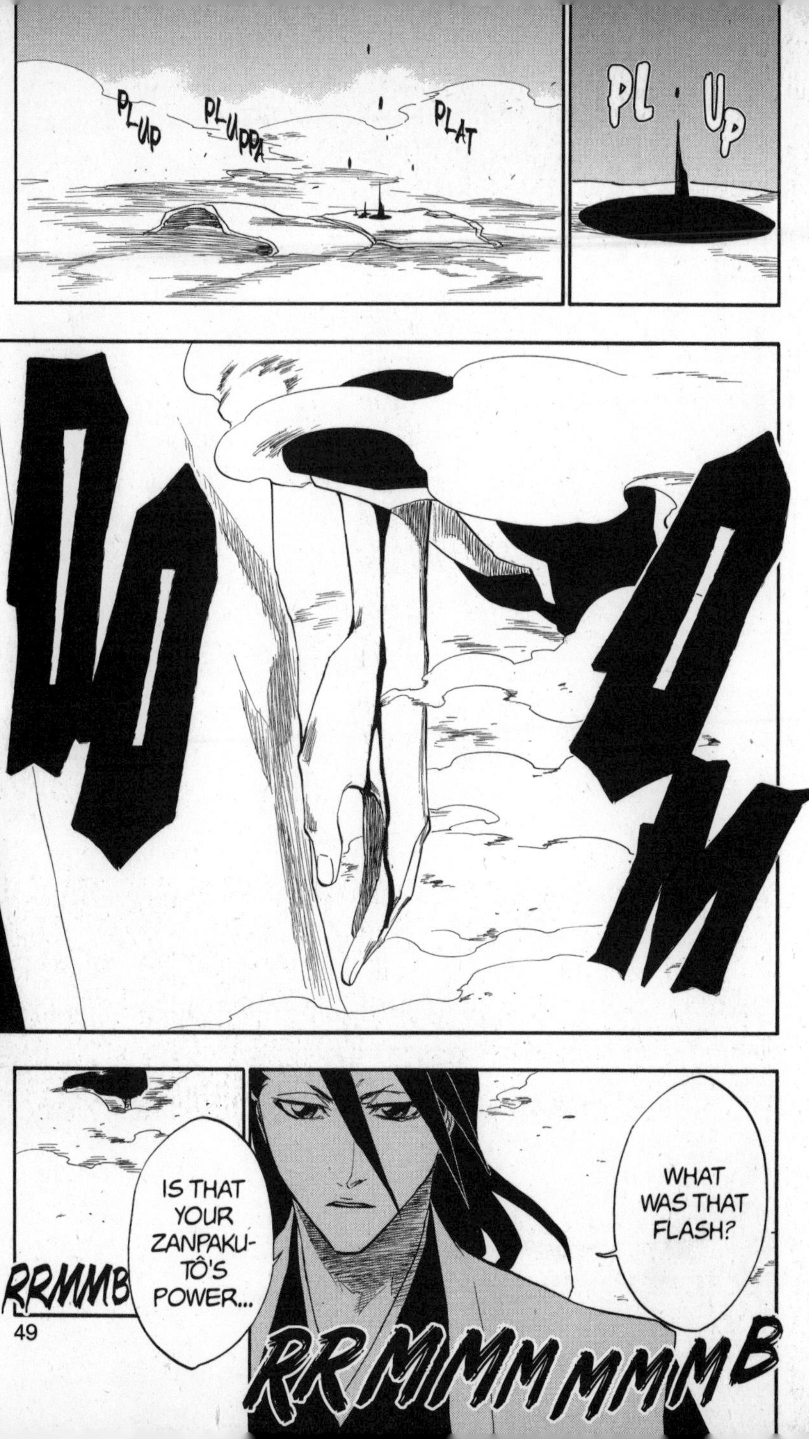
PL UP
PLUP
PLUPPA
PLAT
DOOM
WHAT WAS THAT FLASH?
IS THAT YOUR ZANPAKU-TÔ'S POWER...
RRMMMM MMMB
RRMMB

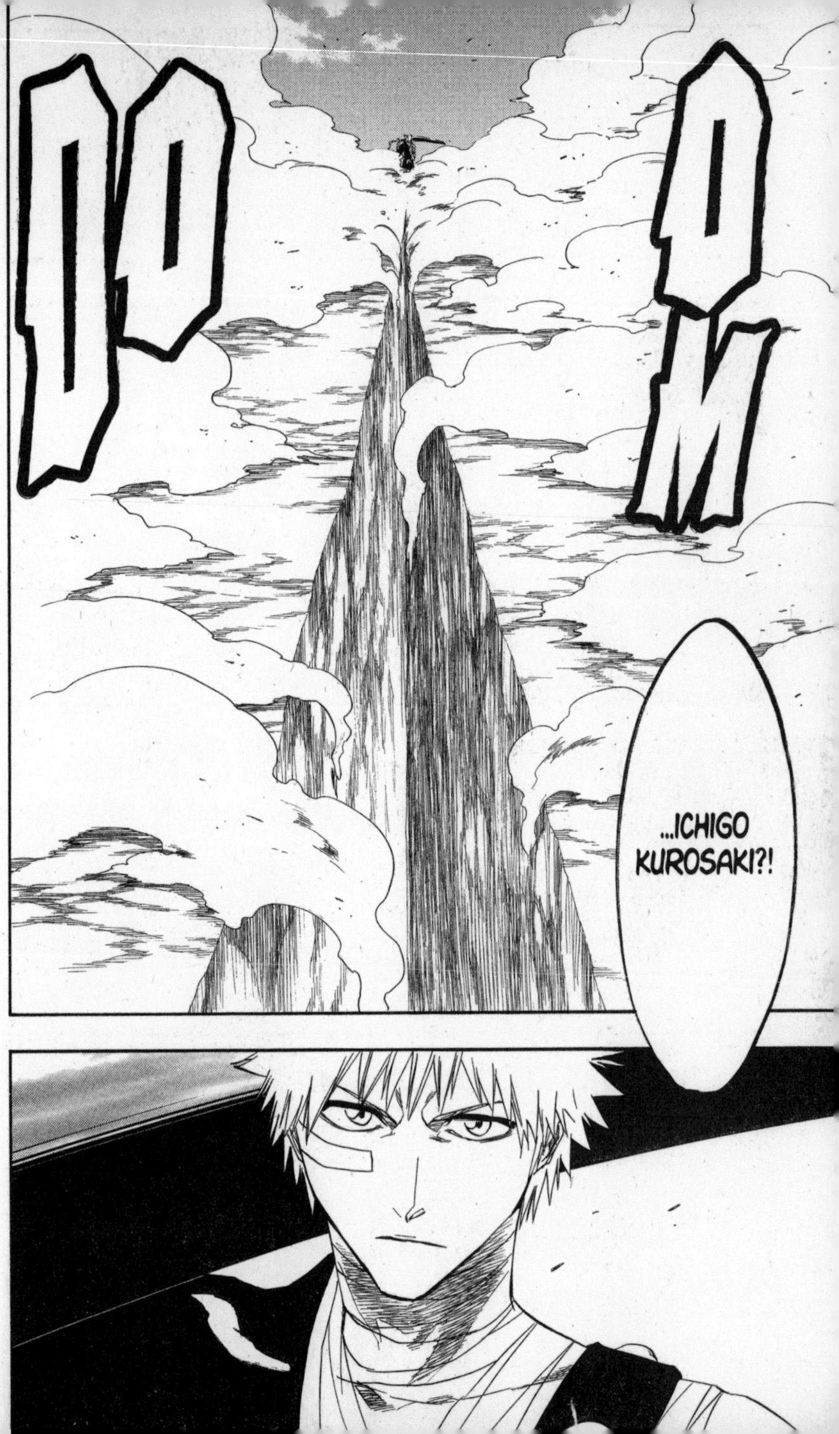
DOOM
...ICHIGO KUROSAKI?!

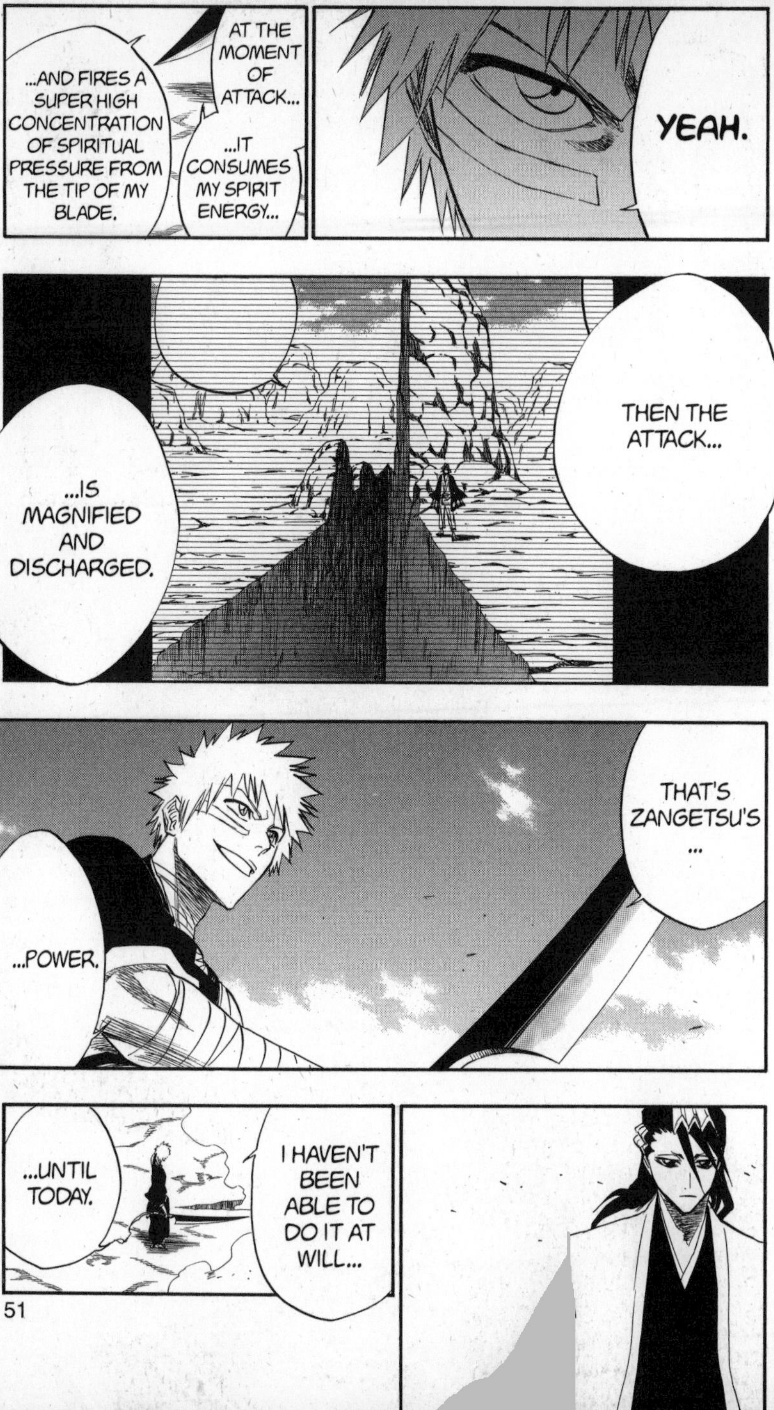
YEAH.
AT THE MOMENT OF ATTACK...
...IT CONSUMES MY SPIRIT ENERGY...
...AND FIRES A SUPER HIGH CONCENTRATION OF SPIRITUAL PRESSURE FROM THE TIP OF MY BLADE.
THEN THE ATTACK...
...IS MAGNIFIED AND DISCHARGED.
THAT'S ZANGETSU'S ...
...POWER.
I HAVEN'T BEEN ABLE TO DO IT AT WILL...
...UNTIL TODAY.

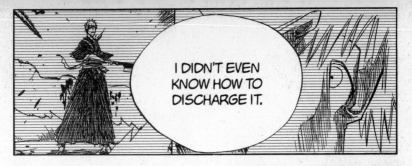

I DIDN'T EVEN KNOW HOW TO DISCHARGE IT.
MR. URAHARA SAID...
TMP
"THE ONLY THING I CAN TEACH YOU IS THE PROPER STATE OF MIND."
AFTER TRAINING WITH ZAN-GETSU...
...I FINALLY UNDER-STOOD.

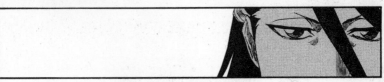

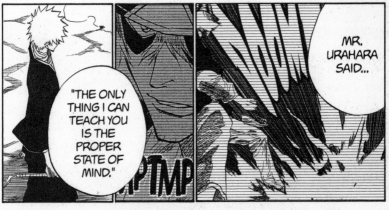

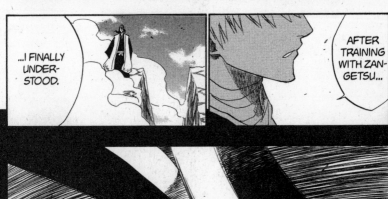

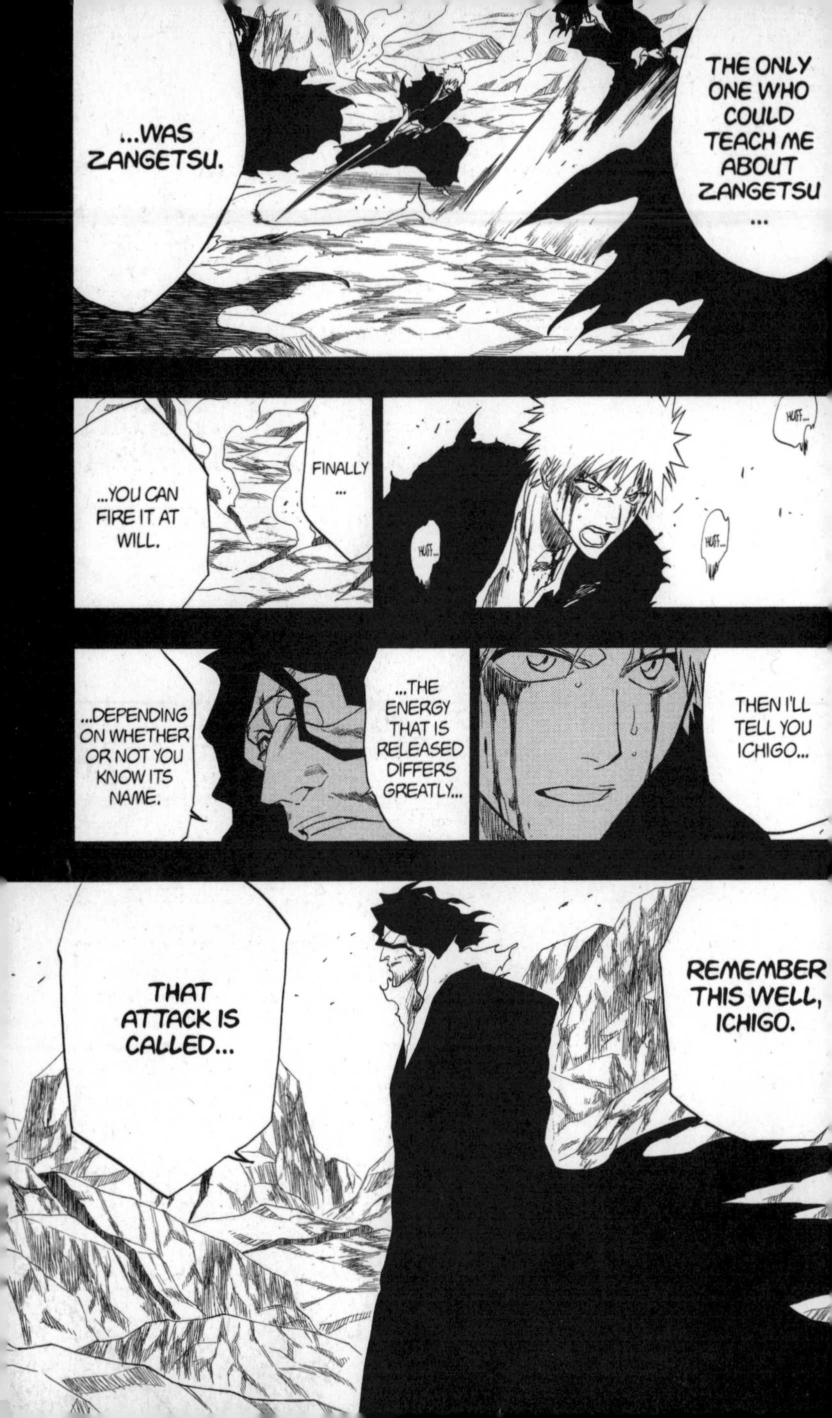
THE ONLY ONE WHO COULD TEACH ME ABOUT ZANGETSU ...
...WAS ZANGETSU.
HUFF...
HUFF...
HUFF...
FINALLY ...
...YOU CAN FIRE IT AT WILL.
THEN I'LL TELL YOU ICHIGO...
...THE ENERGY THAT IS RELEASED DIFFERS GREATLY...
...DEPENDING ON WHETHER OR NOT YOU KNOW ITS NAME.
REMEMBER THIS WELL, ICHIGO.
THAT ATTACK IS CALLED...

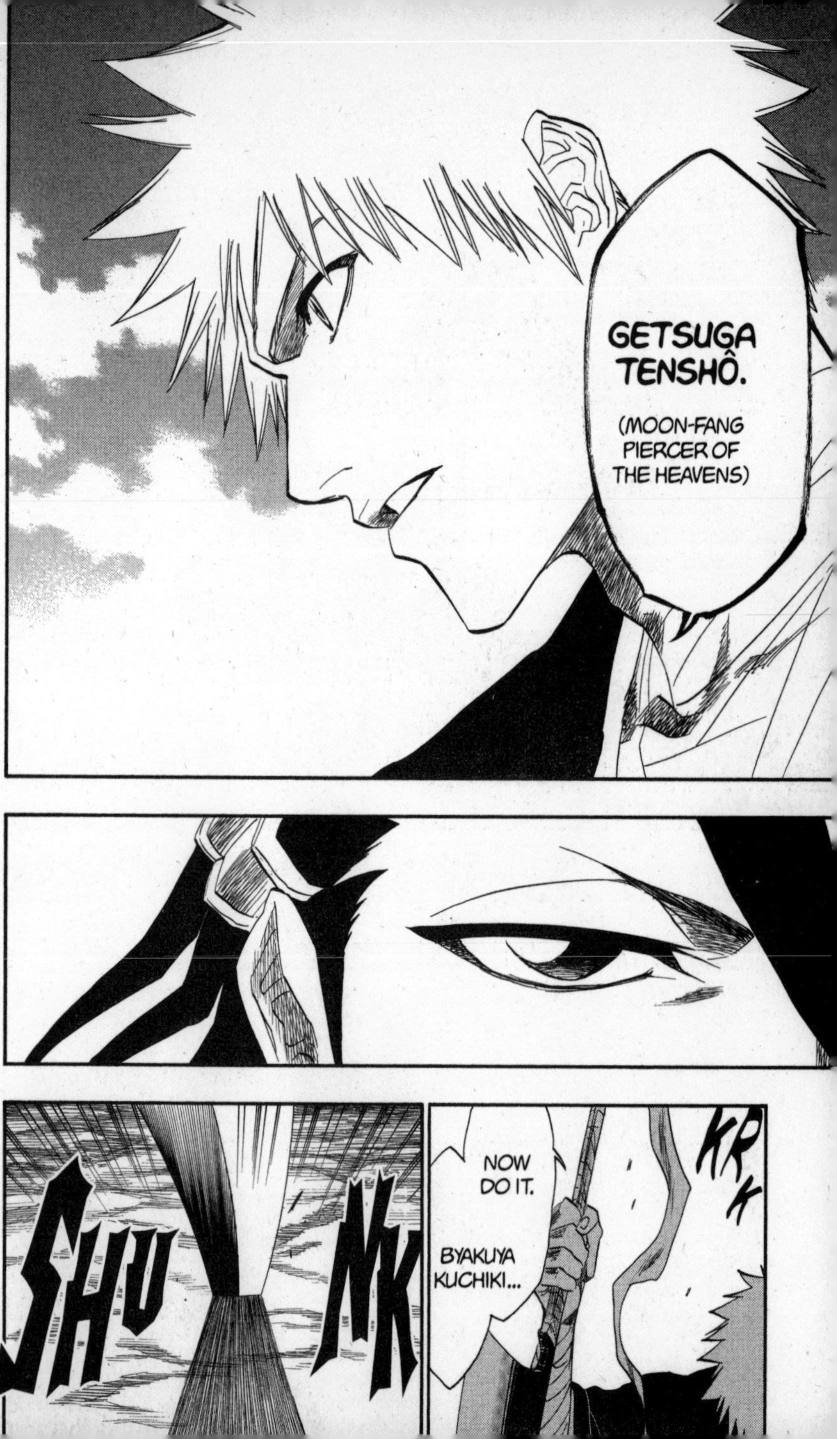
GETSUGA TENSHÔ.
(MOON-FANG PIERCER OF THE HEAVENS)
KR K
NOW DO IT.
BYAKUYA KUCHIKI...
SHUNK

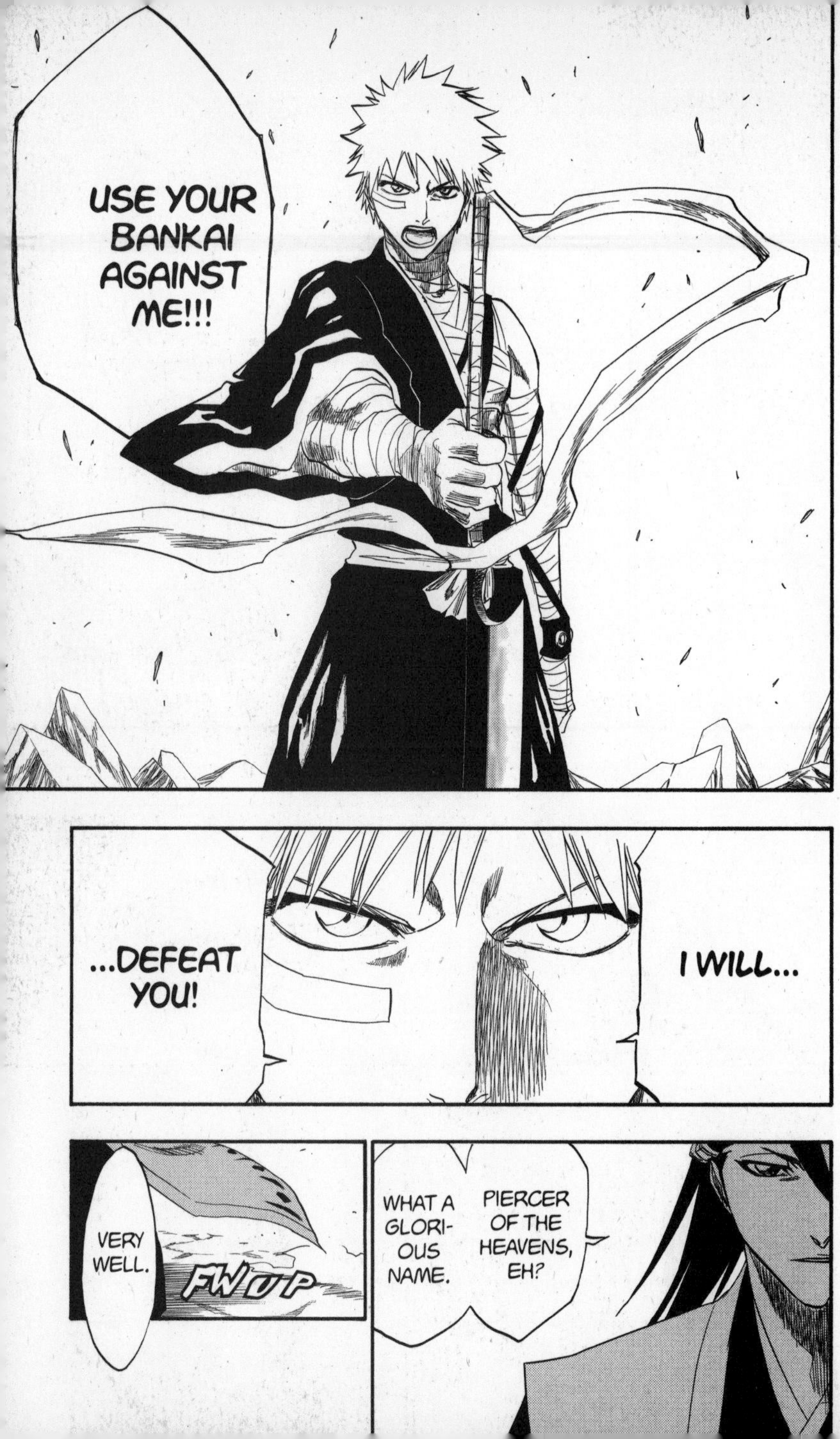
USE YOUR BANKAI AGAINST ME!!!
I WILL...
...DEFEAT YOU!
PIERCER OF THE HEAVENS, EH?
WHAT A GLORIOUS NAME.
FWUP
VERY WELL.

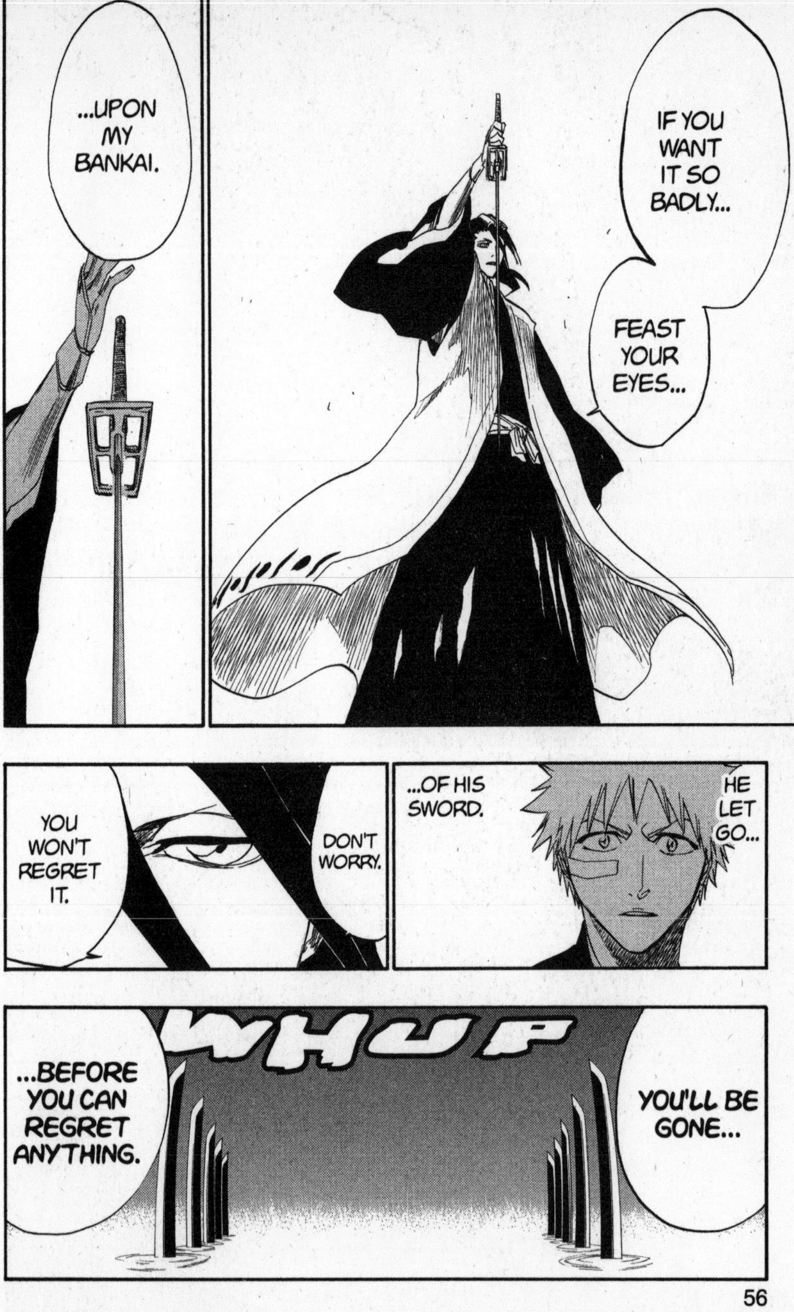
IF YOU WANT IT SO BADLY...
FEAST YOUR EYES...
...UPON MY BANKAI.
HE LET GO...
...OF HIS SWORD.
DON'T WORRY.
YOU WON'T REGRET IT.
WHUP
YOU'LL BE GONE...
...BEFORE YOU CAN REGRET ANYTHING.

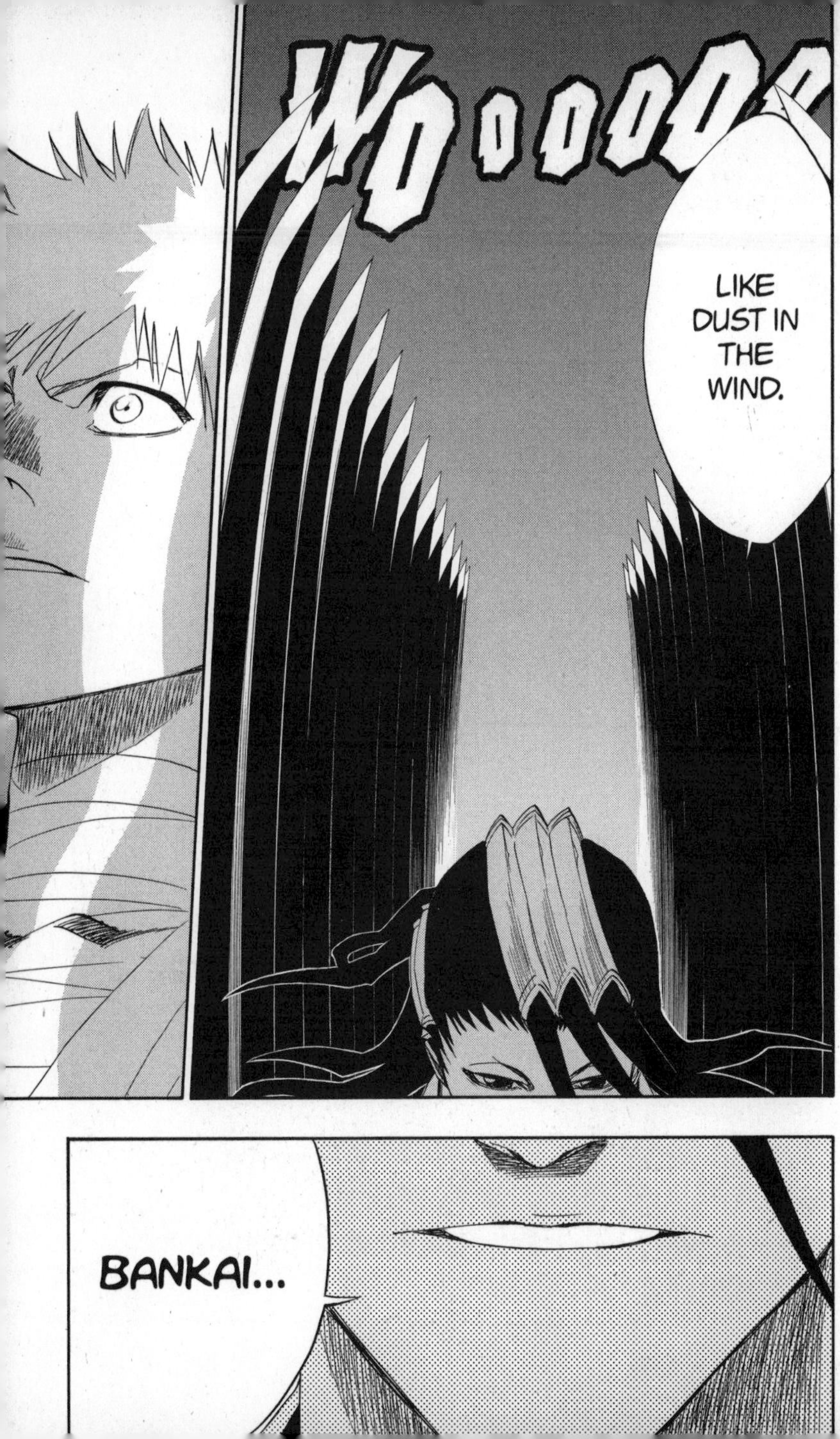
WOOOOOO
LIKE DUST IN THE WIND.
BANKAI...

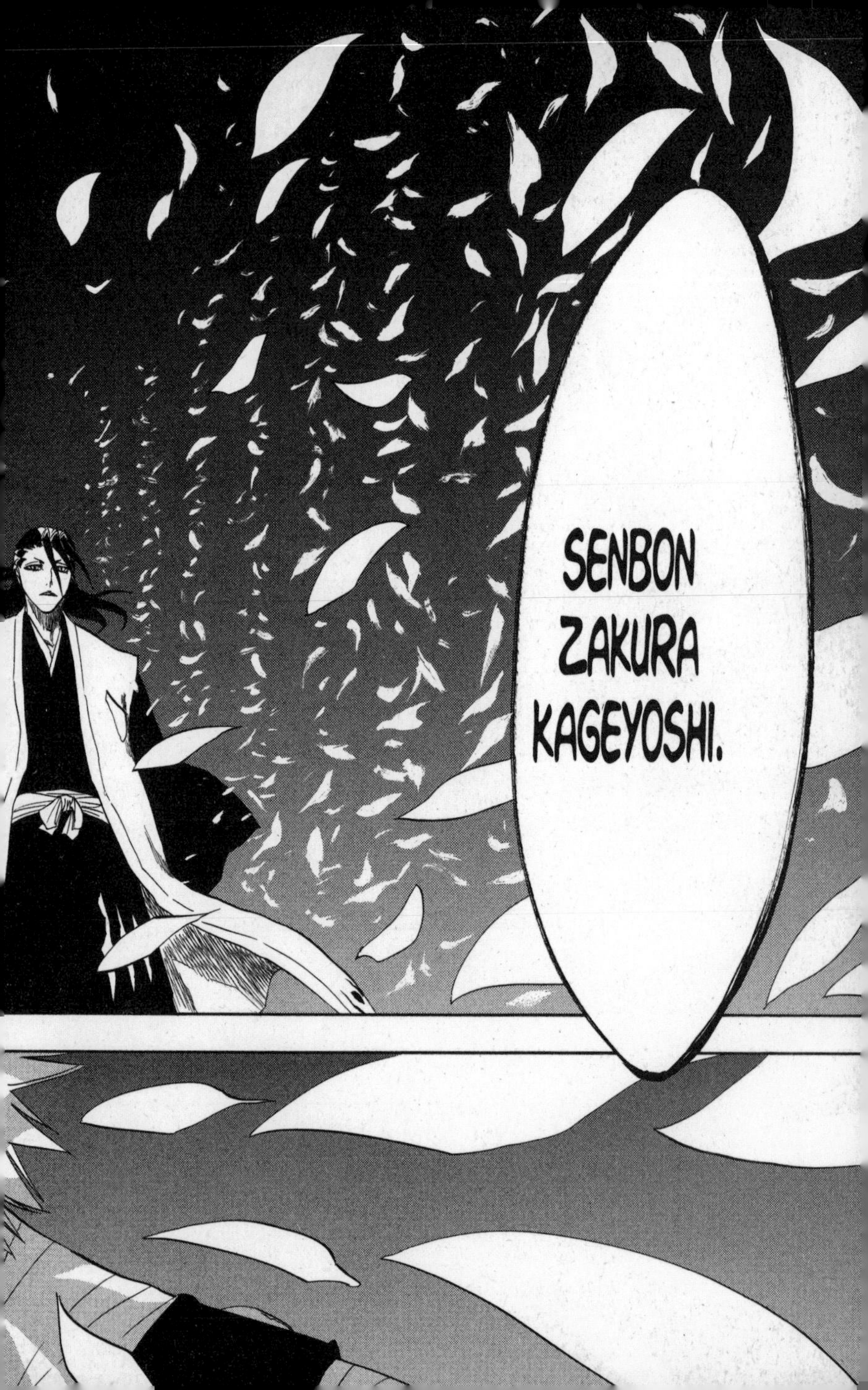
SENBON ZAKURA KAGEYOSHI.

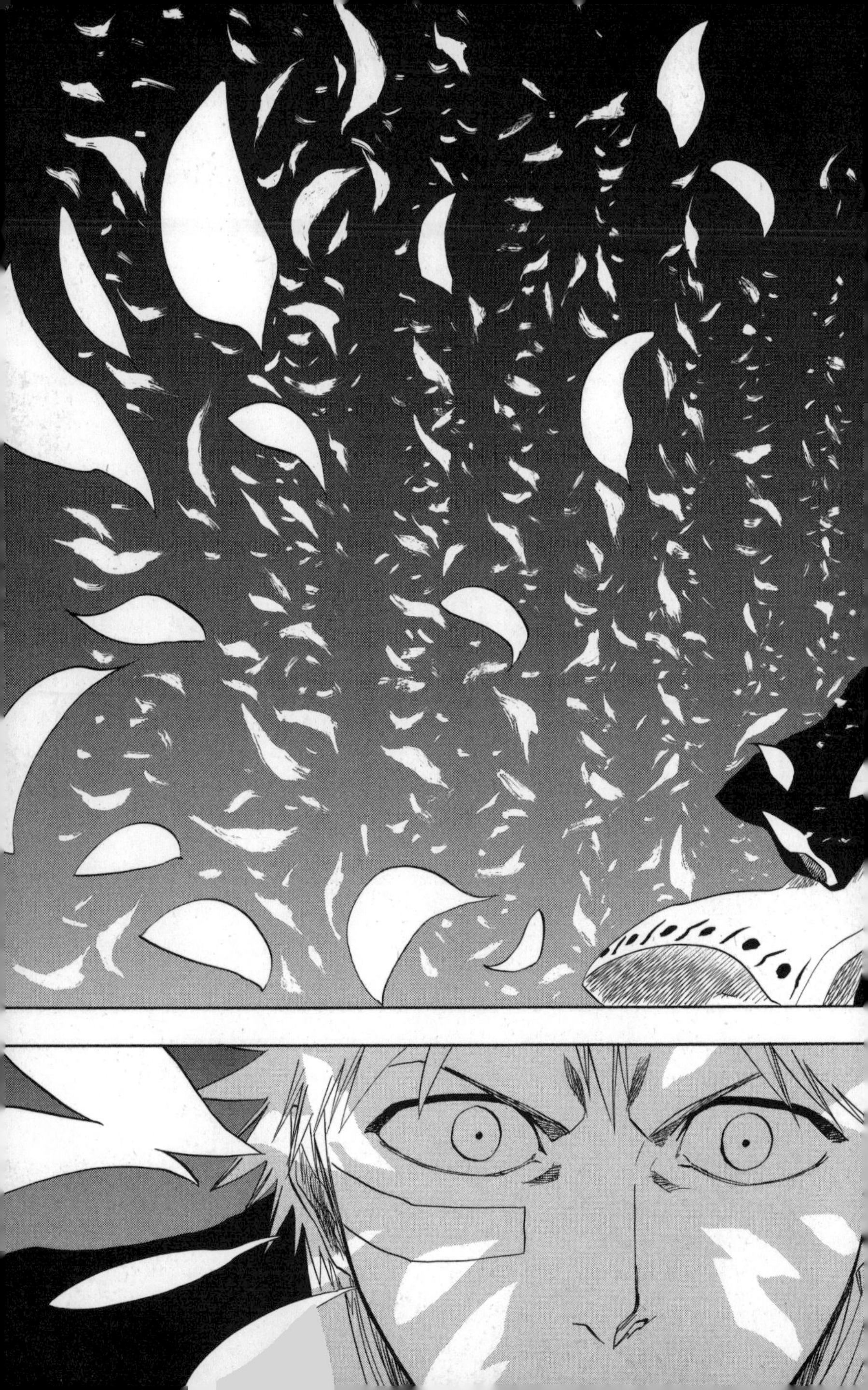

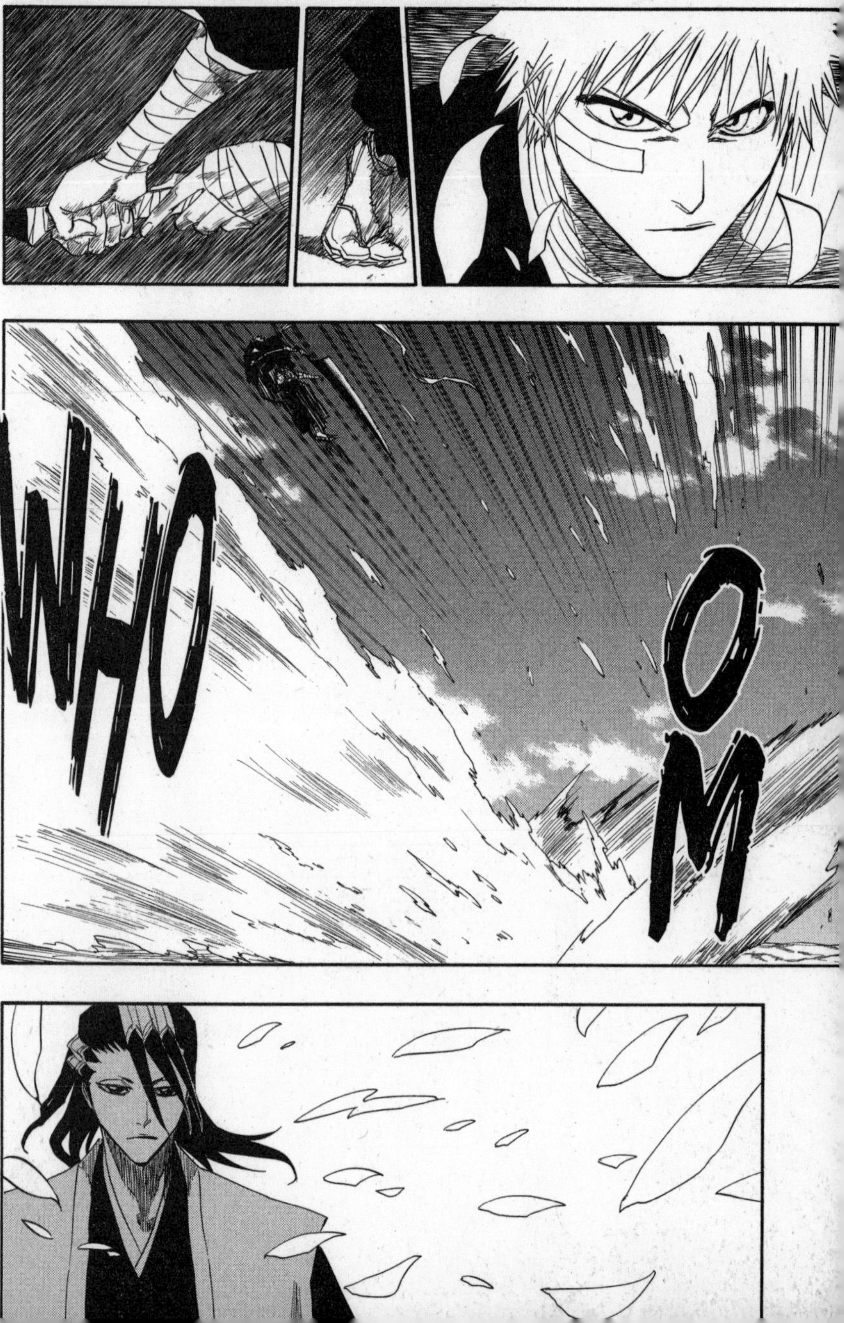
WHOOM

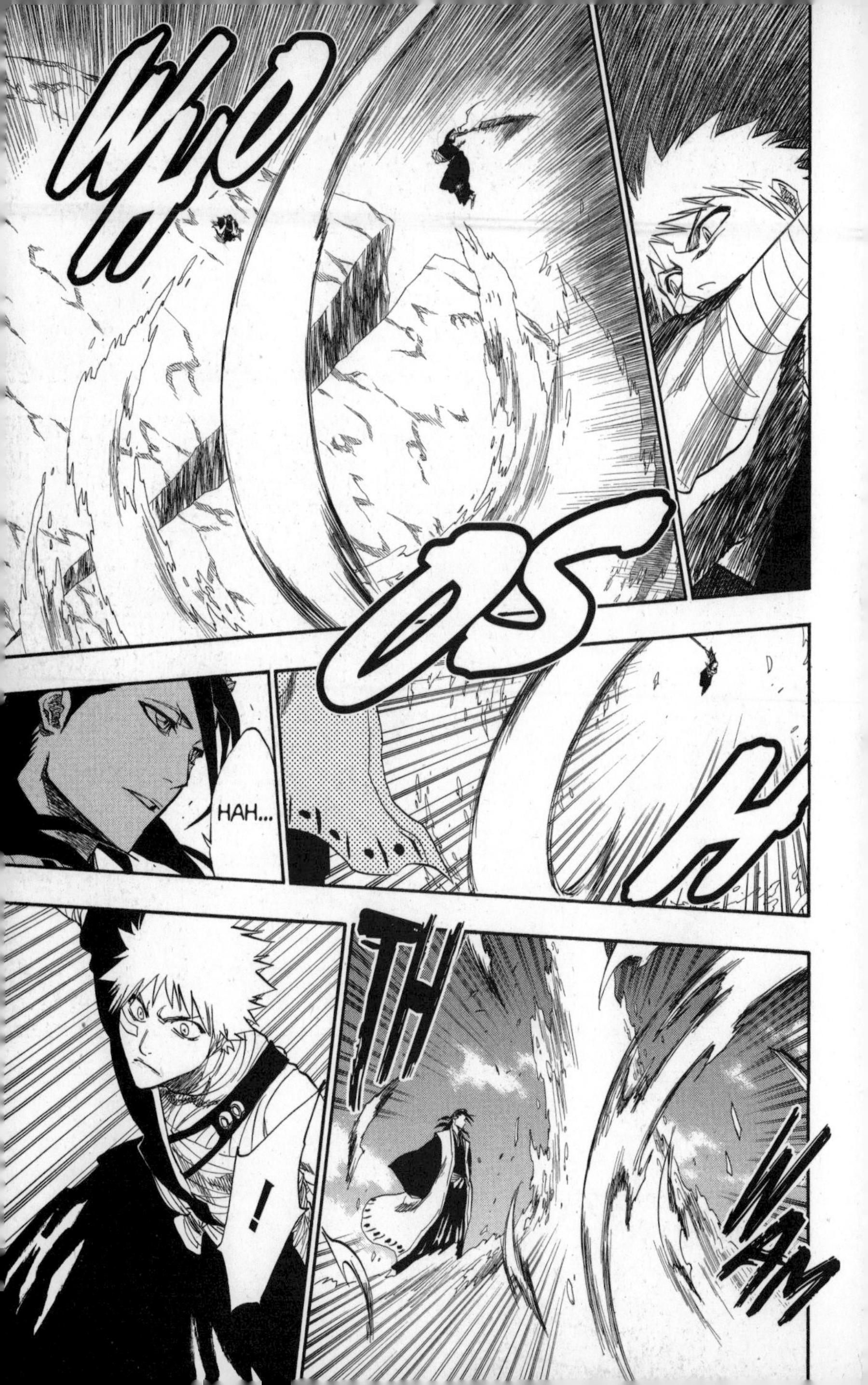
HAH...
!

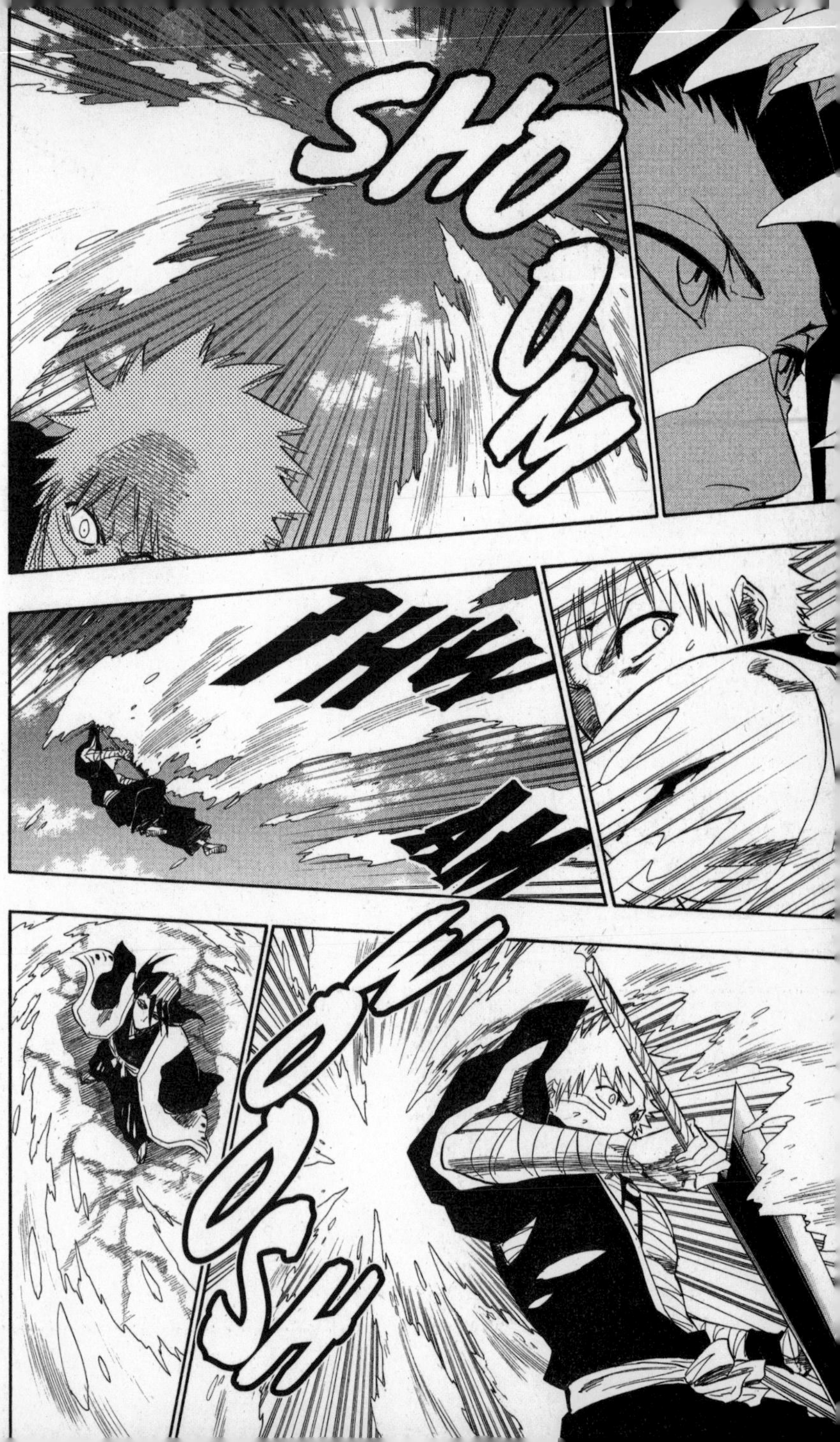
SHOOM
THWAM
WHOOSH

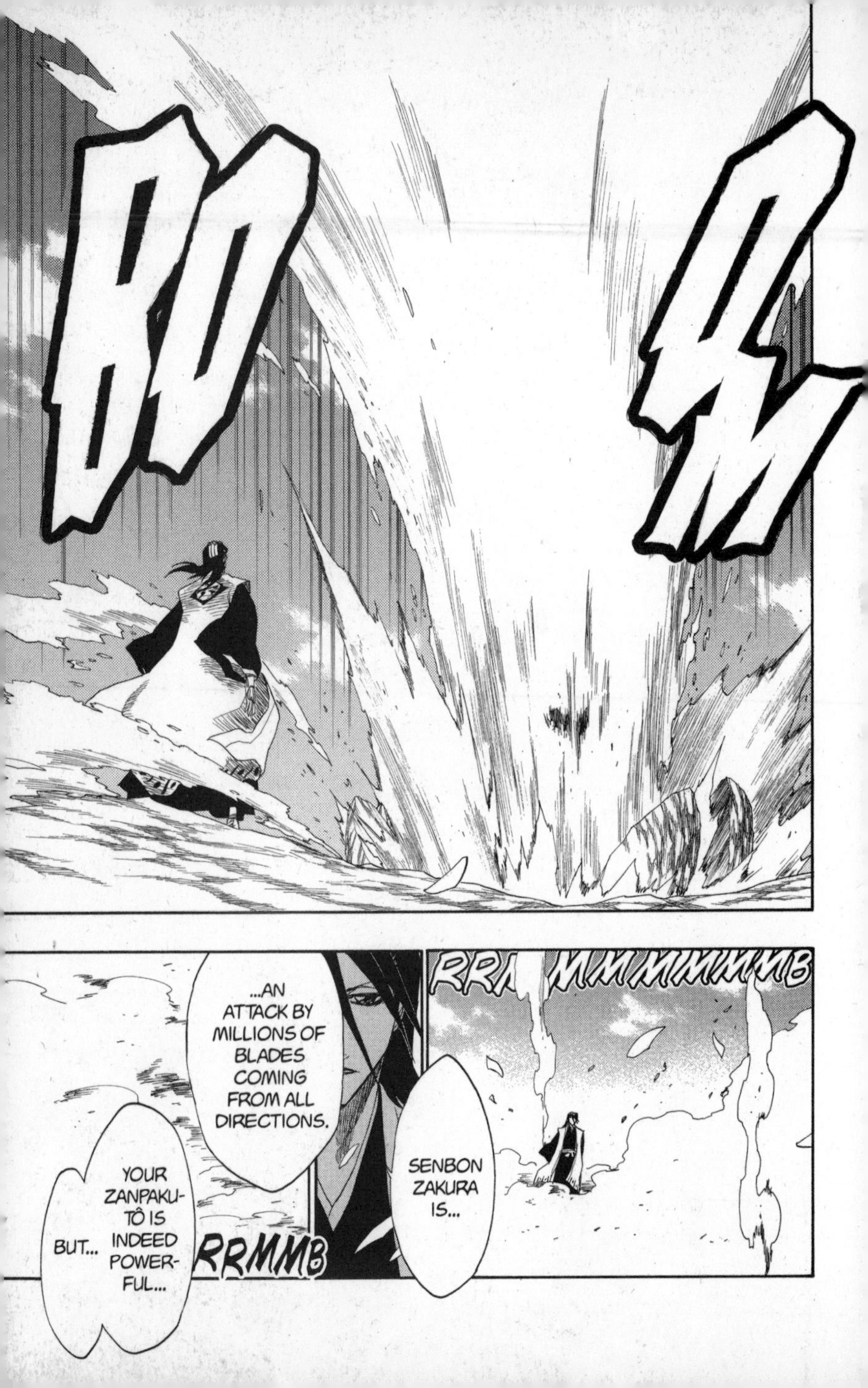
RRMMMMMMMMB
SENBON ZAKURA IS...
...AN ATTACK BY MILLIONS OF BLADES COMING FROM ALL DIRECTIONS.
YOUR ZANPAKU-TÔ IS INDEED POWER-FUL...
BUT...
RRMMB

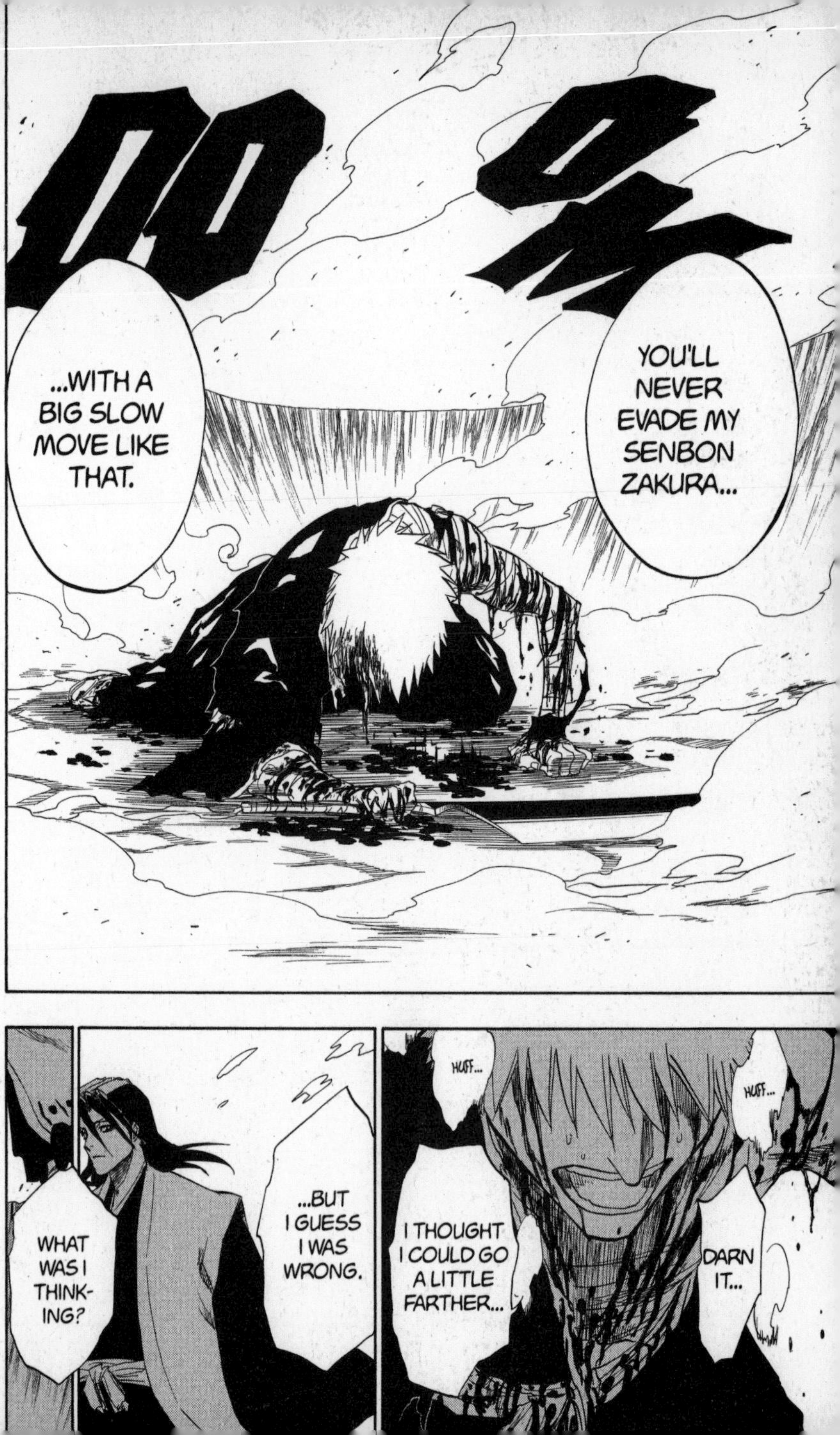
DOOM
YOU'LL NEVER EVADE MY SENBON ZAKURA...
...WITH A BIG SLOW MOVE LIKE THAT.
HUFF...
HUFF...
DARN IT...
I THOUGHT I COULD GO A LITTLE FARTHER...
...BUT I GUESS I WAS WRONG.
WHAT WAS I THINKING?

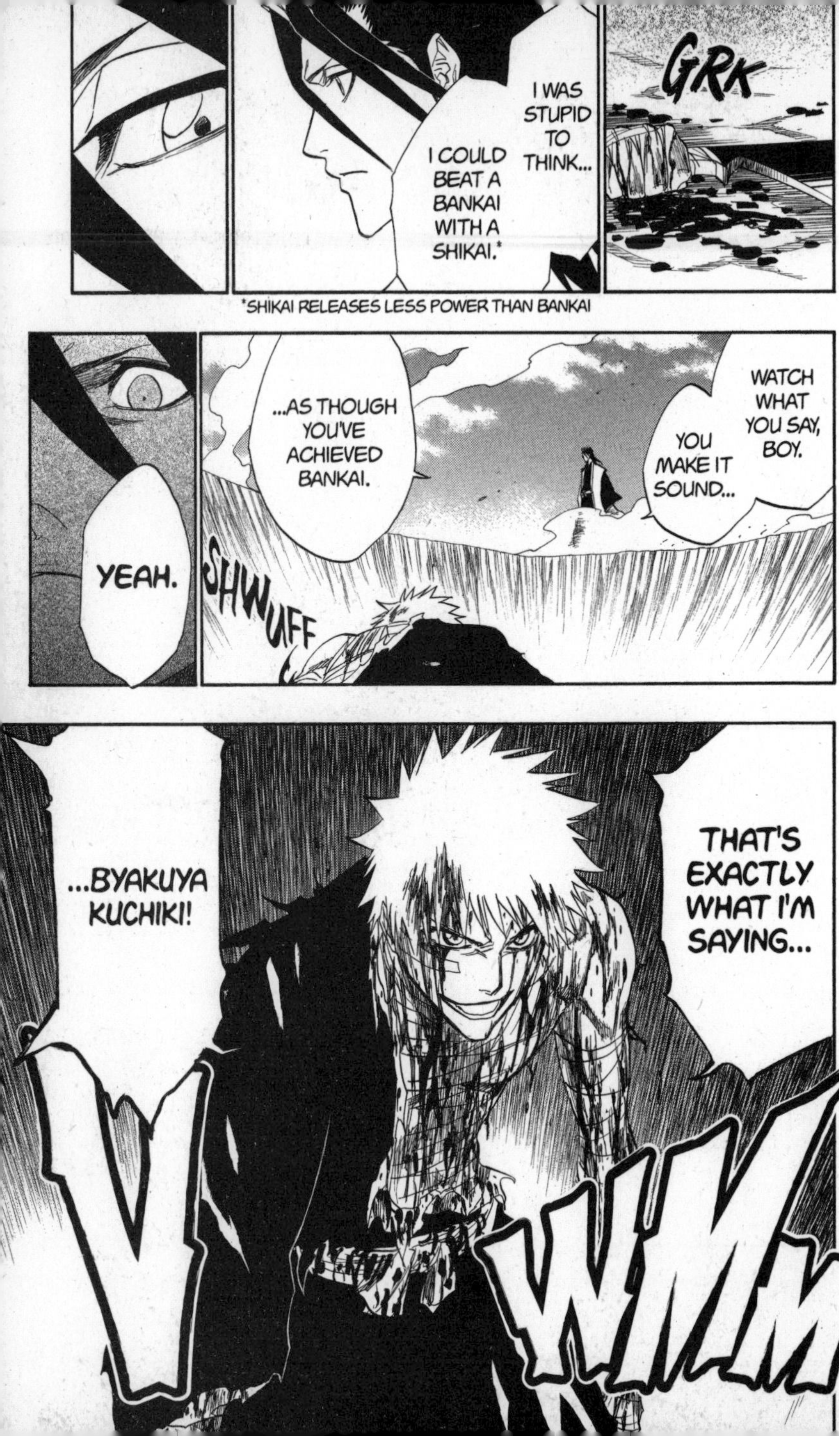
GRK
I WAS STUPID TO THINK...
I COULD BEAT A BANKAI WITH A SHIKAI.*
*SHIKAI RELEASES LESS POWER THAN BANKAI
WATCH WHAT YOU SAY, BOY.
YOU MAKE IT SOUND...
...AS THOUGH YOU'VE ACHIEVED BANKAI.
SHWUFF
YEAH.
THAT'S EXACTLY WHAT I'M SAYING...
...BYAKUYA KUCHIKI!
V
WMM

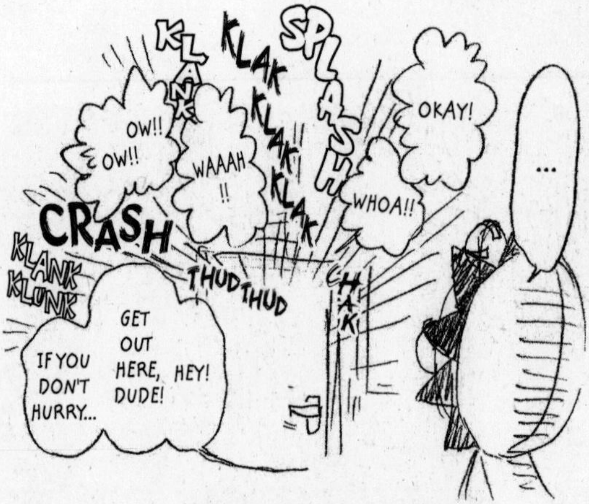
...
OKAY!
WHOA!!
SPLASH
KLAK KLAK KLAK
WAAAH !!
KLANK
OW!! OW!!
CRASH
CHAK
THUD THUD
HEY!
GET OUT HERE, DUDE!
IF YOU DON'T HURRY...
KLANK KLUNK

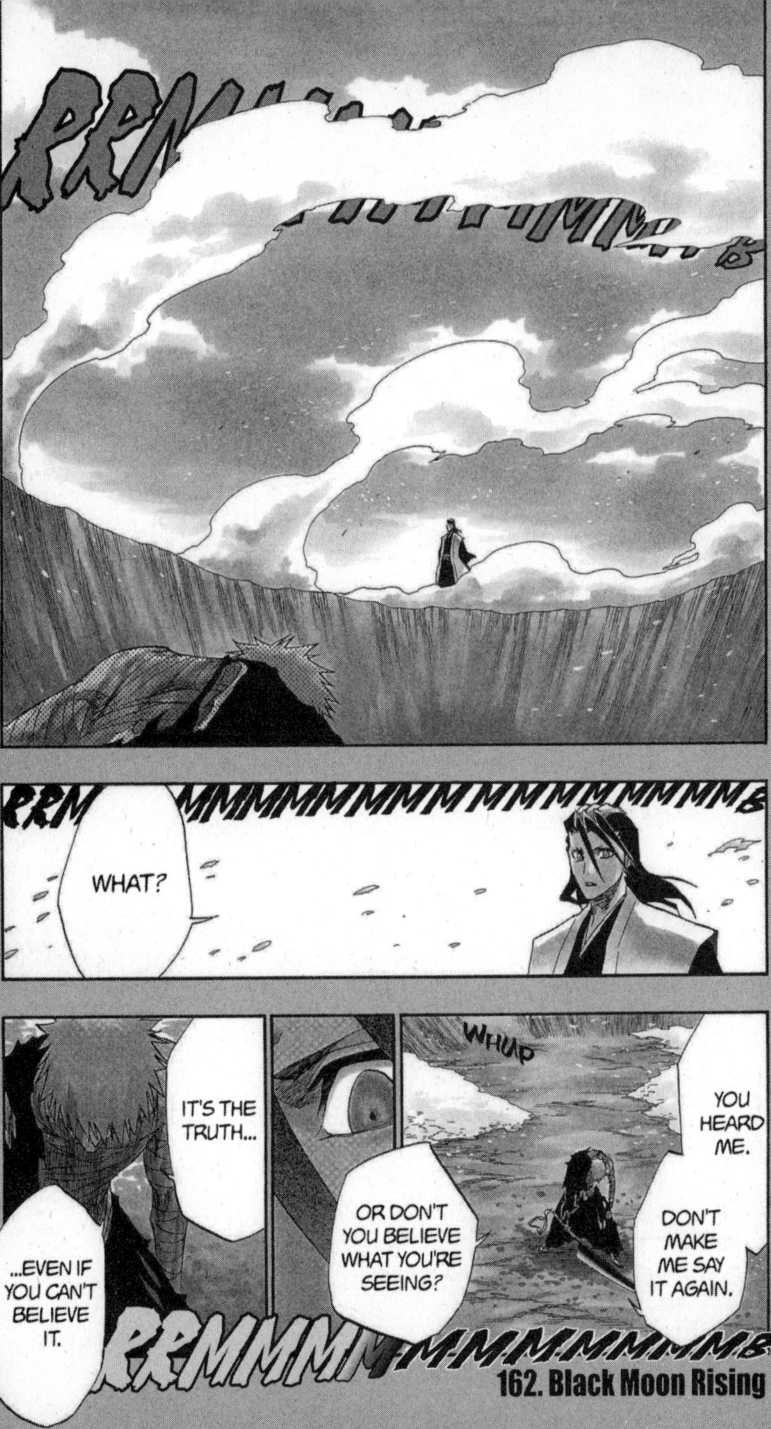
RRMMMMMMMMB
RRMMMMMMMMMMMMMMMMMMMMB
WHAT?
WHUP
YOU HEARD ME.
DON'T MAKE ME SAY IT AGAIN.
OR DON'T YOU BELIEVE WHAT YOU'RE SEEING?
IT'S THE TRUTH...
...EVEN IF YOU CAN'T BELIEVE IT.
RRMMMMMMMMMMMMMMB

162. Black Moon Rising

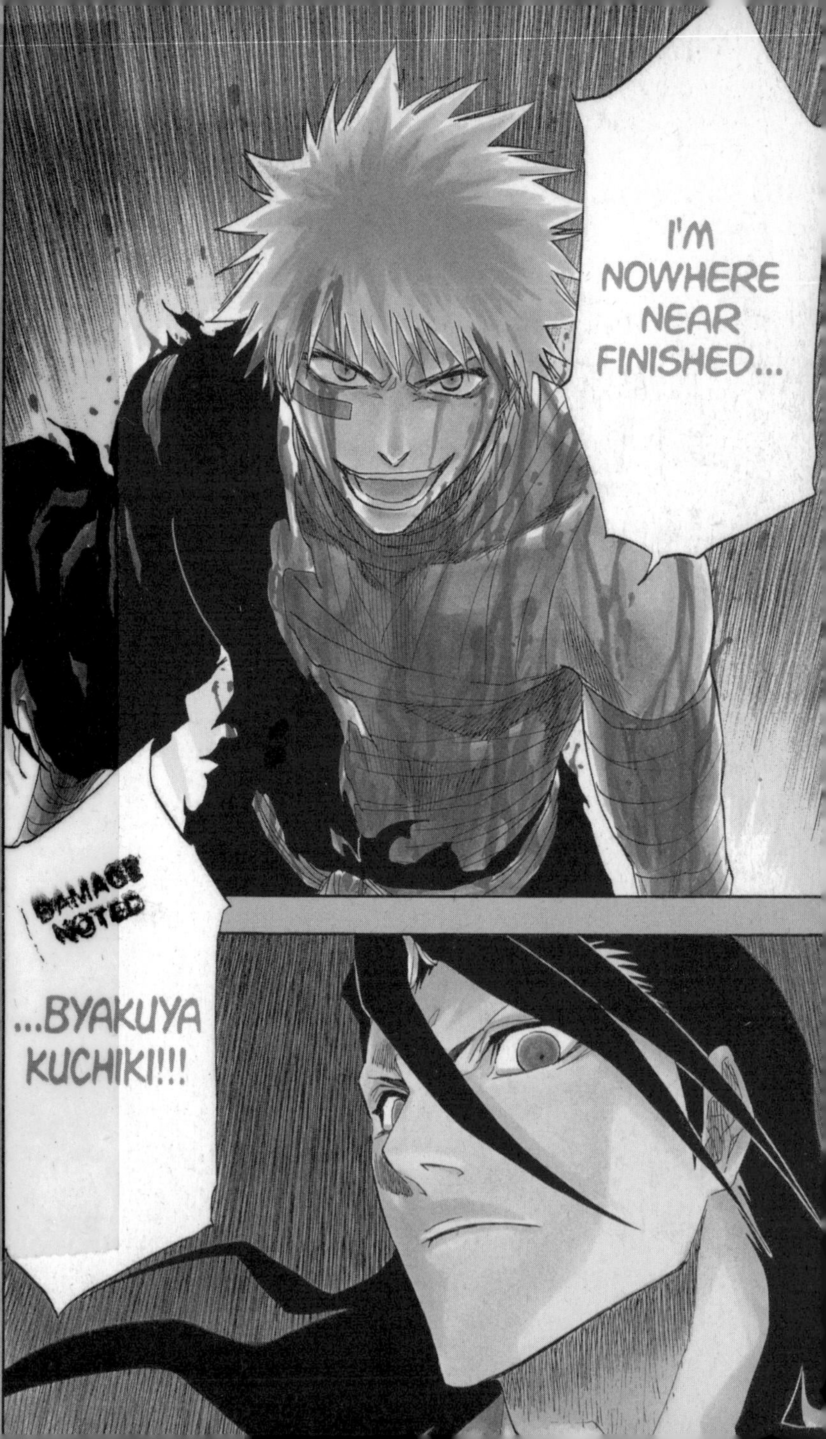
I'M NOWHERE NEAR FINISHED...
...BYAKUYA KUCHIKI!!!

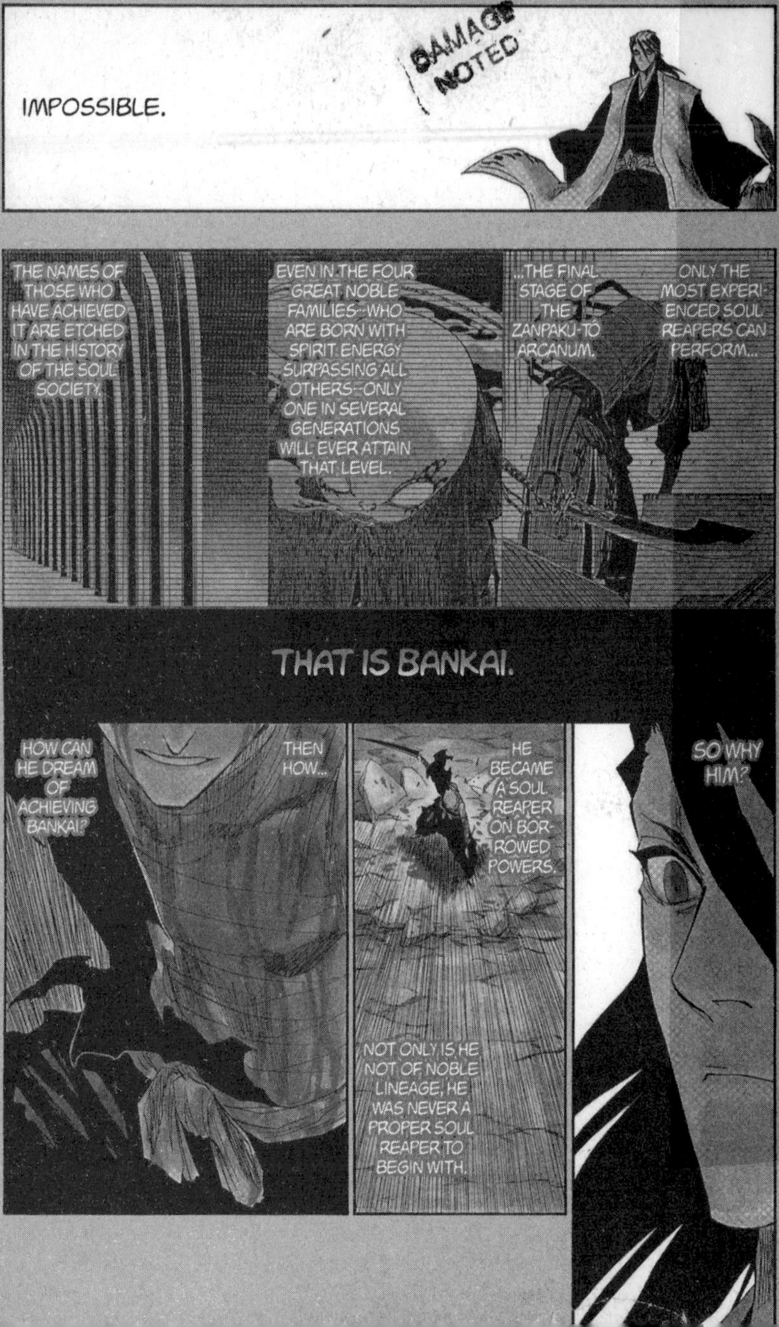
IMPOSSIBLE.
ONLY THE MOST EXPERIENCED SOUL REAPERS CAN PERFORM...
...THE FINAL STAGE OF THE ZANPAKU-TŌ ARCANUM.
EVEN IN THE FOUR GREAT NOBLE FAMILIES--WHO ARE BORN WITH SPIRIT ENERGY SURPASSING ALL OTHERS--ONLY ONE IN SEVERAL GENERATIONS WILL EVER ATTAIN THAT LEVEL.
THE NAMES OF THOSE WHO HAVE ACHIEVED IT ARE ETCHED IN THE HISTORY OF THE SOUL SOCIETY.
THAT IS BANKAI.
SO WHY HIM?
HE BECAME A SOUL REAPER ON BORROWED POWERS.
NOT ONLY IS HE NOT OF NOBLE LINEAGE, HE WAS NEVER A PROPER SOUL REAPER TO BEGIN WITH.
THEN HOW...
HOW CAN HE DREAM OF ACHIEVING BANKAI?

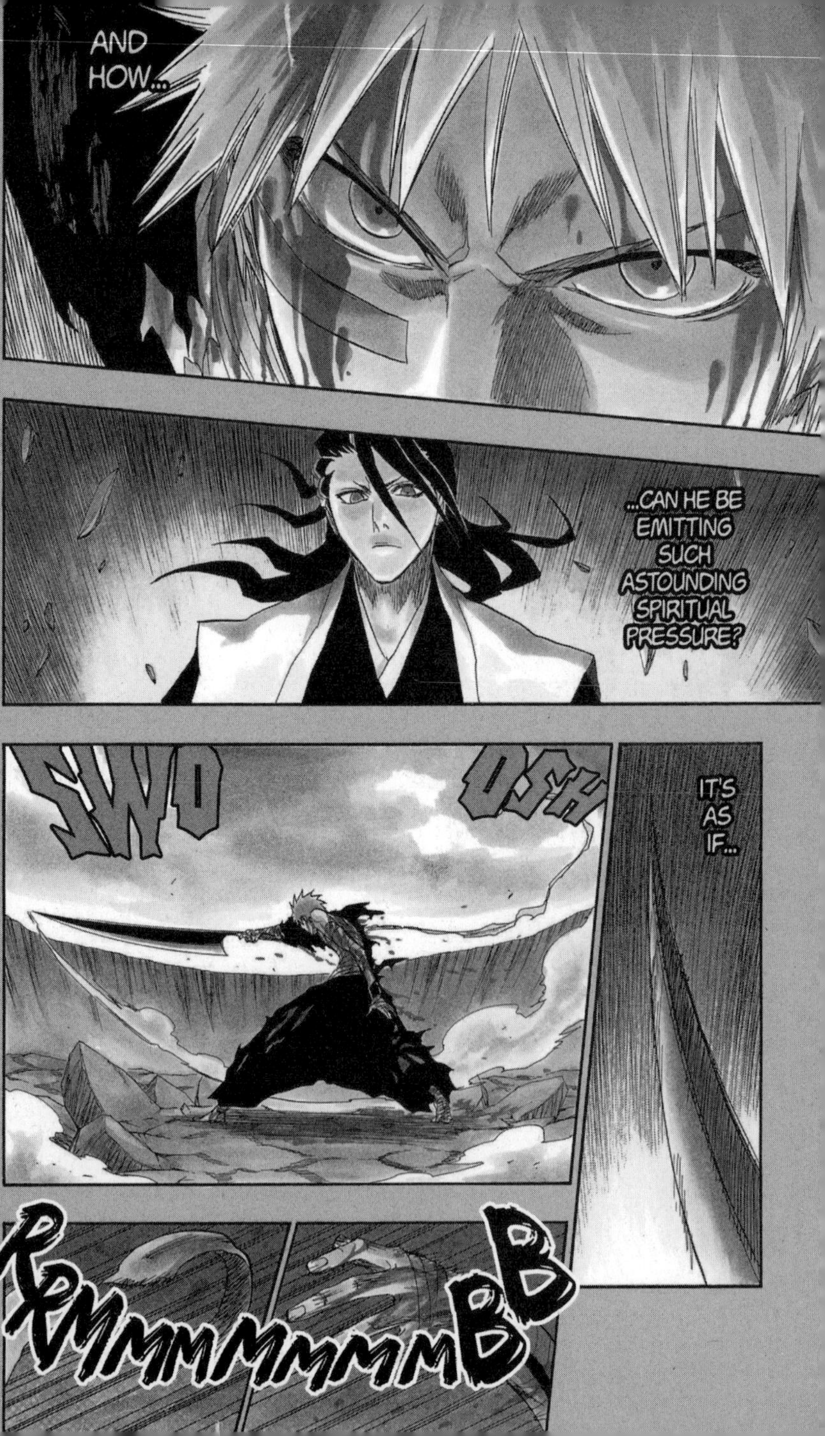
AND HOW...
...CAN HE BE EMITTING SUCH ASTOUNDING SPIRITUAL PRESSURE?
IT'S AS IF...
SWOOSH
RUMMMMMMMMBB

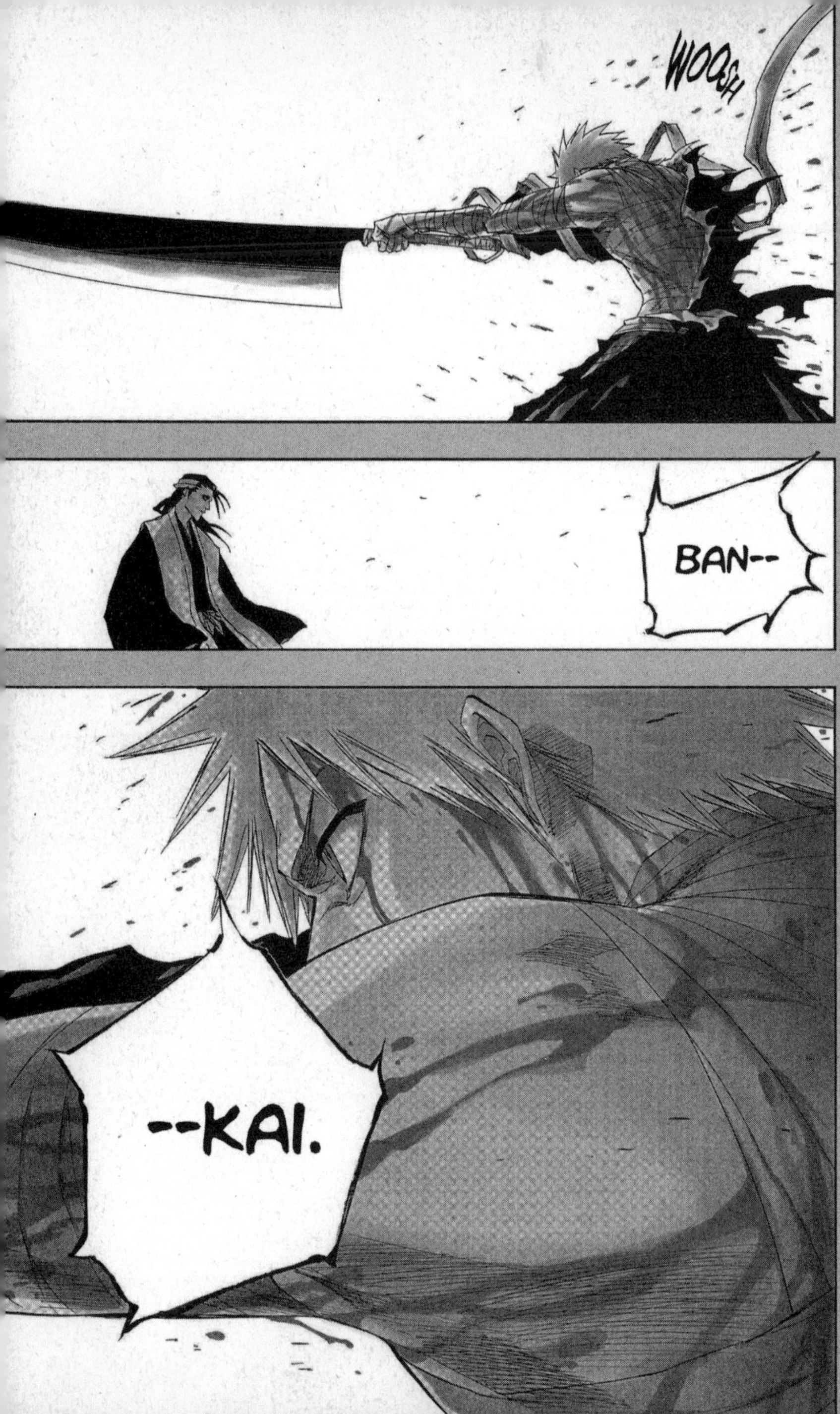
WOOSH
BAN--
--KAI.

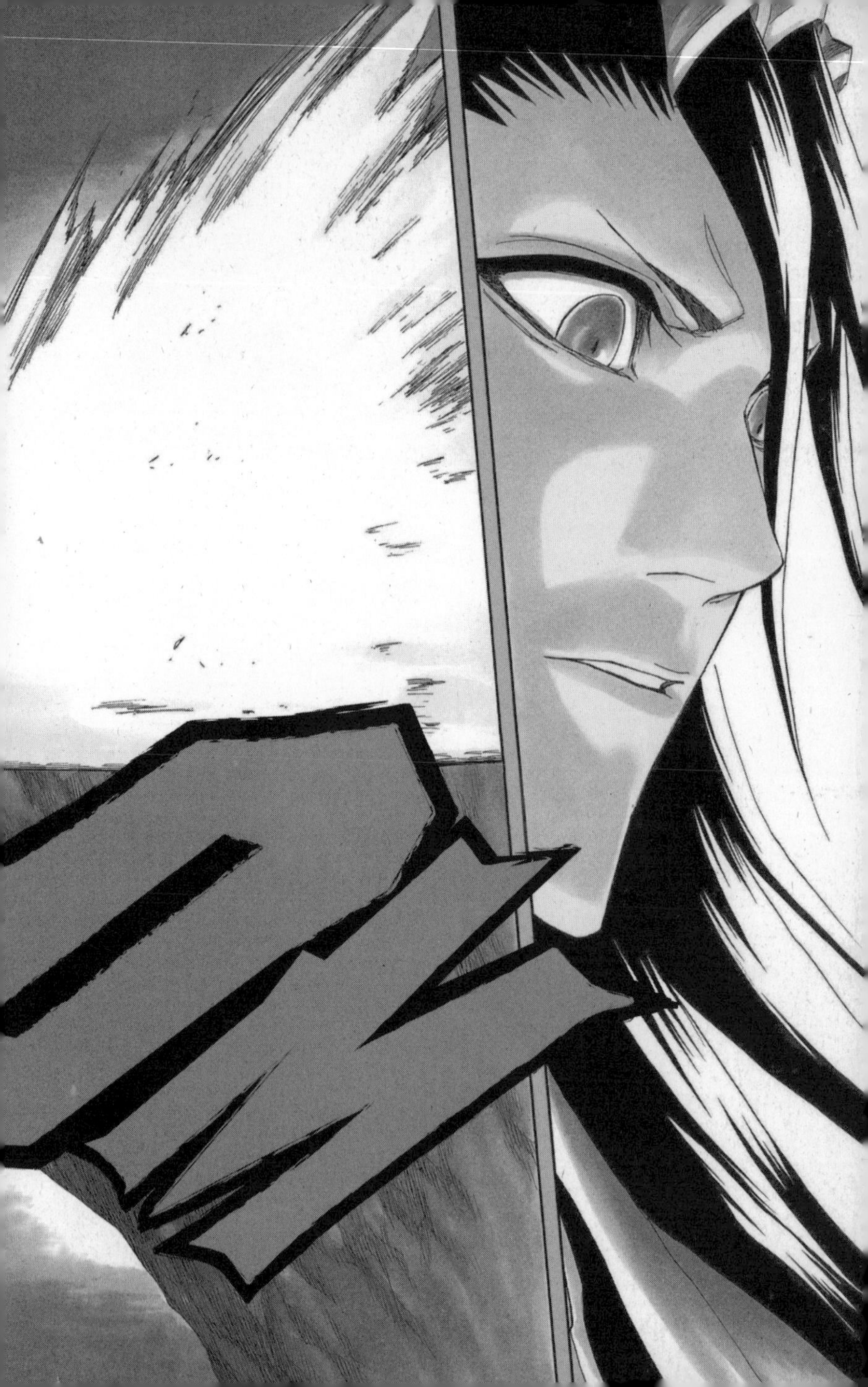

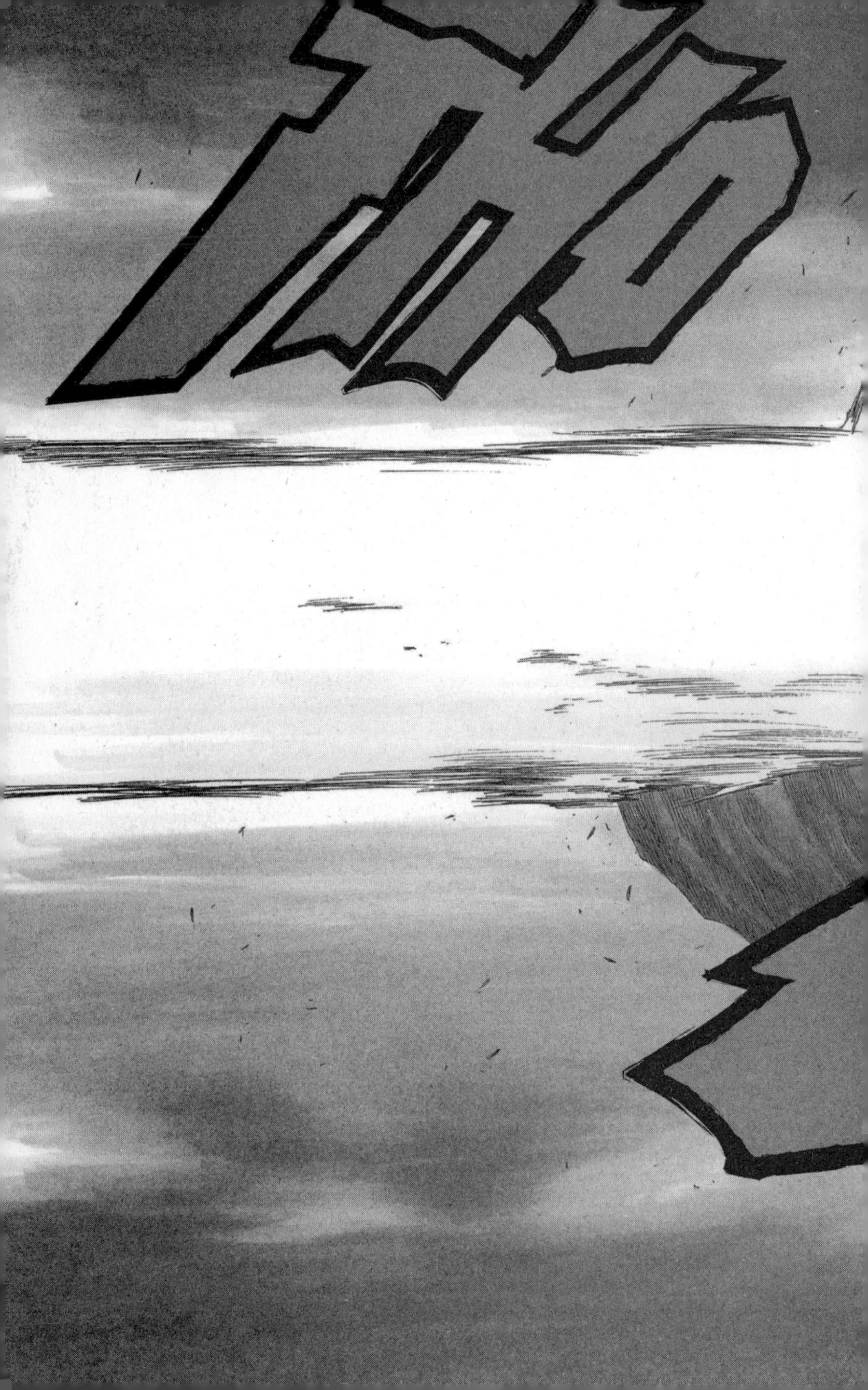

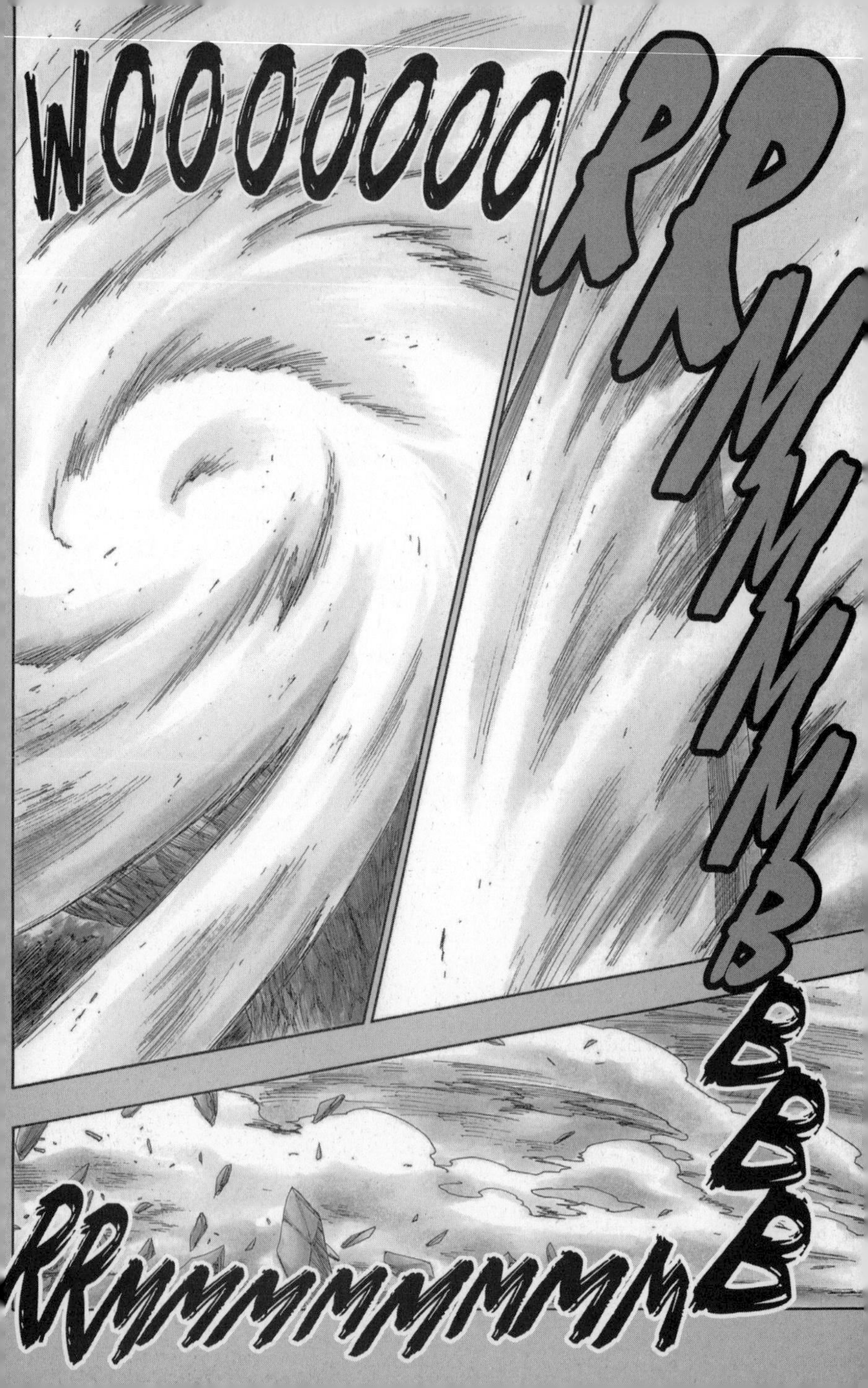
PRMMMMMBBBBB
WOOOOOOO
RRMMMMMMMMB

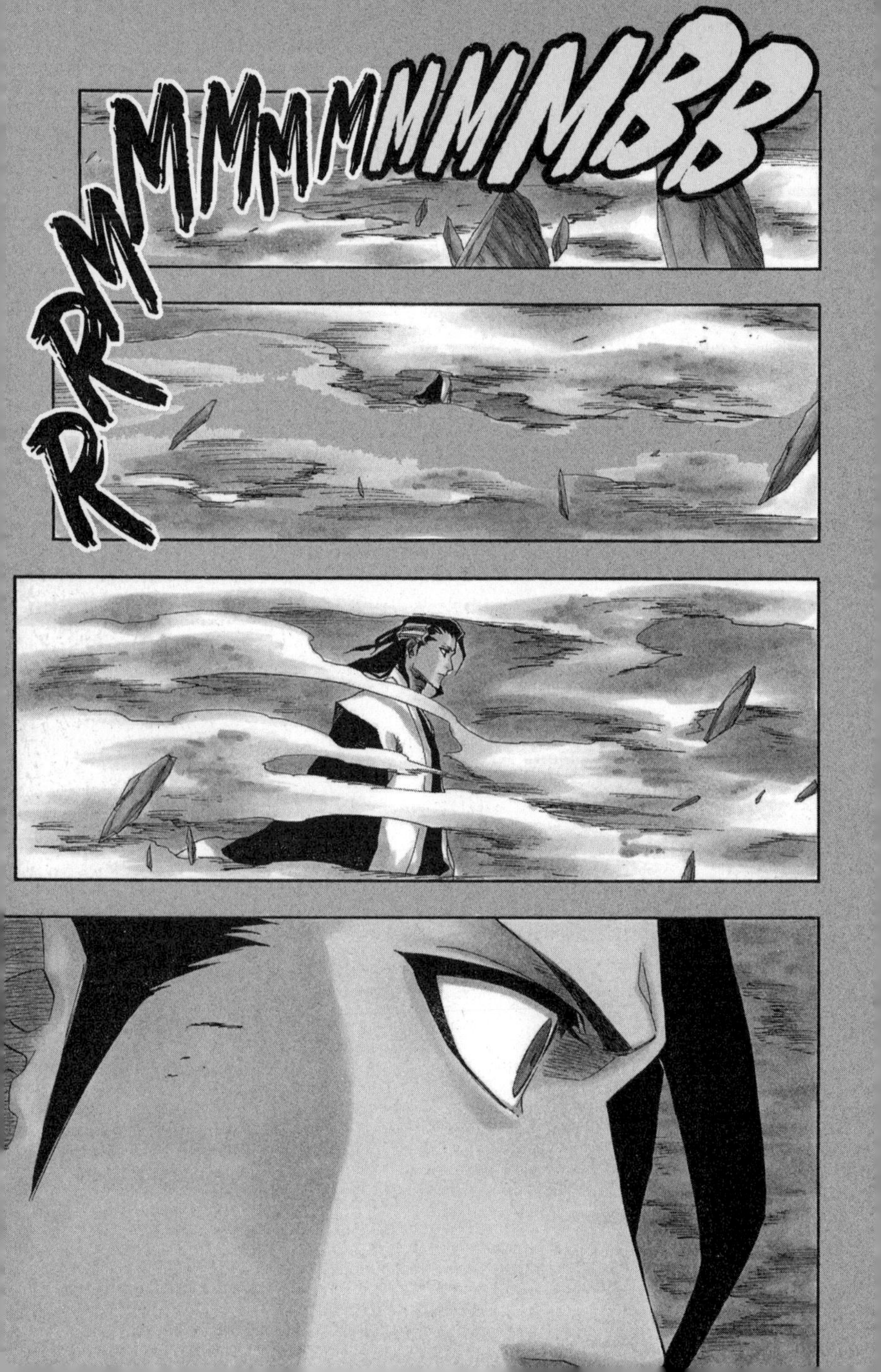
RRMMMMMMMMMMMBB

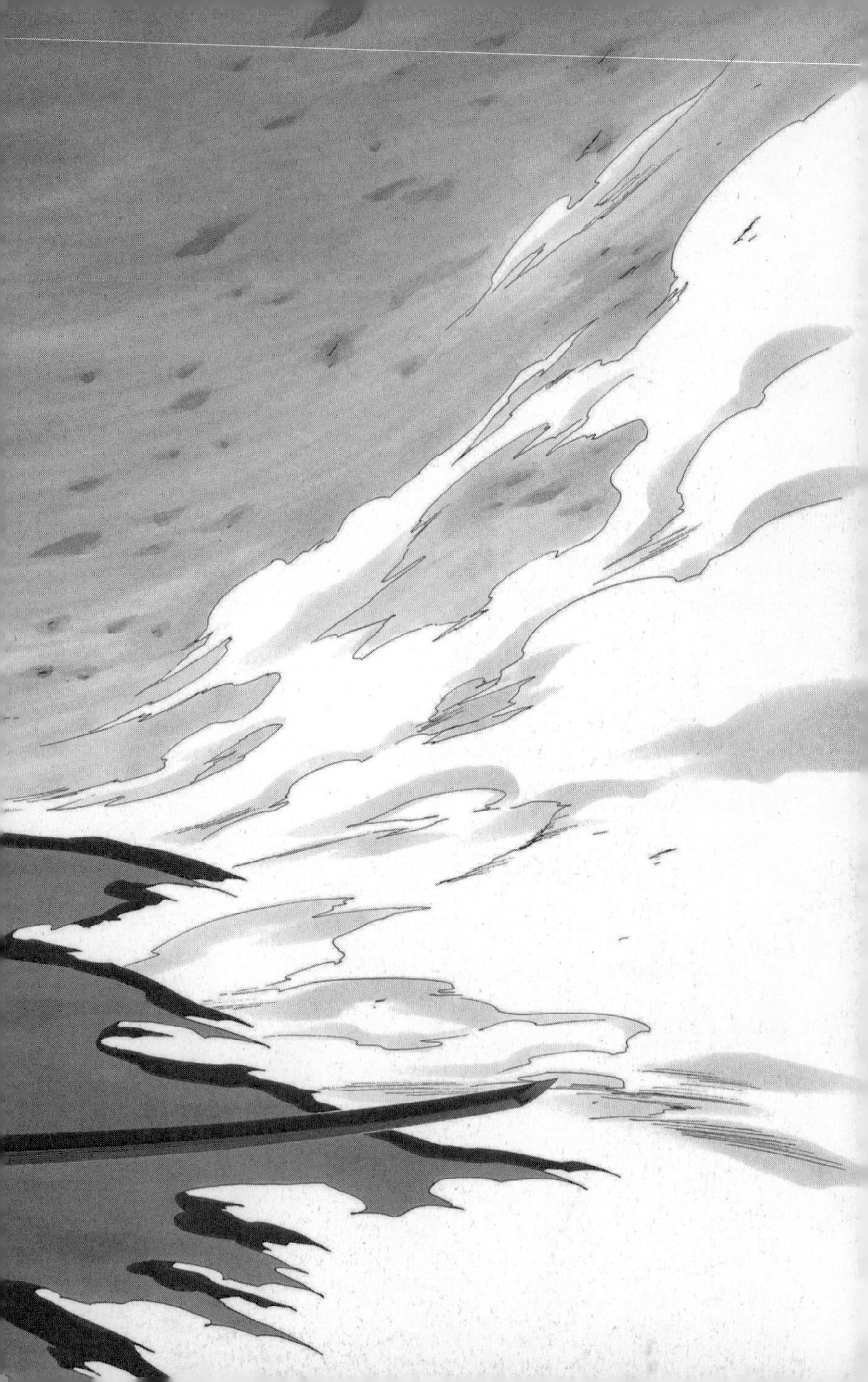

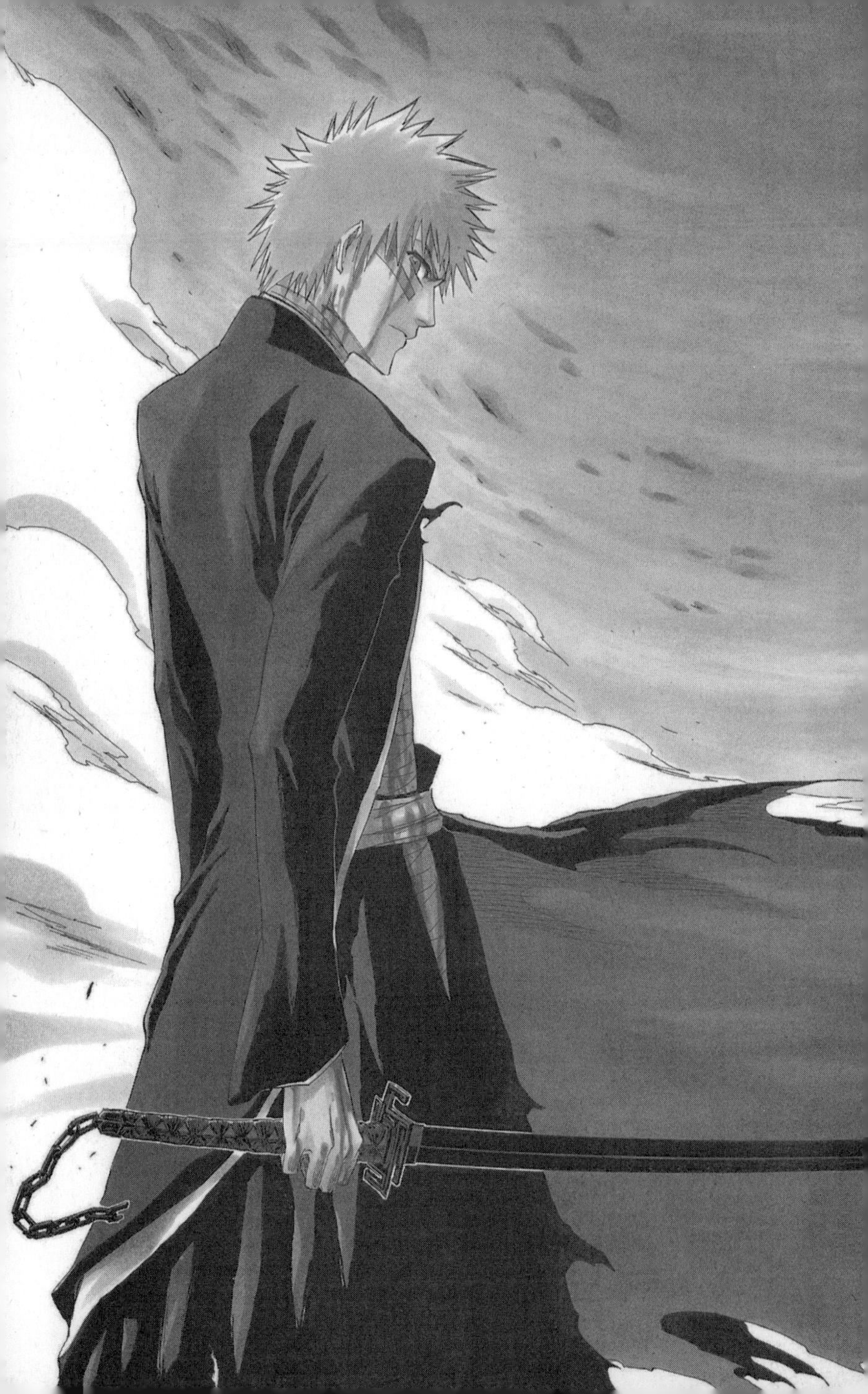

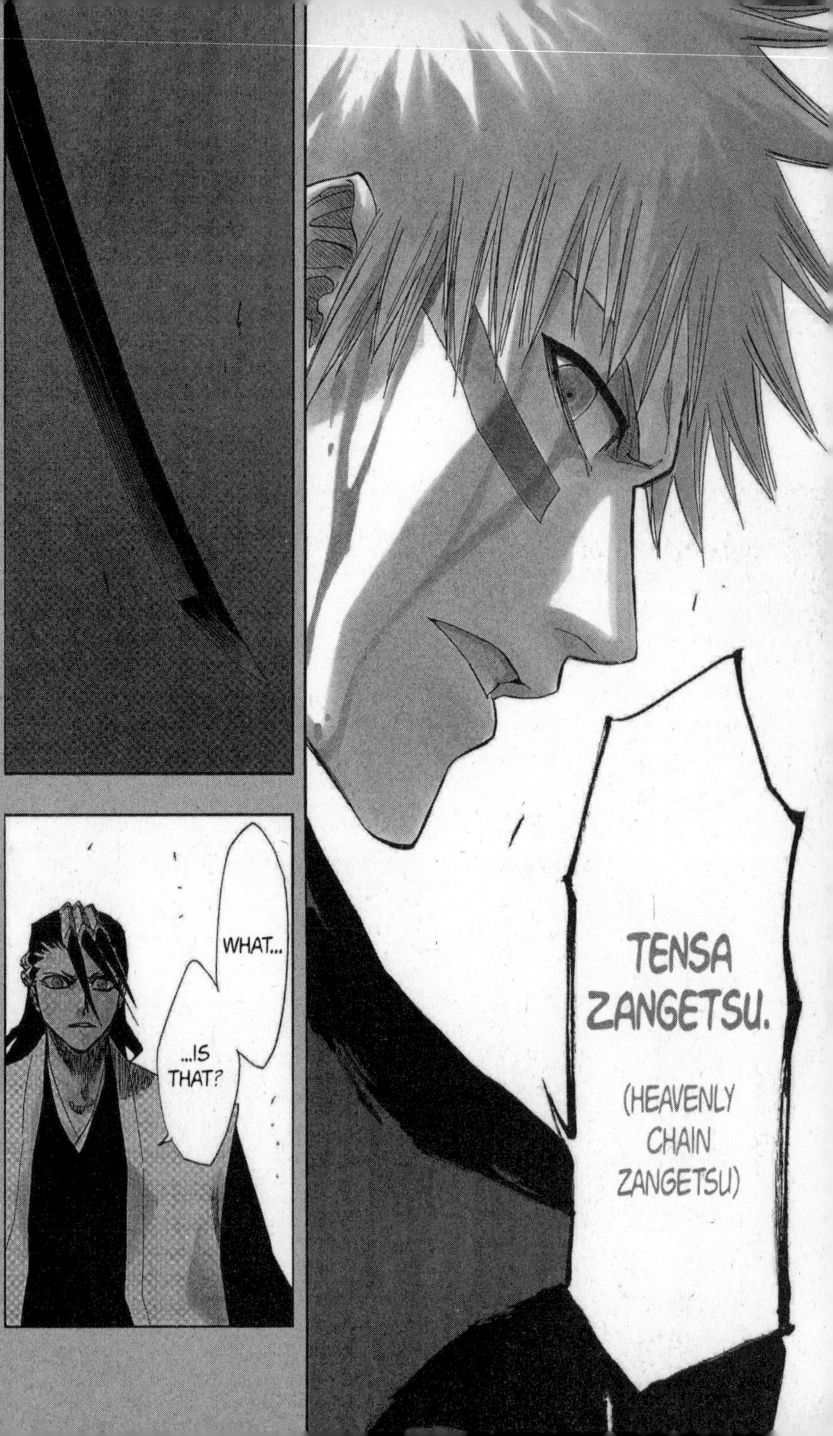
TENSA ZANGETSU.
(HEAVENLY CHAIN ZANGETSU)
WHAT...
...IS THAT?

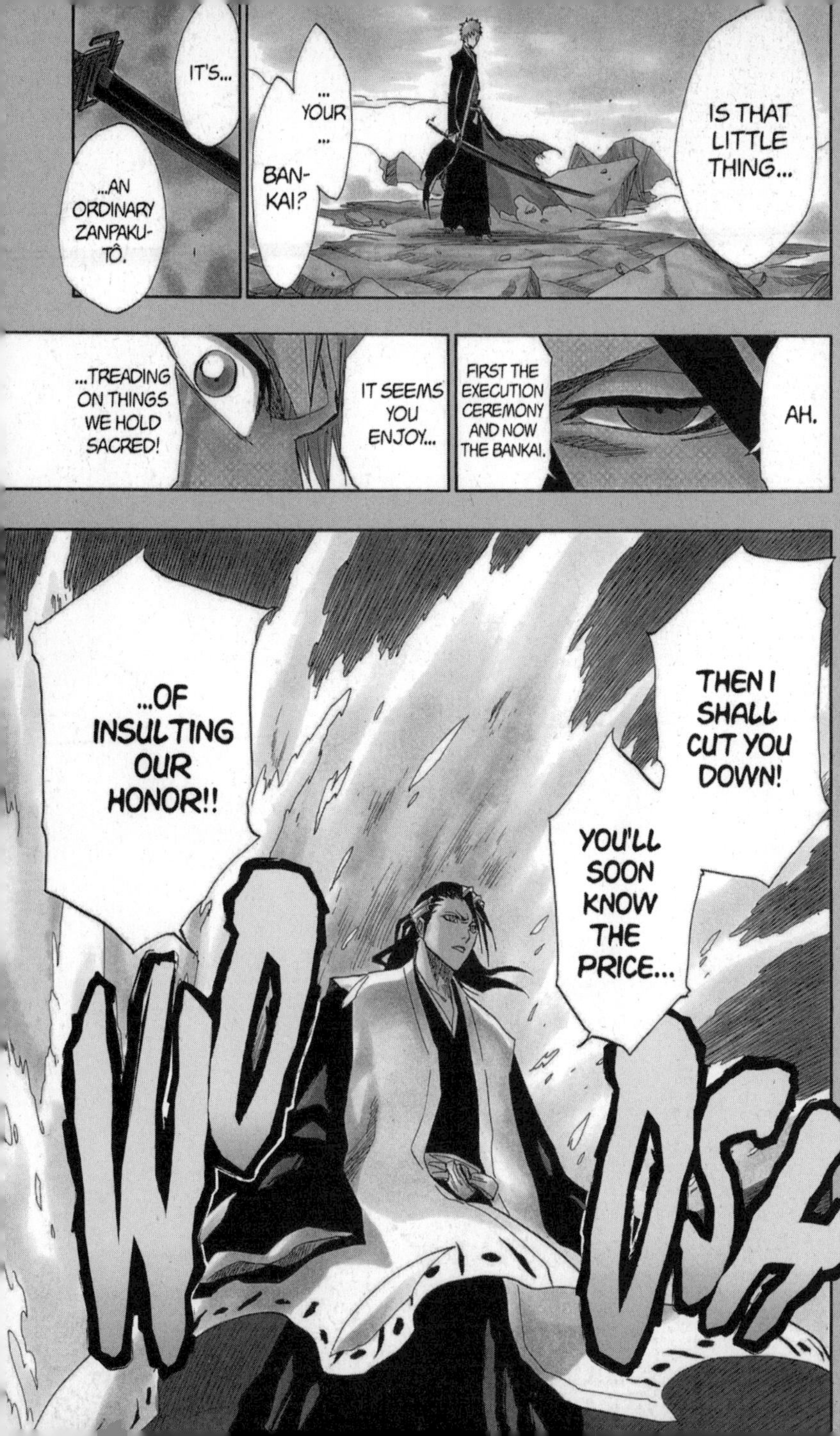
IS THAT LITTLE THING...
... YOUR ...
BAN-KAI?
IT'S...
...AN ORDINARY ZANPAKU-TÔ.
AH.
FIRST THE EXECUTION CEREMONY AND NOW THE BANKAI.
IT SEEMS YOU ENJOY...
...TREADING ON THINGS WE HOLD SACRED!
THEN I SHALL CUT YOU DOWN!
YOU'LL SOON KNOW THE PRICE...
...OF INSULTING OUR HONOR!!
WOOSH

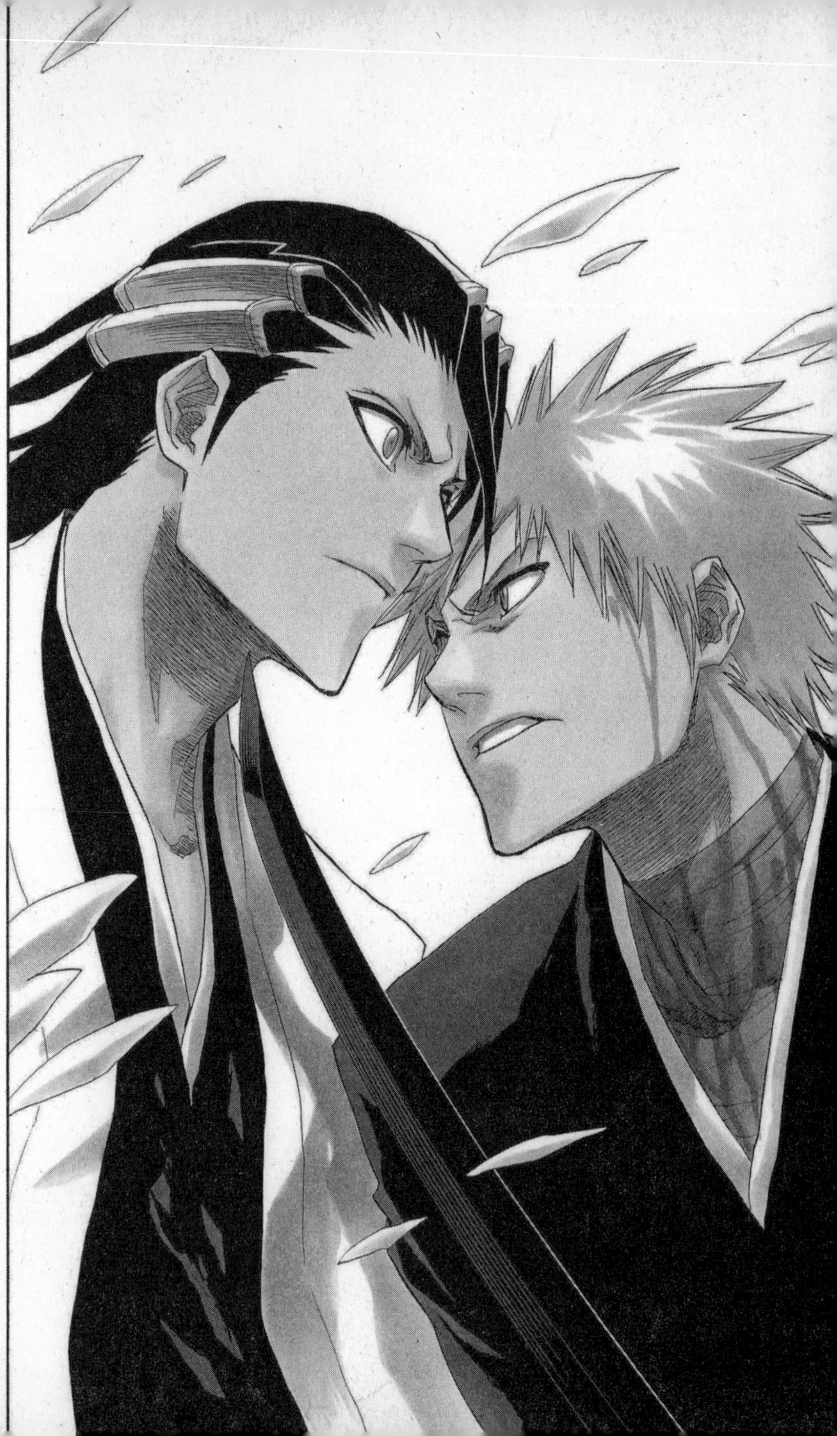

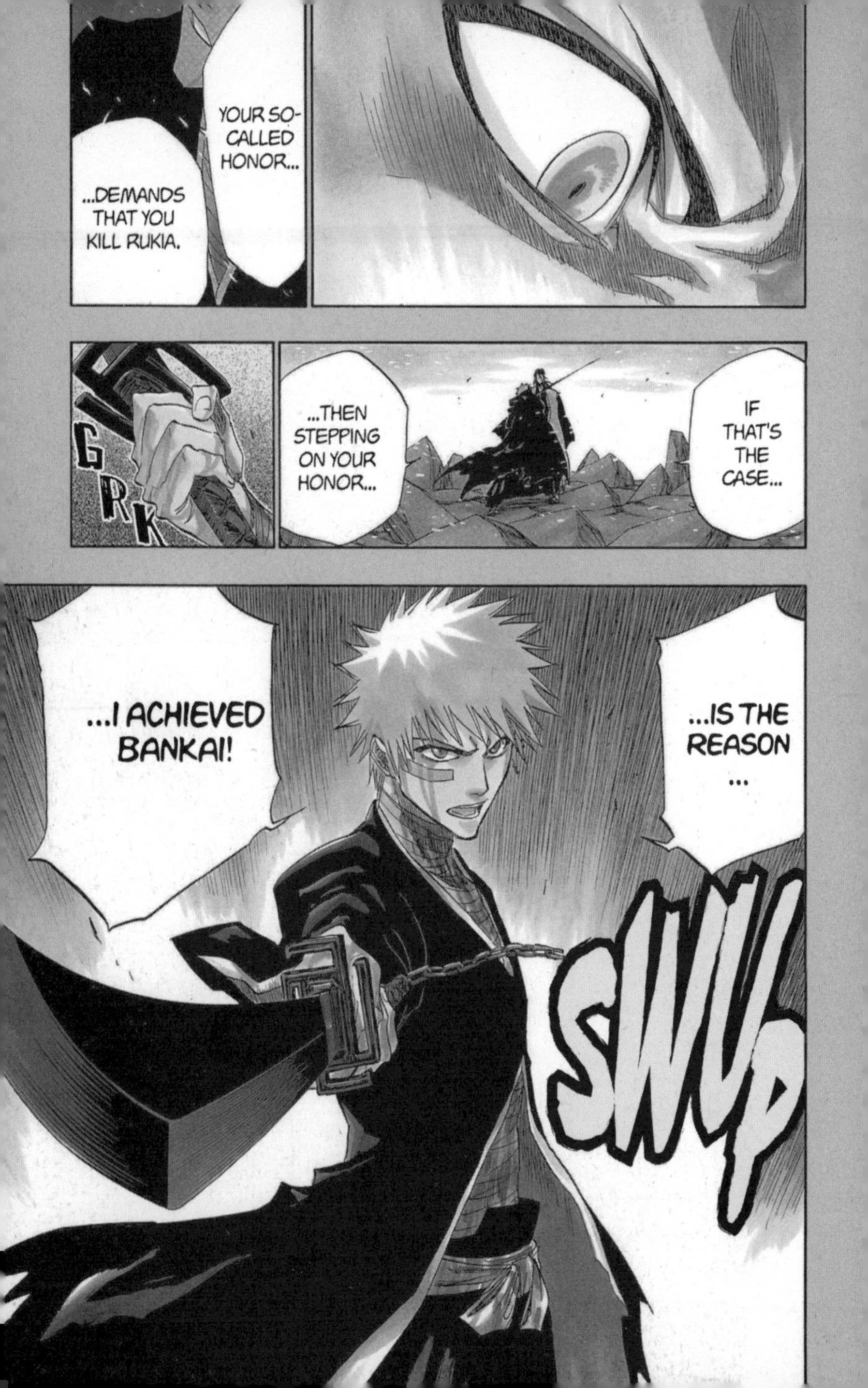
YOUR SO-CALLED HONOR...
...DEMANDS THAT YOU KILL RUKIA.
IF THAT'S THE CASE...
...THEN STEPPING ON YOUR HONOR...
GRK
...IS THE REASON ...
...I ACHIEVED BANKAI!
SWUP

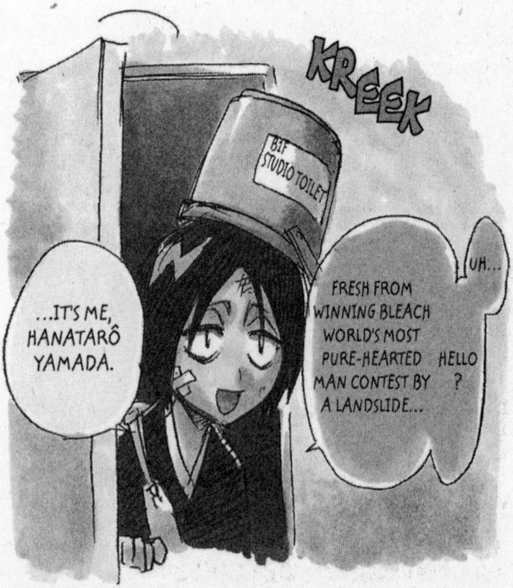
KREEEK
B1F STUDIO TOILET
UH... HELLO ?
FRESH FROM WINNING BLEACH WORLD'S MOST PURE-HEARTED MAN CONTEST BY A LANDSLIDE...
...IT'S ME, HANATARÔ YAMADA.

FOR AN INSTANT...

...I LOST SIGHT OF HIM.

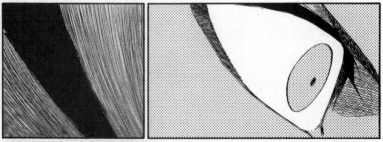

163. THE Speed Phantom 2
(Denial by Pride, Contradiction by Power)

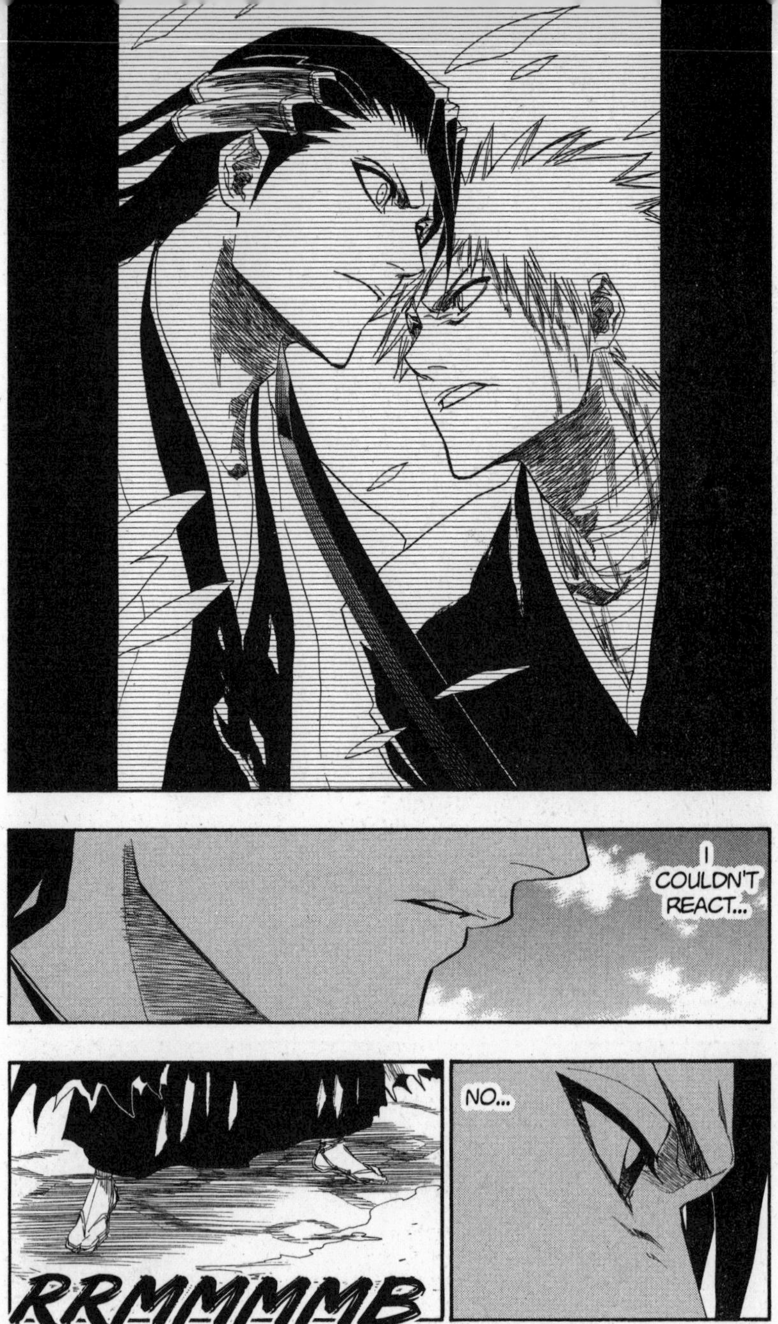
I COULDN'T REACT...
NO...
RRMMMMMB

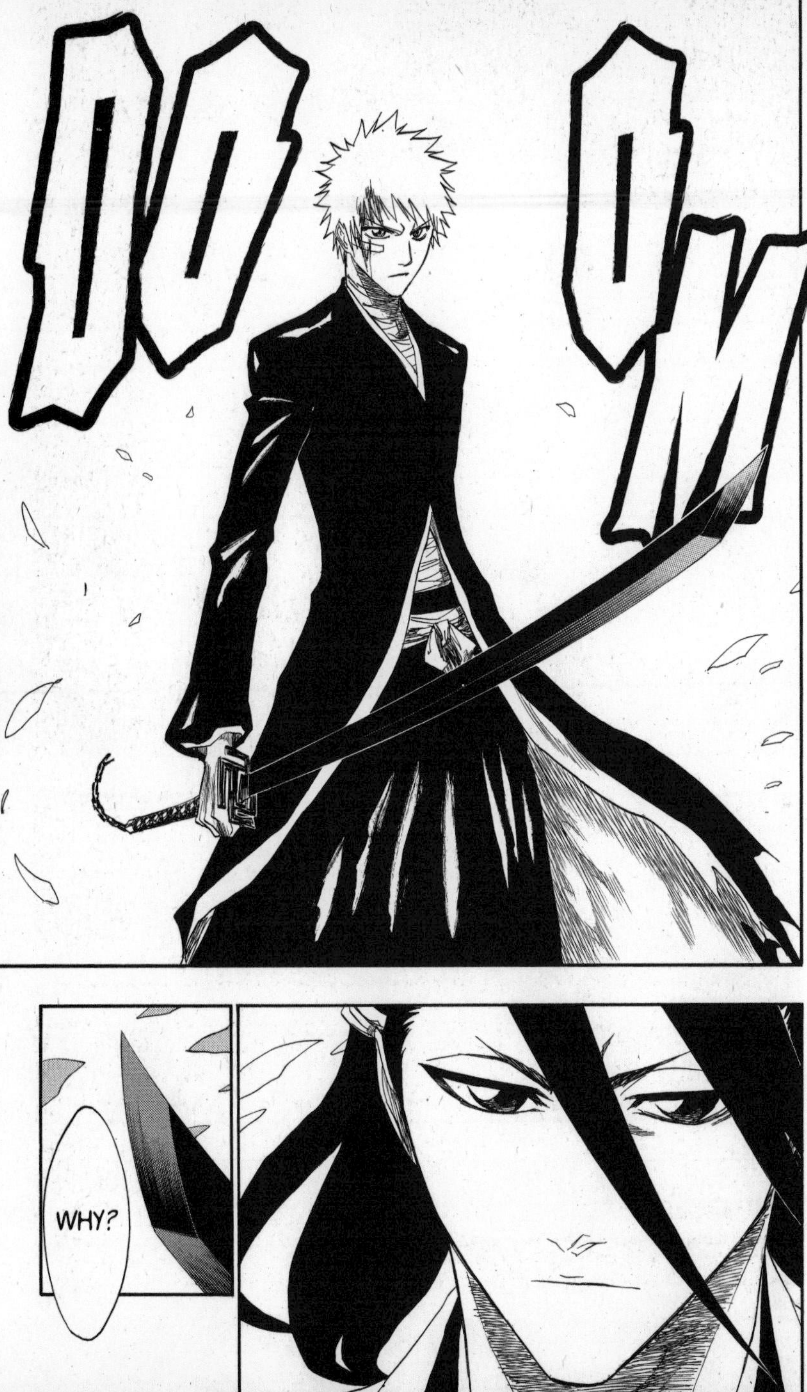
DOOM
WHY?

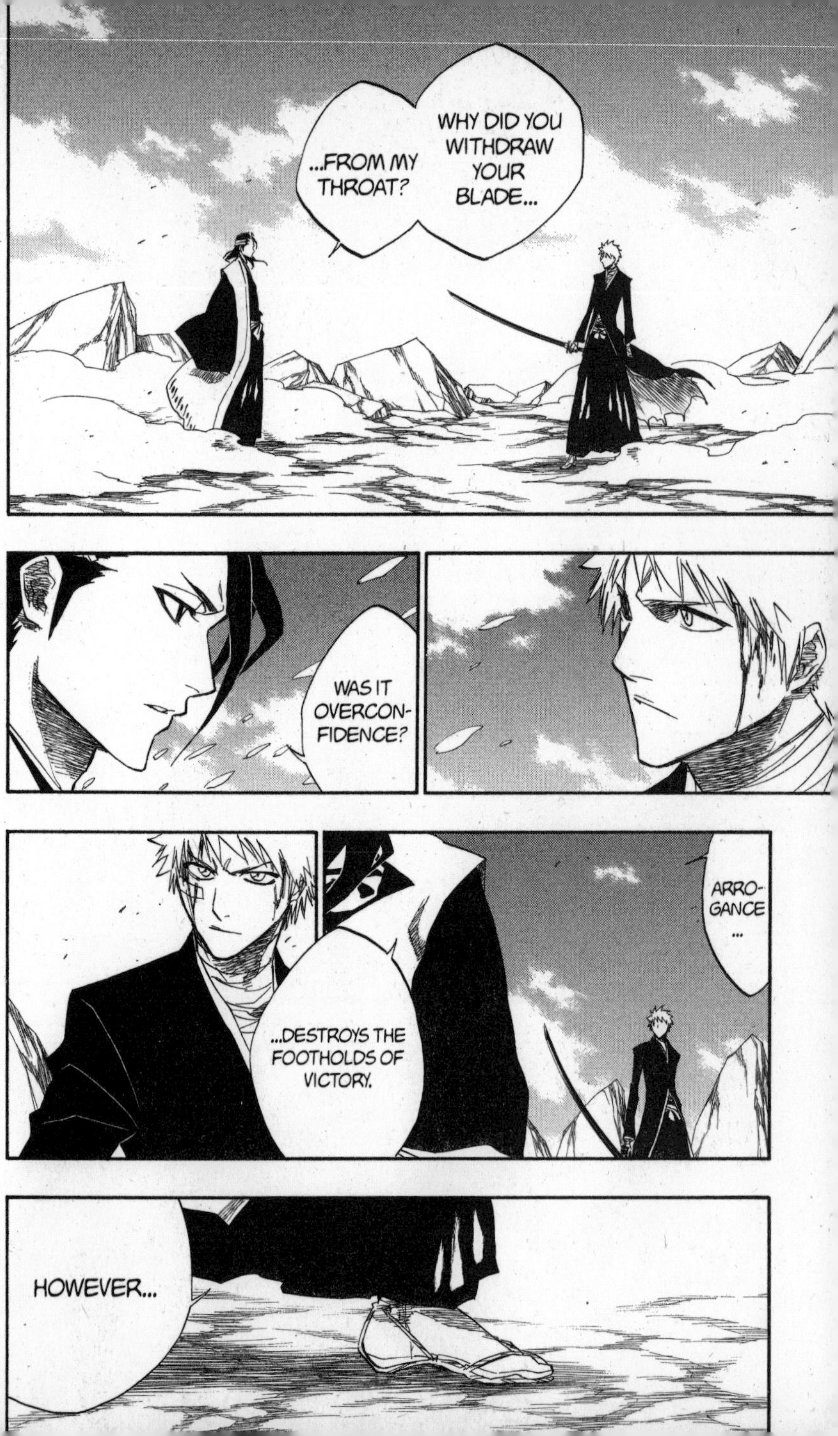
WHY DID YOU WITHDRAW YOUR BLADE...
...FROM MY THROAT?
WAS IT OVERCON-FIDENCE?
ARRO-GANCE...
...DESTROYS THE FOOTHOLDS OF VICTORY.
HOWEVER...

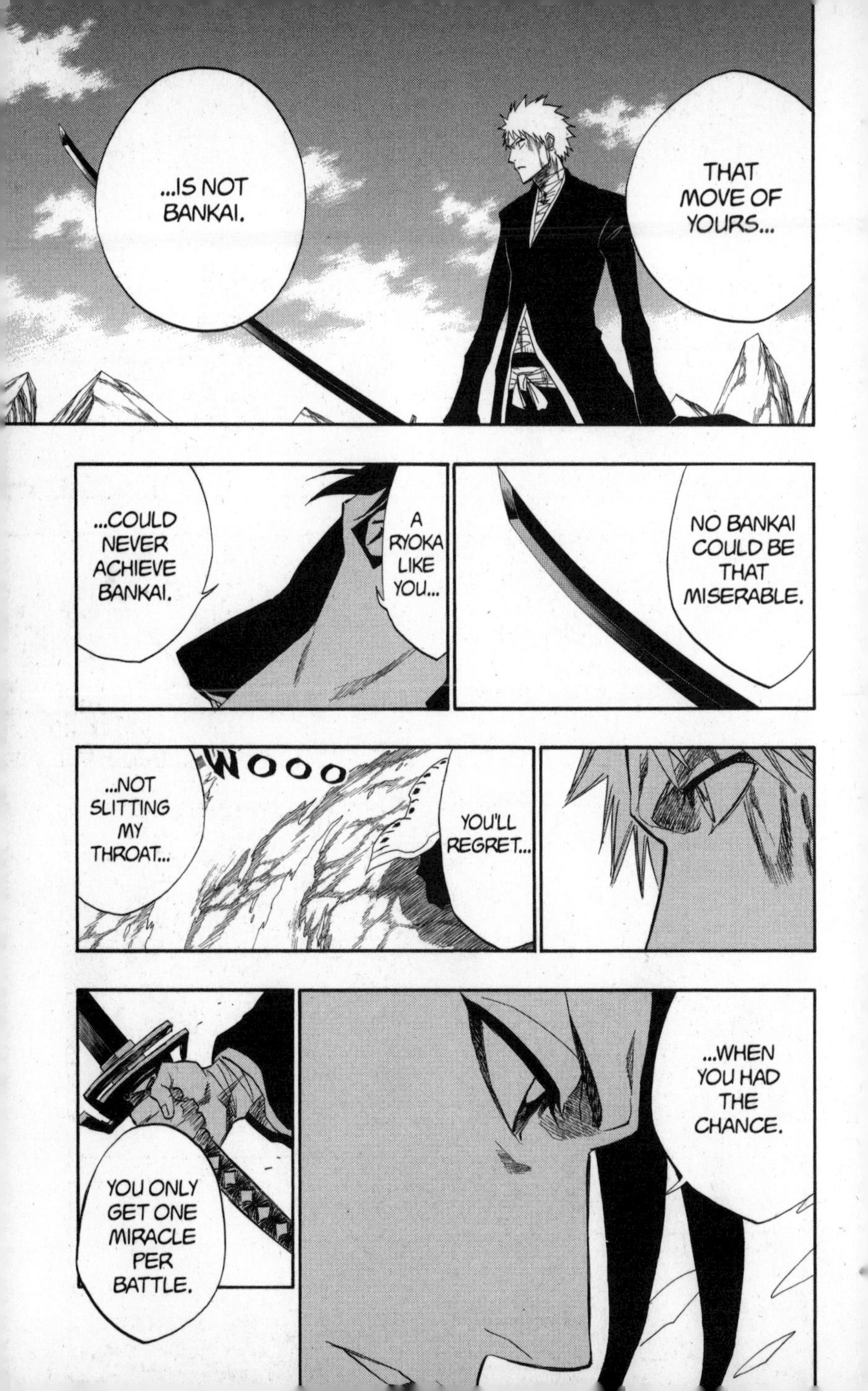
THAT MOVE OF YOURS...
...IS NOT BANKAI.
NO BANKAI COULD BE THAT MISERABLE.
A RYOKA LIKE YOU...
...COULD NEVER ACHIEVE BANKAI.
YOU'LL REGRET...
WOOO
...NOT SLITTING MY THROAT...
...WHEN YOU HAD THE CHANCE.
YOU ONLY GET ONE MIRACLE PER BATTLE.

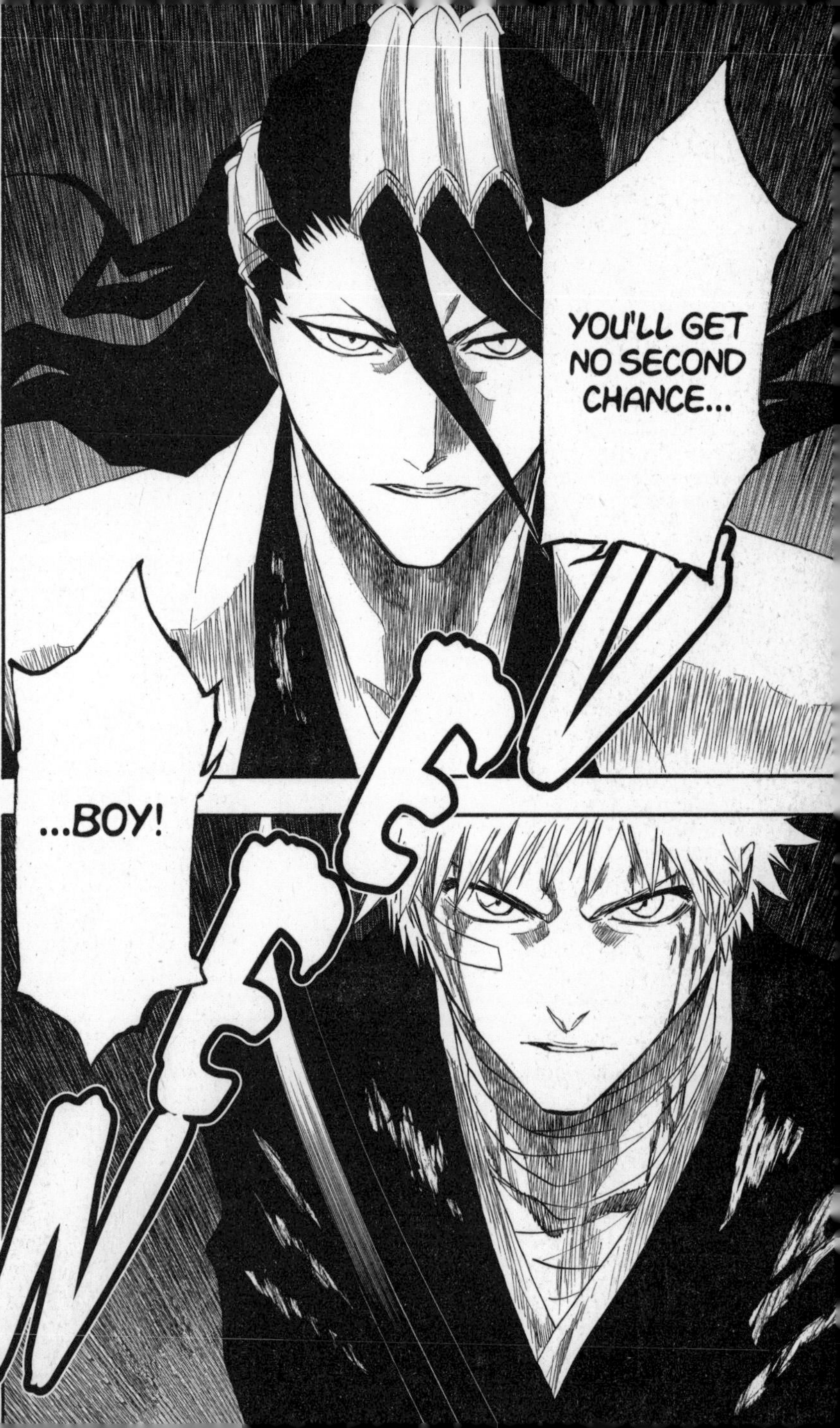
YOU'LL GET NO SECOND CHANCE...
...BOY!

BLEACH —ブリーチ—

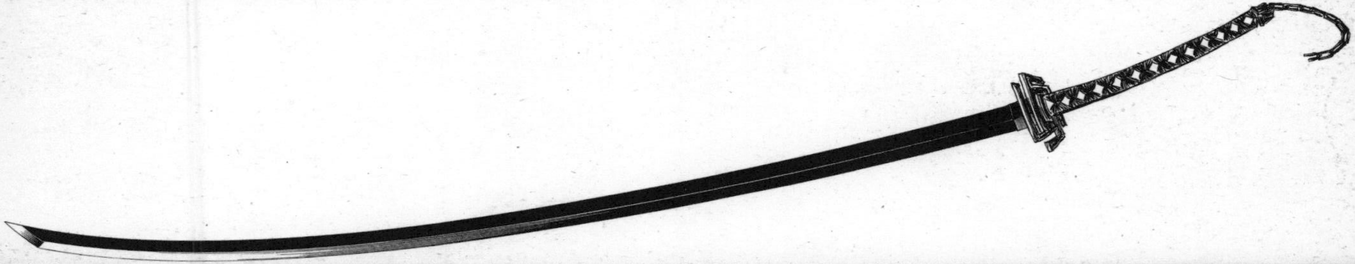

163. THE Speed Phantom 2
(Denial by Pride, Contradiction by Power)

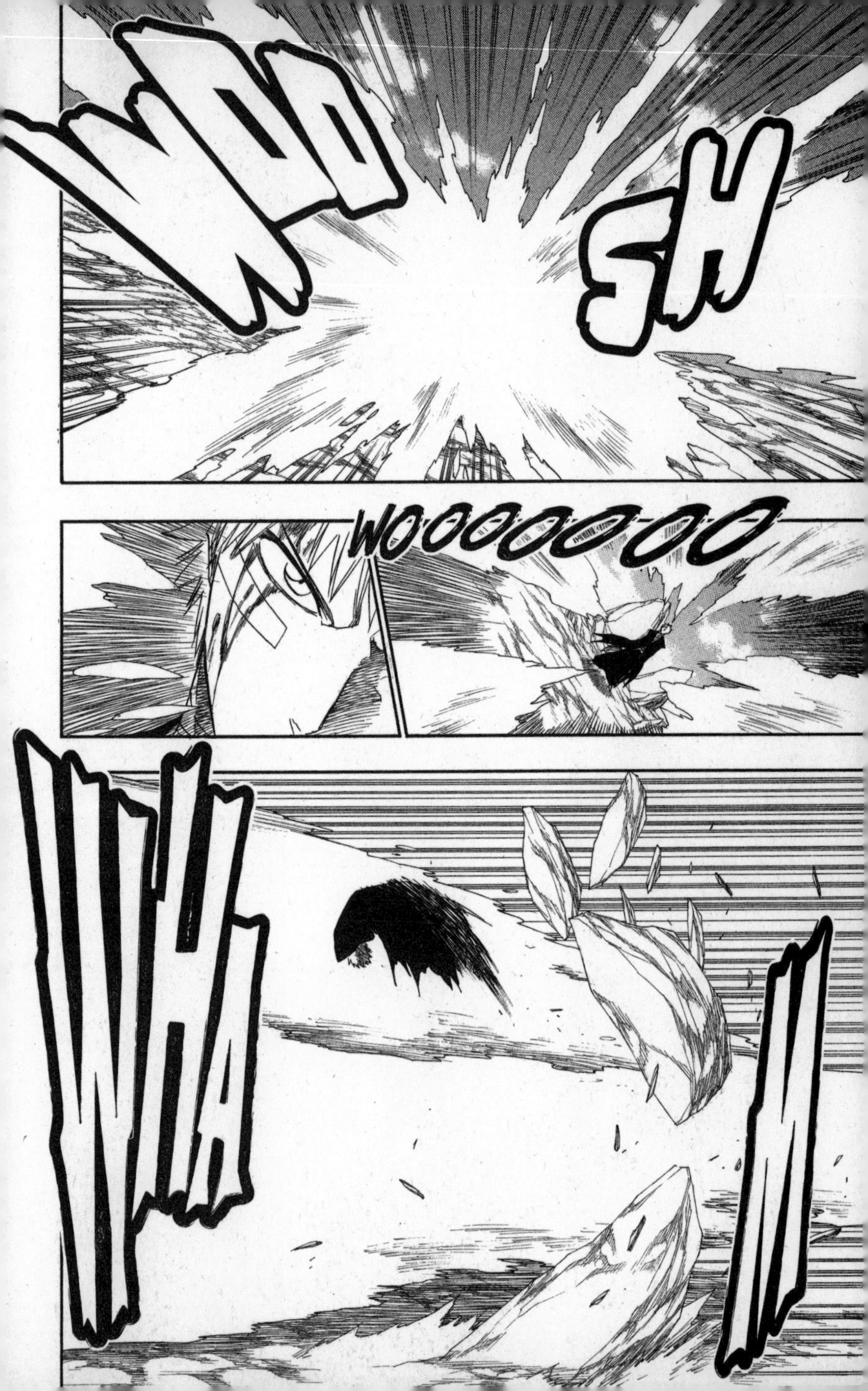
WOOSH
WOOOOOOOO
WHAM

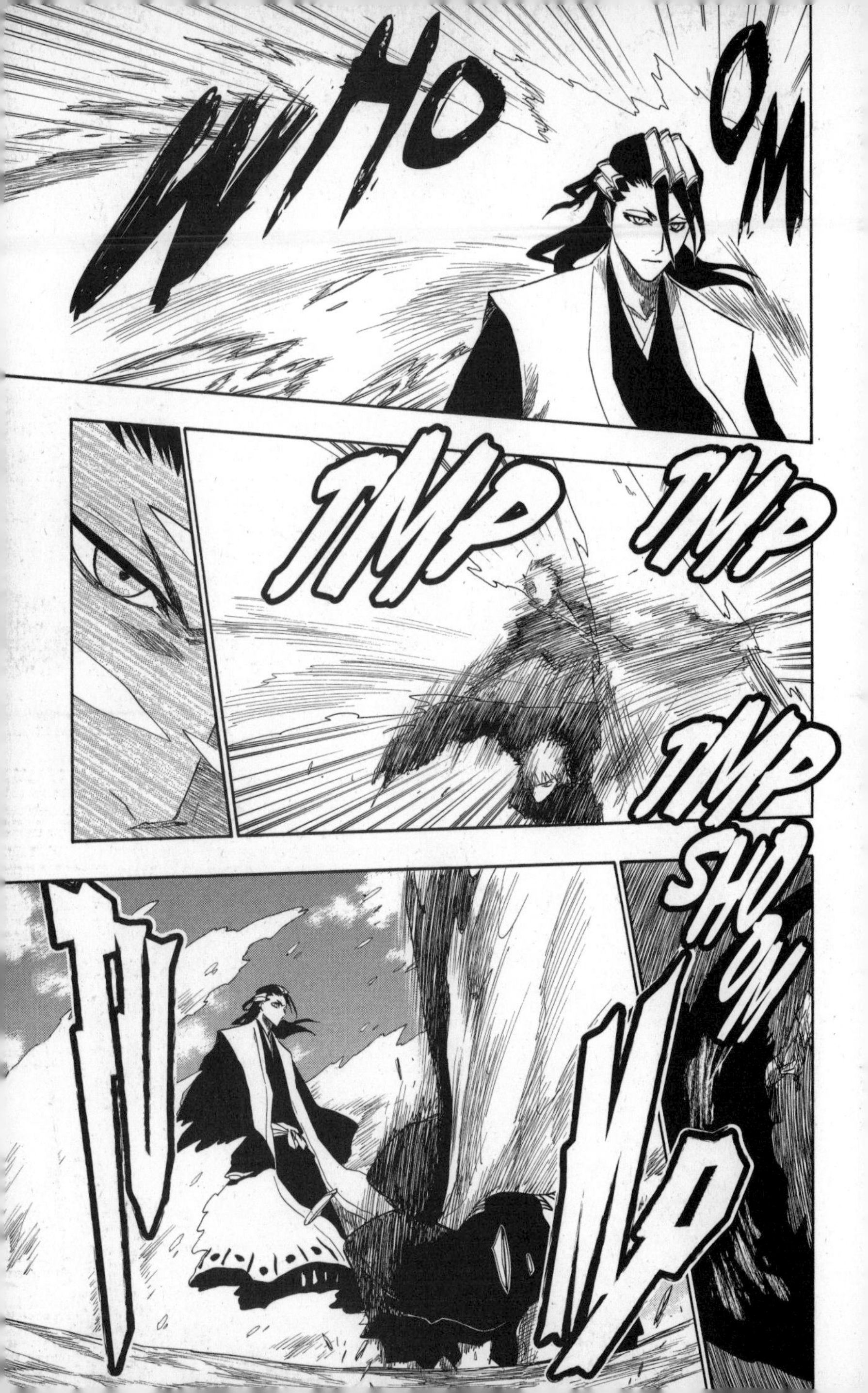
WHOOM
TMP
TMP
TMP
SHOOM
TUMP

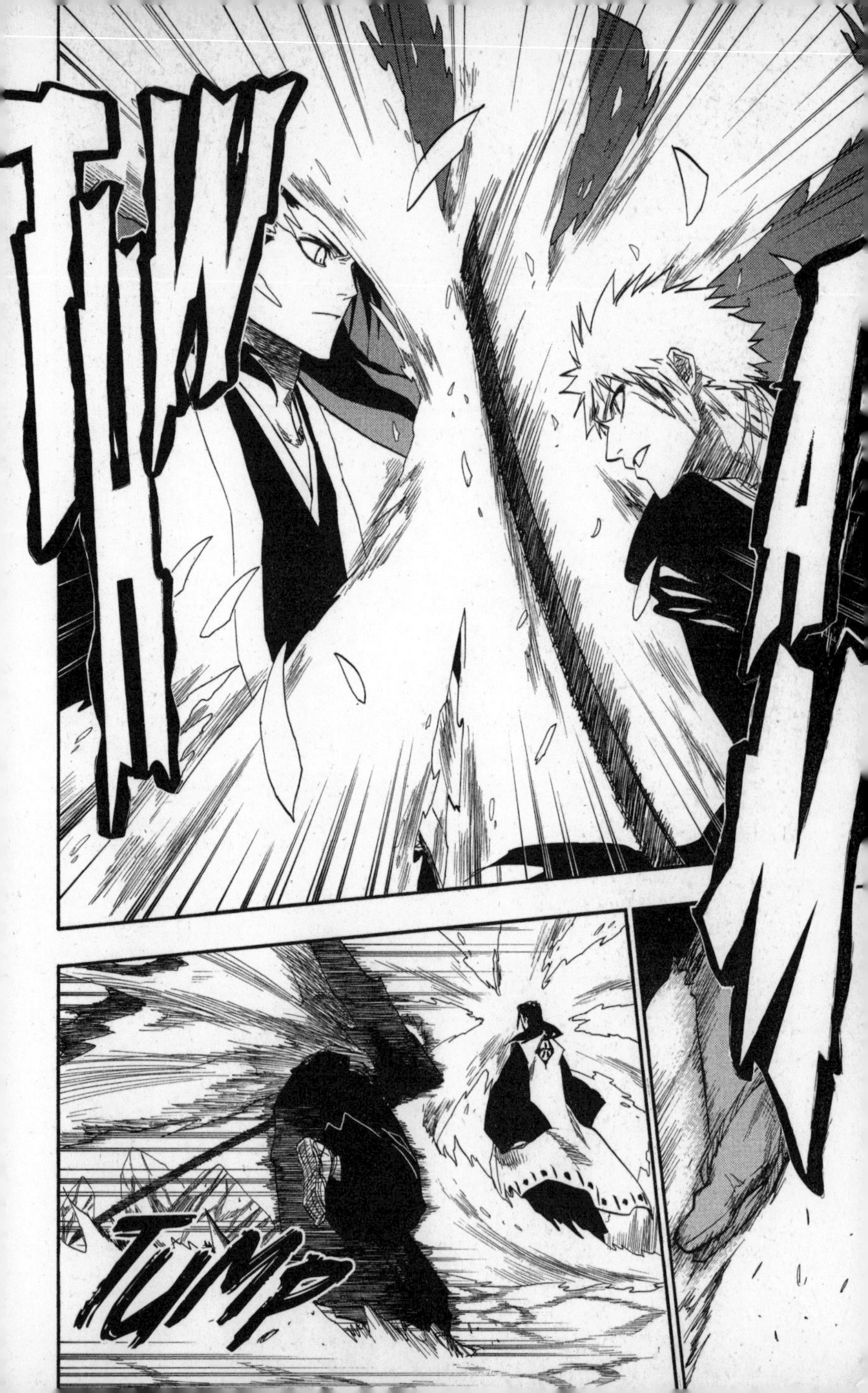
THWAM
TUMP

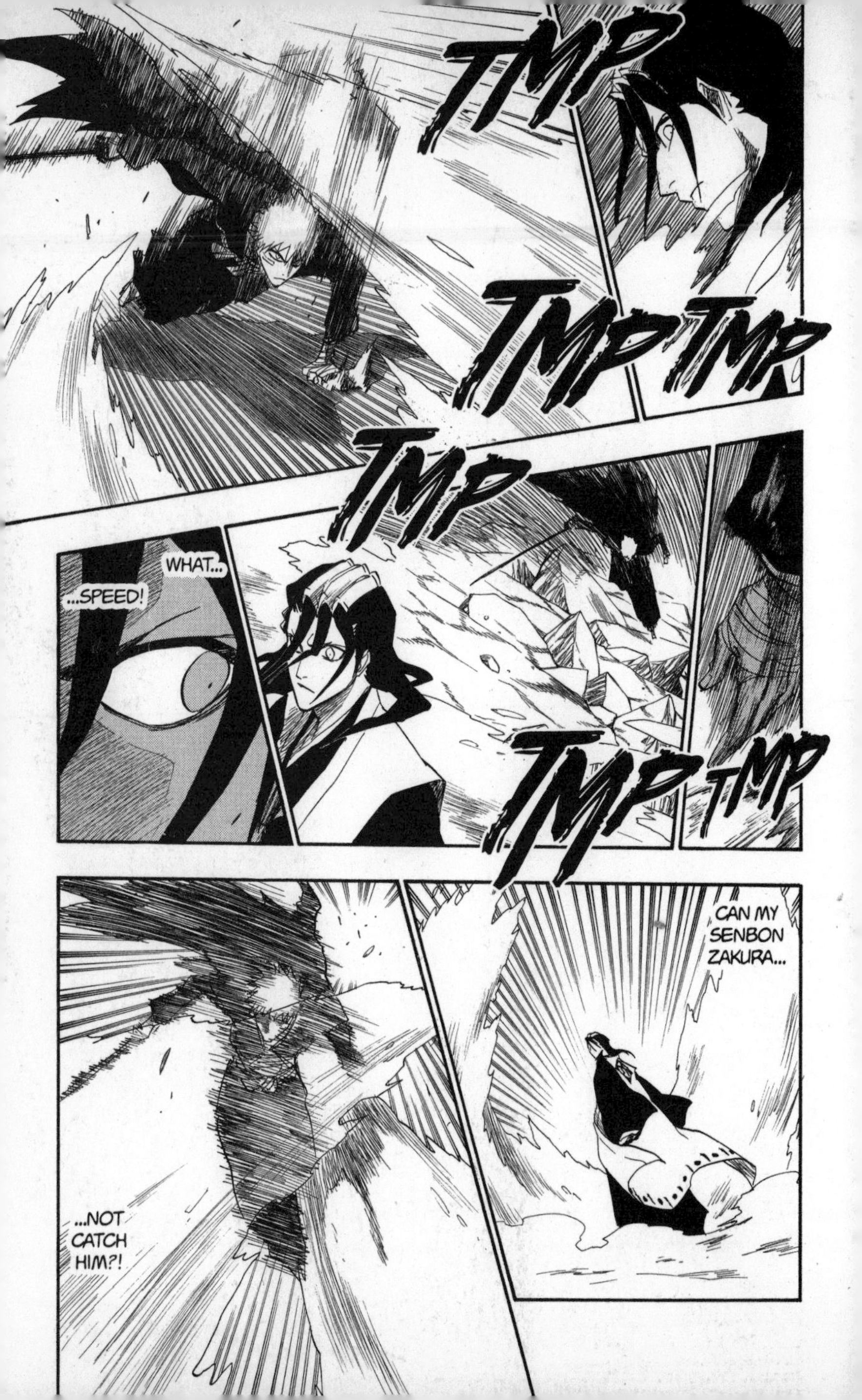
TMP
TMP TMP
TMP
TMP TMP
WHAT...
...SPEED!
CAN MY SENBON ZAKURA...
...NOT CATCH HIM?!

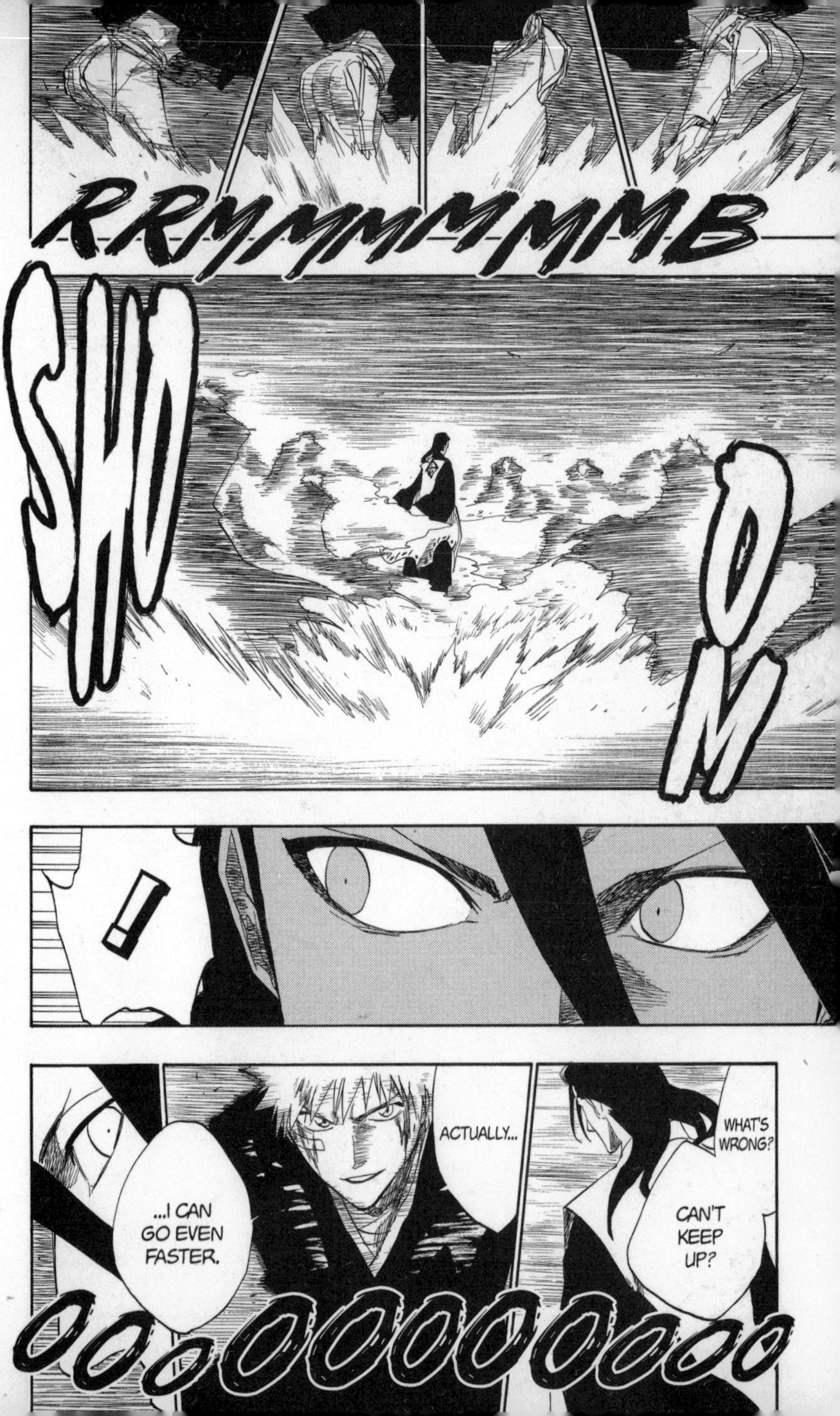
RRMMMMMMB
SHO
OM
!
WHAT'S WRONG?
CAN'T KEEP UP?
ACTUALLY...
...I CAN GO EVEN FASTER.
OOOOOOOOOOO

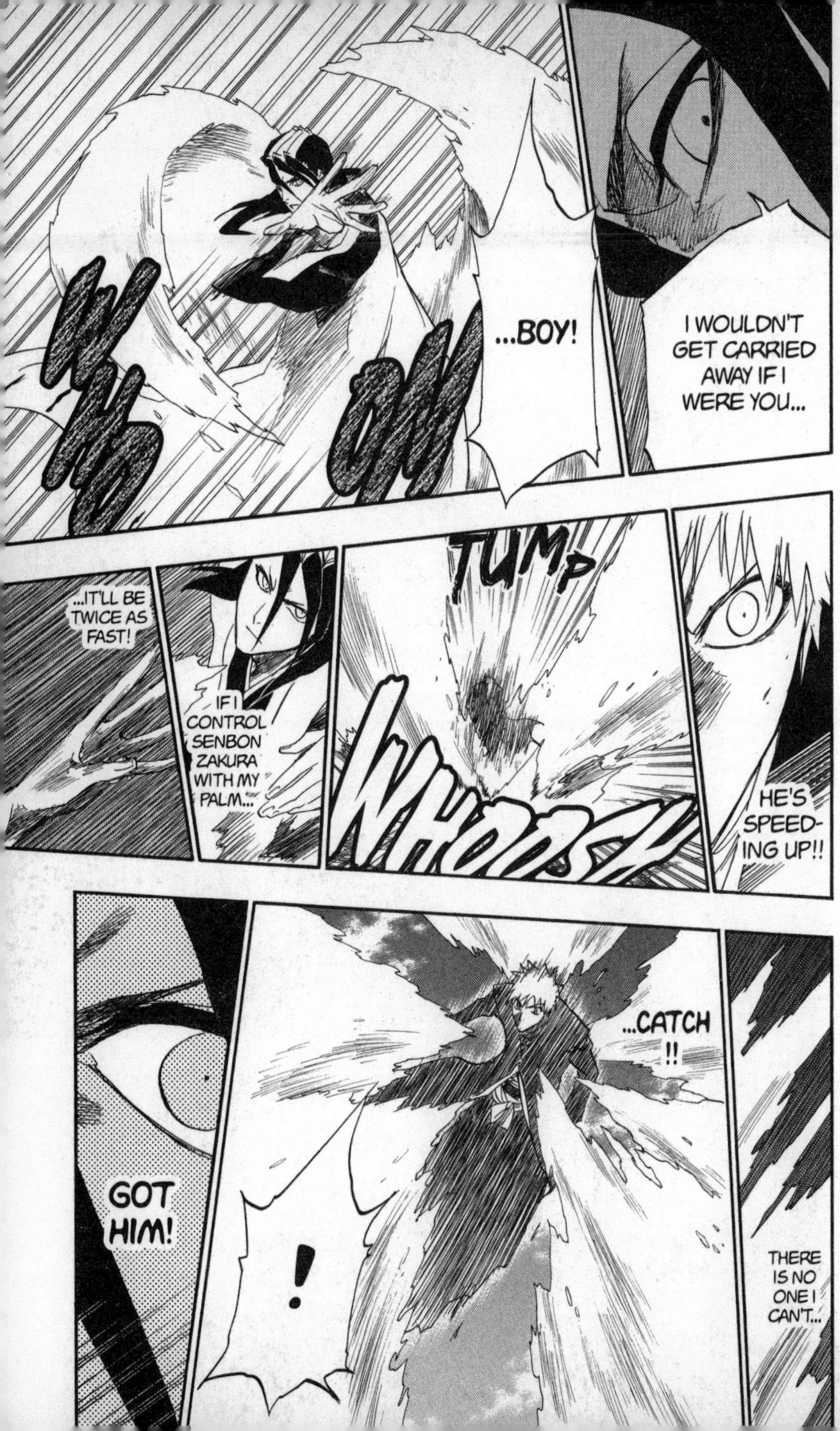
I WOULDN'T GET CARRIED AWAY IF I WERE YOU...
...BOY!
WHOOM
HE'S SPEEDING UP!!
TUMP
WHOOSH
IF I CONTROL SENBON ZAKURA WITH MY PALM...
...IT'LL BE TWICE AS FAST!
THERE IS NO ONE I CAN'T...
...CATCH!!
!
GOT HIM!

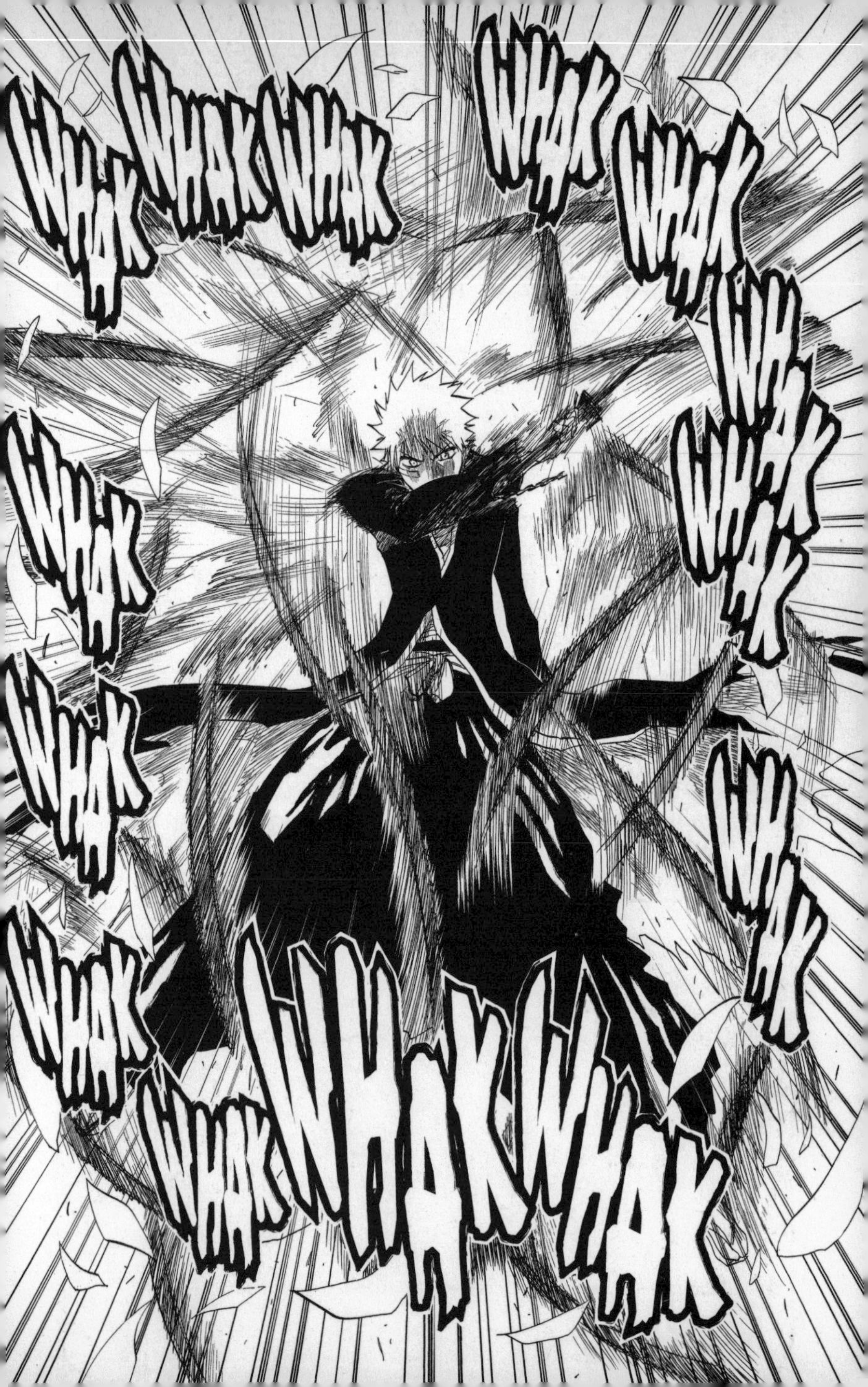
WHAK
WHAK
WHAK
WHAK
WHAK
WHAK
WHAK
WHAK
WHAK
WHAK
WHAK
WHAK
WHAK
WHAK

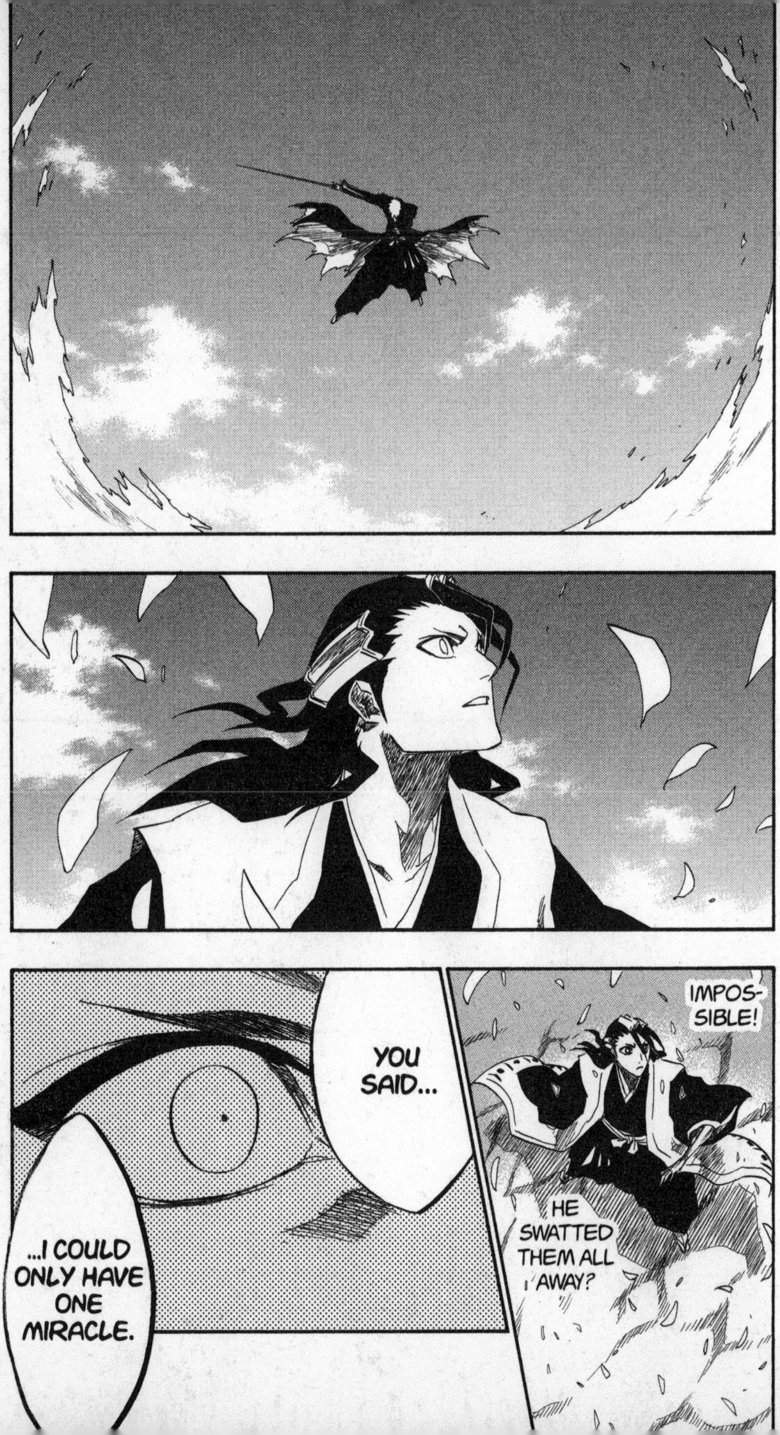
IMPOSSIBLE!
HE SWATTED THEM ALL AWAY?
YOU SAID...
...I COULD ONLY HAVE ONE MIRACLE.

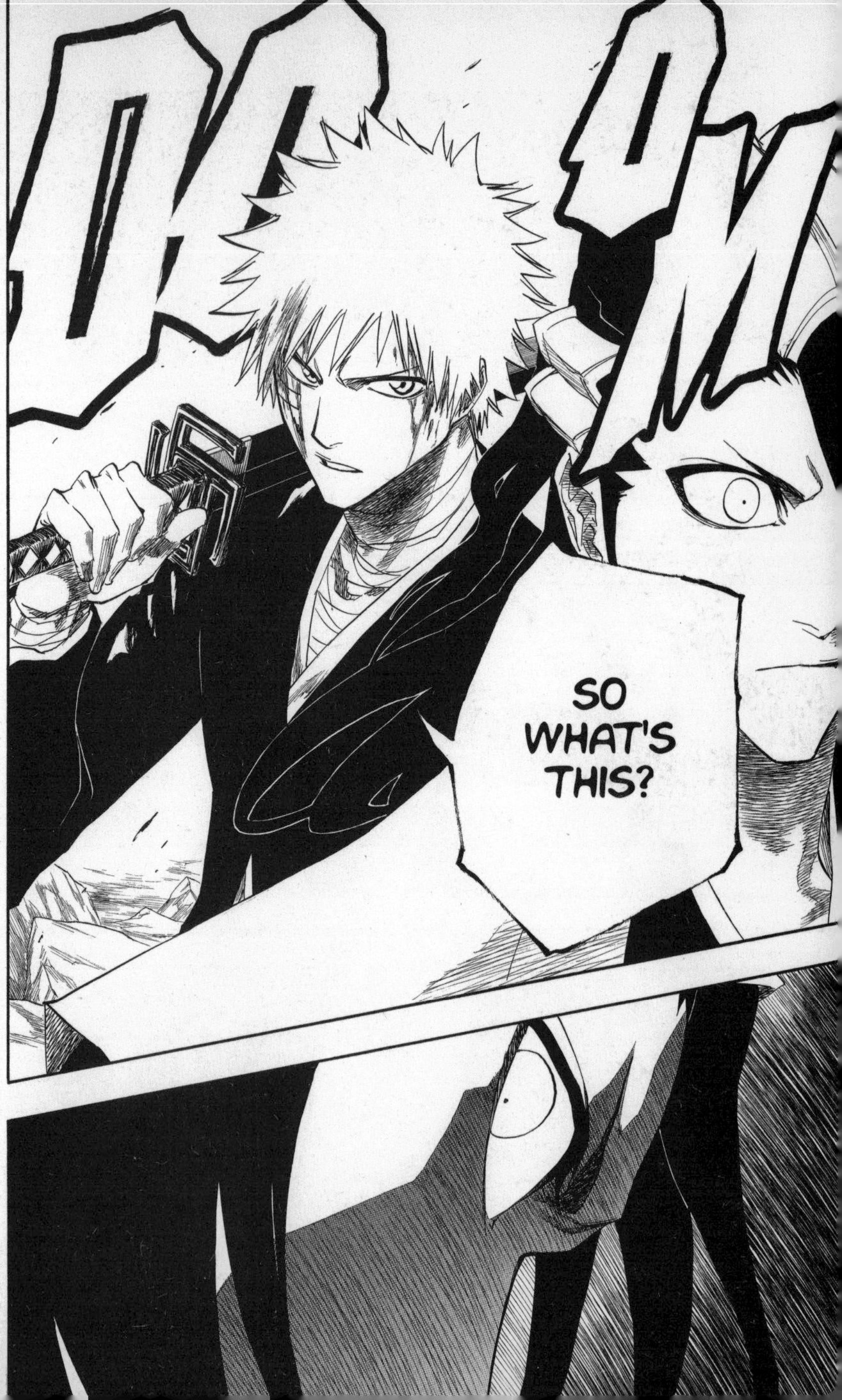
SO WHAT'S THIS?

READ THIS WAY

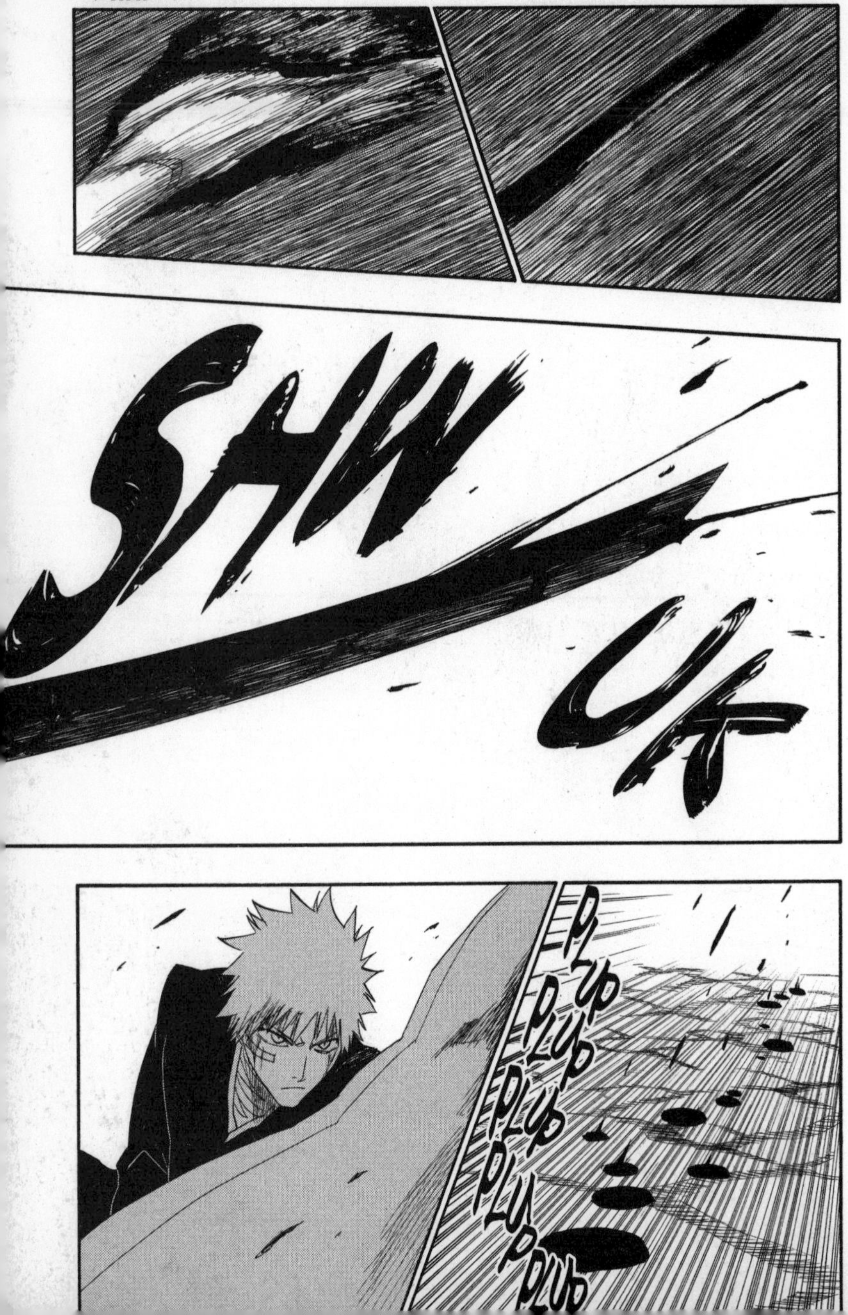
SHWUK
PLUP PLUP PLUP PLUP

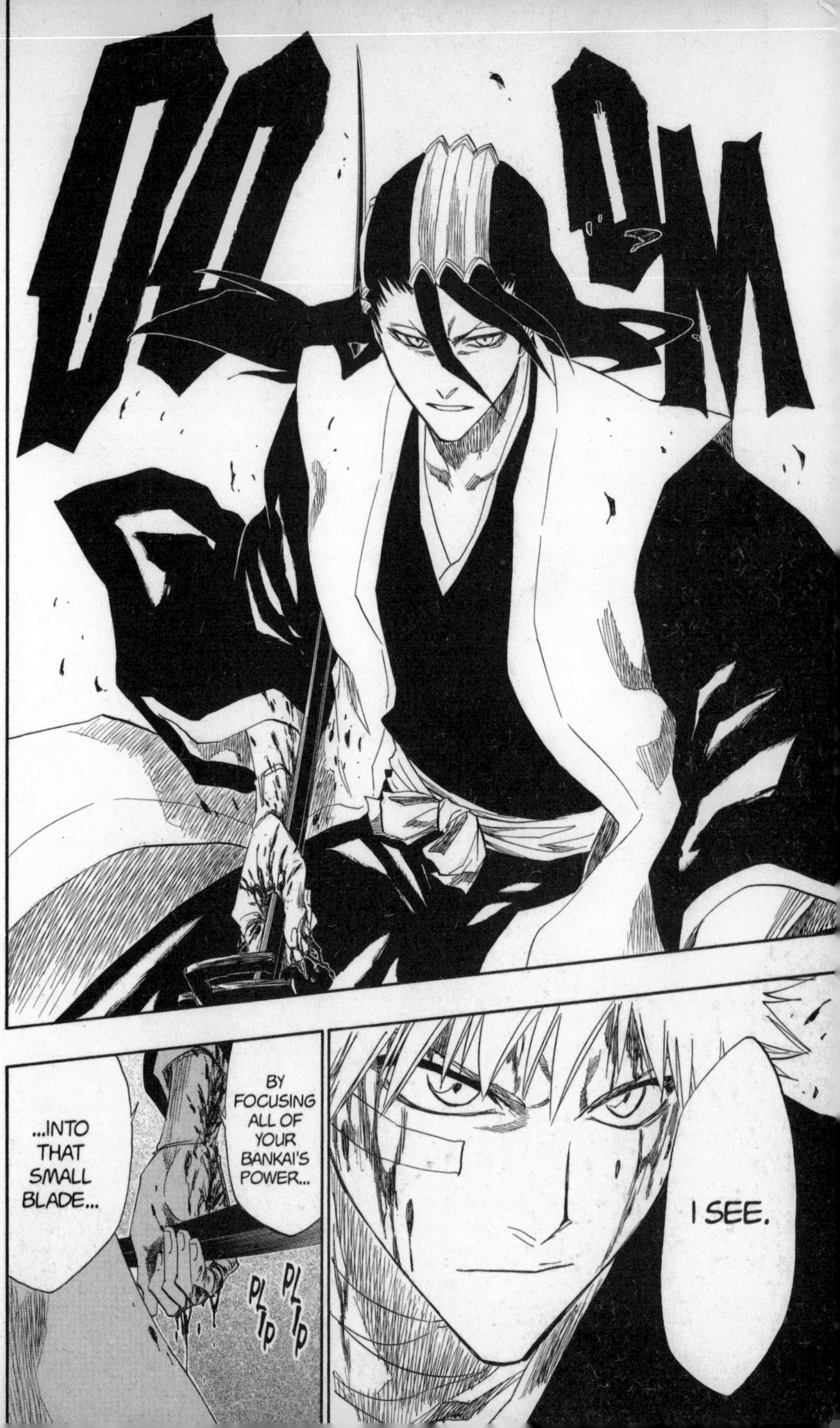
I SEE.
BY FOCUSING ALL OF YOUR BANKAI'S POWER...
...INTO THAT SMALL BLADE...
PLIP PLIP

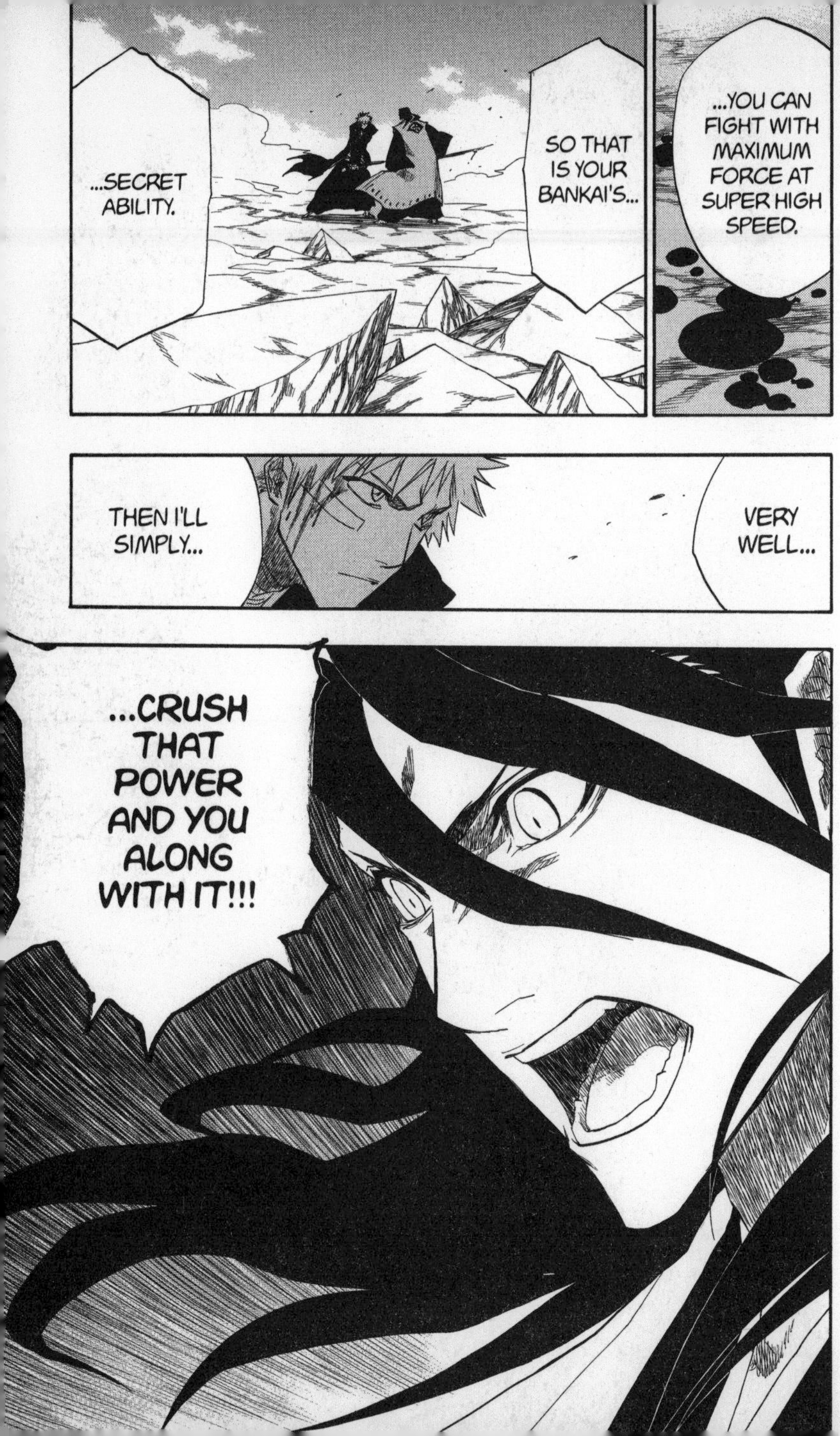
...YOU CAN FIGHT WITH MAXIMUM FORCE AT SUPER HIGH SPEED.
SO THAT IS YOUR BANKAI'S...
...SECRET ABILITY.
VERY WELL...
THEN I'LL SIMPLY...
...CRUSH THAT POWER AND YOU ALONG WITH IT!!!

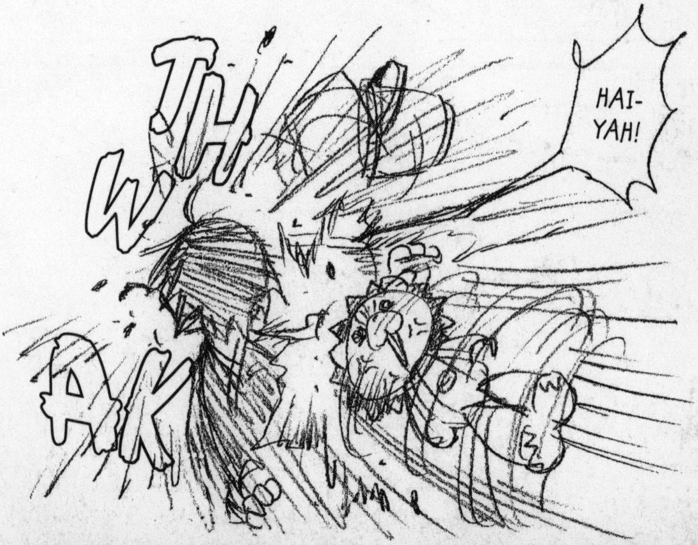
HAI-
YAH!
THWAK

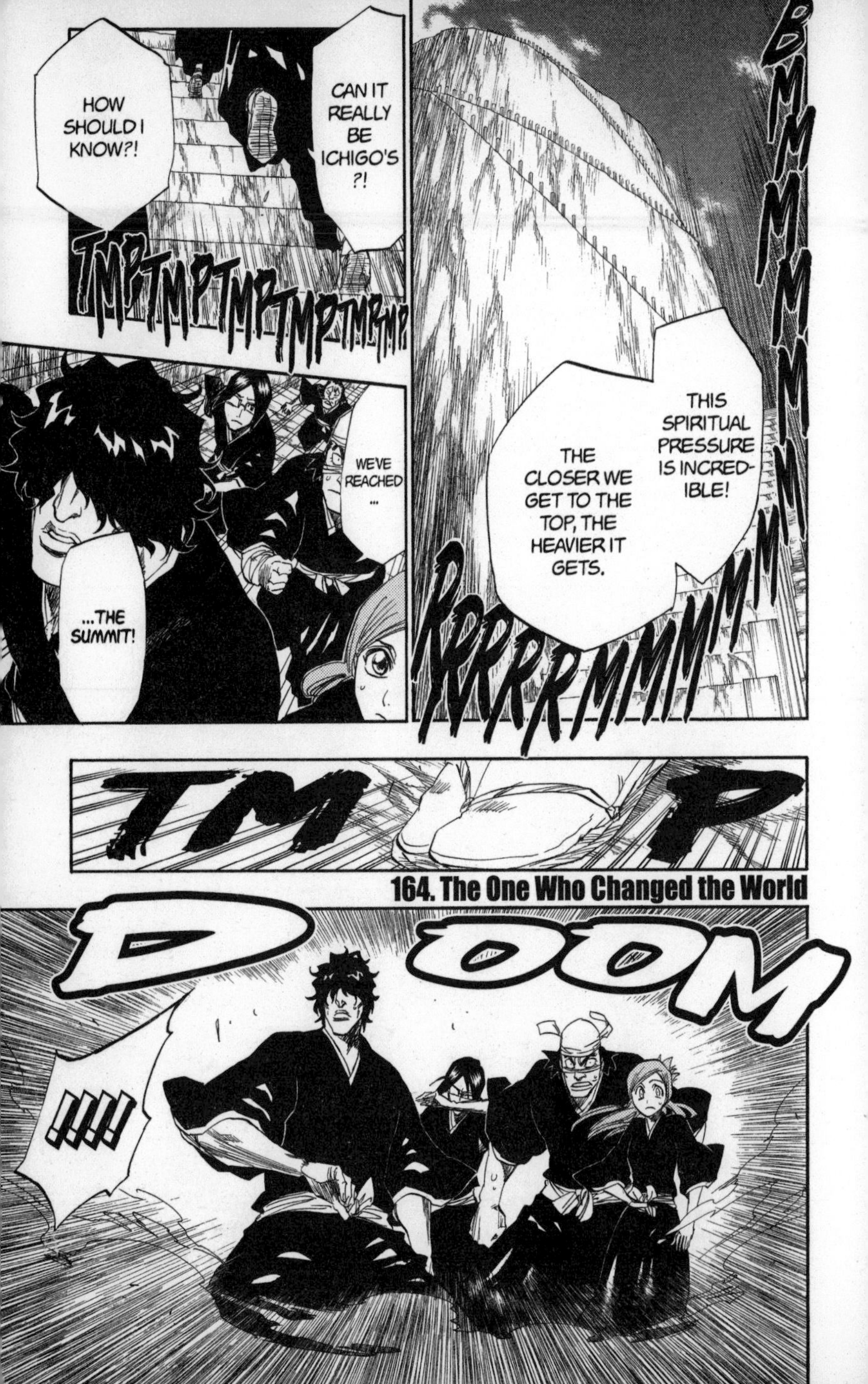
BMMMMMMMM
THIS SPIRITUAL PRESSURE IS INCREDIBLE!
THE CLOSER WE GET TO THE TOP, THE HEAVIER IT GETS.
RRRRRMMMM
CAN IT REALLY BE ICHIGO'S ?!
HOW SHOULD I KNOW?!
TMPTMPTMPTMPTMPTMP
WE'VE REACHED ...
...THE SUMMIT!
TMP
DOOM
!!!!

164. The One Who Changed the World

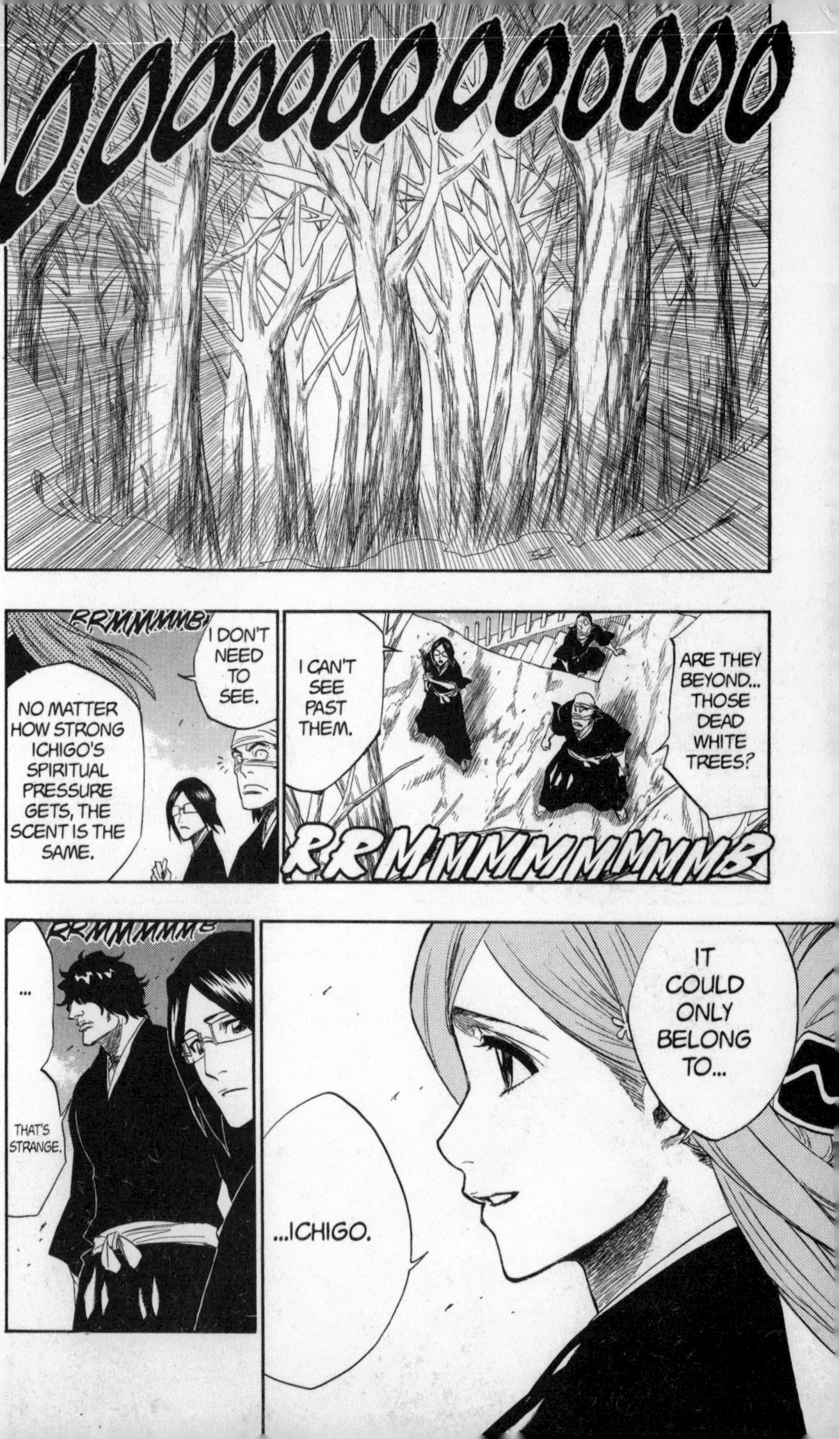
OOOOOOOOOOOO
ARE THEY BEYOND... THOSE DEAD WHITE TREES?
I CAN'T SEE PAST THEM.
RRMMMMMMMMMB
RRMMMMB
I DON'T NEED TO SEE.
NO MATTER HOW STRONG ICHIGO'S SPIRITUAL PRESSURE GETS, THE SCENT IS THE SAME.
IT COULD ONLY BELONG TO...
...ICHIGO.
RRMMMMMB
...
THAT'S STRANGE.

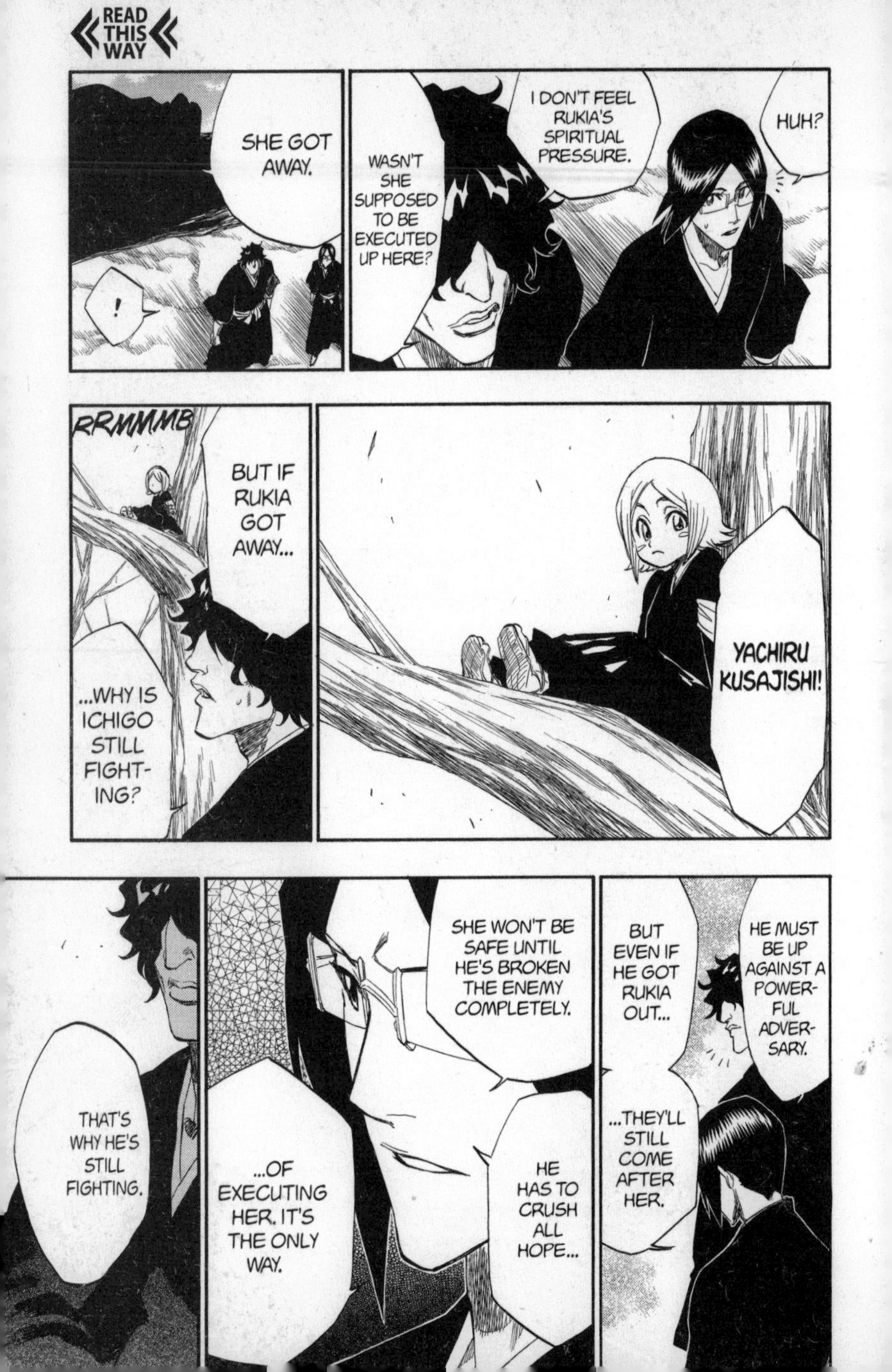
READ THIS WAY
HUH?
I DON'T FEEL RUKIA'S SPIRITUAL PRESSURE.
WASN'T SHE SUPPOSED TO BE EXECUTED UP HERE?
SHE GOT AWAY.
!
YACHIRU KUSAJISHI!
RRMMMB
BUT IF RUKIA GOT AWAY...
...WHY IS ICHIGO STILL FIGHT-ING?
HE MUST BE UP AGAINST A POWER-FUL ADVER-SARY.
BUT EVEN IF HE GOT RUKIA OUT...
...THEY'LL STILL COME AFTER HER.
SHE WON'T BE SAFE UNTIL HE'S BROKEN THE ENEMY COMPLETELY.
HE HAS TO CRUSH ALL HOPE...
...OF EXECUTING HER. IT'S THE ONLY WAY.
THAT'S WHY HE'S STILL FIGHTING.

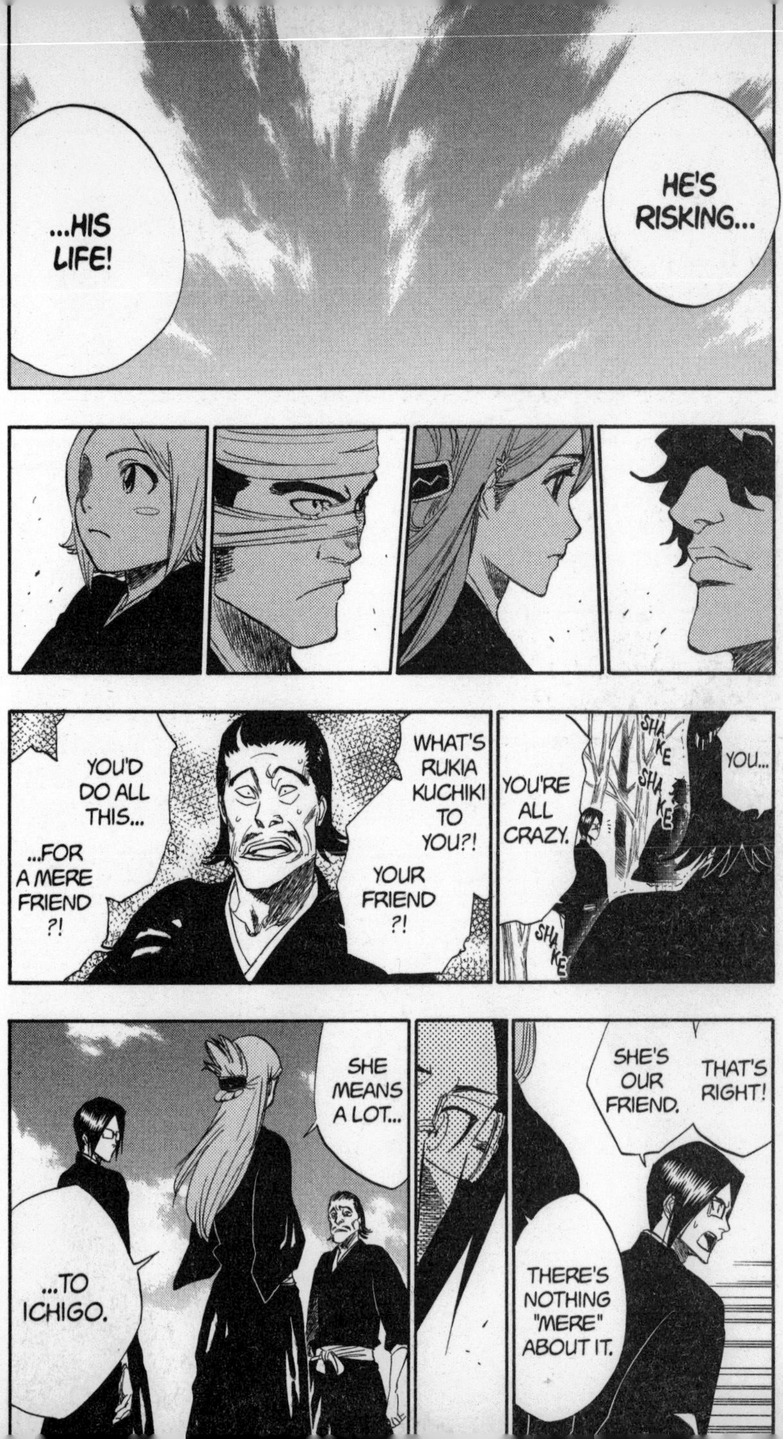
HE'S RISKING...
...HIS LIFE!
YOU...
SHAKE
SHAKE
YOU'RE ALL CRAZY.
SHAKE
WHAT'S RUKIA KUCHIKI TO YOU?!
YOUR FRIEND ?!
YOU'D DO ALL THIS...
...FOR A MERE FRIEND ?!
THAT'S RIGHT!
SHE'S OUR FRIEND.
THERE'S NOTHING "MERE" ABOUT IT.
SHE MEANS A LOT...
...TO ICHIGO.

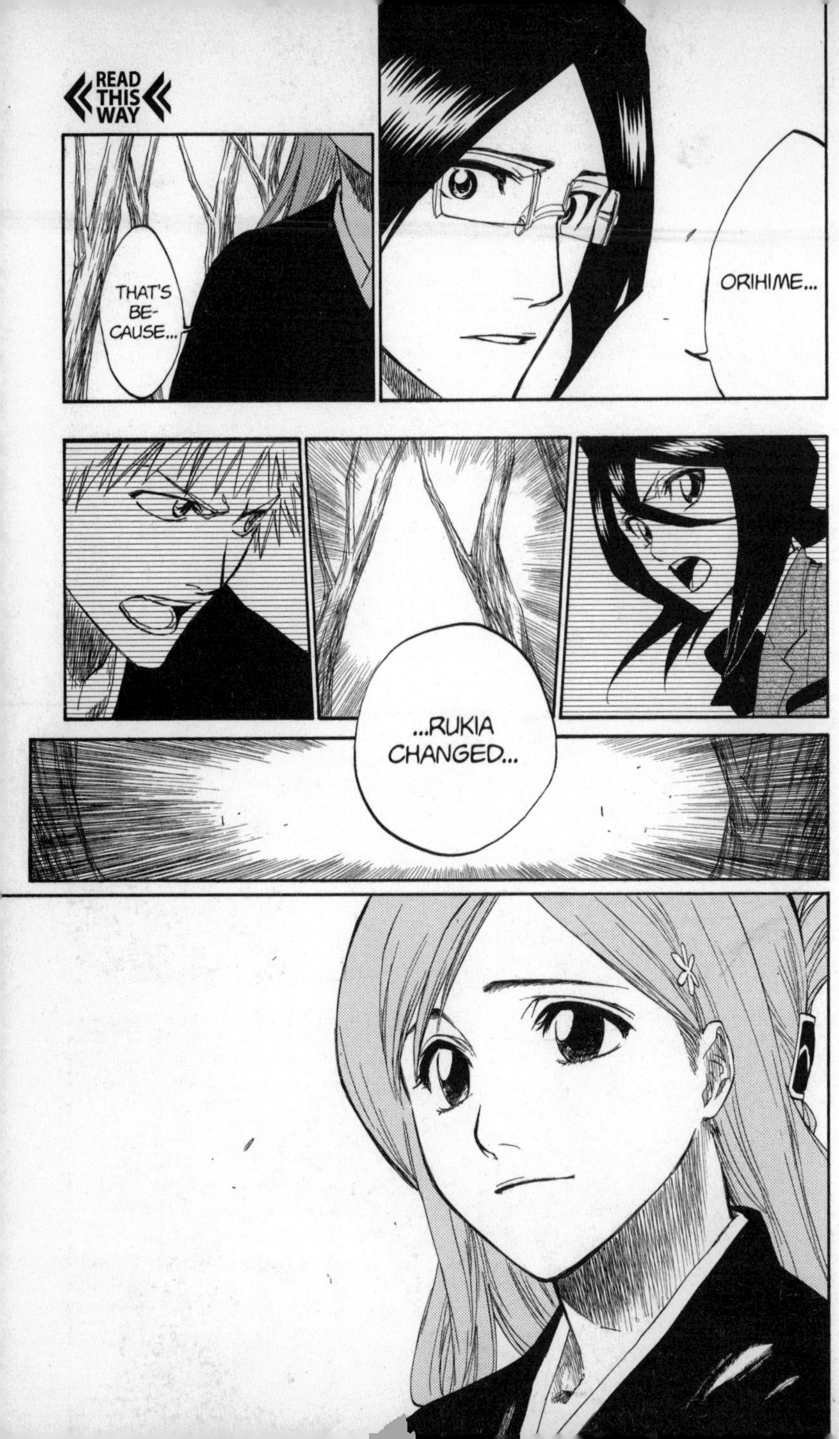
READ THIS WAY
ORIHIME...
THAT'S BE-CAUSE...
...RUKIA CHANGED...

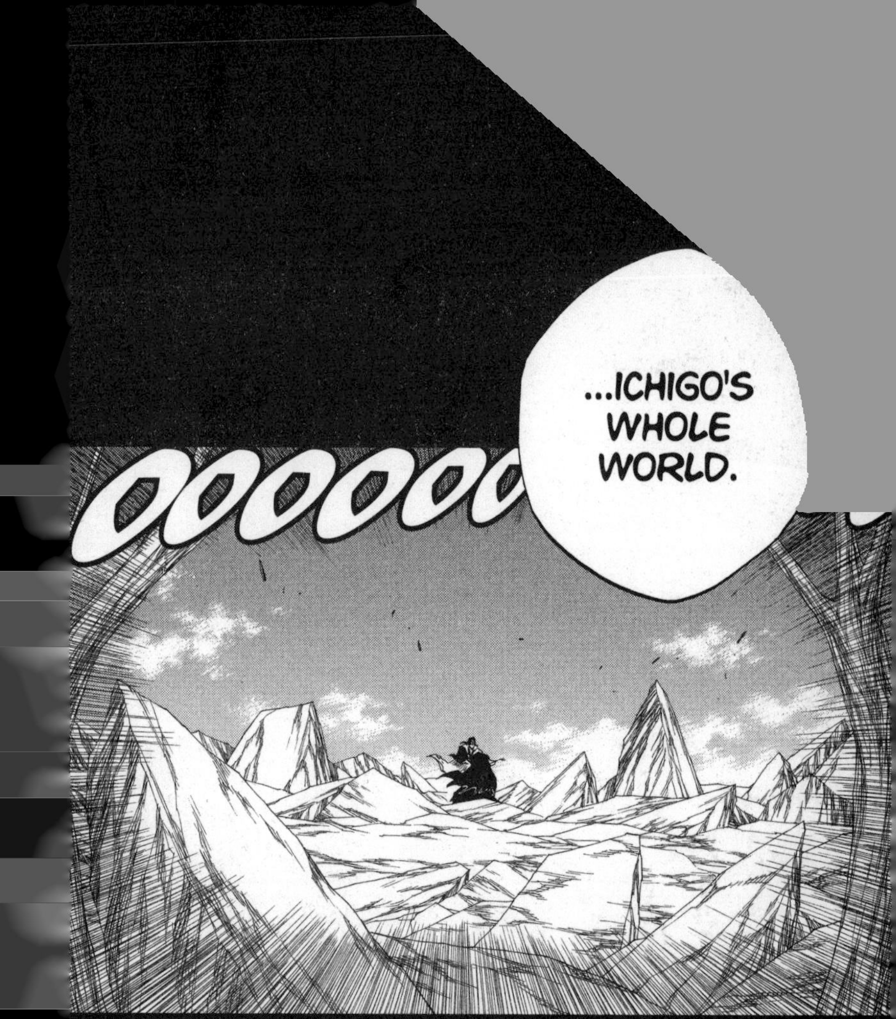

164. The One Who Changed the World

BLEACH -ブリーチ-

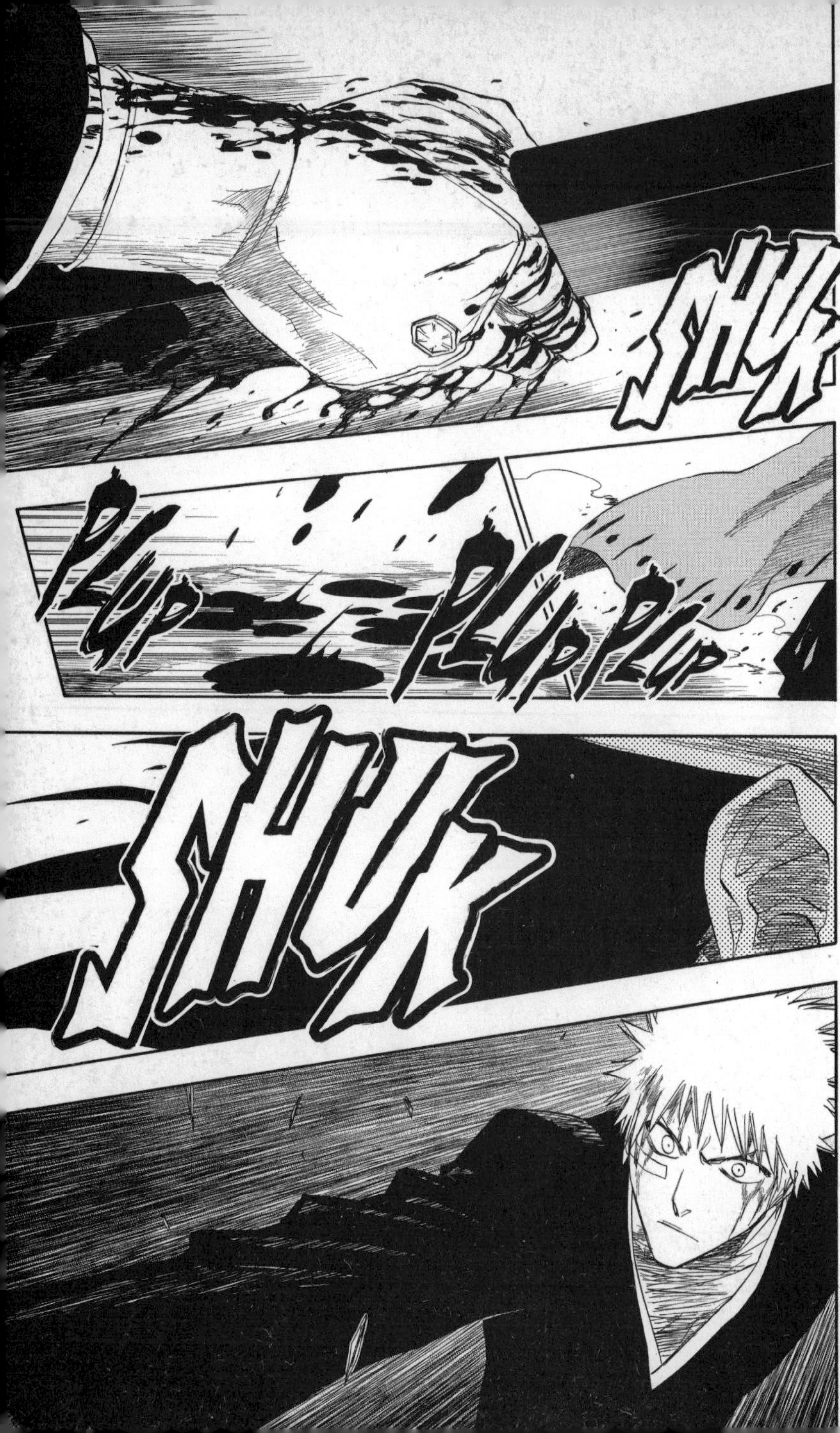
SHUK
PLUP PLUP PLUP
PLUP
SHUK

...ICHIGO KUROSAKI.

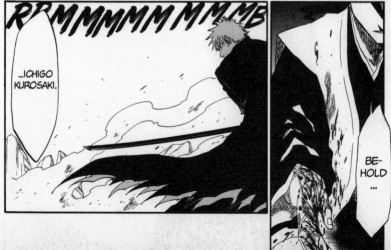

BE-HOLD...

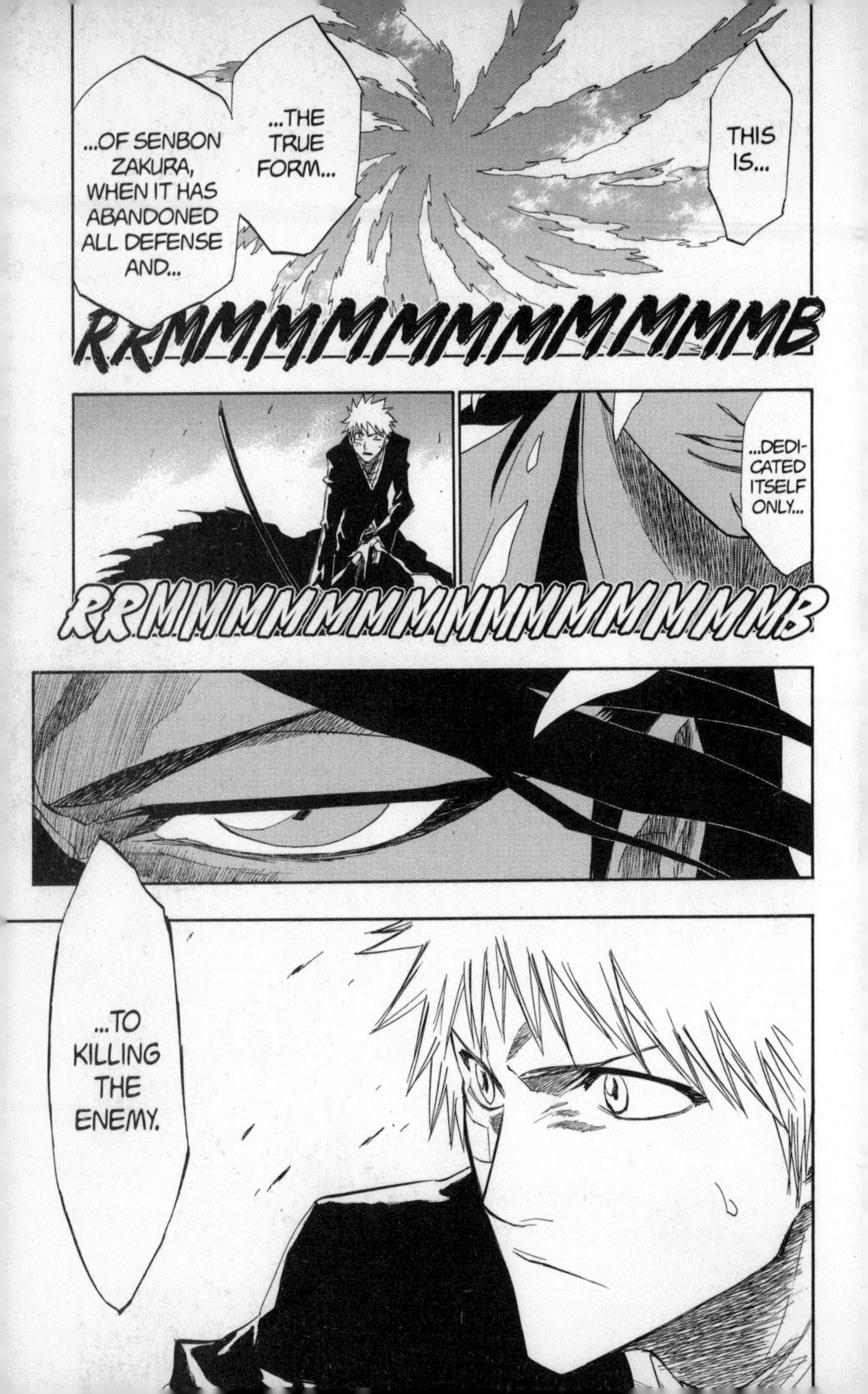
THIS IS...
...THE TRUE FORM...
...OF SENBON ZAKURA, WHEN IT HAS ABANDONED ALL DEFENSE AND...
RRMMMMMMMMMMMMMB
...DEDICATED ITSELF ONLY...
RRMMMMMMMMMMMMMMMMB
...TO KILLING THE ENEMY.

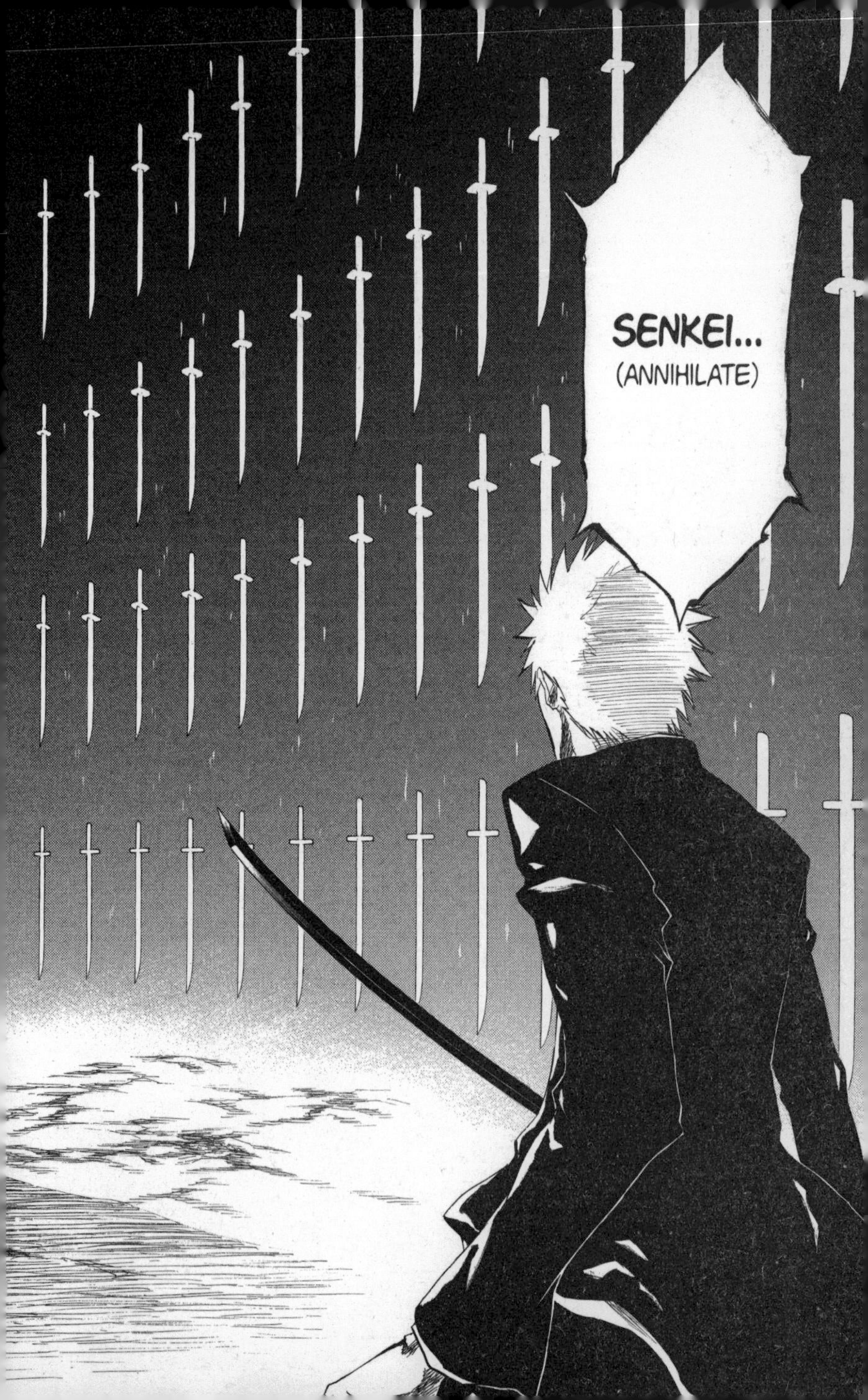
SENKEI...
(ANNIHILATE)

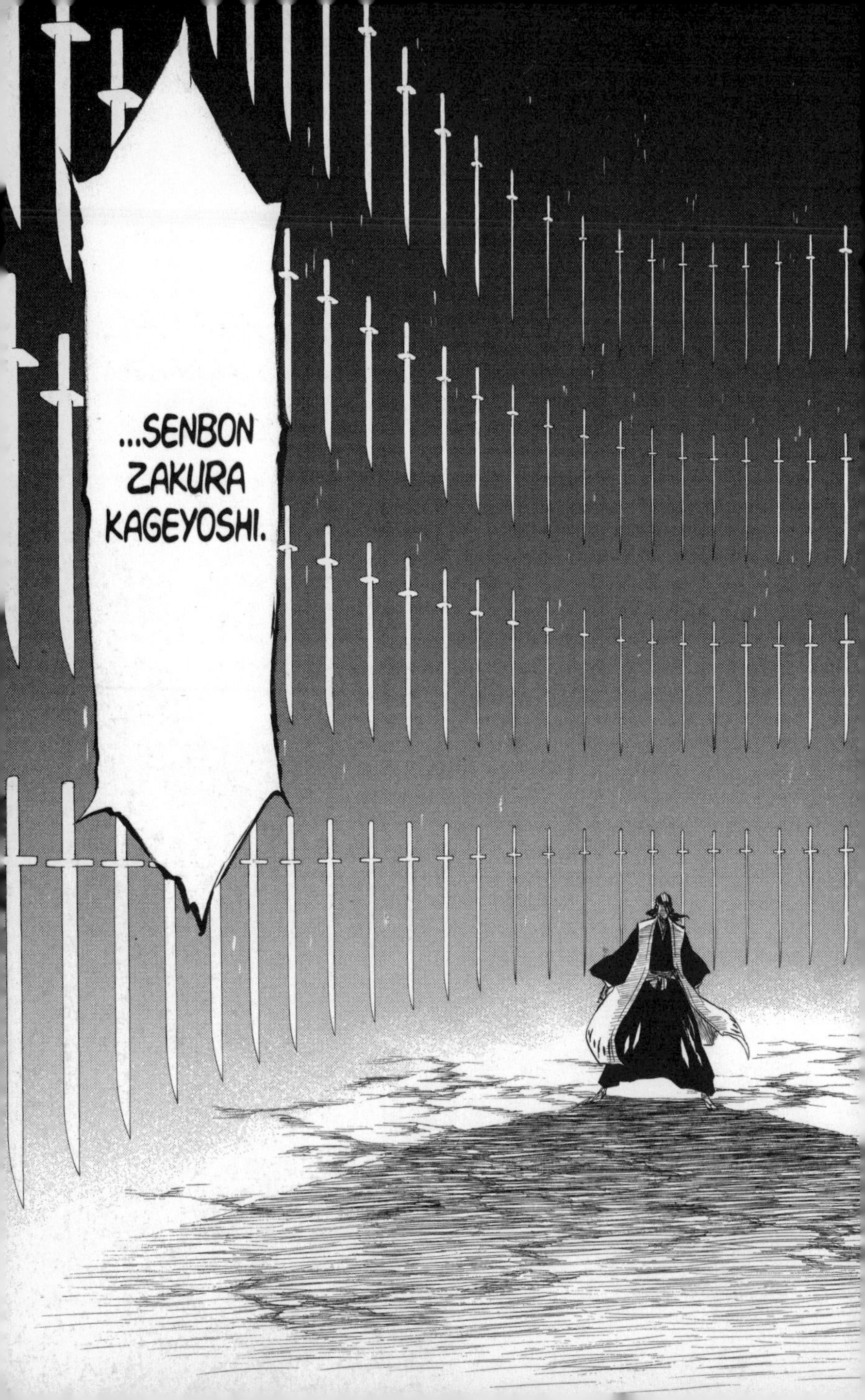
...SENBON ZAKURA KAGEYOSHI.

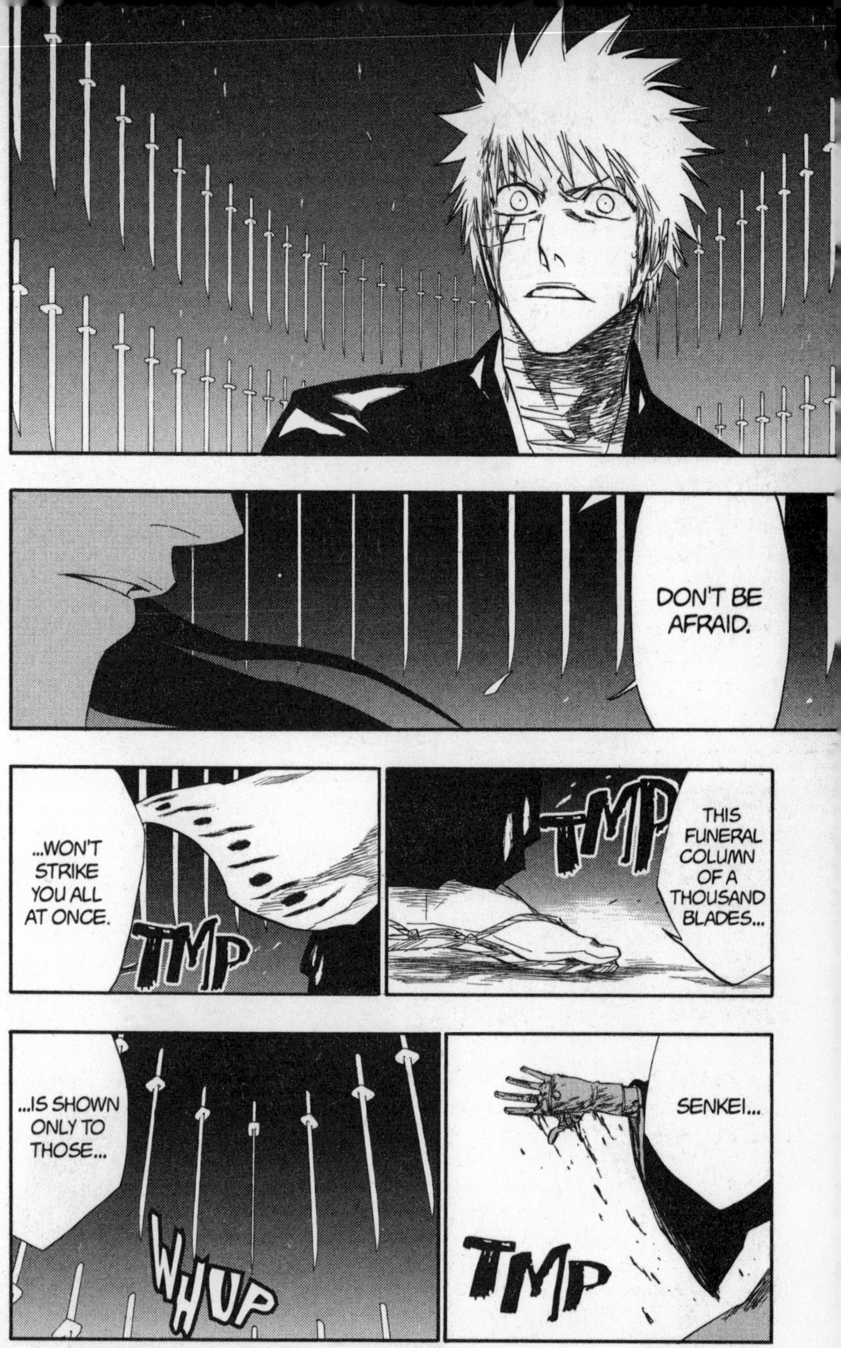
DON'T BE AFRAID.
TMP
THIS FUNERAL COLUMN OF A THOUSAND BLADES...
...WON'T STRIKE YOU ALL AT ONCE.
TMP
SENKEI...
TMP
...IS SHOWN ONLY TO THOSE...
WHUP

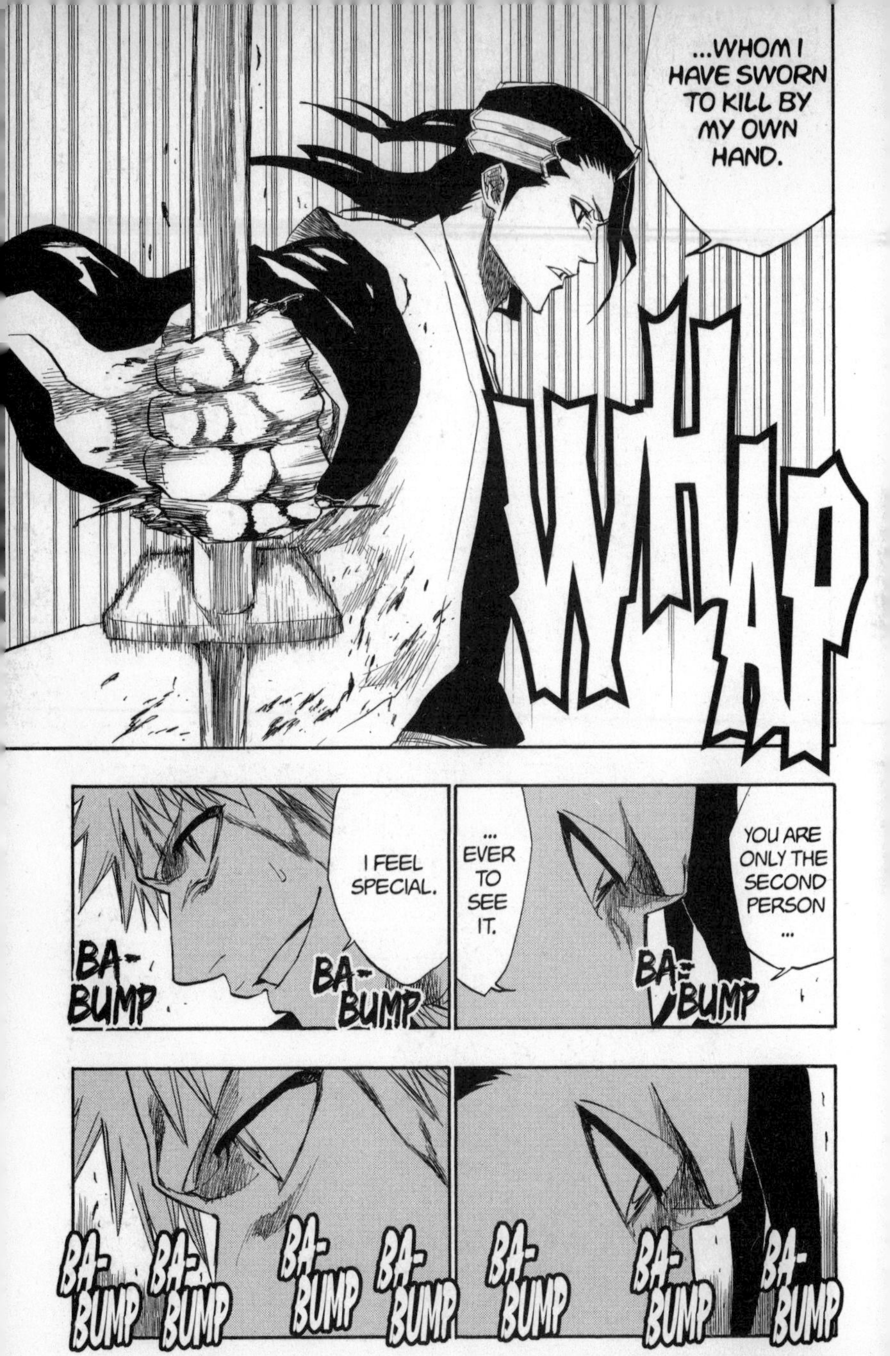
...WHOM I HAVE SWORN TO KILL BY MY OWN HAND.
WHAP
YOU ARE ONLY THE SECOND PERSON ...
... EVER TO SEE IT.
BA-BUMP
I FEEL SPECIAL.
BA-BUMP
BA-BUMP
BA-BUMP
BA-BUMP
BA-BUMP
BA-BUMP
BA-BUMP
BA-BUMP
BA-BUMP

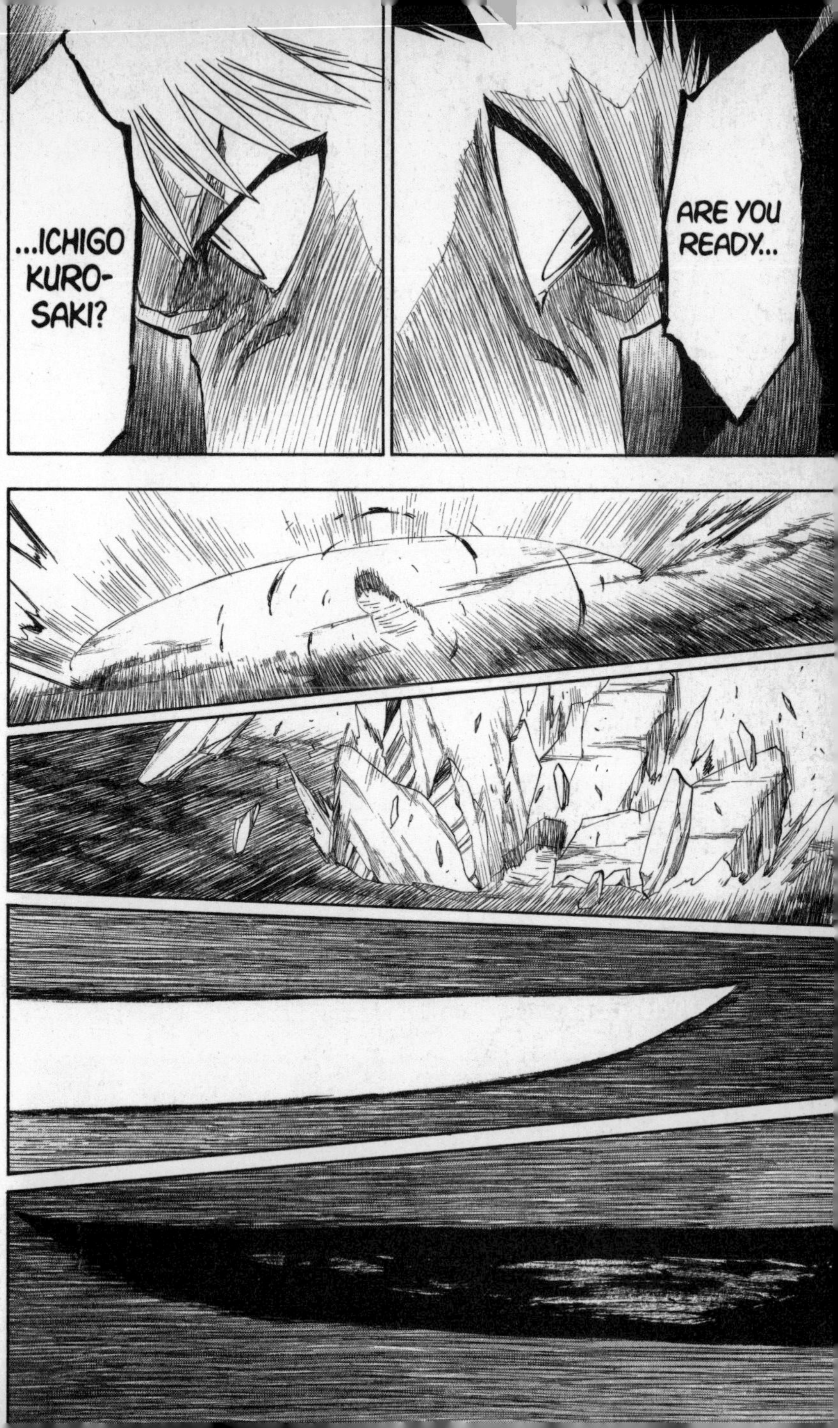
ARE YOU READY...
...ICHIGO KURO-SAKI?

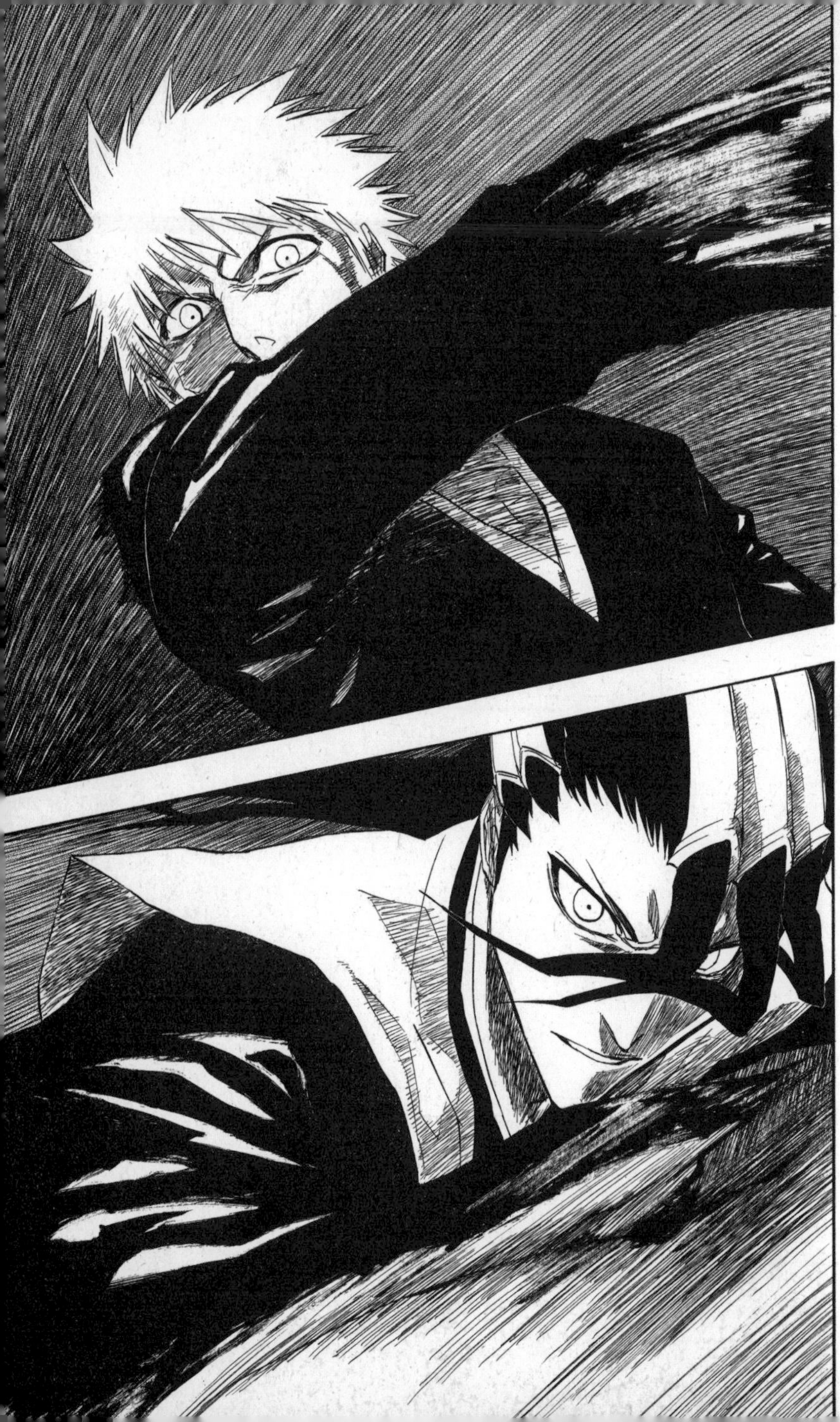

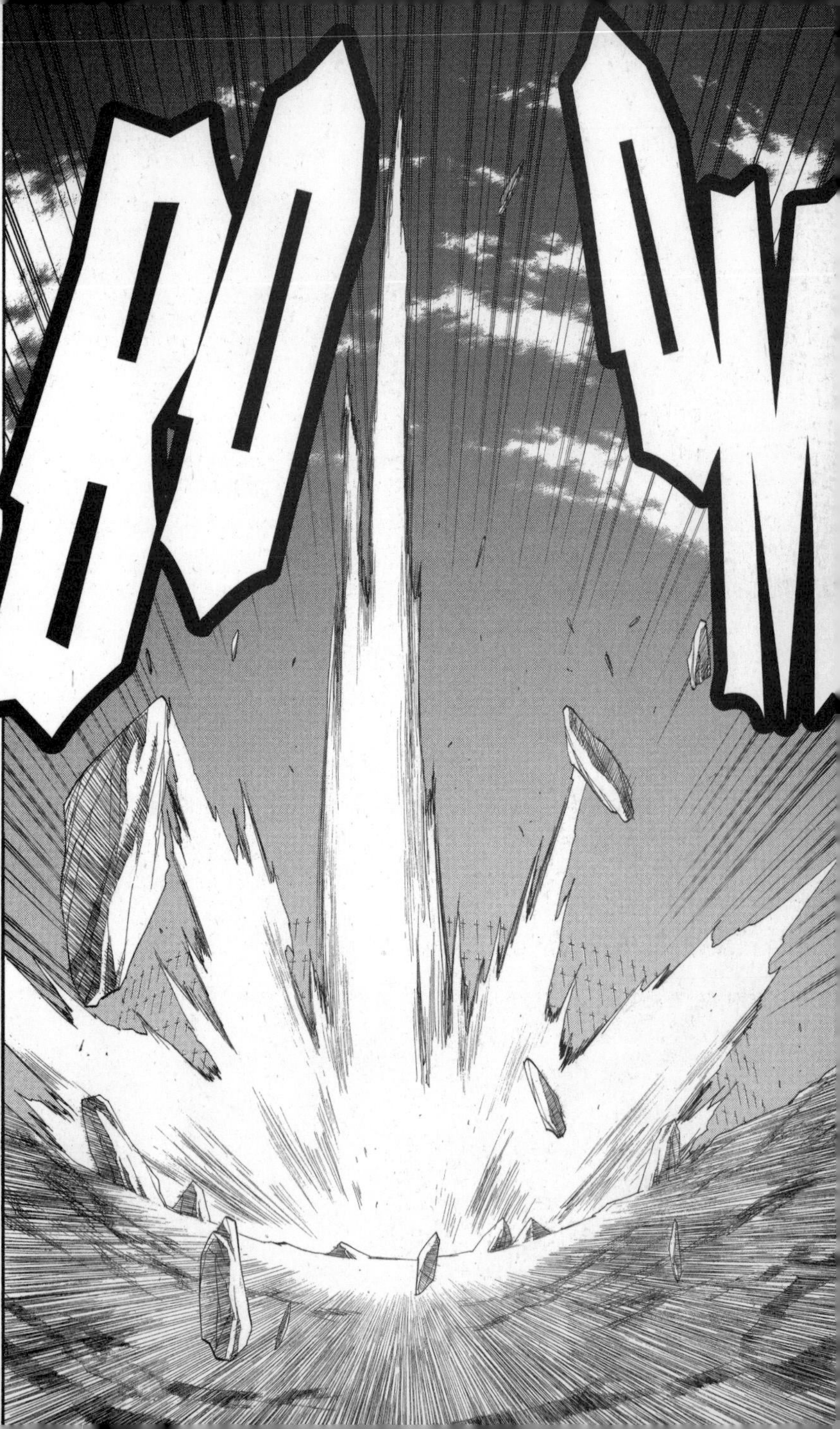
BOOM

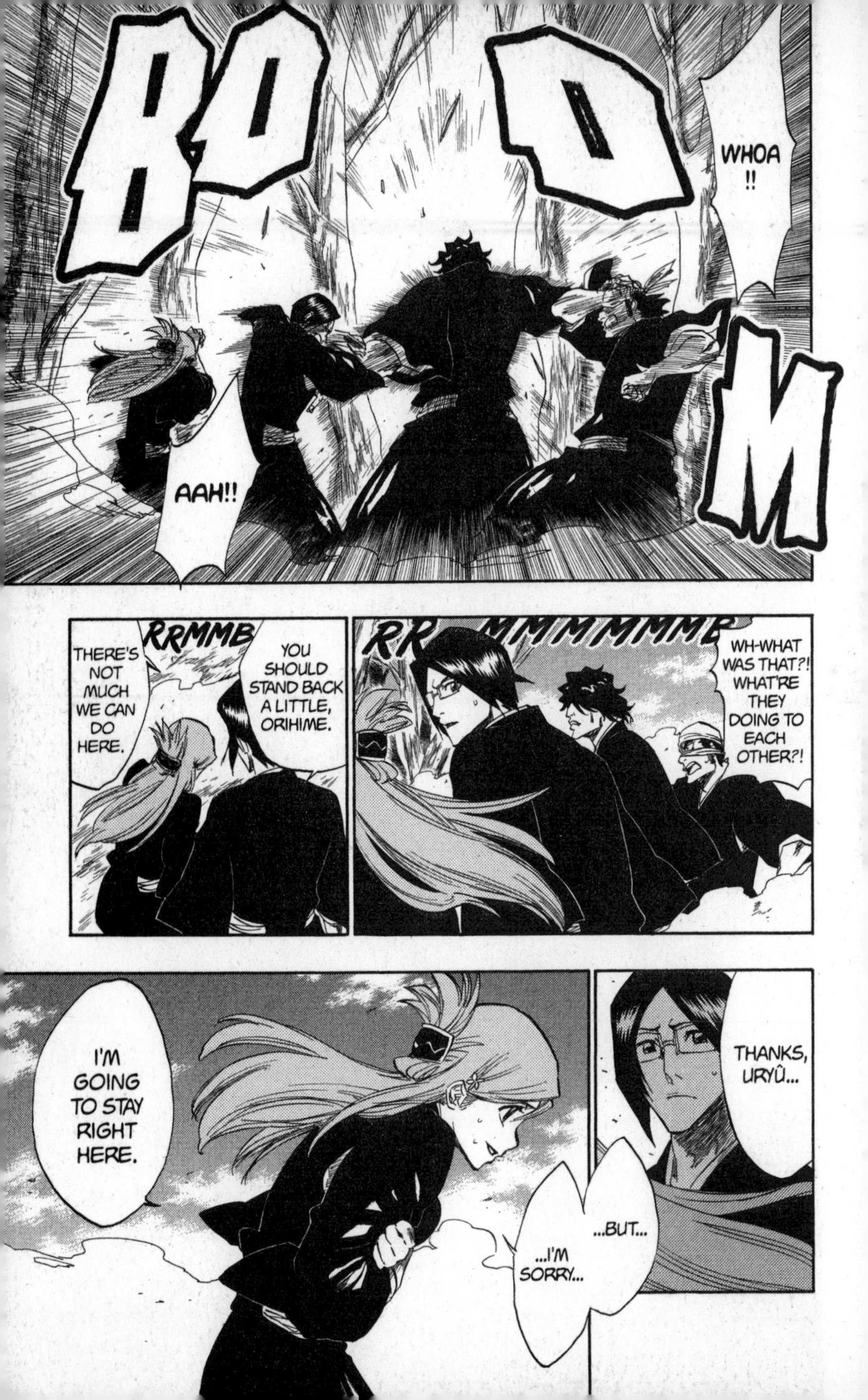

BOOM
WHOA!!
AAH!!
RRMMMMMMMB
WH-WHAT WAS THAT?! WHAT'RE THEY DOING TO EACH OTHER?!
RRMMB
YOU SHOULD STAND BACK A LITTLE, ORIHIME.
THERE'S NOT MUCH WE CAN DO HERE.
THANKS, URYÛ...
...BUT...
I'M GOING TO STAY RIGHT HERE.
...I'M SORRY...

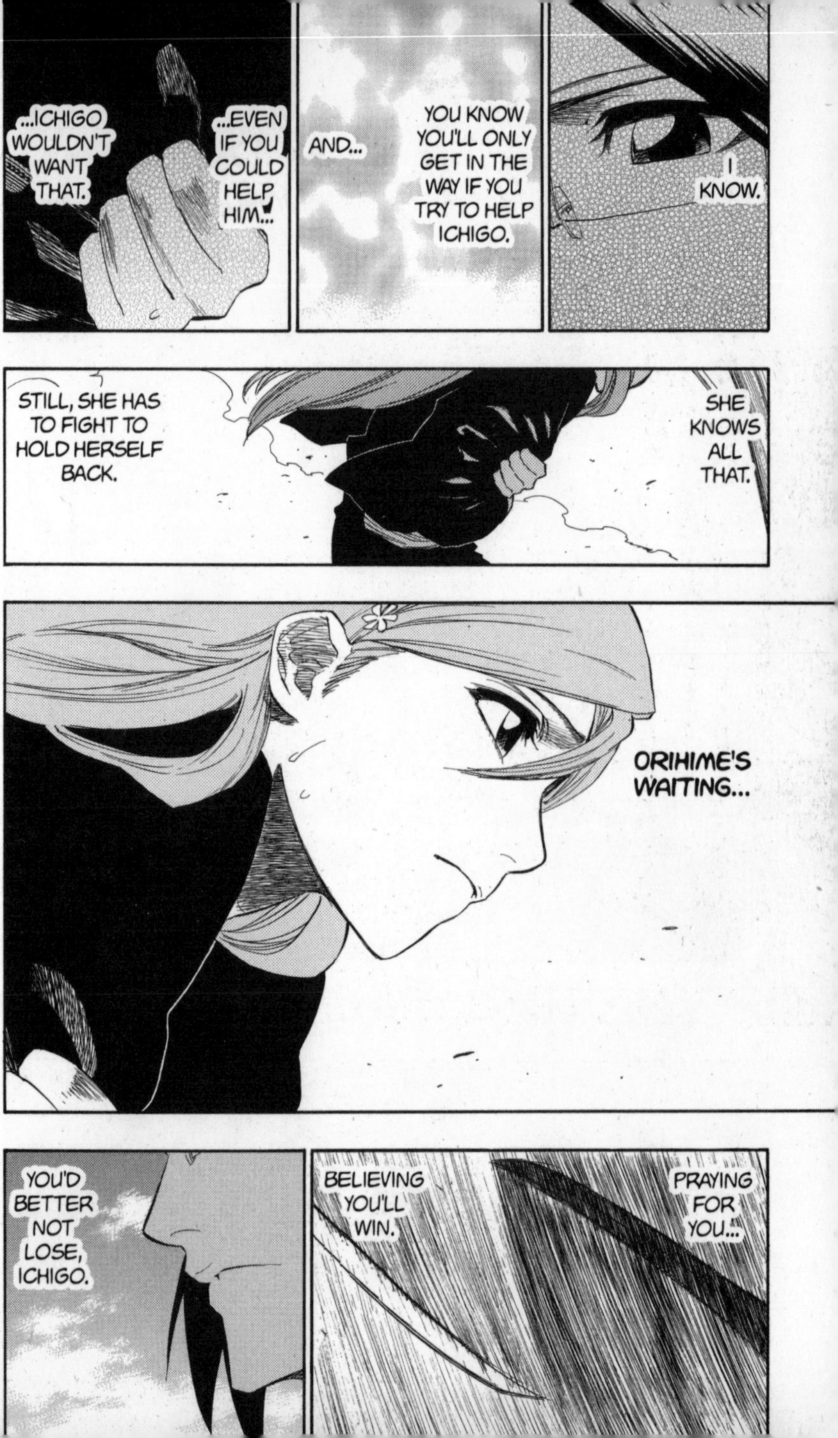
I KNOW.
YOU KNOW YOU'LL ONLY GET IN THE WAY IF YOU TRY TO HELP ICHIGO.
AND...
...EVEN IF YOU COULD HELP HIM...
...ICHIGO WOULDN'T WANT THAT.
SHE KNOWS ALL THAT.
STILL, SHE HAS TO FIGHT TO HOLD HERSELF BACK.
ORIHIME'S WAITING...
PRAYING FOR YOU...
BELIEVING YOU'LL WIN.
YOU'D BETTER NOT LOSE, ICHIGO.

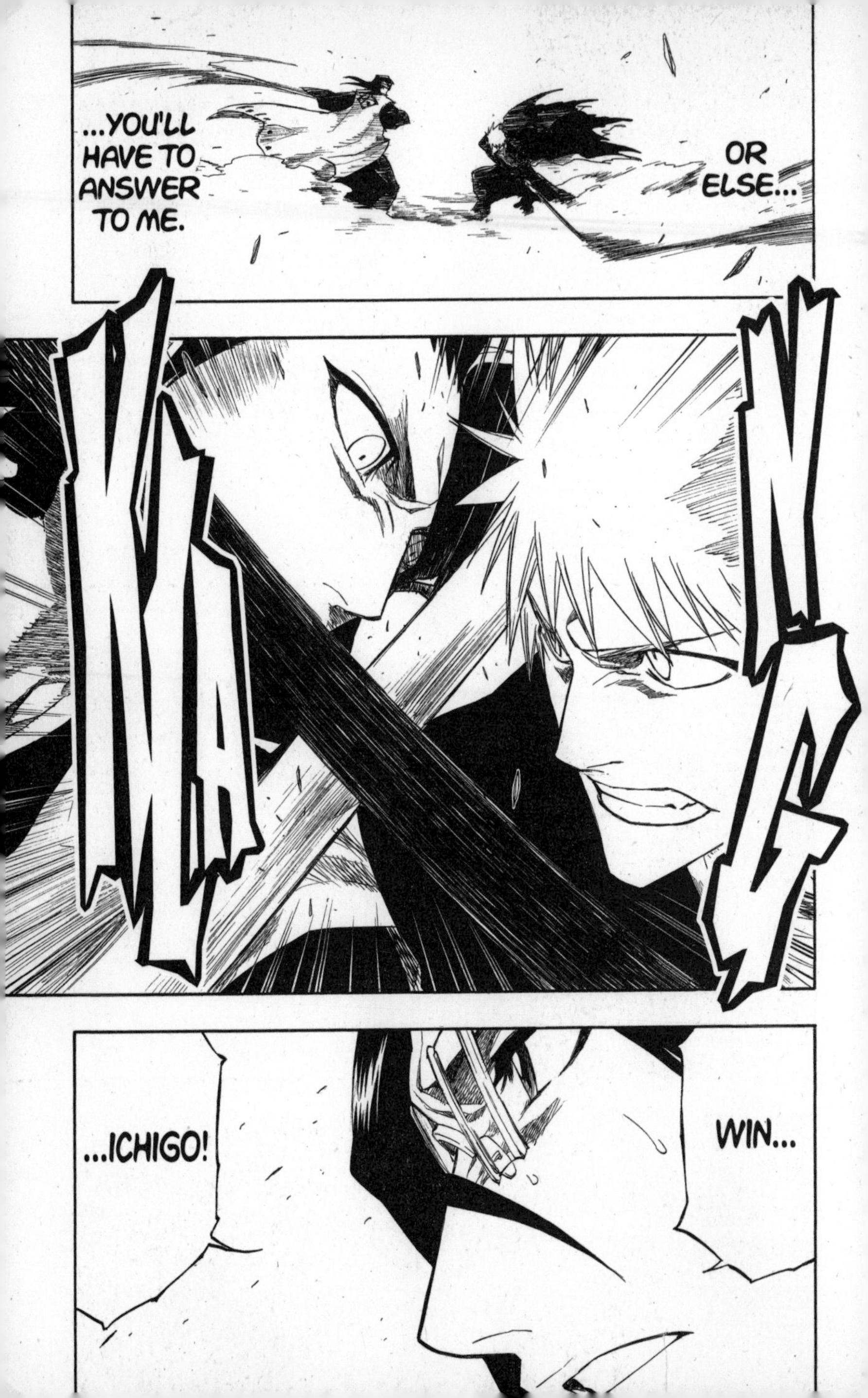
OR ELSE...
...YOU'LL HAVE TO ANSWER TO ME.
WIN...
...ICHIGO!

LOOK WHAT YOU DID!!
BECAUSE YOU TOOK YOUR OWN SWEET TIME, THE PRECIOUS COLOR PAGES STARTED WITH A CLOSE-UP OF YOU!!
MAN!!
THE COLOR PAGES ARE OVER ALREADY!! DARN!!!
CRAP.
WHY DOES HE GET ALL THE ATTENTION WHILE I GET STUCK WITH THIS?
IT'S NOT FAIR! IT'S NOT FAIR!!
FINE, I'LL JUST...!!

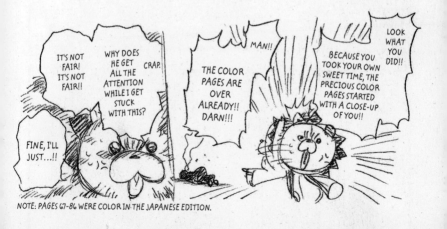

NOTE: PAGES 67-86 WERE COLOR IN THE JAPANESE EDITION.

165. The Dark Side of the Universe 2

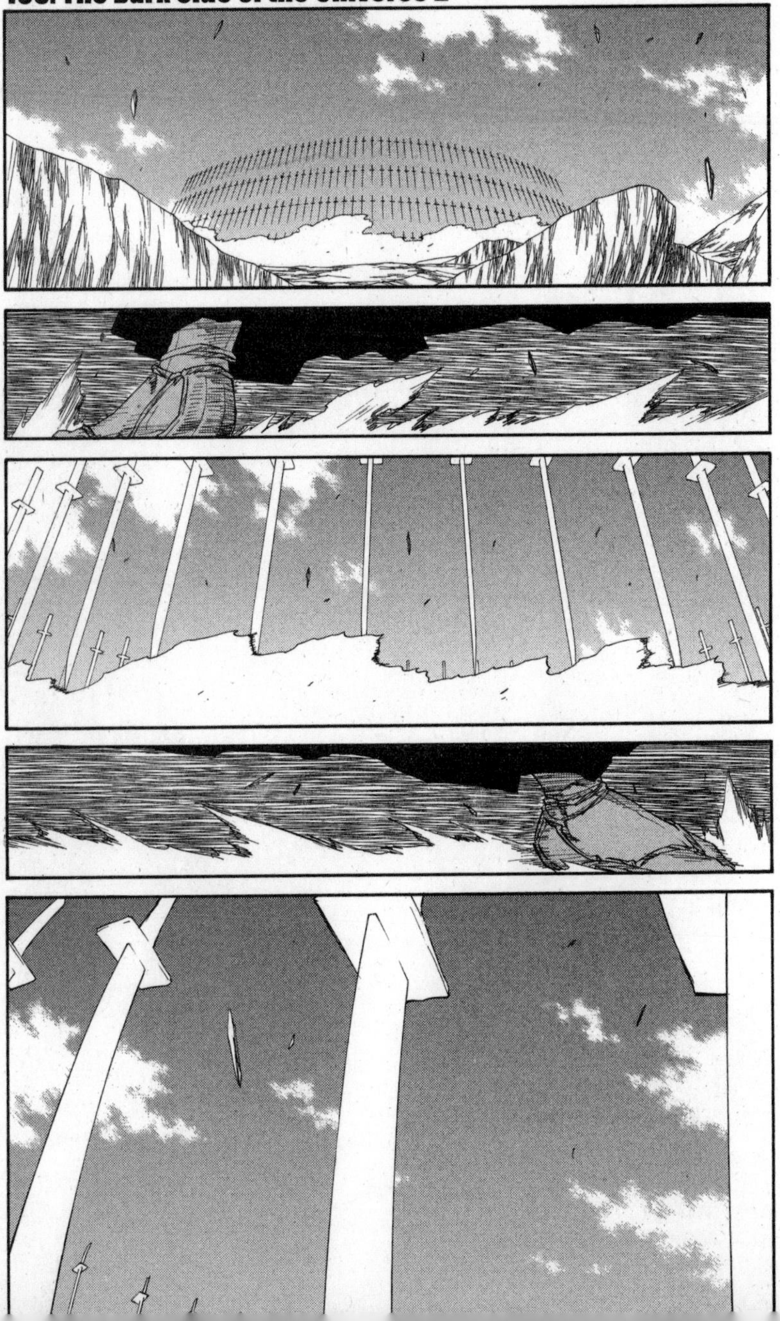

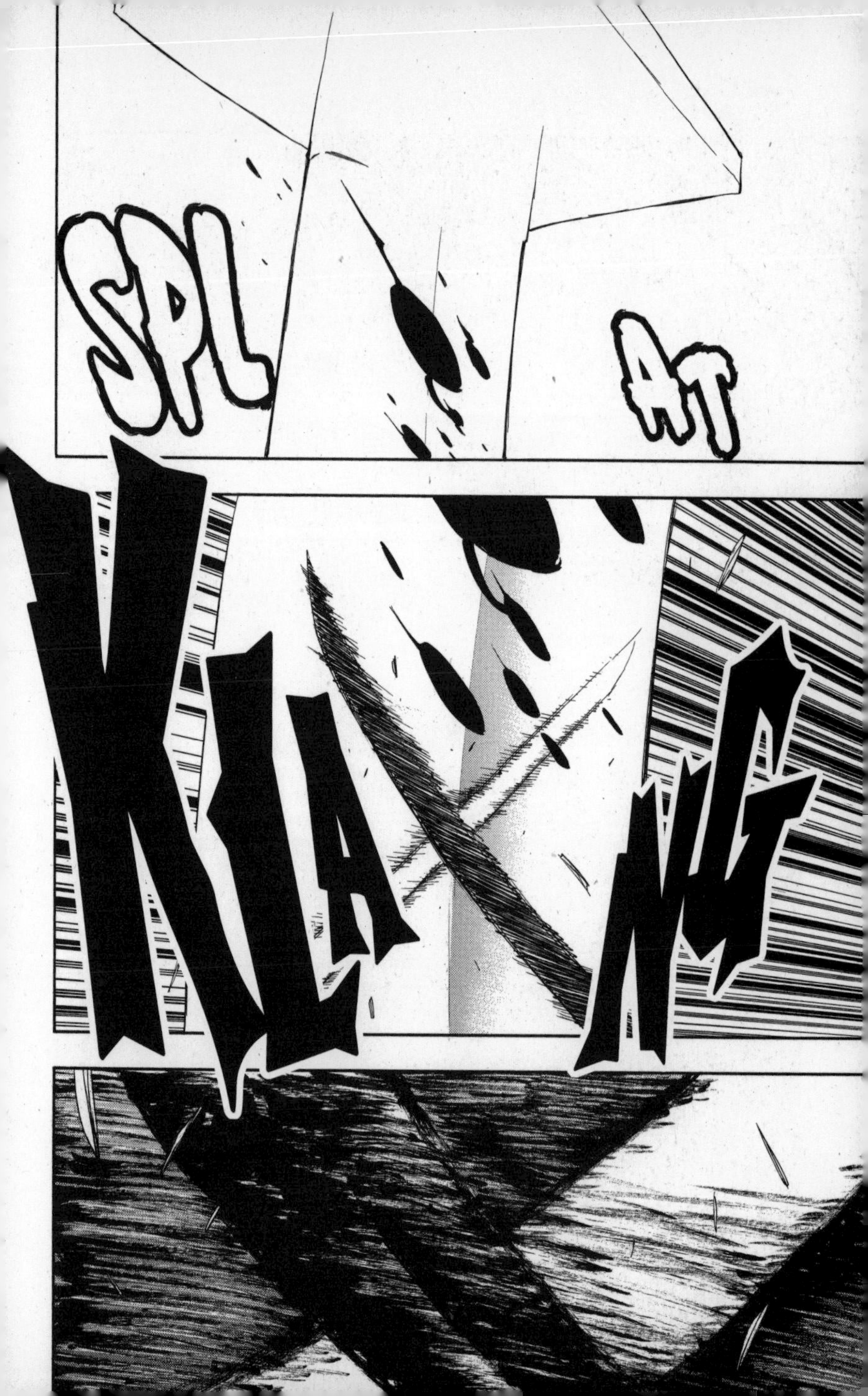
SPL AT
KLANG

READ THIS WAY

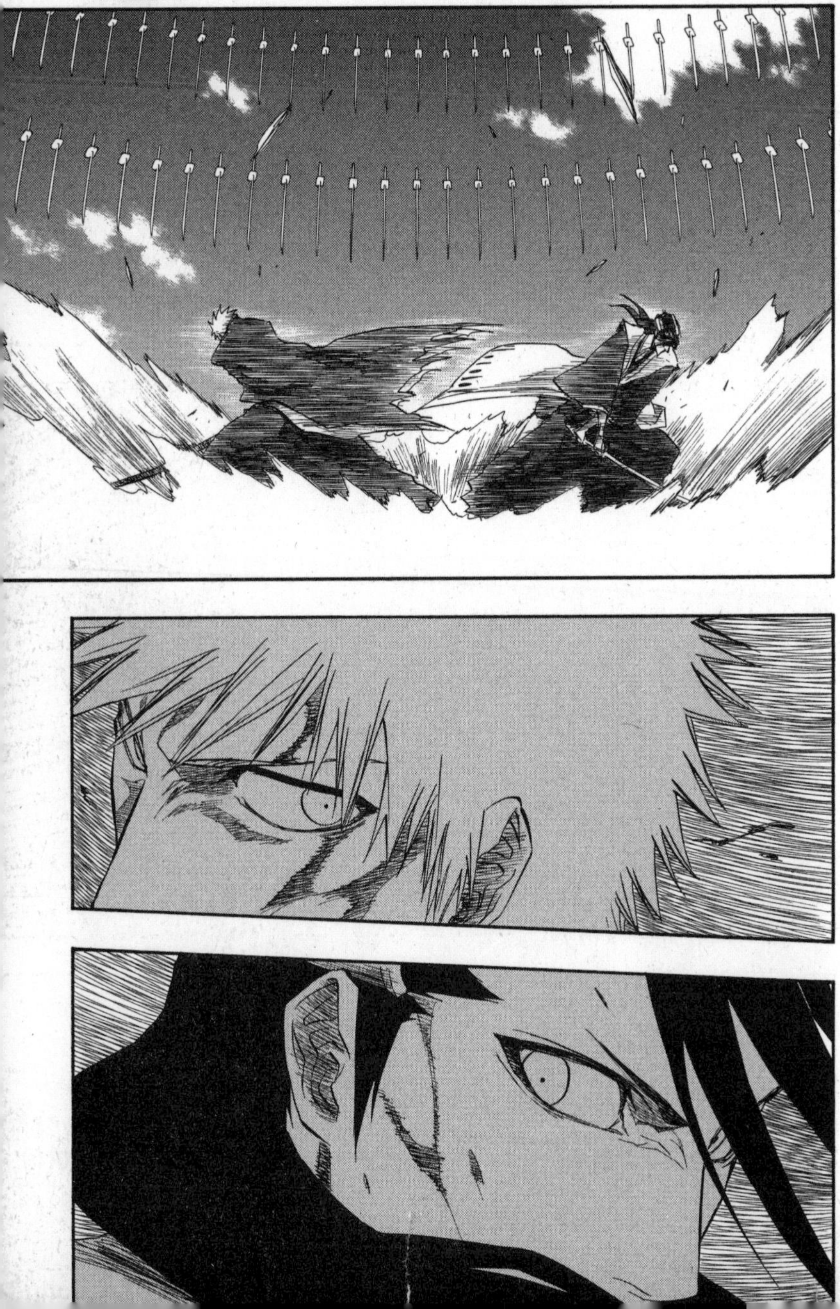

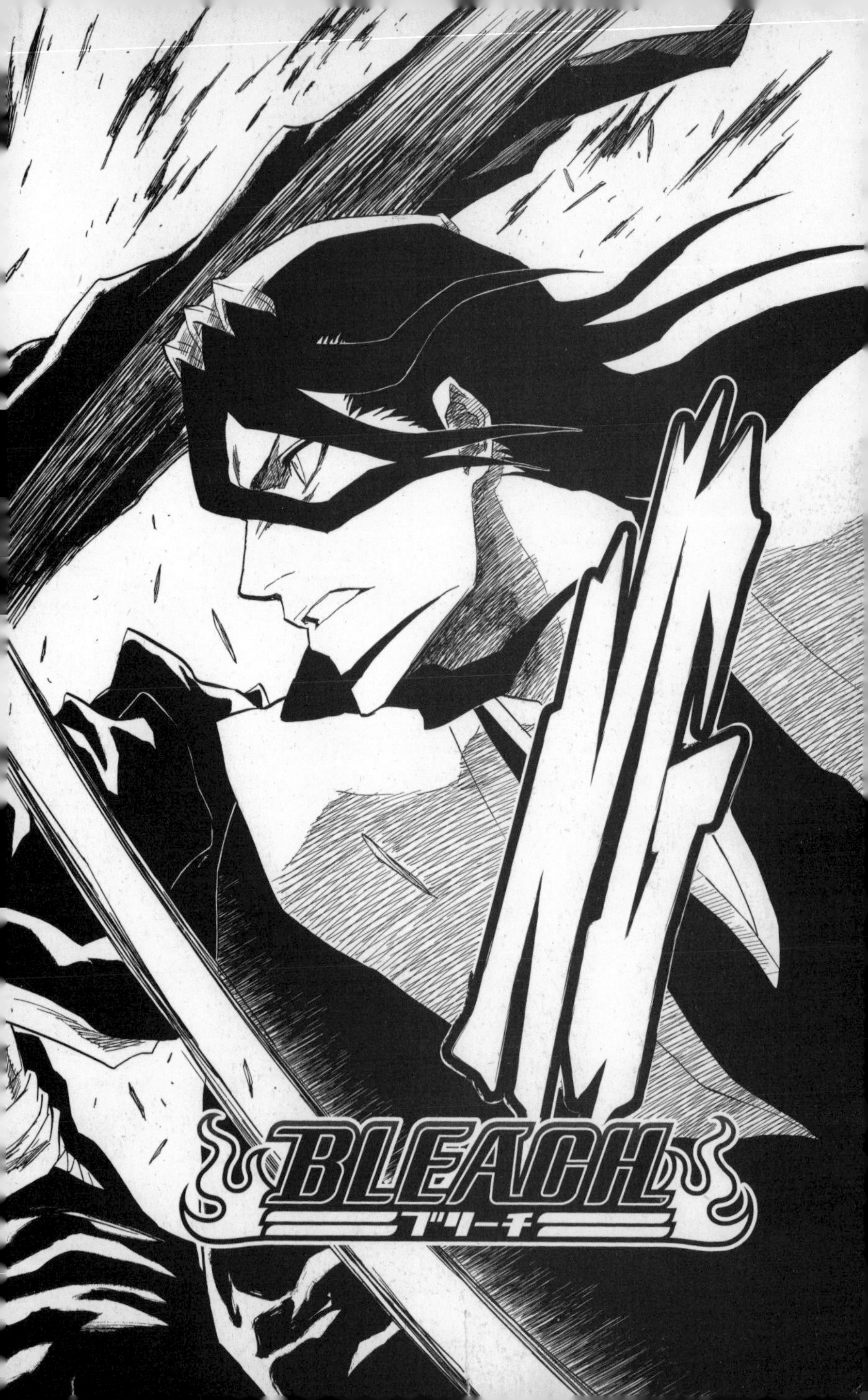
BLEACH
ブリーチ

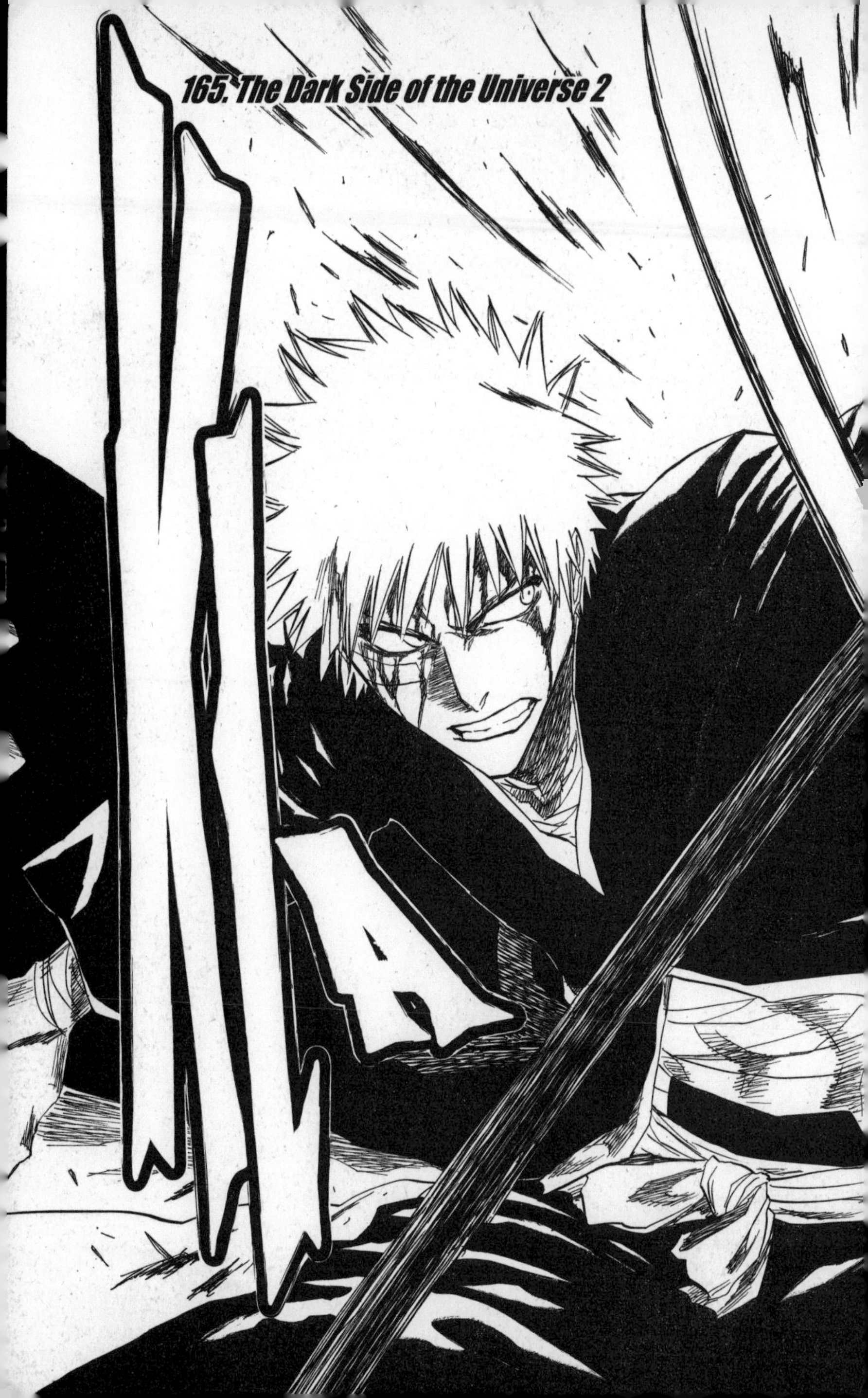
165. The Dark Side of the Universe 2

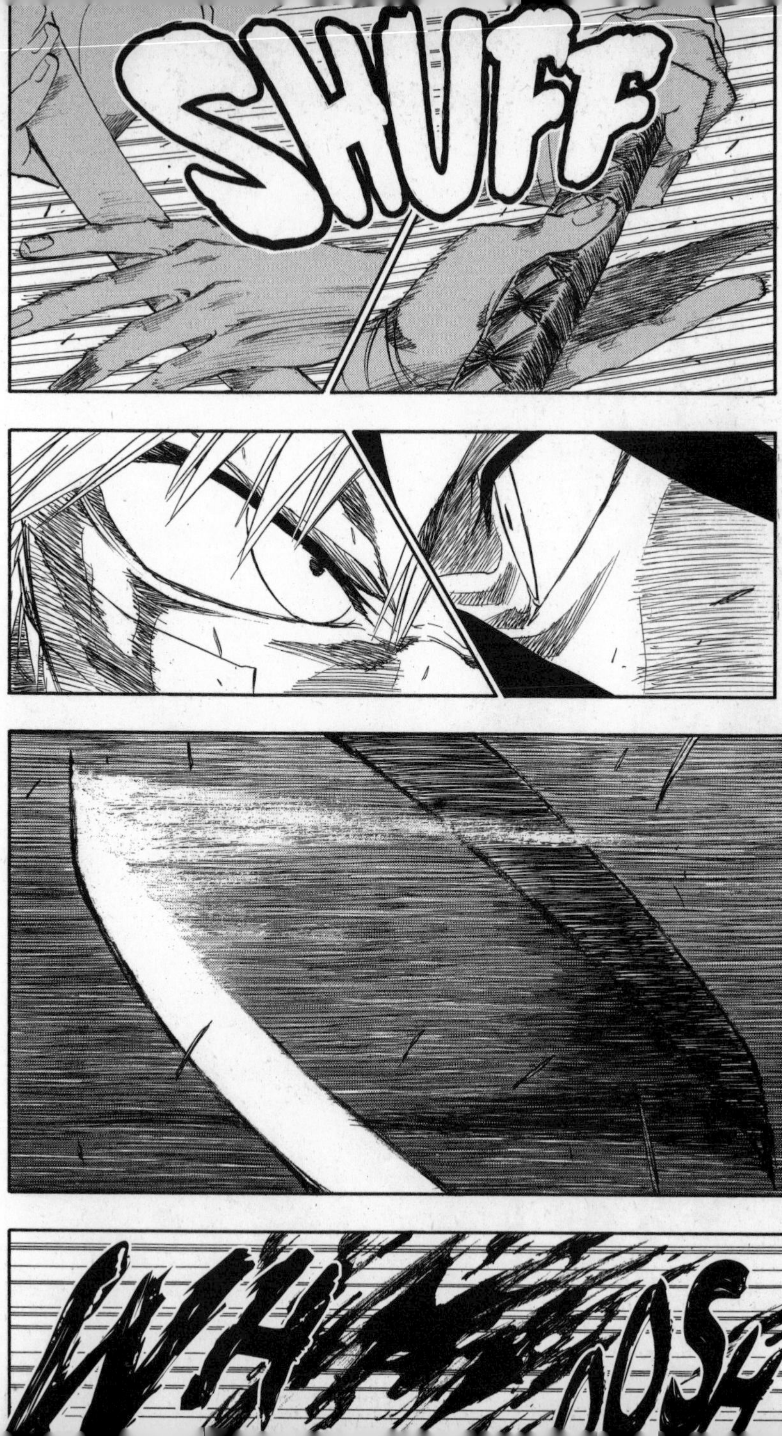
SHUFF
WHOOSH

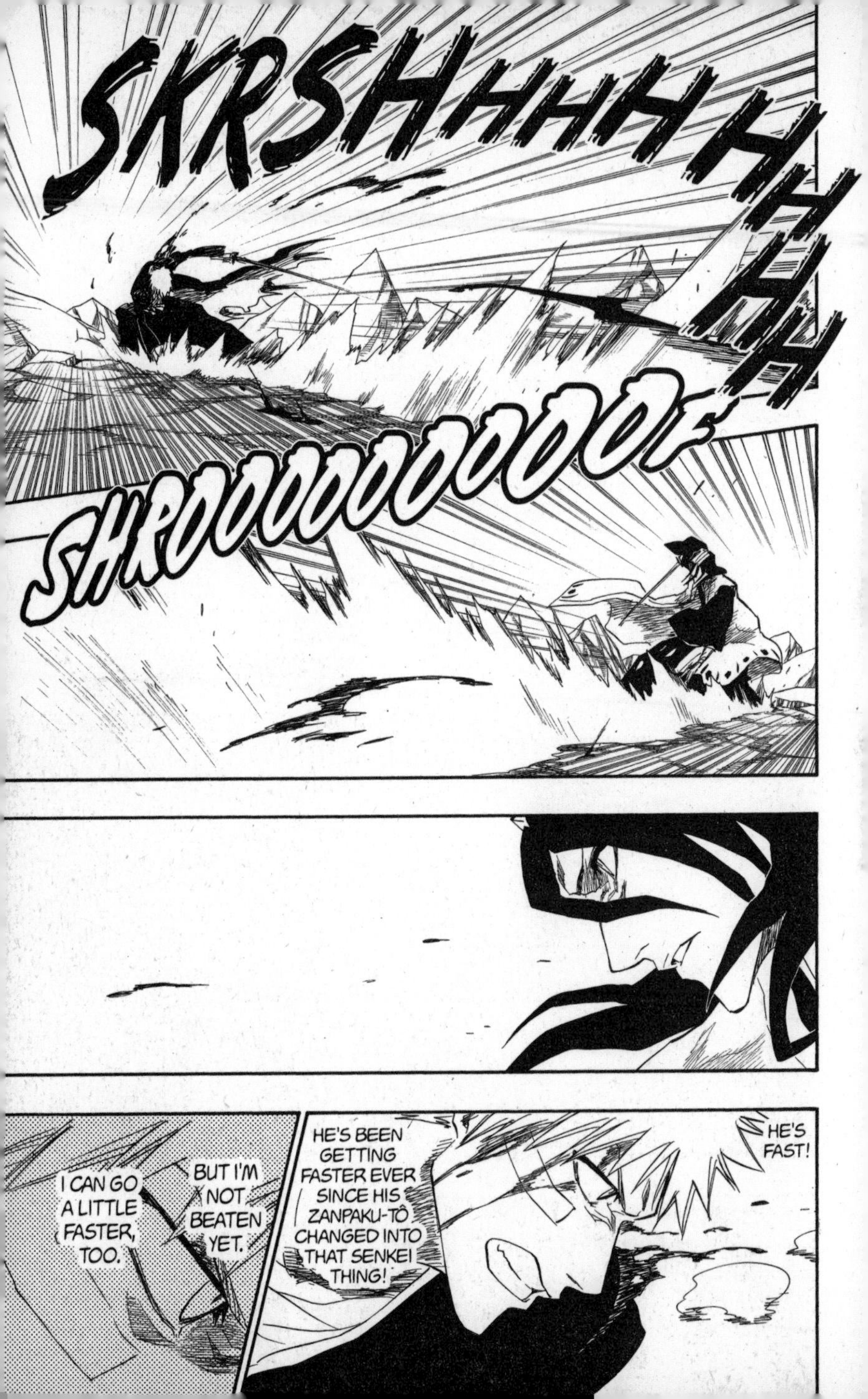
SKRSHHHHHHHH
SHROOOOOOOOO
HE'S FAST!
HE'S BEEN GETTING FASTER EVER SINCE HIS ZANPAKU-TÔ CHANGED INTO THAT SENKEI THING!
BUT I'M NOT BEATEN YET.
I CAN GO A LITTLE FASTER, TOO.

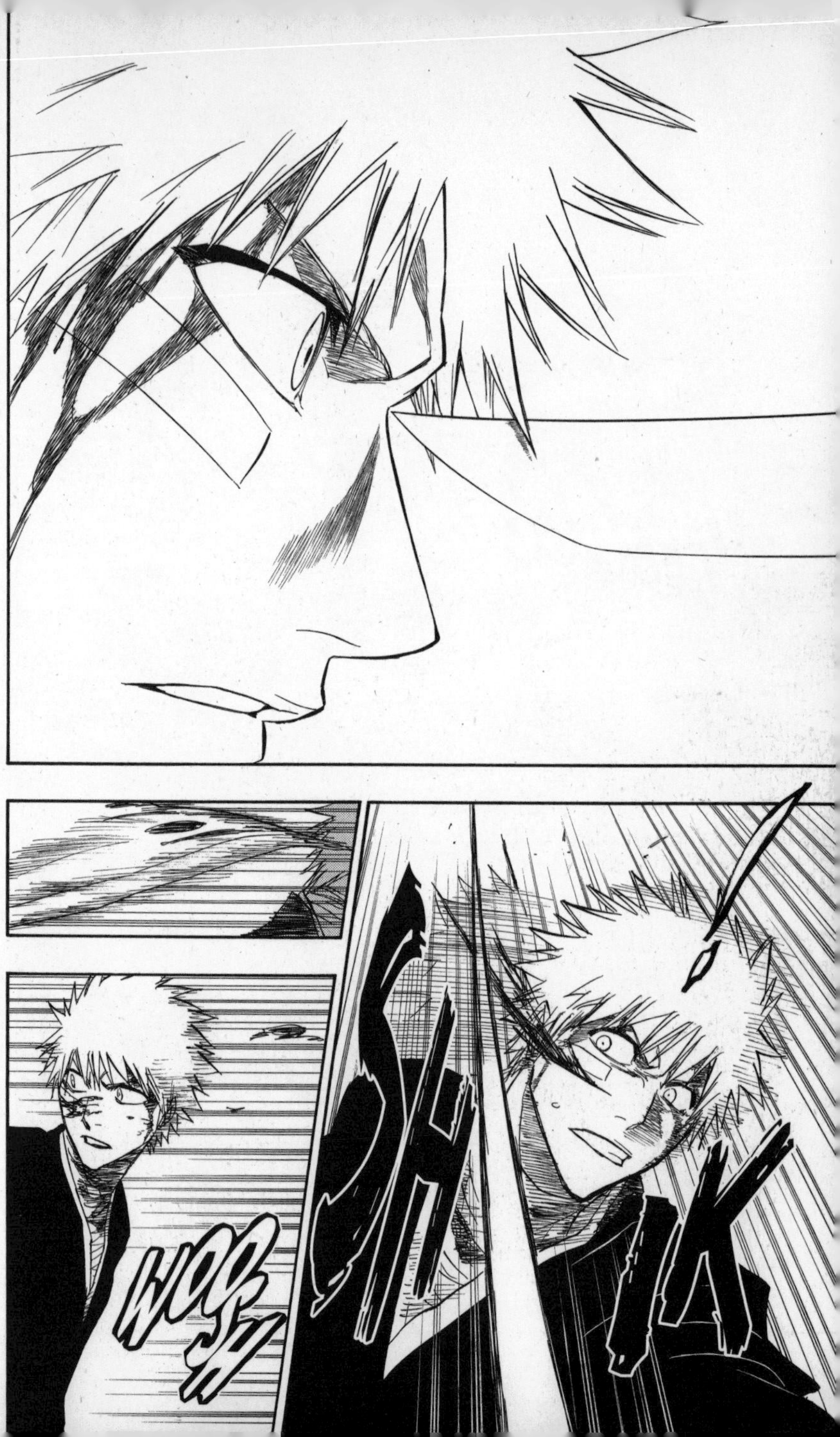

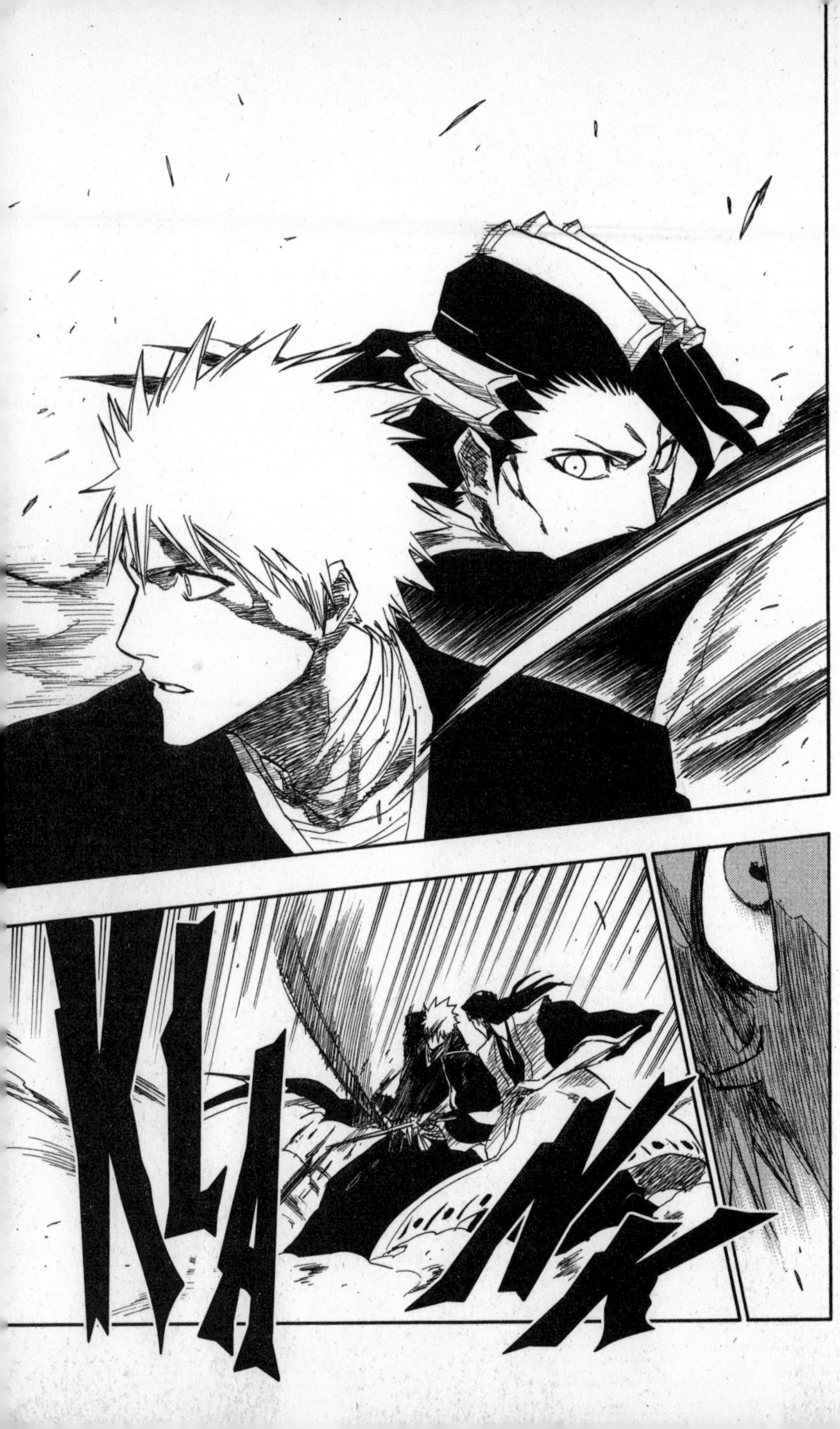
KLANK

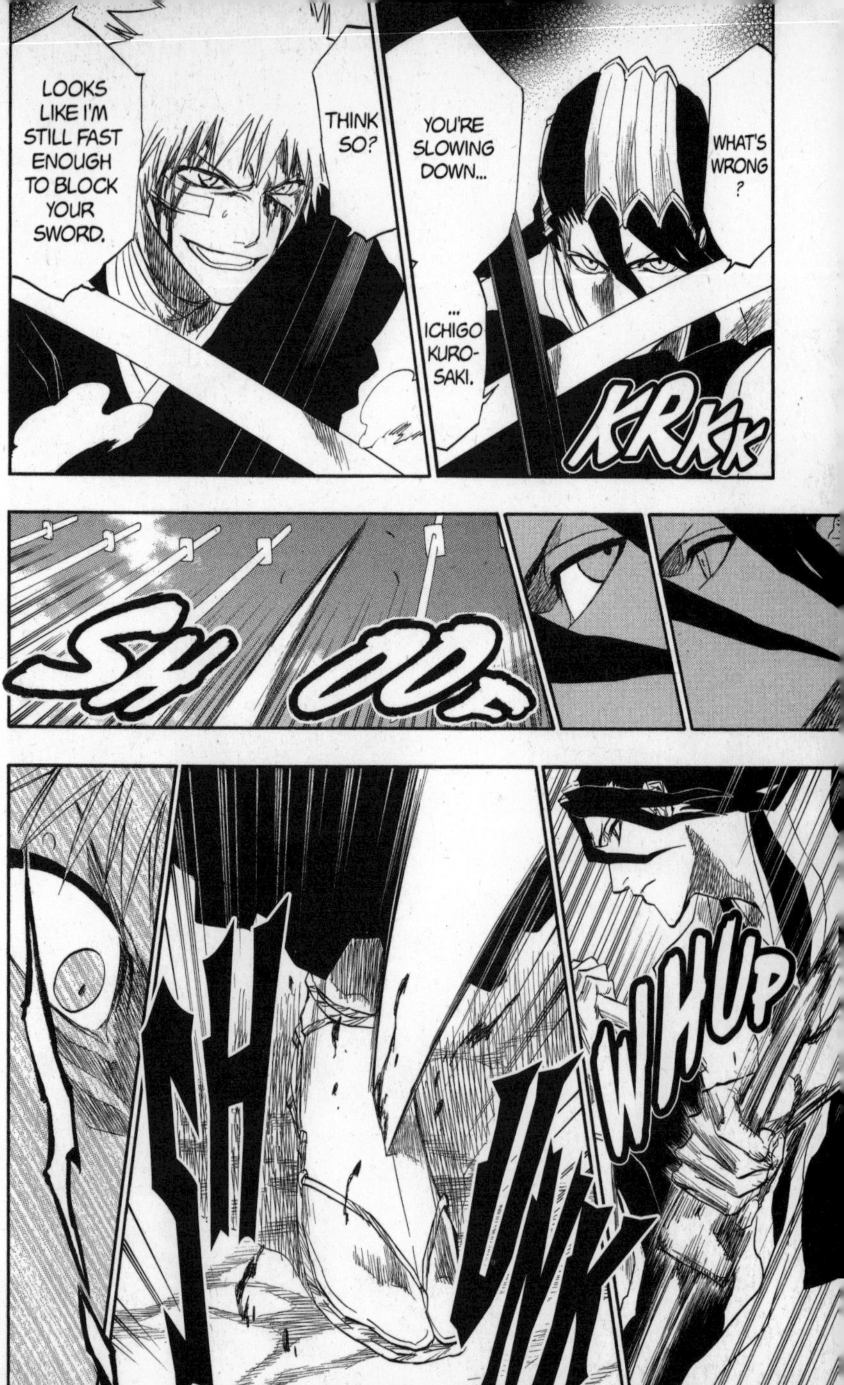
WHAT'S WRONG?
YOU'RE SLOWING DOWN...
...ICHIGO KUROSAKI.
KRKKK
THINK SO?
LOOKS LIKE I'M STILL FAST ENOUGH TO BLOCK YOUR SWORD.
SHOO
WHUP

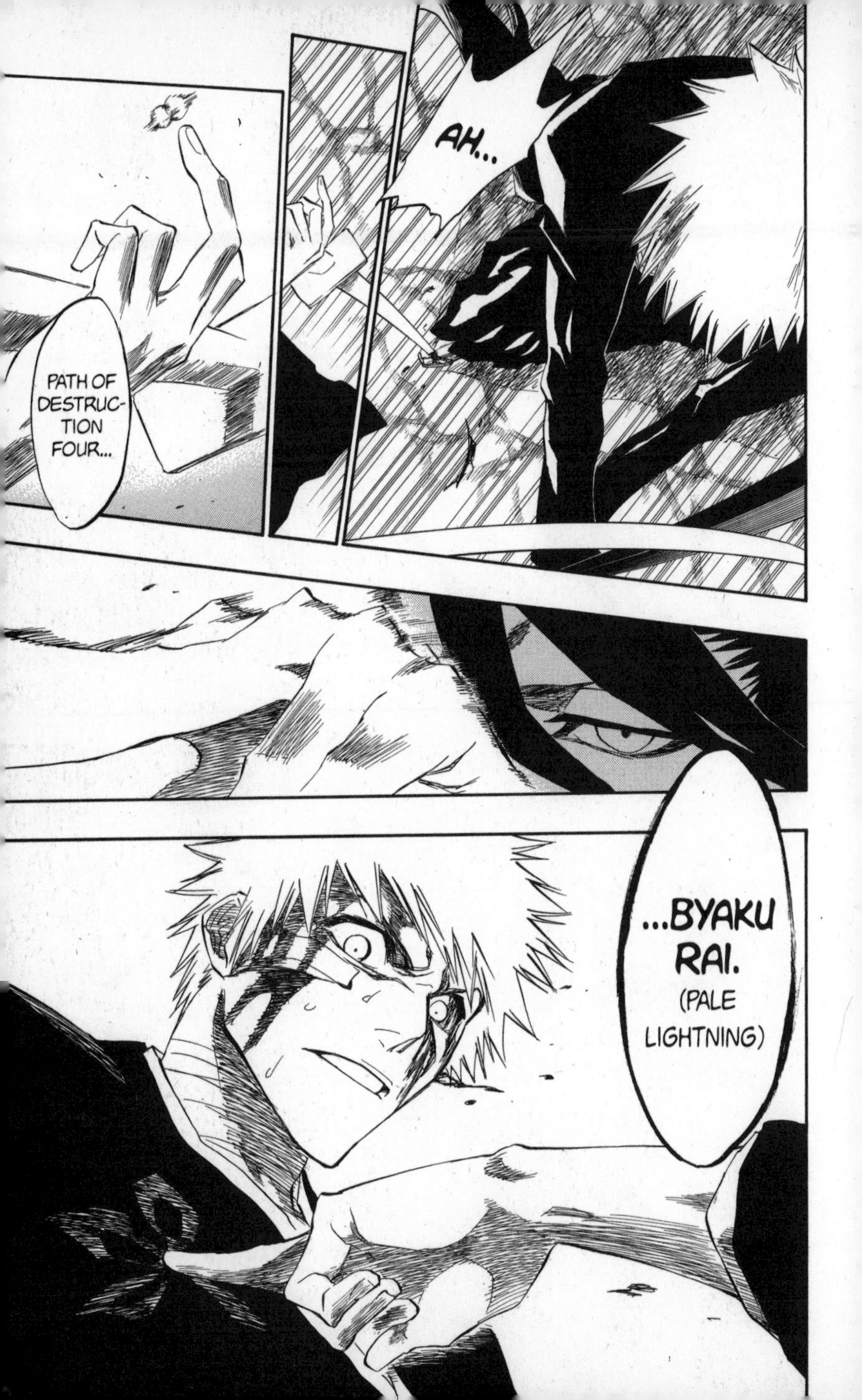
AH...
PATH OF DESTRUCTION FOUR...
...BYAKU RAI.
(PALE LIGHTNING)

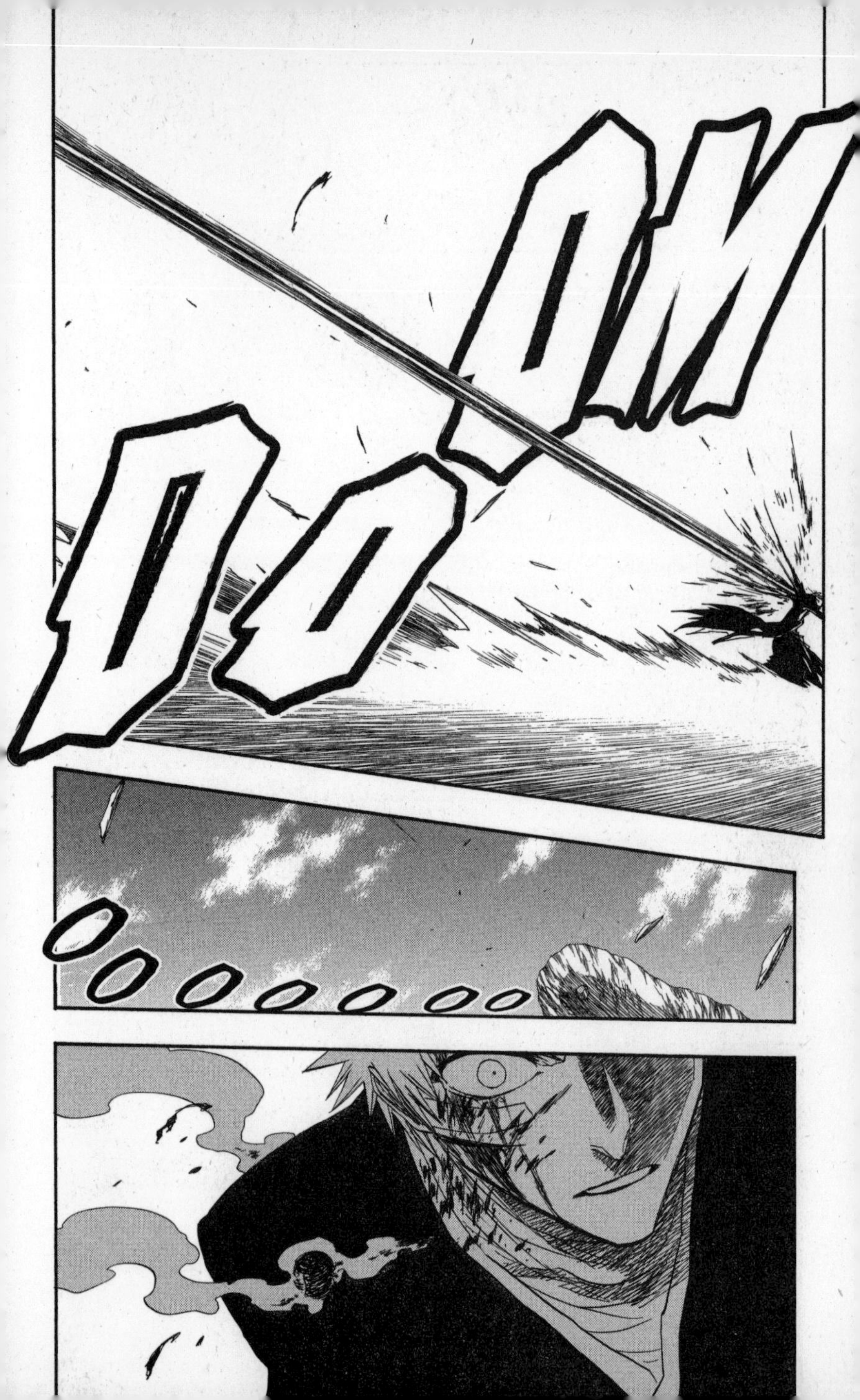
DOOM
OOOOOOOOO

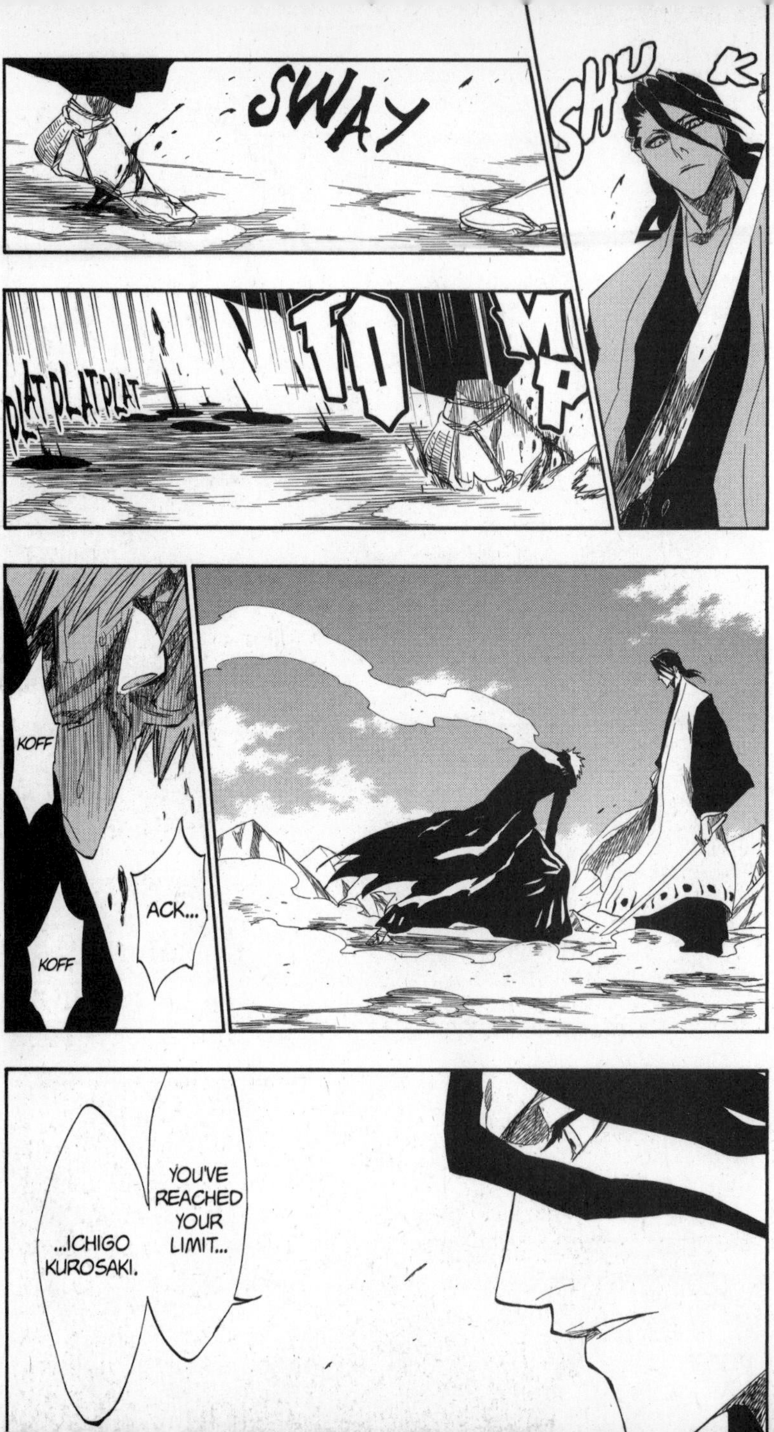
SHUNK
SWAY
TOMP
PLAT PLAT PLAT
KOFF
ACK...
KOFF
YOU'VE REACHED YOUR LIMIT...
...ICHIGO KUROSAKI.

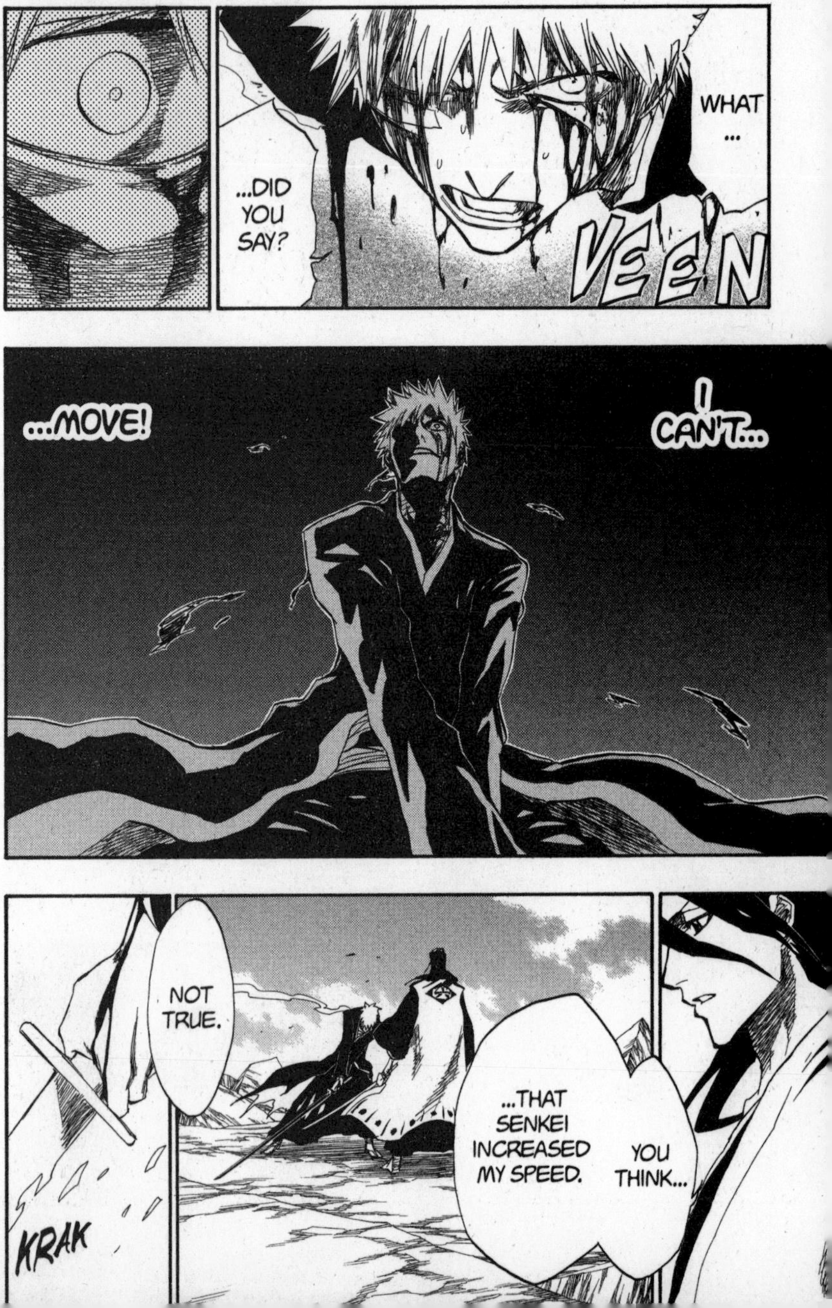
WHAT ...
...DID YOU SAY?
VEEN
I CAN'T...
...MOVE!
YOU THINK...
...THAT SENKEI INCREASED MY SPEED.
NOT TRUE.
KRAK

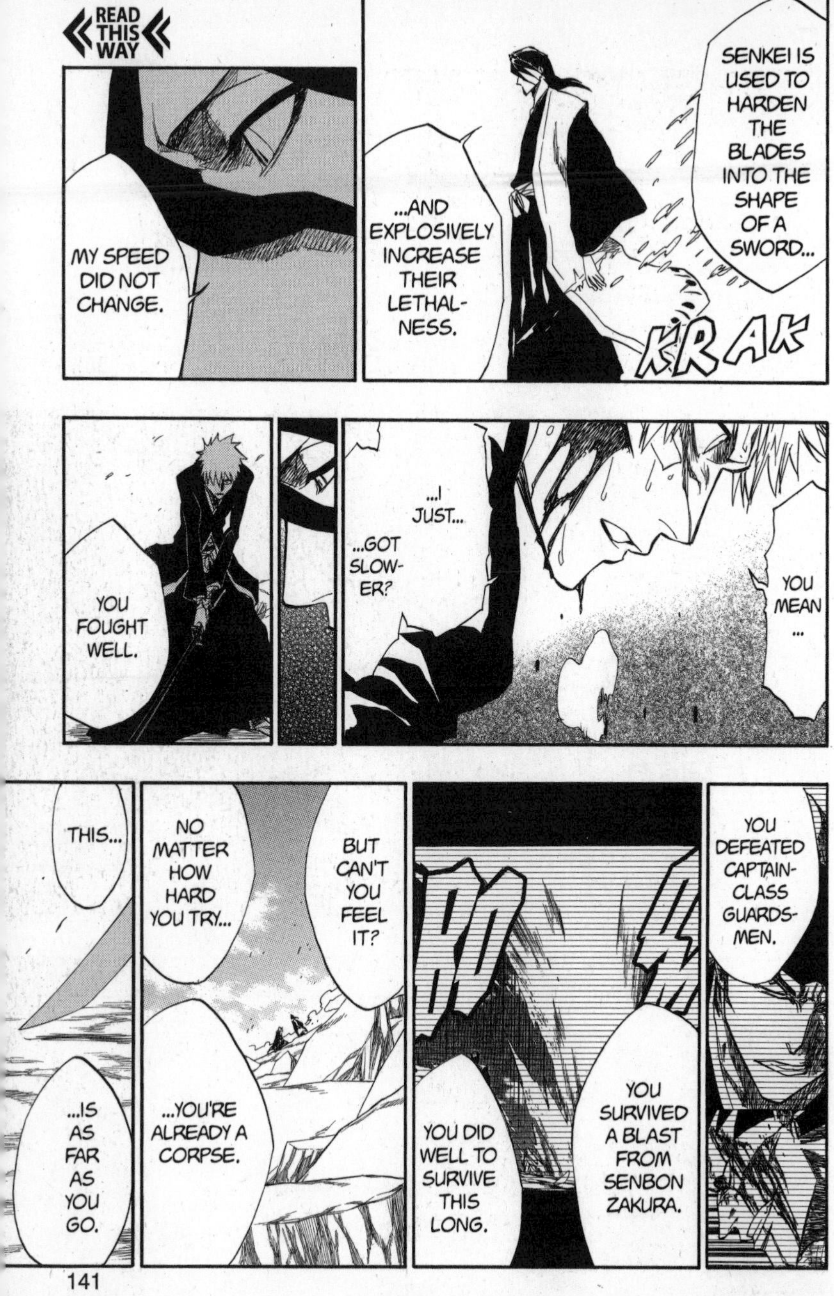
READ THIS WAY
SENKEI IS USED TO HARDEN THE BLADES INTO THE SHAPE OF A SWORD...
...AND EXPLOSIVELY INCREASE THEIR LETHAL-NESS.
KRAK
MY SPEED DID NOT CHANGE.
YOU MEAN...
...I JUST...
...GOT SLOW-ER?
YOU FOUGHT WELL.
YOU DEFEATED CAPTAIN-CLASS GUARDS-MEN.
YOU SURVIVED A BLAST FROM SENBON ZAKURA.
YOU DID WELL TO SURVIVE THIS LONG.
BUT CAN'T YOU FEEL IT?
NO MATTER HOW HARD YOU TRY...
...YOU'RE ALREADY A CORPSE.
THIS...
...IS AS FAR AS YOU GO.

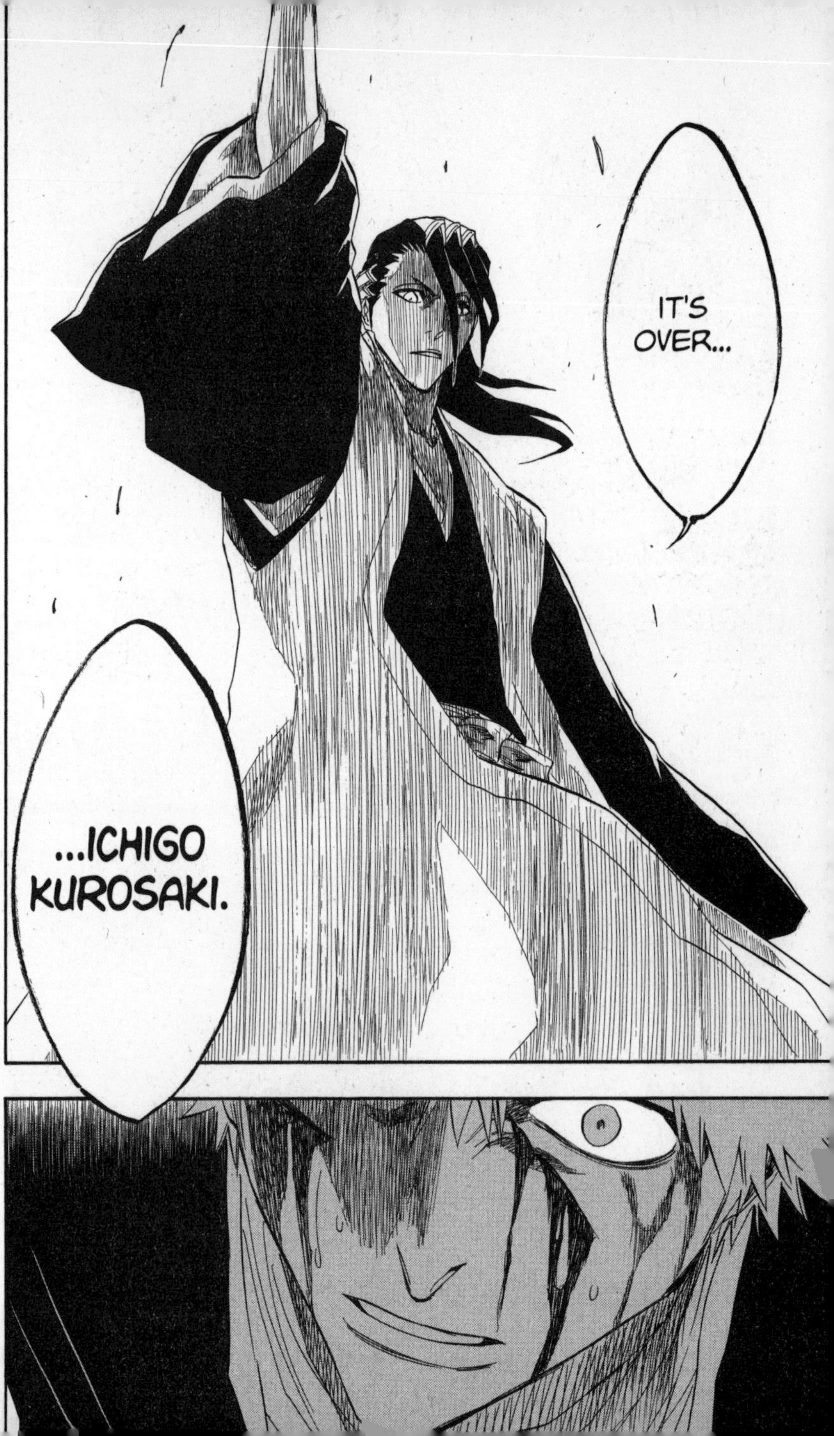
IT'S OVER...
...ICHIGO KUROSAKI.

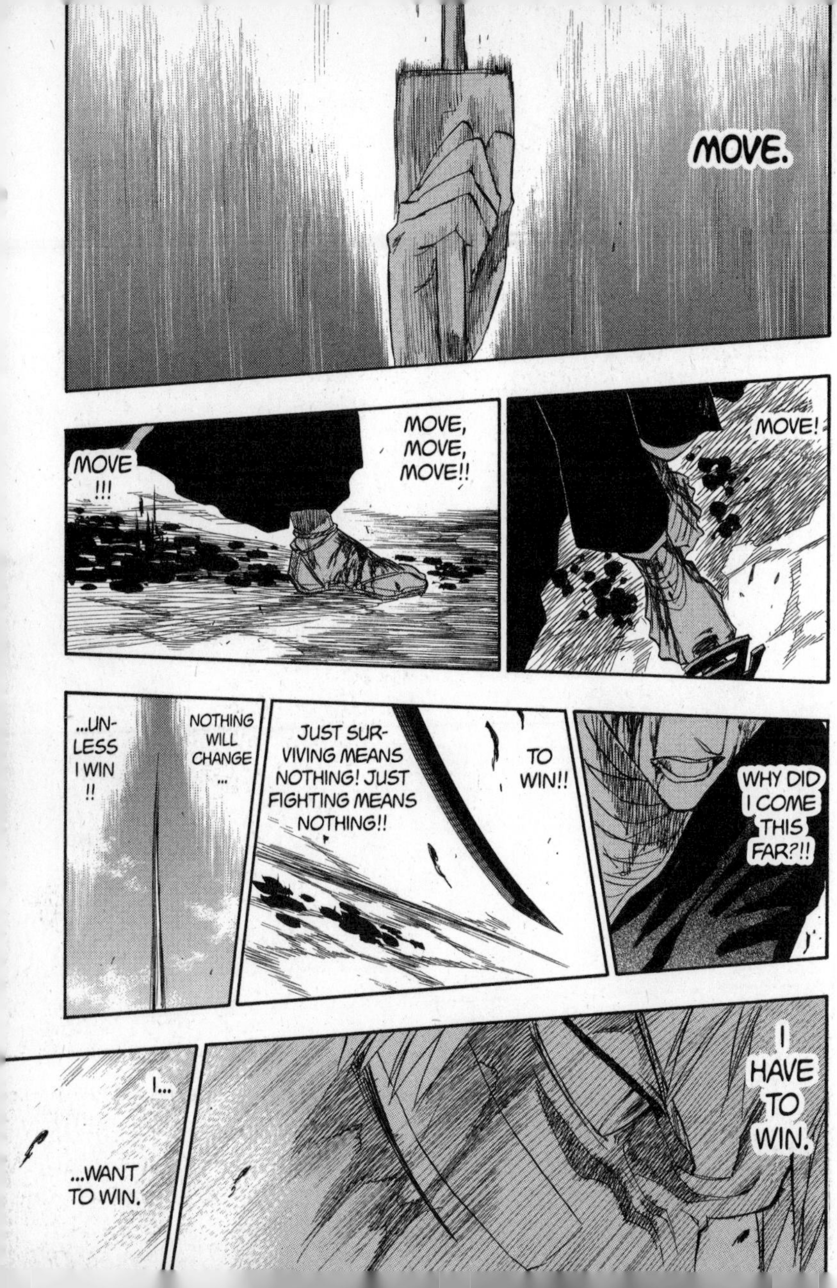
MOVE.
MOVE!
MOVE, MOVE, MOVE!!
MOVE !!!
WHY DID I COME THIS FAR?!!
TO WIN!!
JUST SUR-VIVING MEANS NOTHING! JUST FIGHTING MEANS NOTHING!!
NOTHING WILL CHANGE ...
...UN-LESS I WIN !!
I HAVE TO WIN.
I...
...WANT TO WIN.

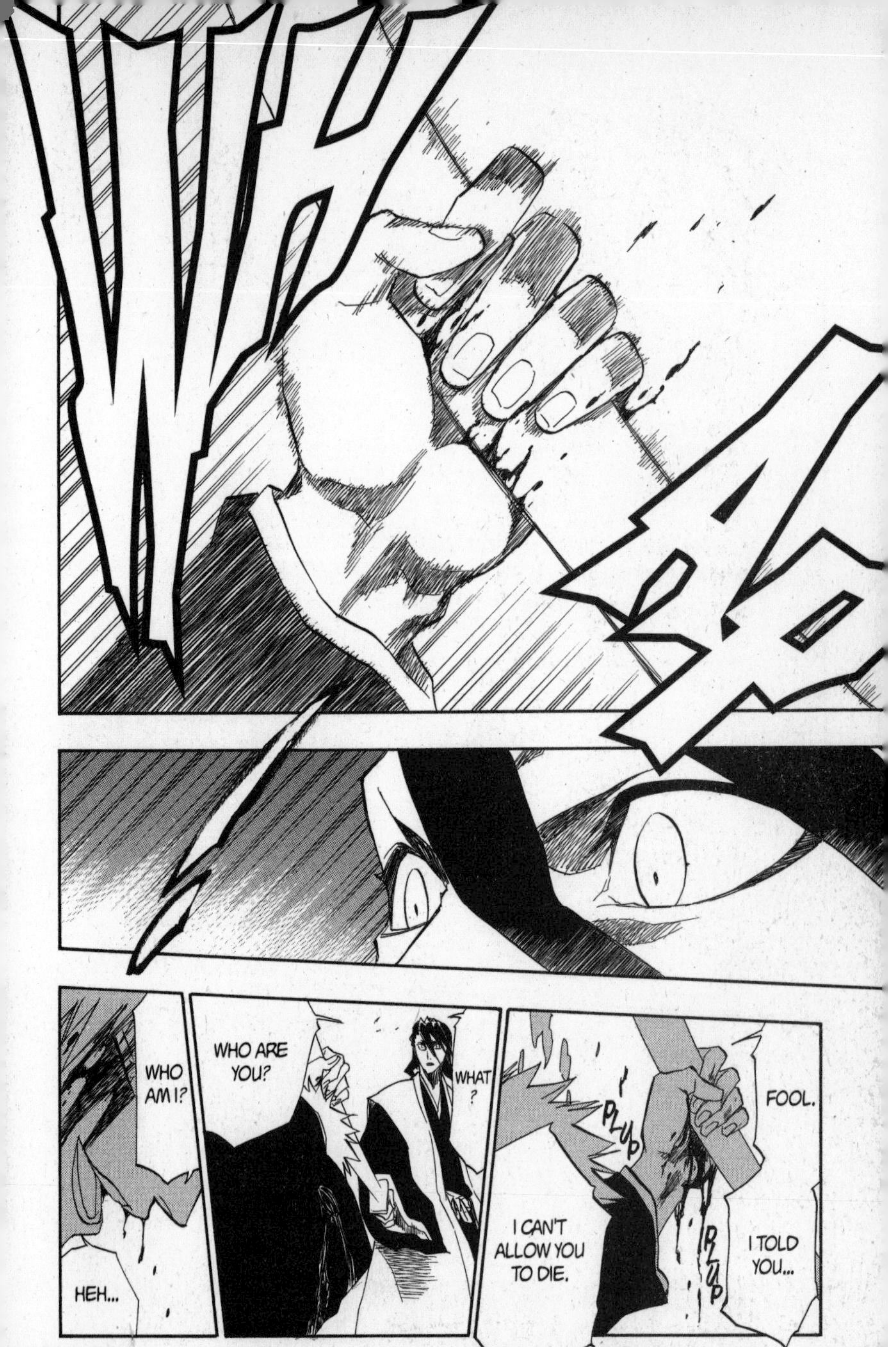
FOOL.
PLUP
I TOLD YOU...
PLUP
I CAN'T ALLOW YOU TO DIE.
WHAT?
WHO ARE YOU?
WHO AM I?
HEH...

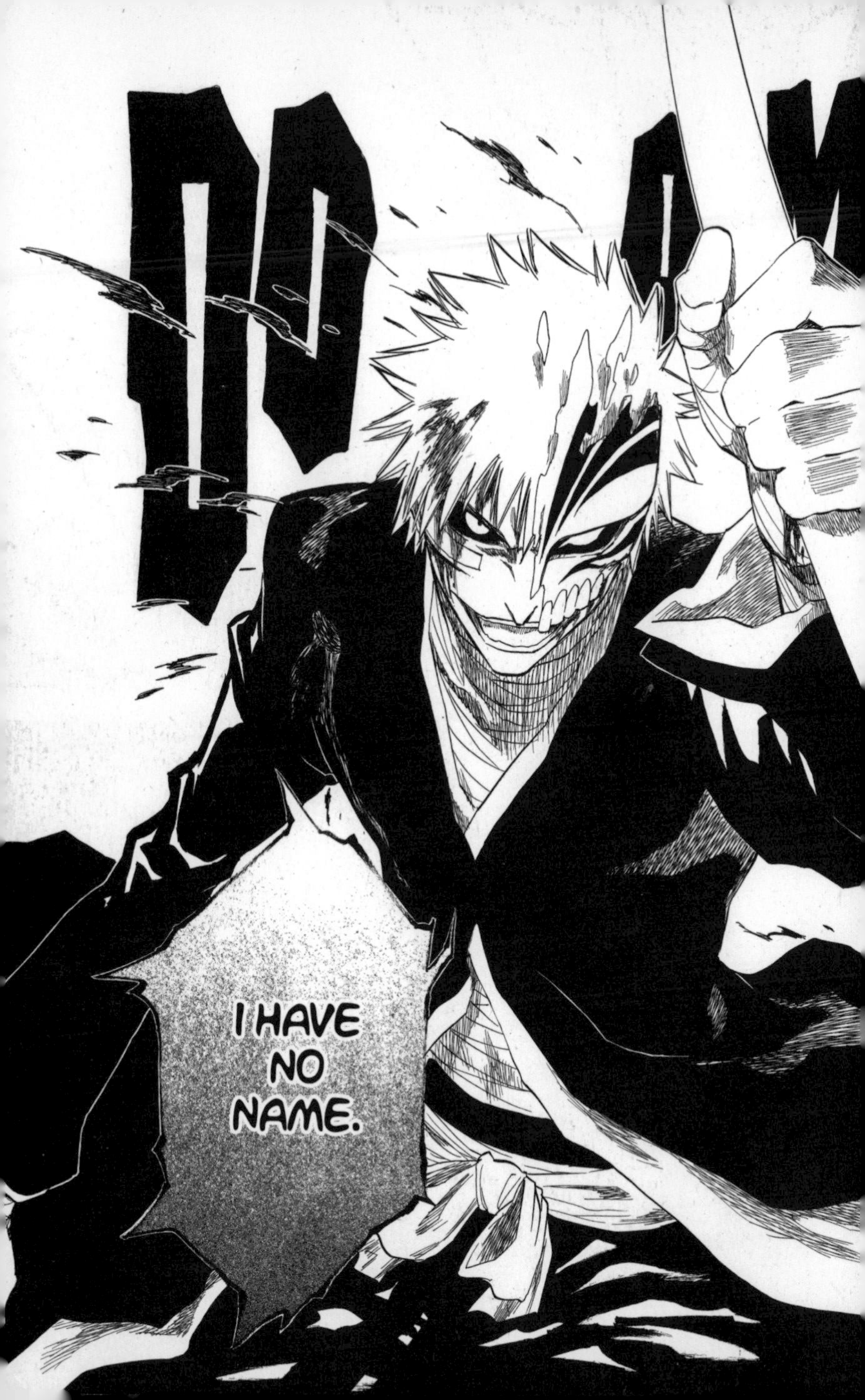
I HAVE NO NAME.

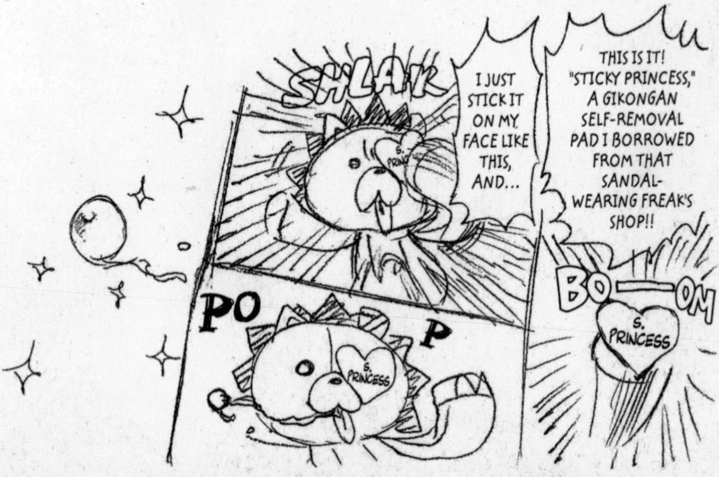
THIS IS IT! "STICKY PRINCESS," A GIKONGAN SELF-REMOVAL PAD I BORROWED FROM THAT SANDAL-WEARING FREAK'S SHOP!!
BO—OM
S. PRINCESS
I JUST STICK IT ON MY FACE LIKE THIS, AND...
SHLAK
PO
P
S. PRINCESS

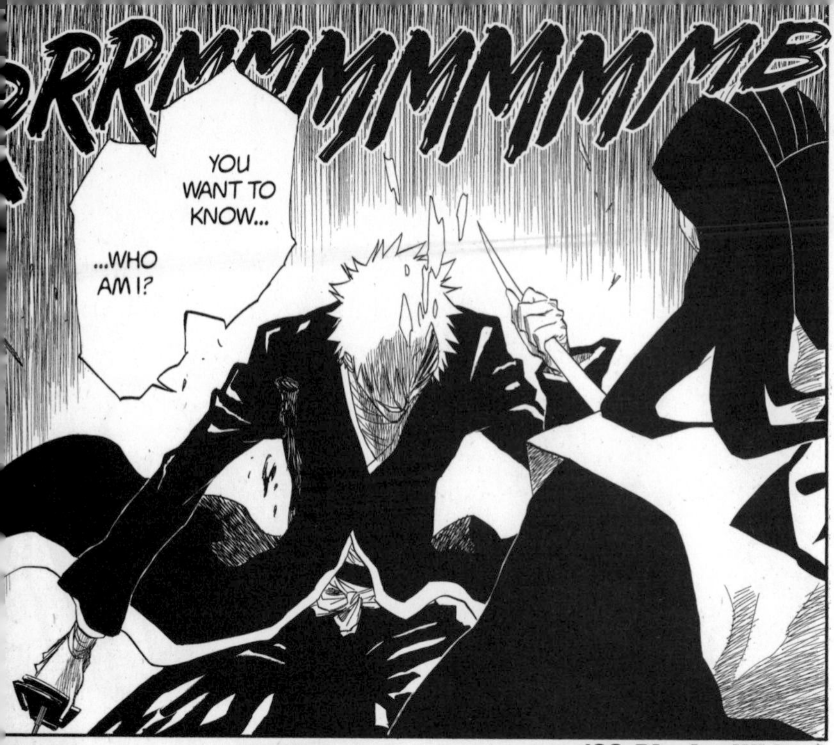
RRMMMMMMMMB
YOU WANT TO KNOW...
...WHO AM I?

166. Black & White 2

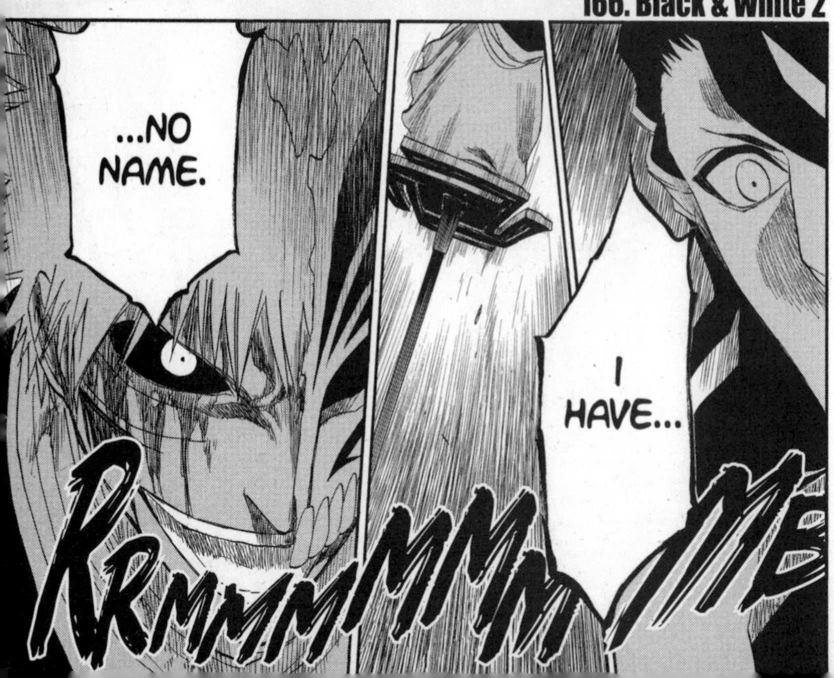
I HAVE...
...NO NAME.
RMMMMMMMMB

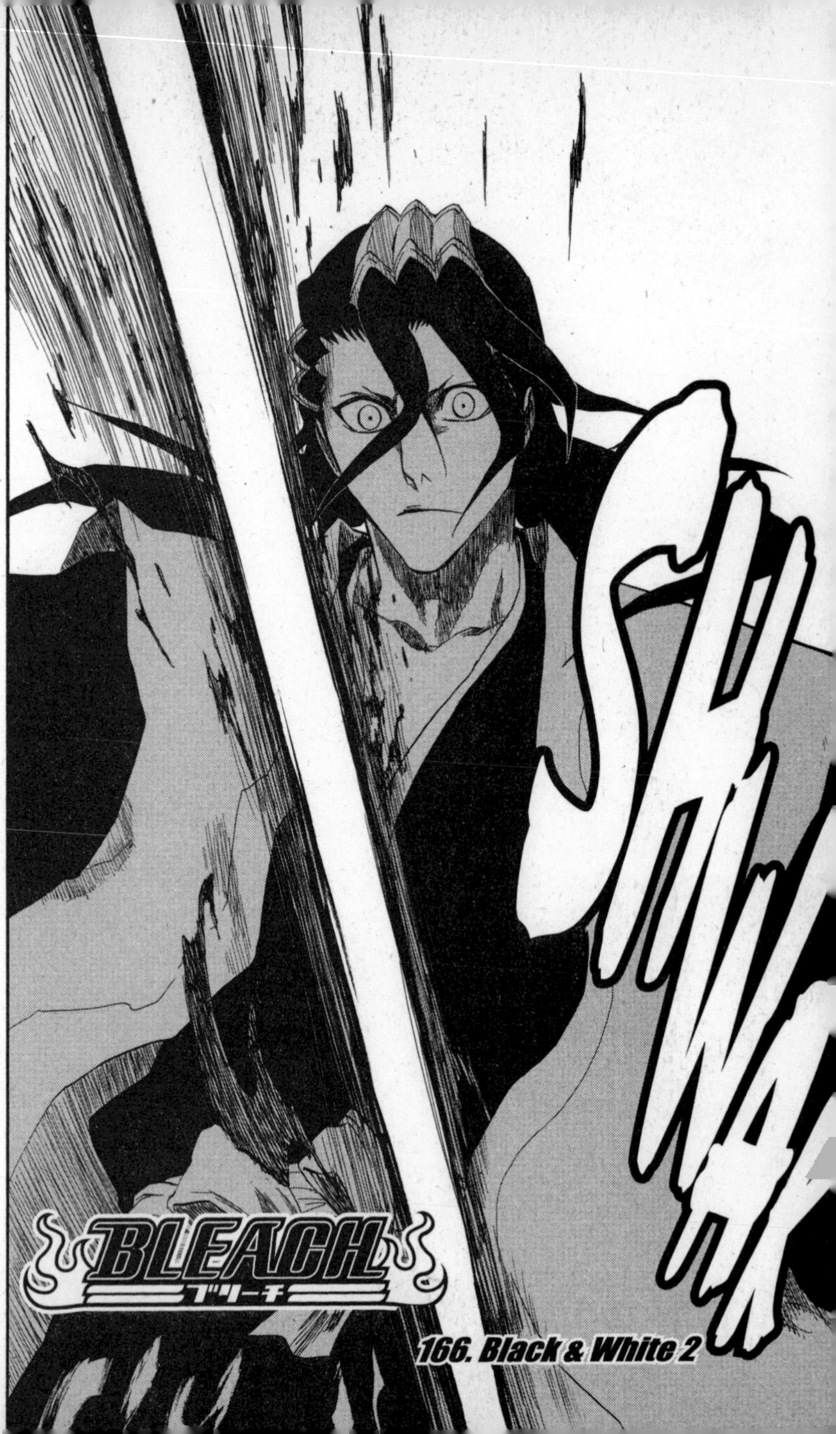
SHWA

166. Black & White 2

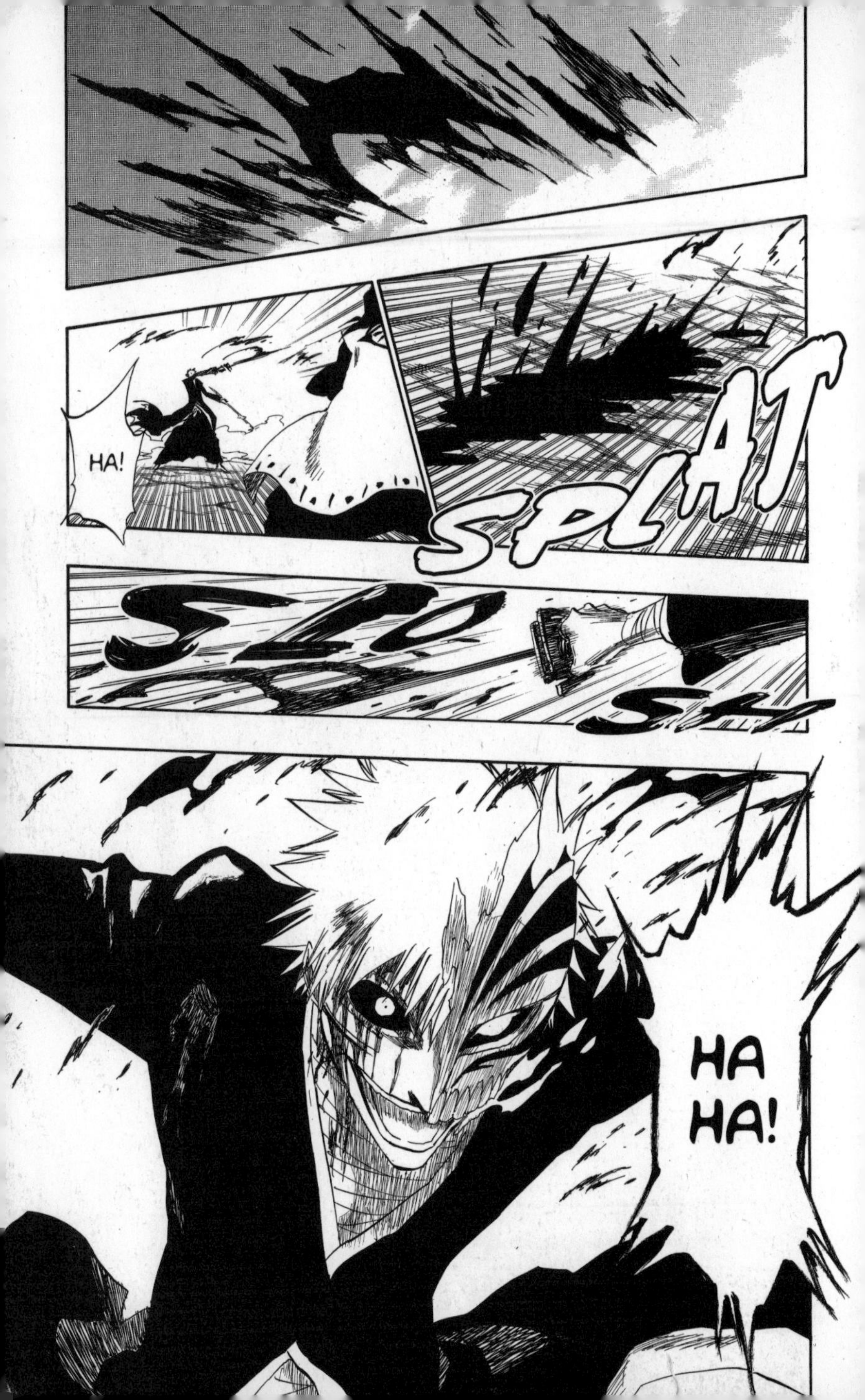
SPLAT
HA!
HA HA!

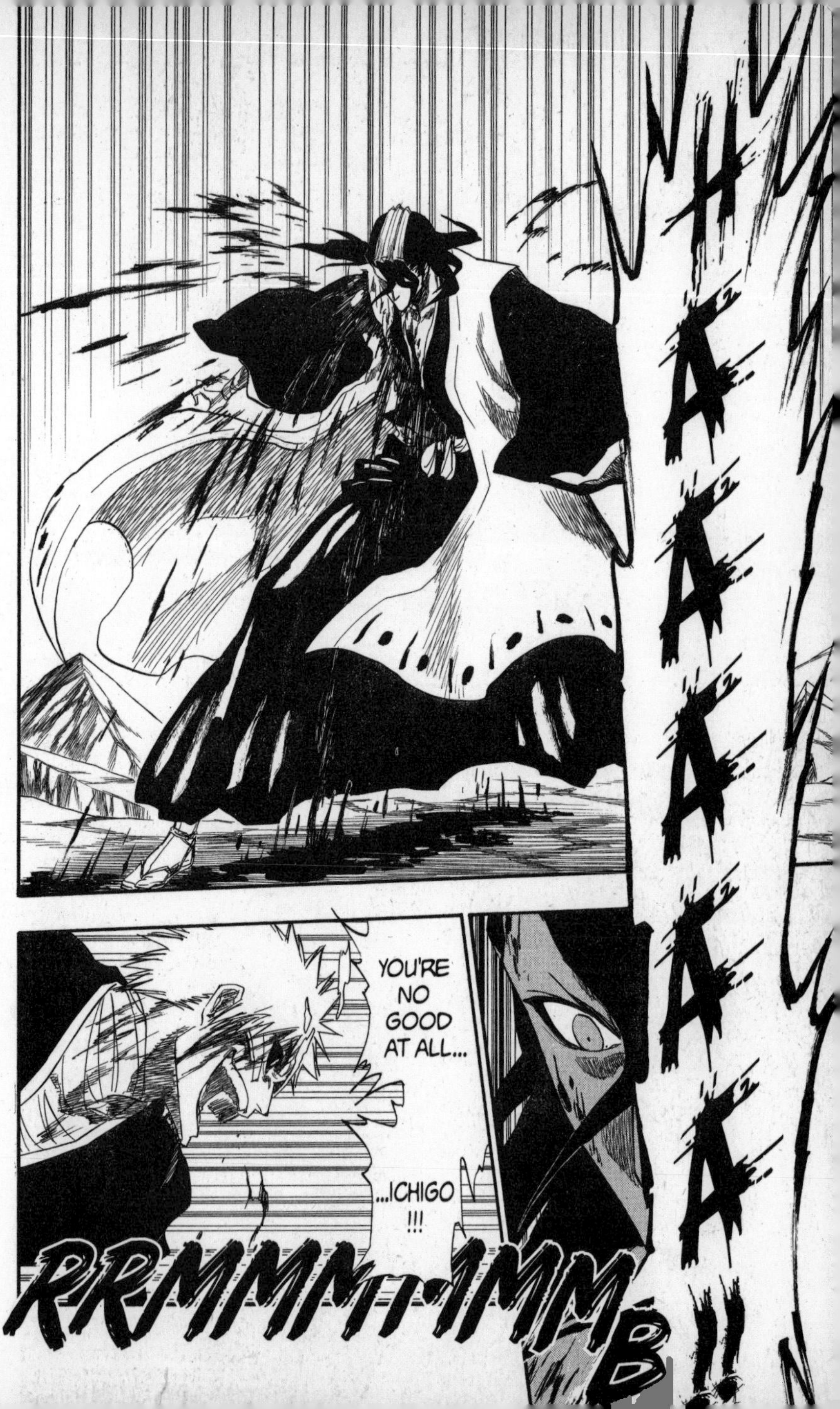
YOU'RE NO GOOD AT ALL...
...ICHIGO !!!

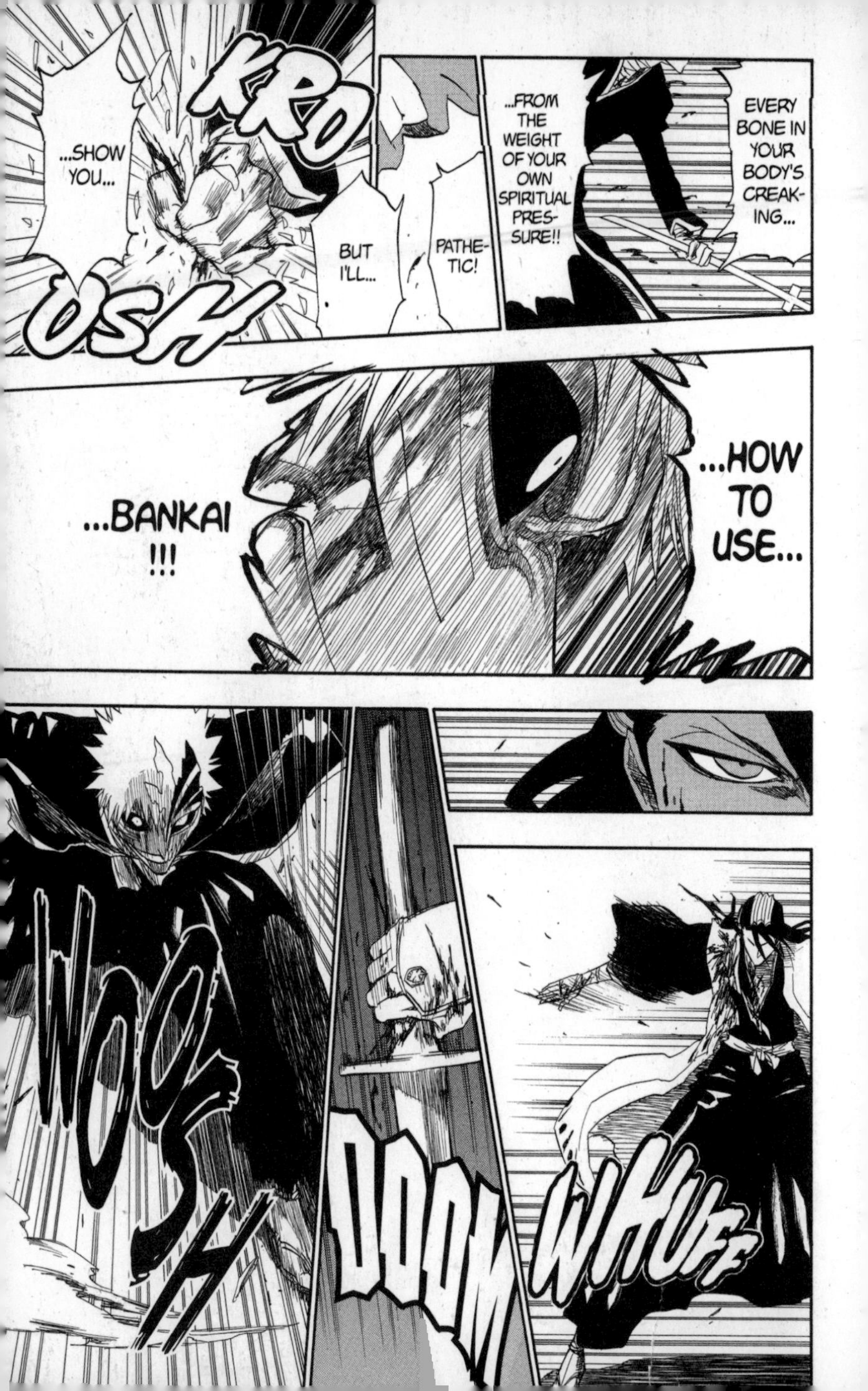
EVERY BONE IN YOUR BODY'S CREAK-ING...
...FROM THE WEIGHT OF YOUR OWN SPIRITUAL PRES-SURE!!
PATHE-TIC!
BUT I'LL...
KRO
...SHOW YOU...
OSH
...HOW TO USE...
...BANKAI !!!
WHUF
DOOM
WOOSH

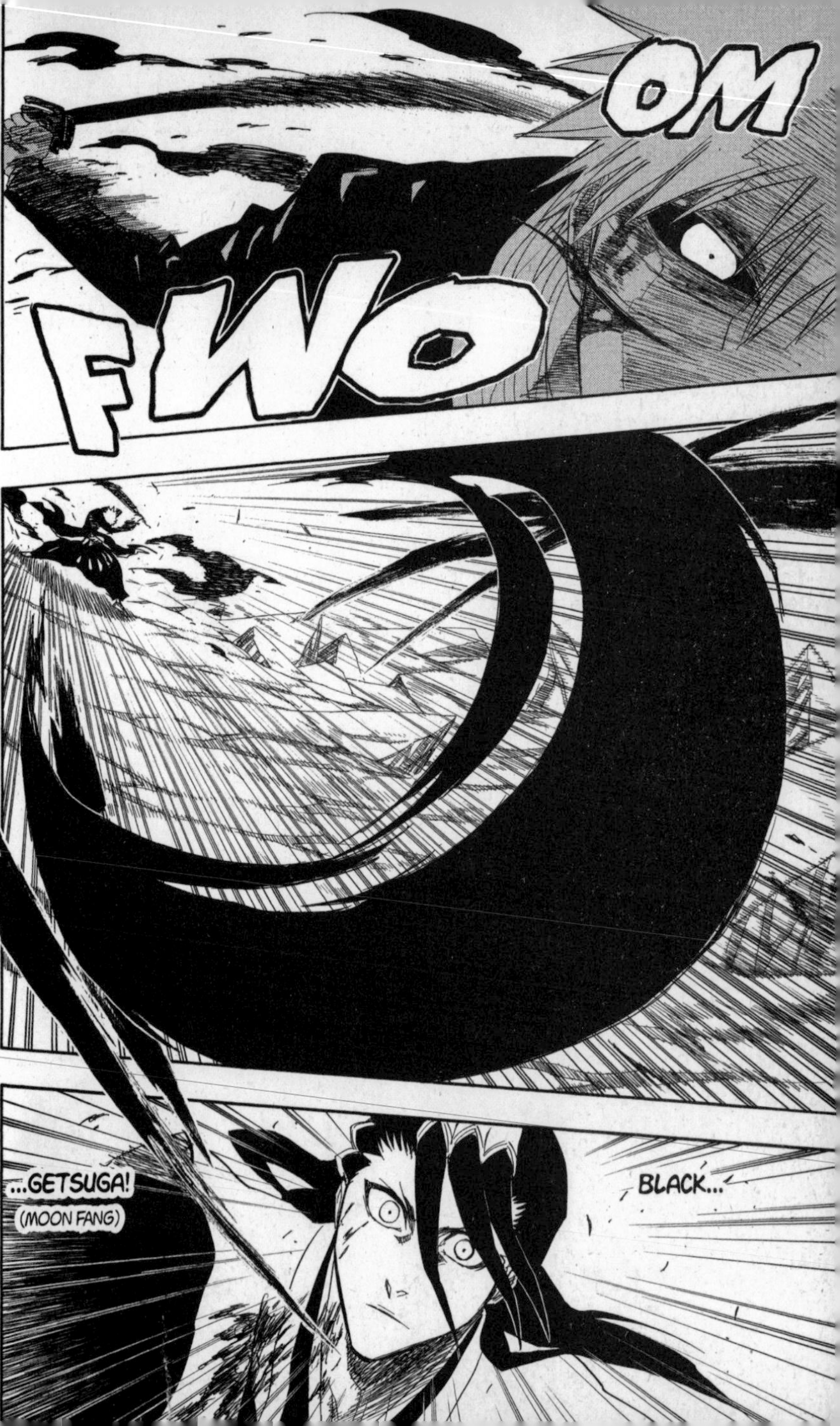
FWOOM
BLACK...
...GETSUGA!
(MOON FANG)

READ THIS WAY

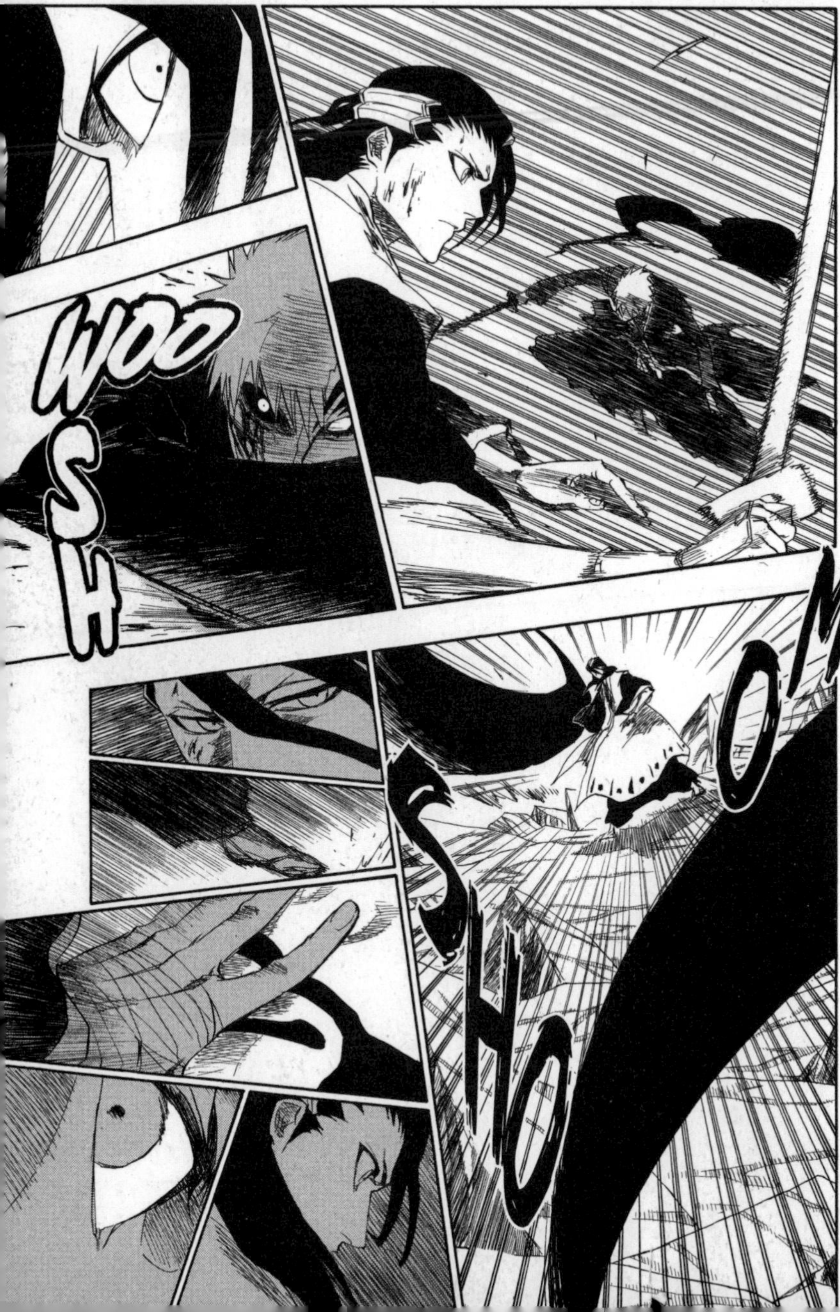
WOOSH
SHOOM

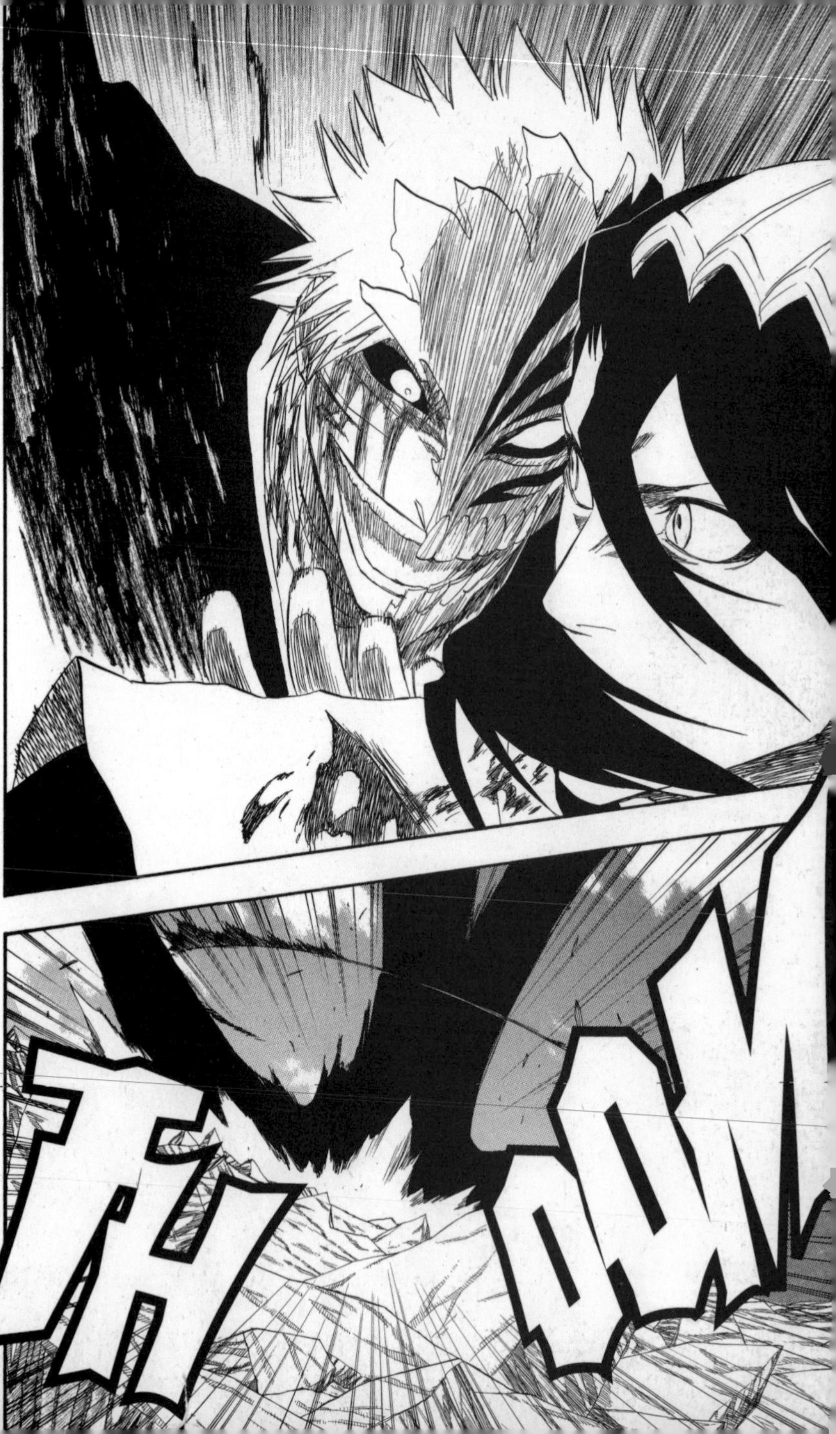
THOOM

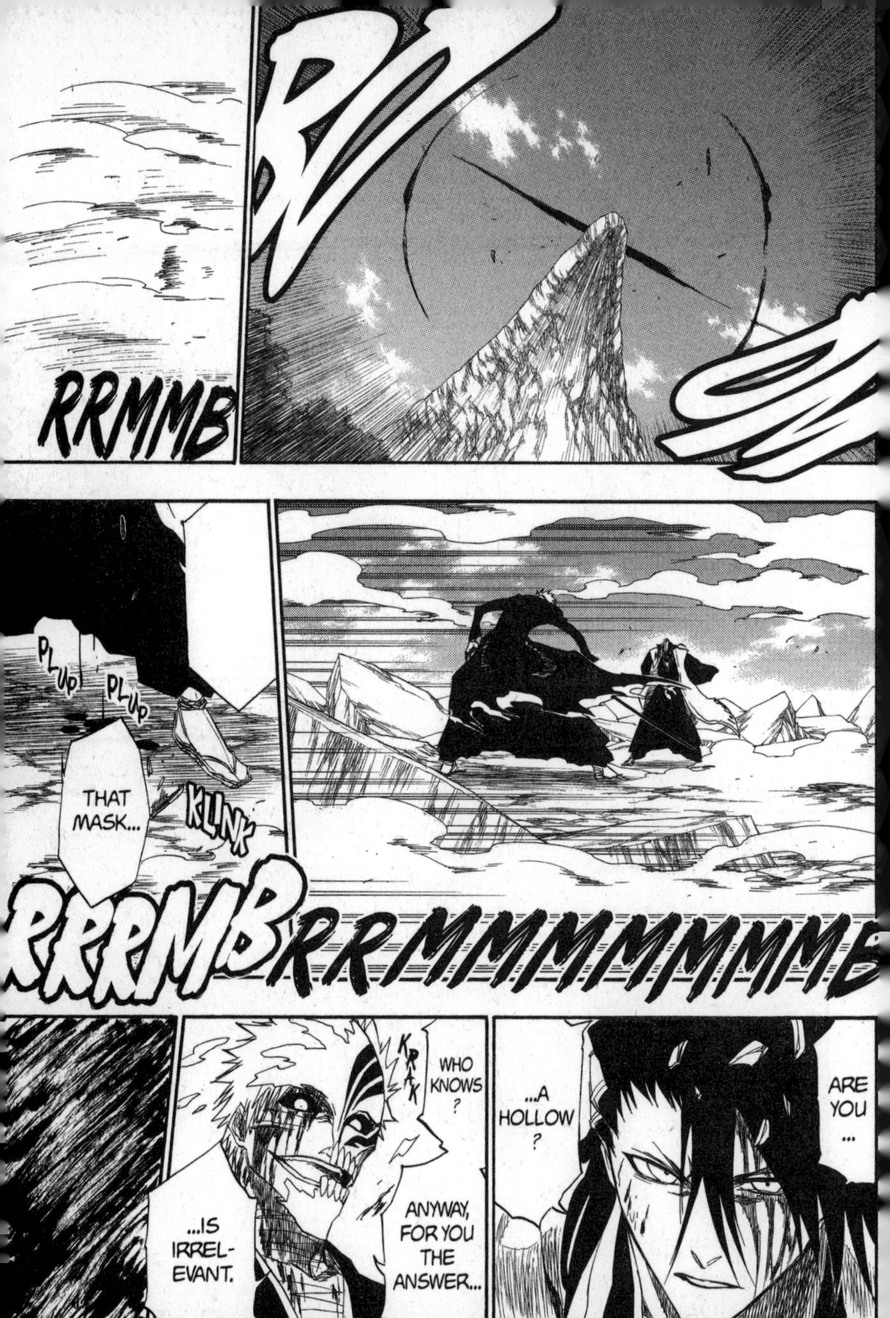
RRMMB
PLUP
PLUP
KLINK
THAT MASK...
RRRMB
RRRMMMMMMMMMB
ARE YOU...
...A HOLLOW?
KRAK
WHO KNOWS?
ANYWAY, FOR YOU THE ANSWER...
...IS IRREL-EVANT.

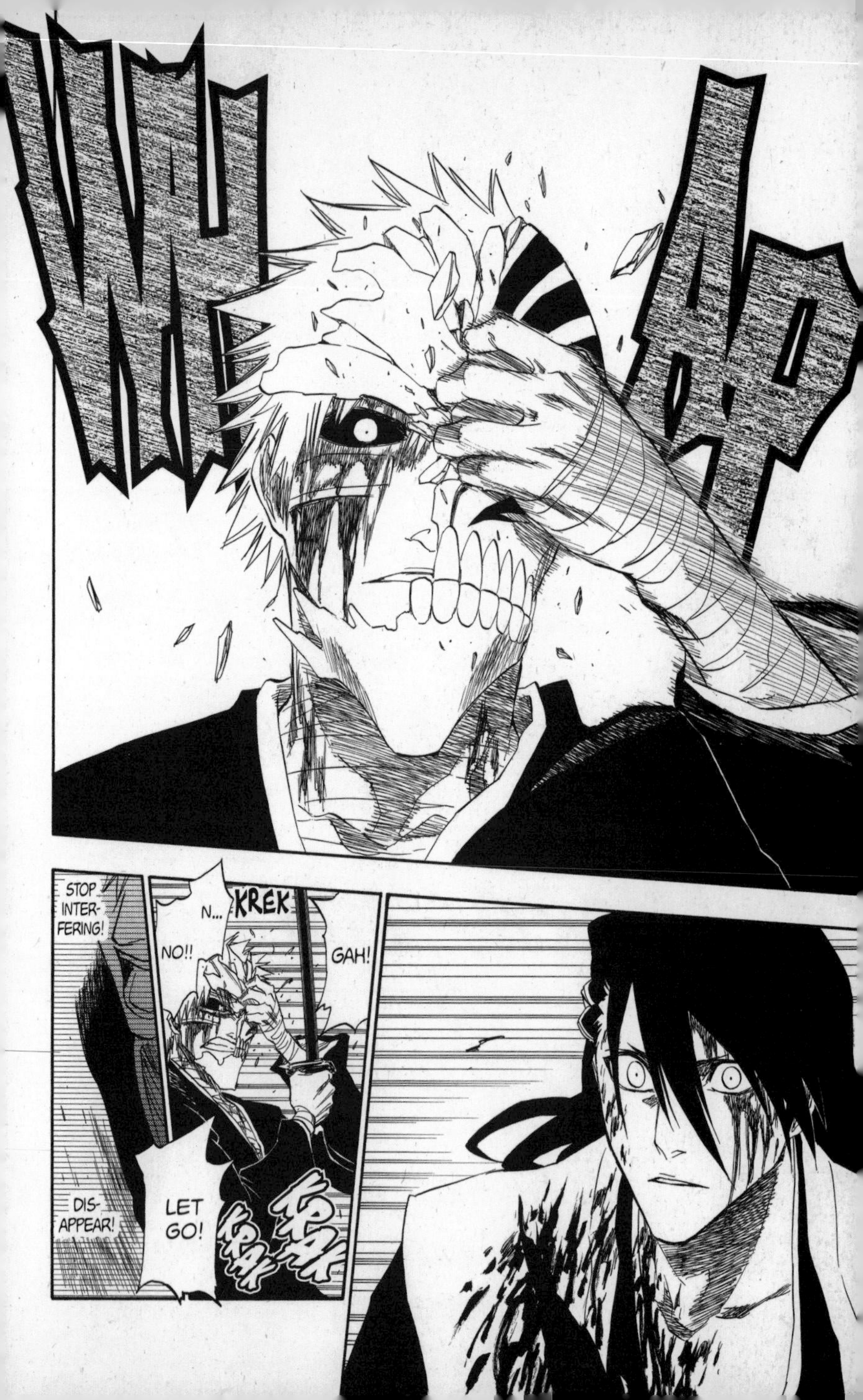
WHAP
KREK
N...
GAH!
NO!!
KRAK KRAK
LET GO!
STOP INTERFERING!
DIS-APPEAR!

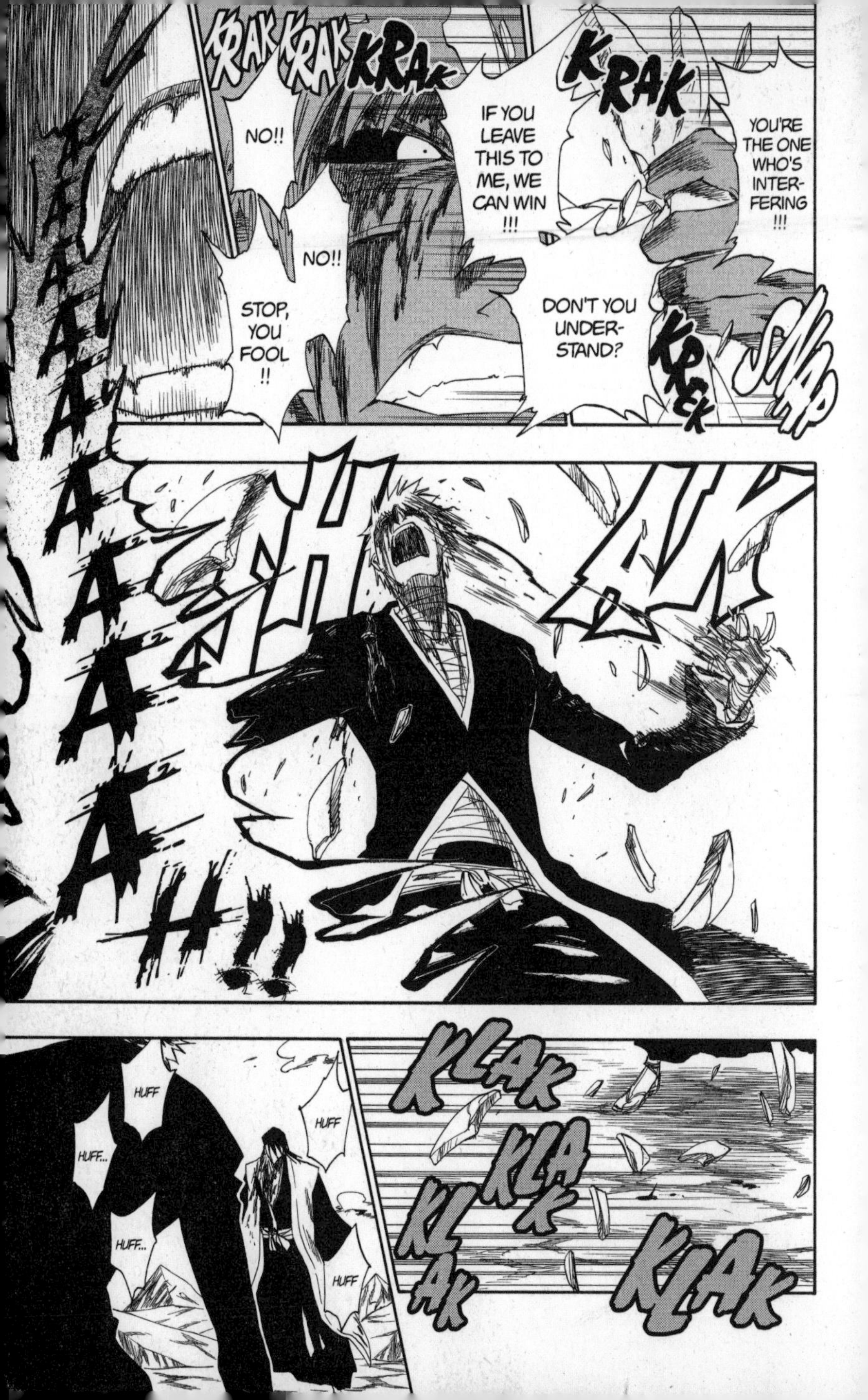

KRAK
YOU'RE THE ONE WHO'S INTERFERING!!!
IF YOU LEAVE THIS TO ME, WE CAN WIN!!!
KRAK KRAK KRAK
NO!!
NO!!
SNAP
KREK
DON'T YOU UNDERSTAND?
STOP, YOU FOOL!!
AH
AAAAAAH!!
KLAK
KLAK
KLAK
KLAK
HUFF
HUFF
HUFF...
HUFF...
HUFF

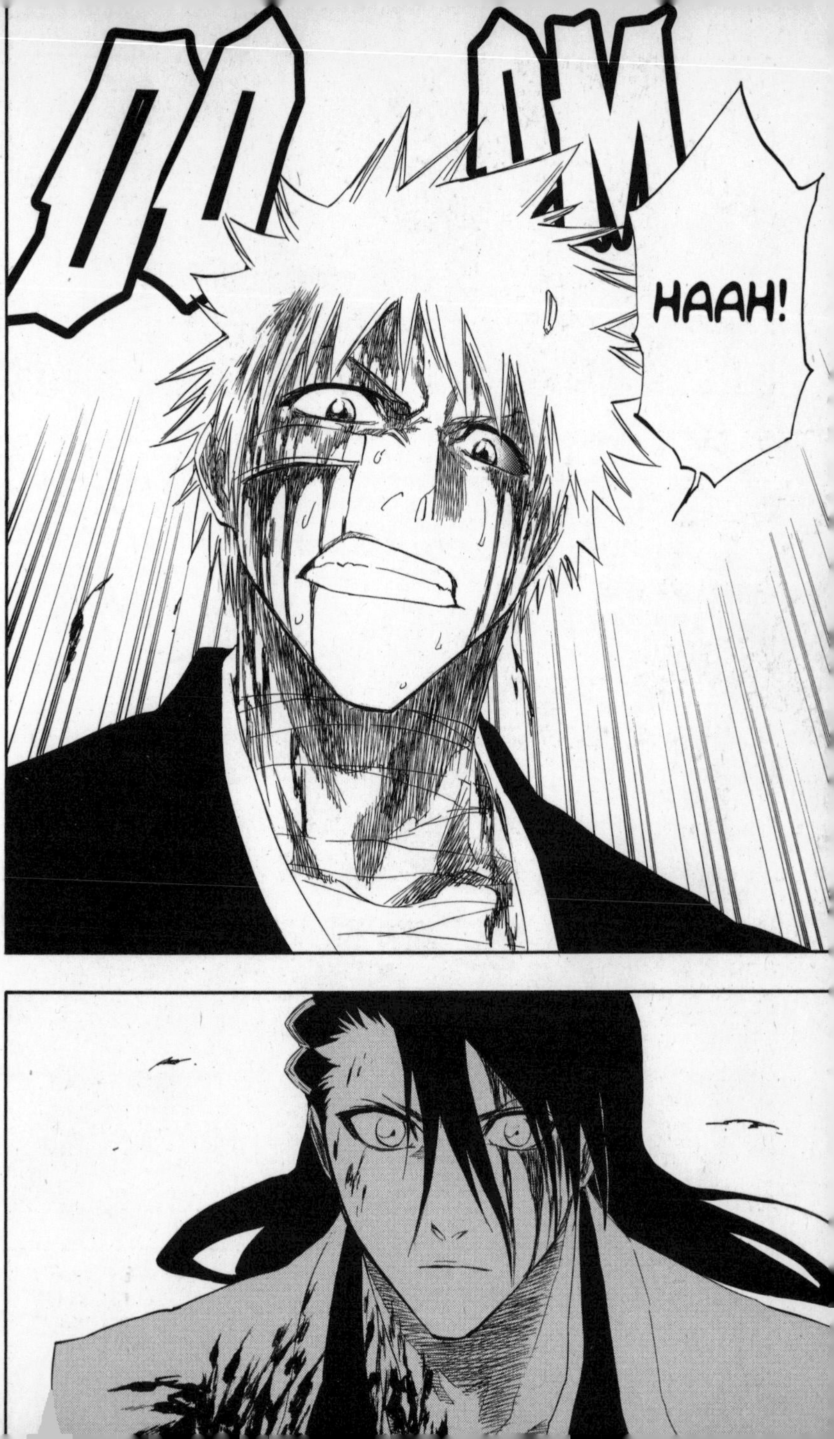
DOOM
HAAH!

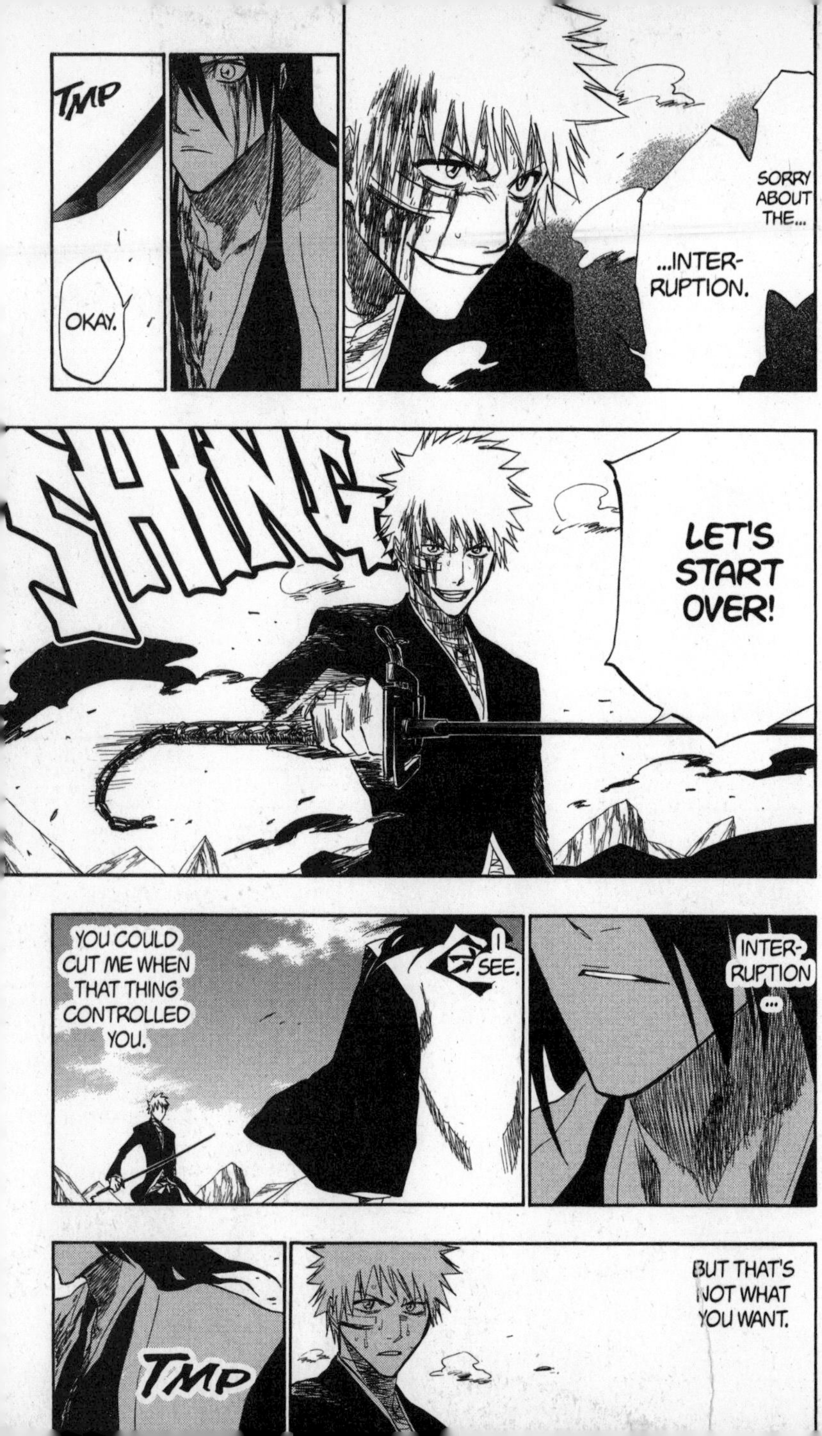
SORRY ABOUT THE...
...INTER-RUPTION.
TMP
OKAY.
LET'S START OVER!
SHING
INTER-RUPTION ...
I SEE.
YOU COULD CUT ME WHEN THAT THING CONTROLLED YOU.
BUT THAT'S NOT WHAT YOU WANT.
TMP

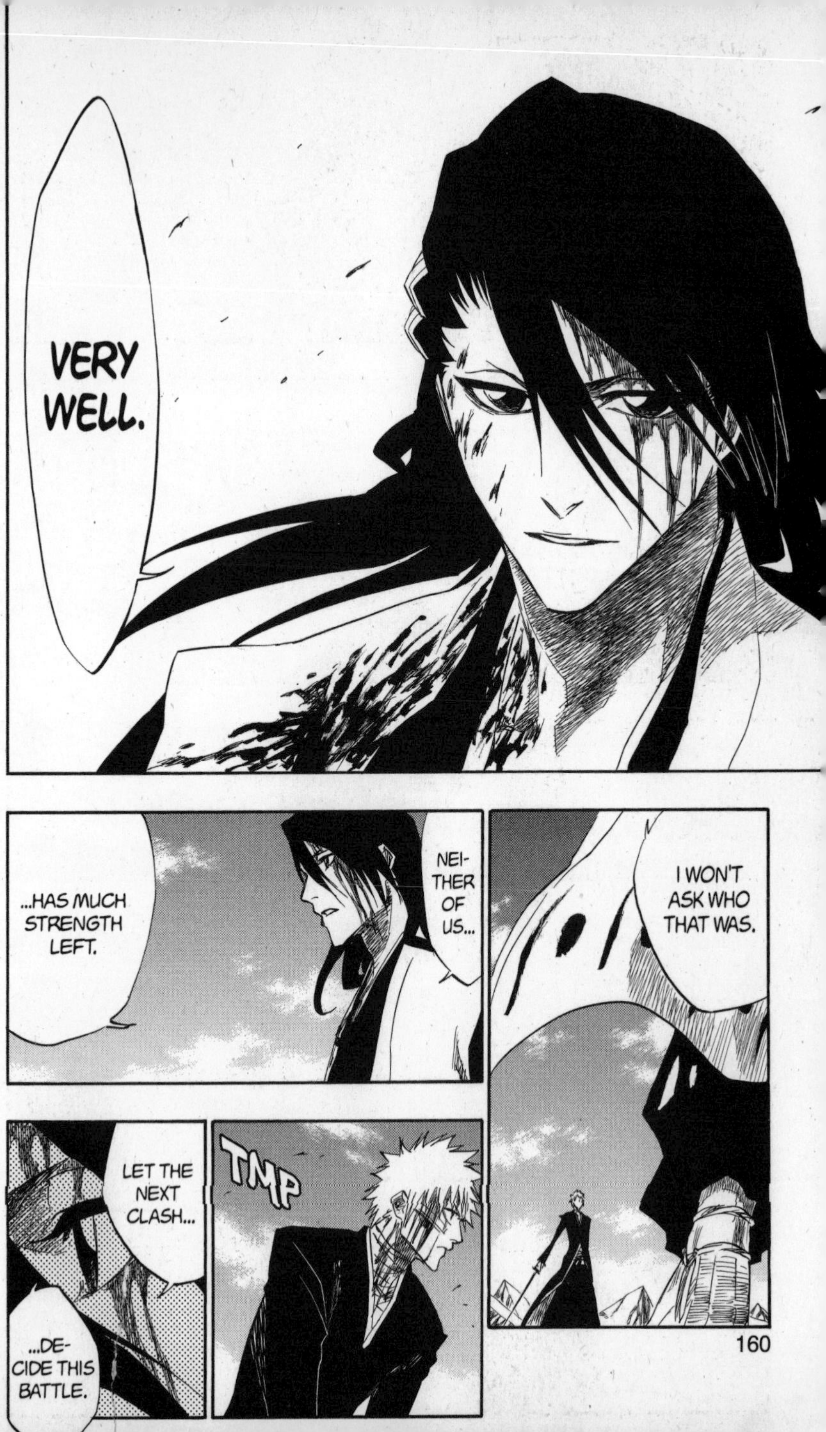
VERY WELL.
I WON'T ASK WHO THAT WAS.
NEI-THER OF US...
...HAS MUCH STRENGTH LEFT.
TMP
LET THE NEXT CLASH...
...DE-CIDE THIS BATTLE.

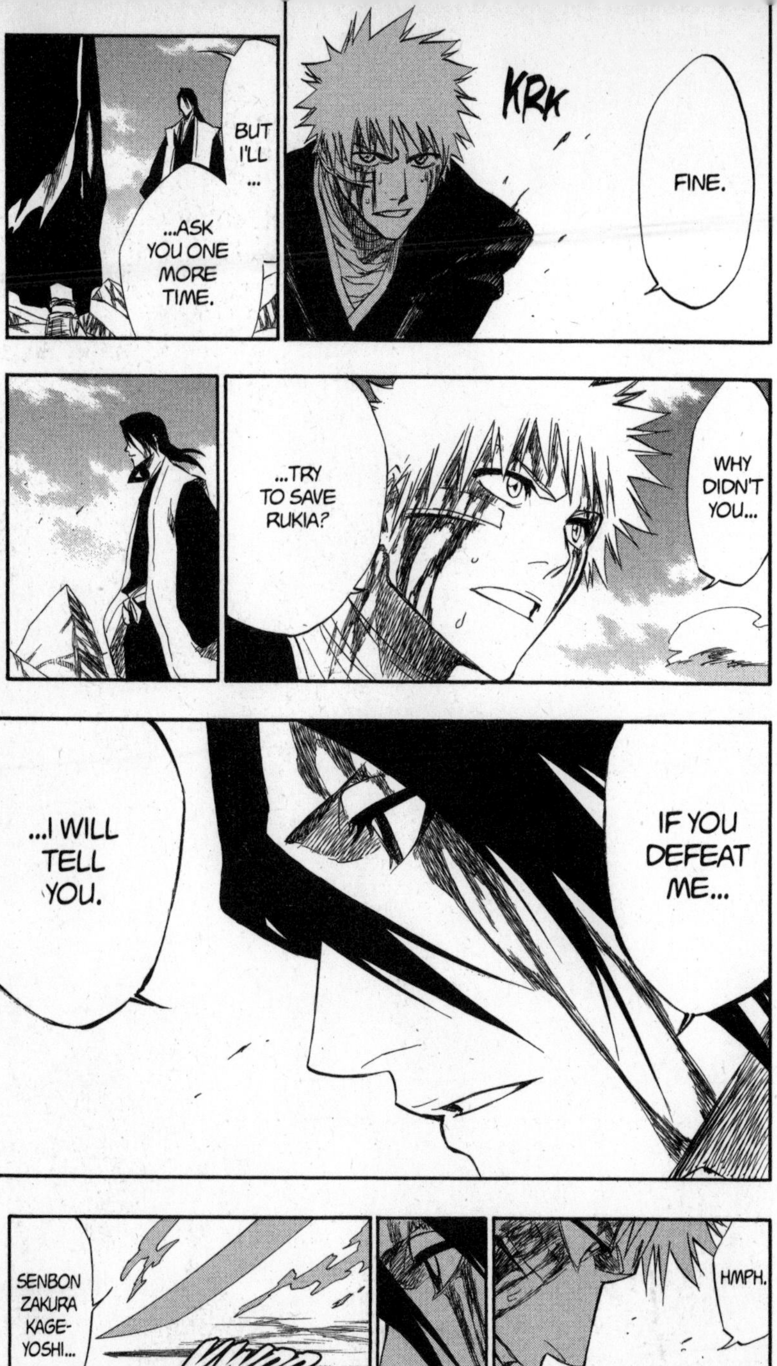

KRK
FINE.
BUT I'LL ...
...ASK YOU ONE MORE TIME.
WHY DIDN'T YOU...
...TRY TO SAVE RUKIA?
IF YOU DEFEAT ME...
...I WILL TELL YOU.
HMPH.
SENBON ZAKURA KAGE-YOSHI...
VWOO

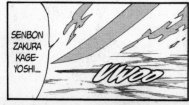

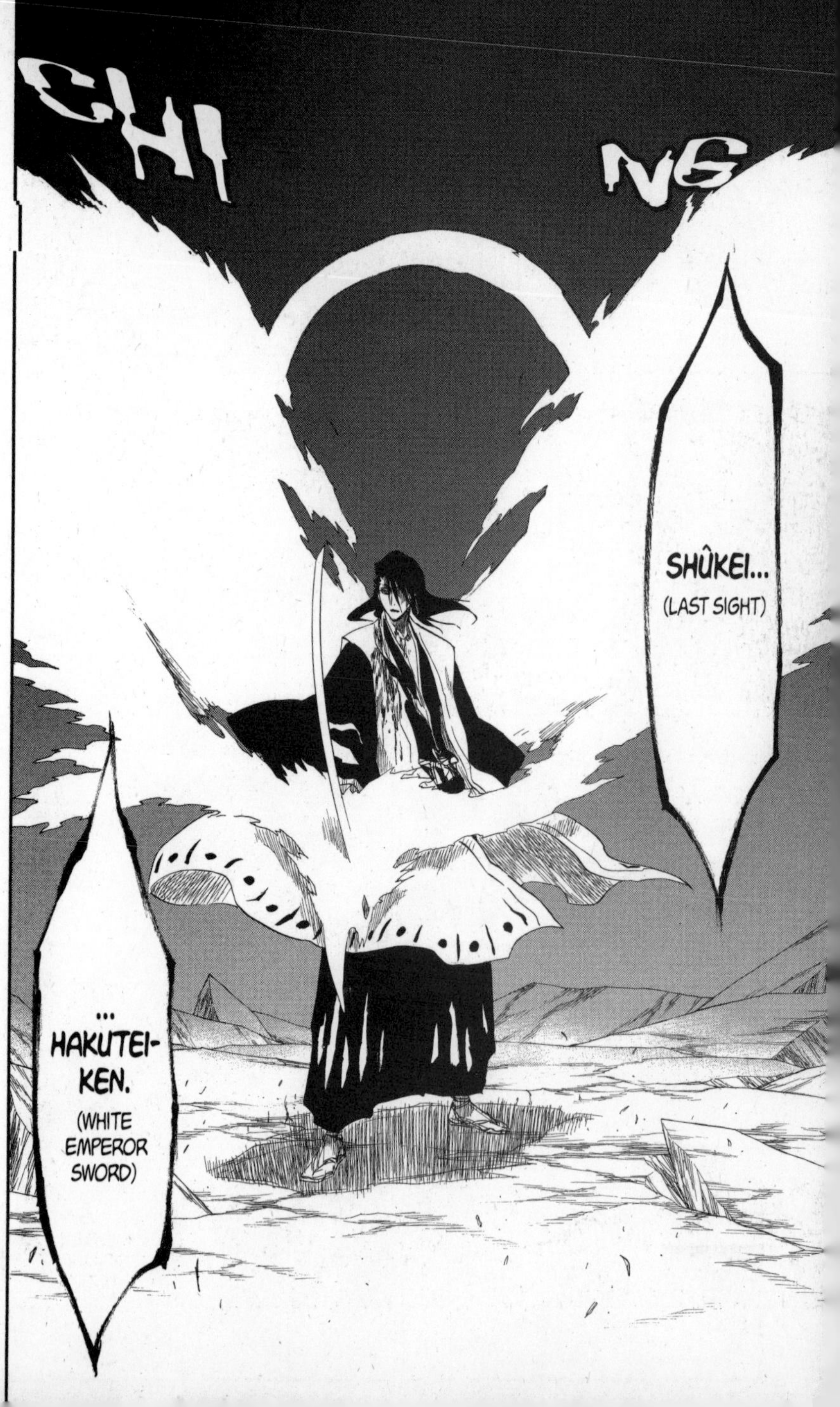
CHI NG
SHÛKEI...
(LAST SIGHT)
...HAKUTEI-
KEN.
(WHITE
EMPEROR
SWORD)

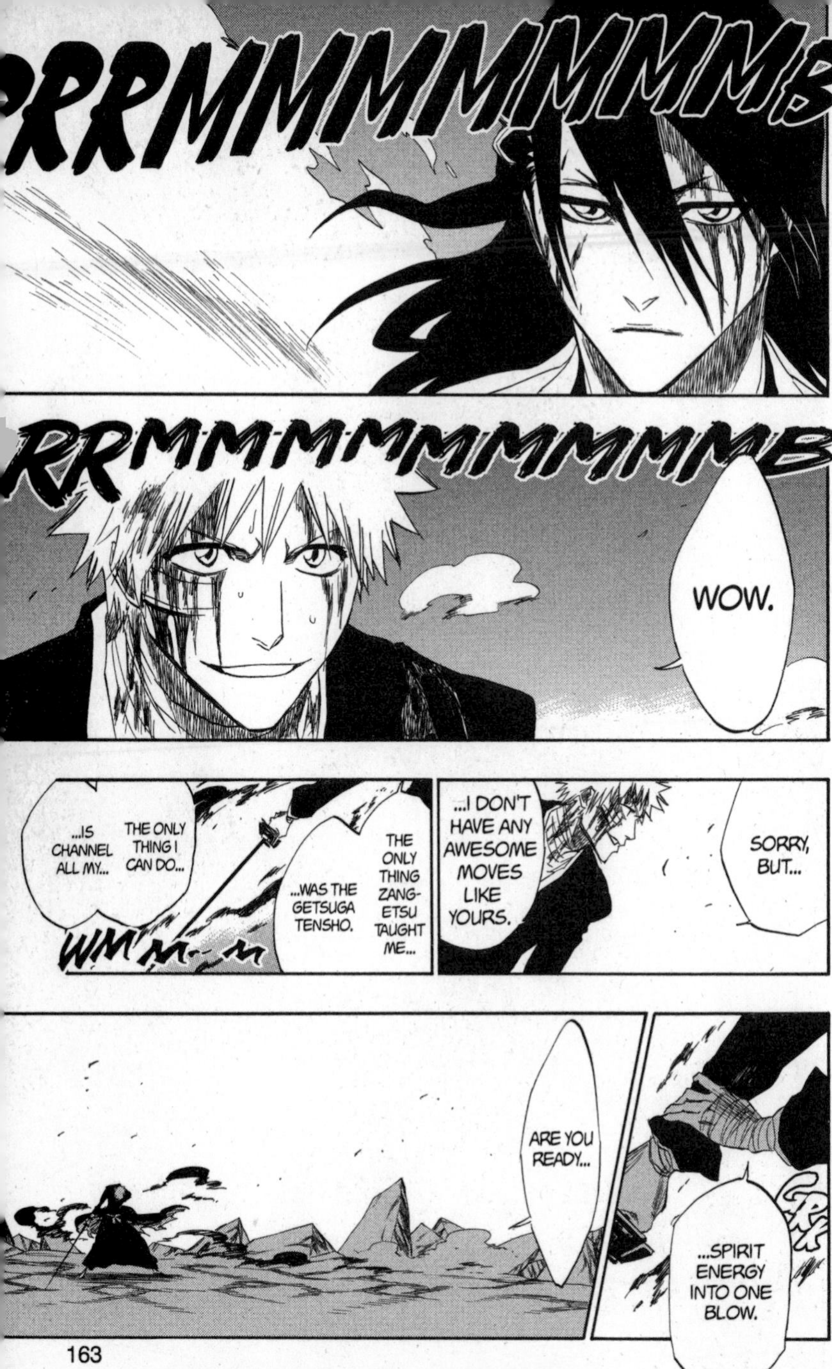
RRMMMMMMMMB
RRMMMMMMMMMMMB
WOW.
SORRY, BUT...
...I DON'T HAVE ANY AWESOME MOVES LIKE YOURS.
THE ONLY THING ZANG-ETSU TAUGHT ME...
...WAS THE GETSUGA TENSHO.
THE ONLY THING I CAN DO...
...IS CHANNEL ALL MY...
WMM
...SPIRIT ENERGY INTO ONE BLOW.
GRK
ARE YOU READY...

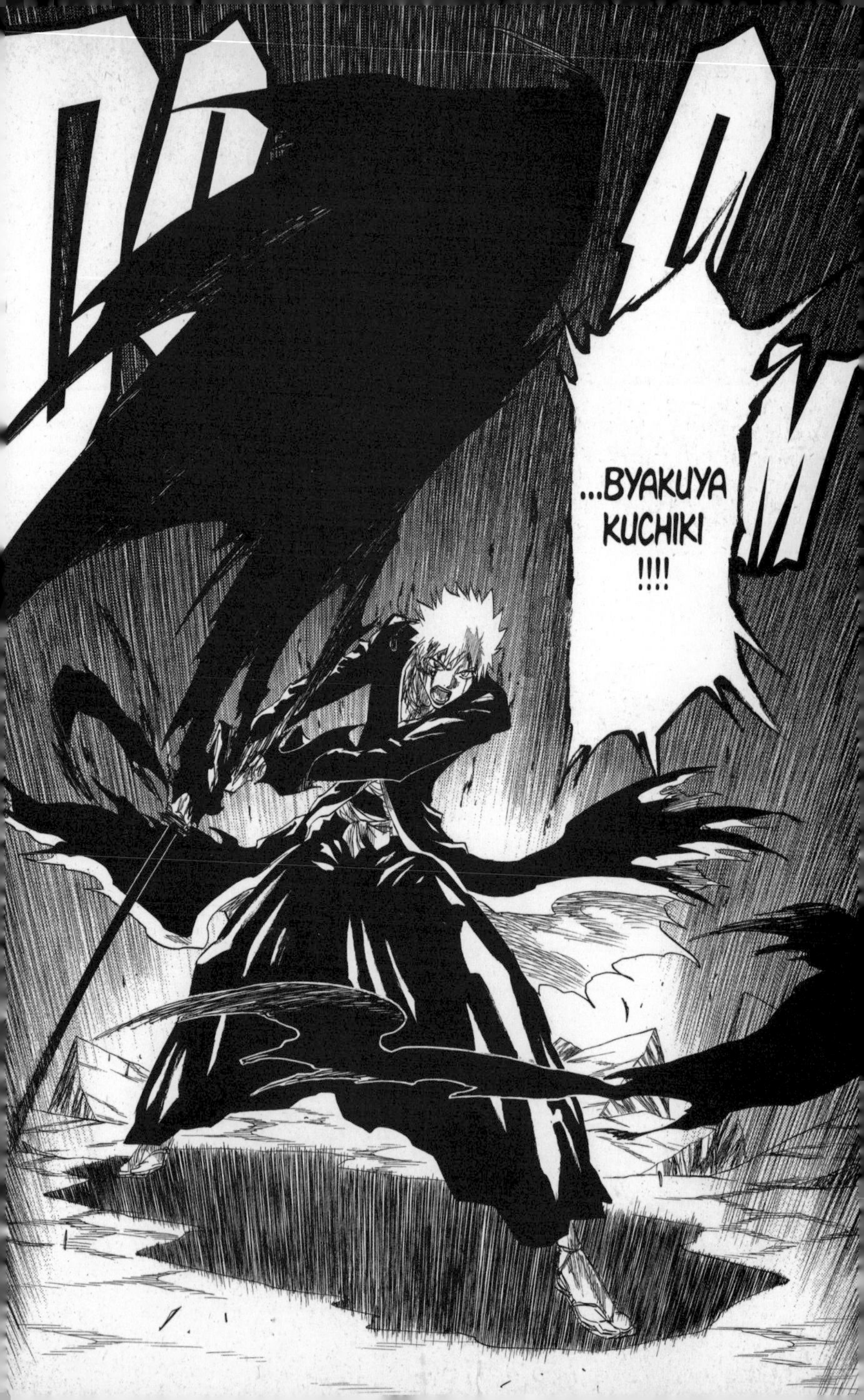
DOOM
...BYAKUYA KUCHIKI !!!!

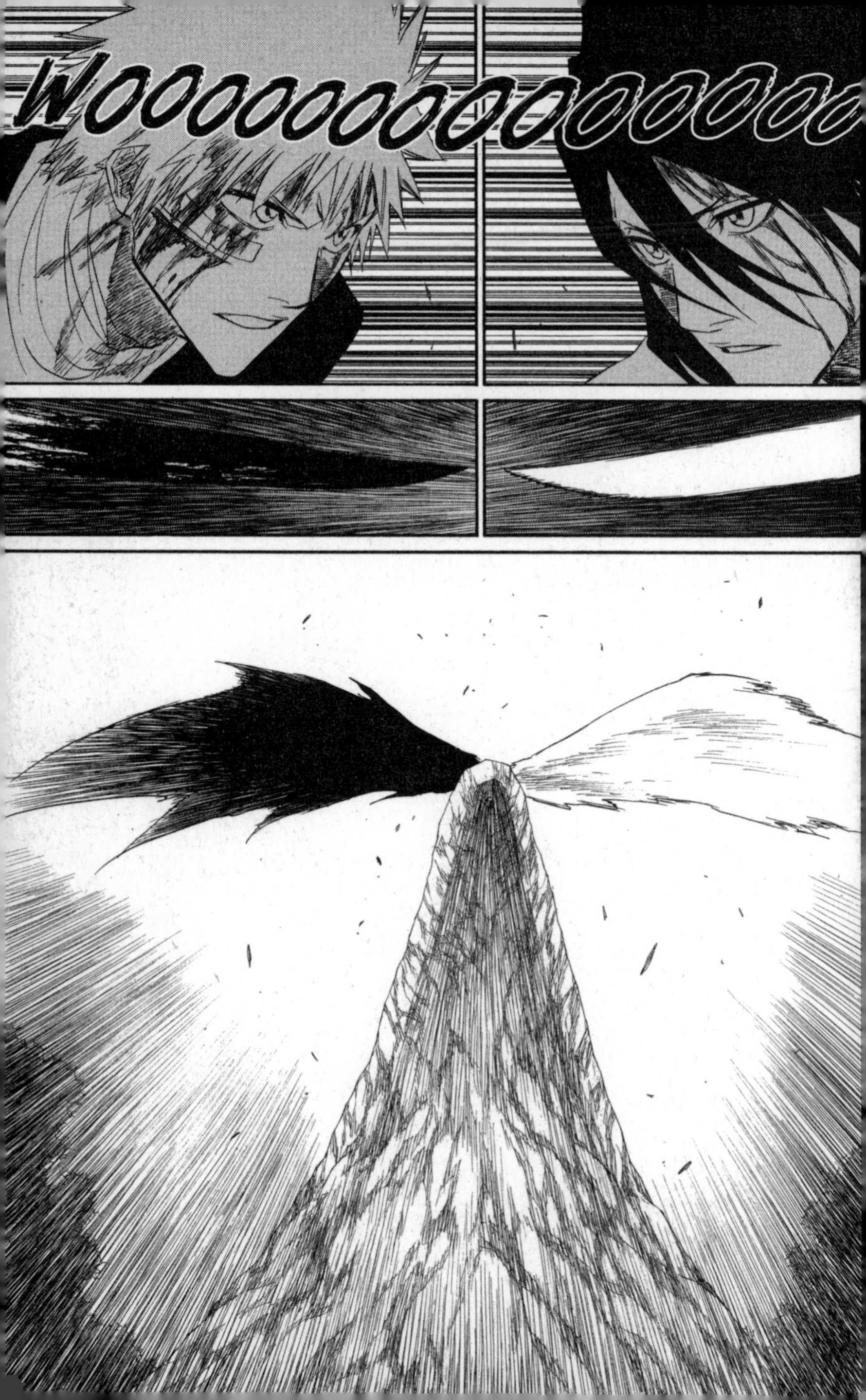
WOOOOOOOOOOOOOOO

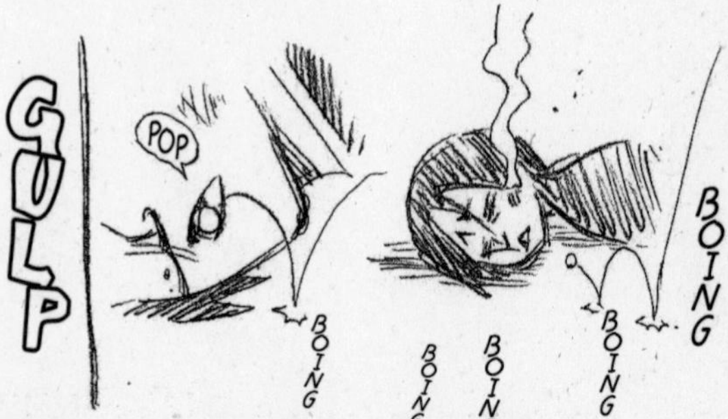
BOING
BOING
BOING
BOING
BOING
POP
GULP

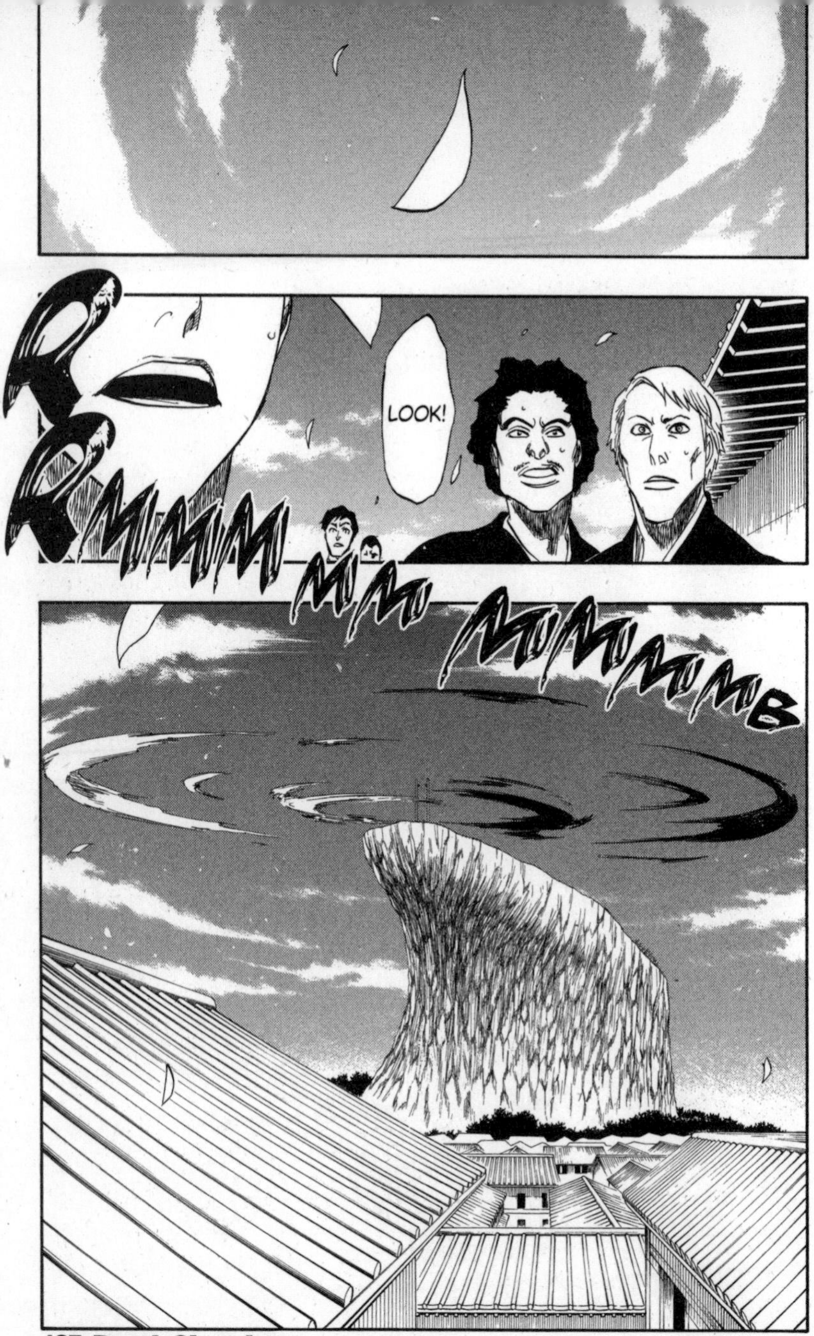
LOOK!

167. Death Chamber

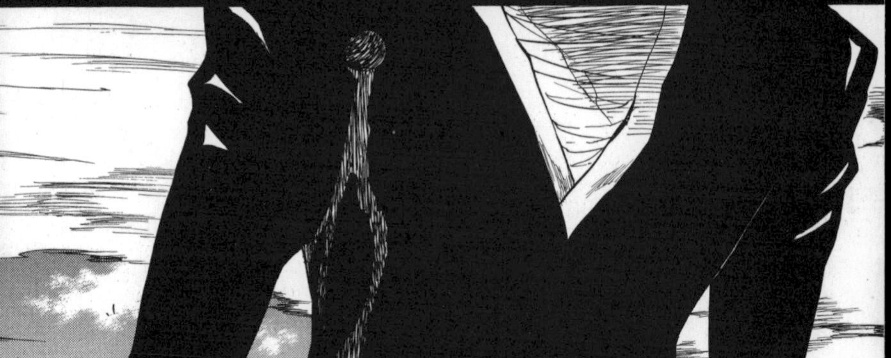

BLEACH

ブリーチ

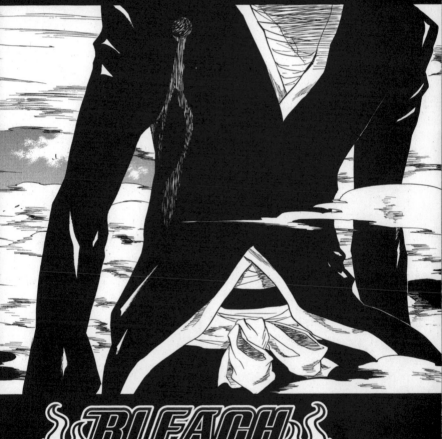

167. Death Chamber

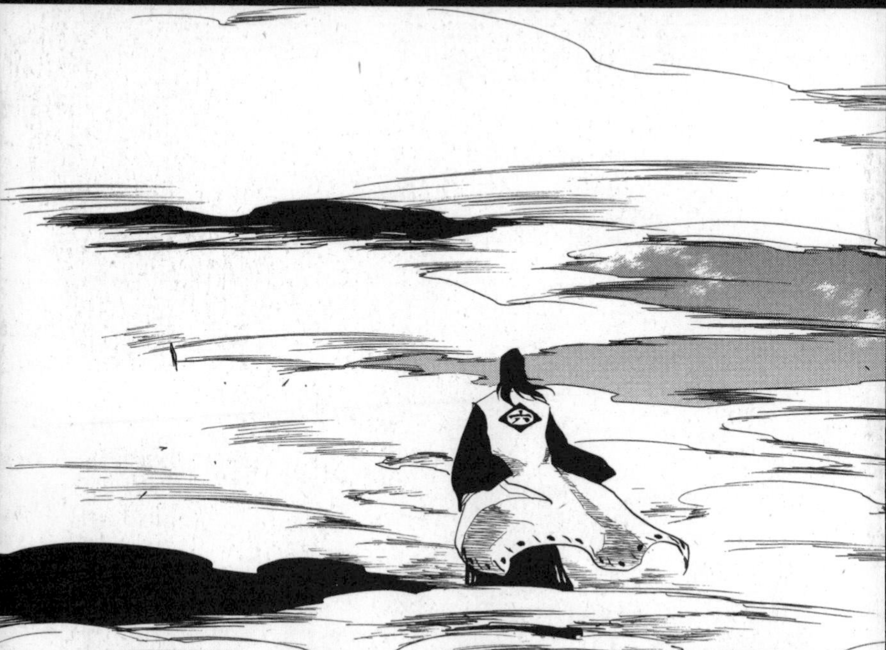

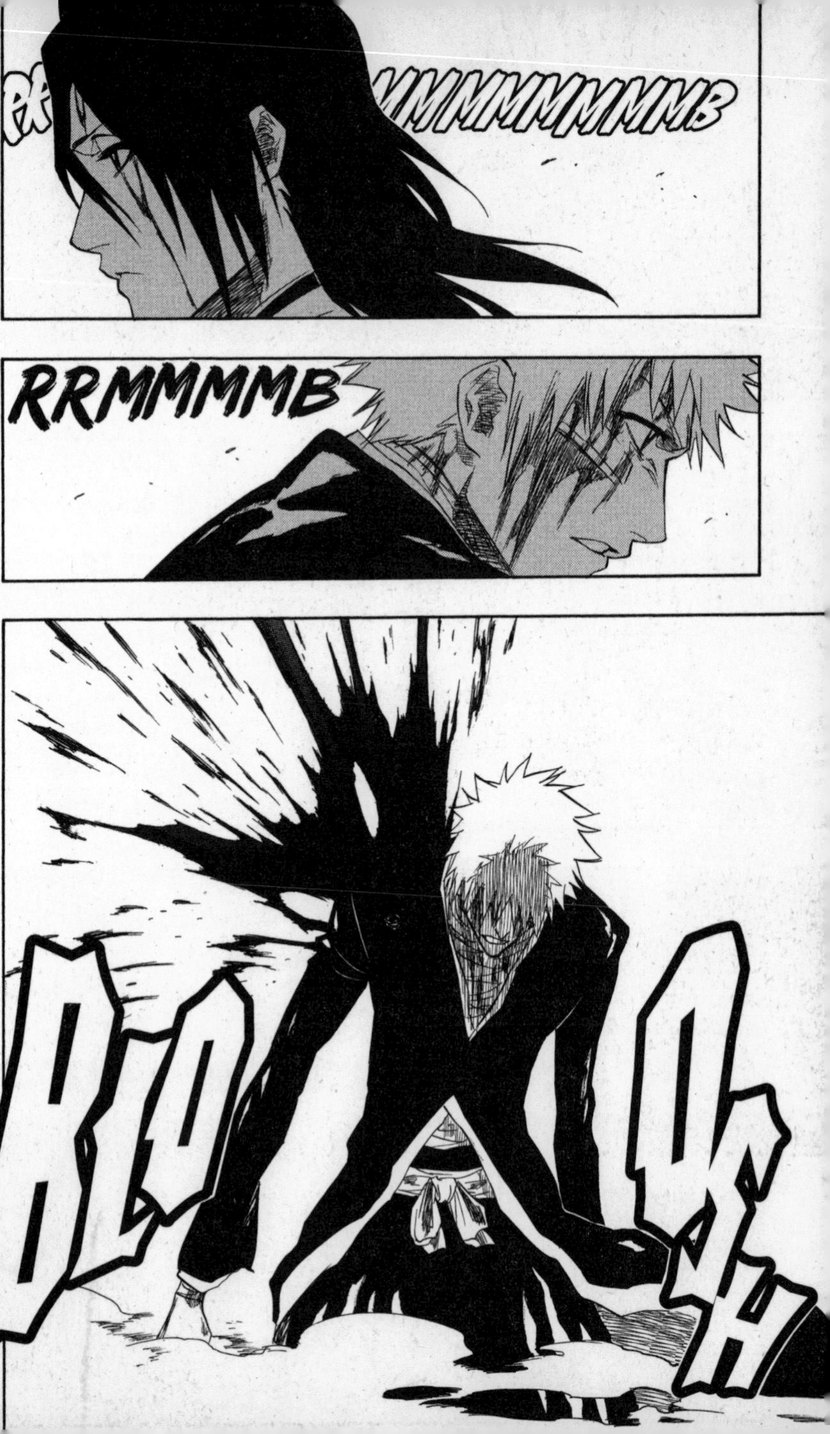
MMMMMMMMMB
RRMMMMMB

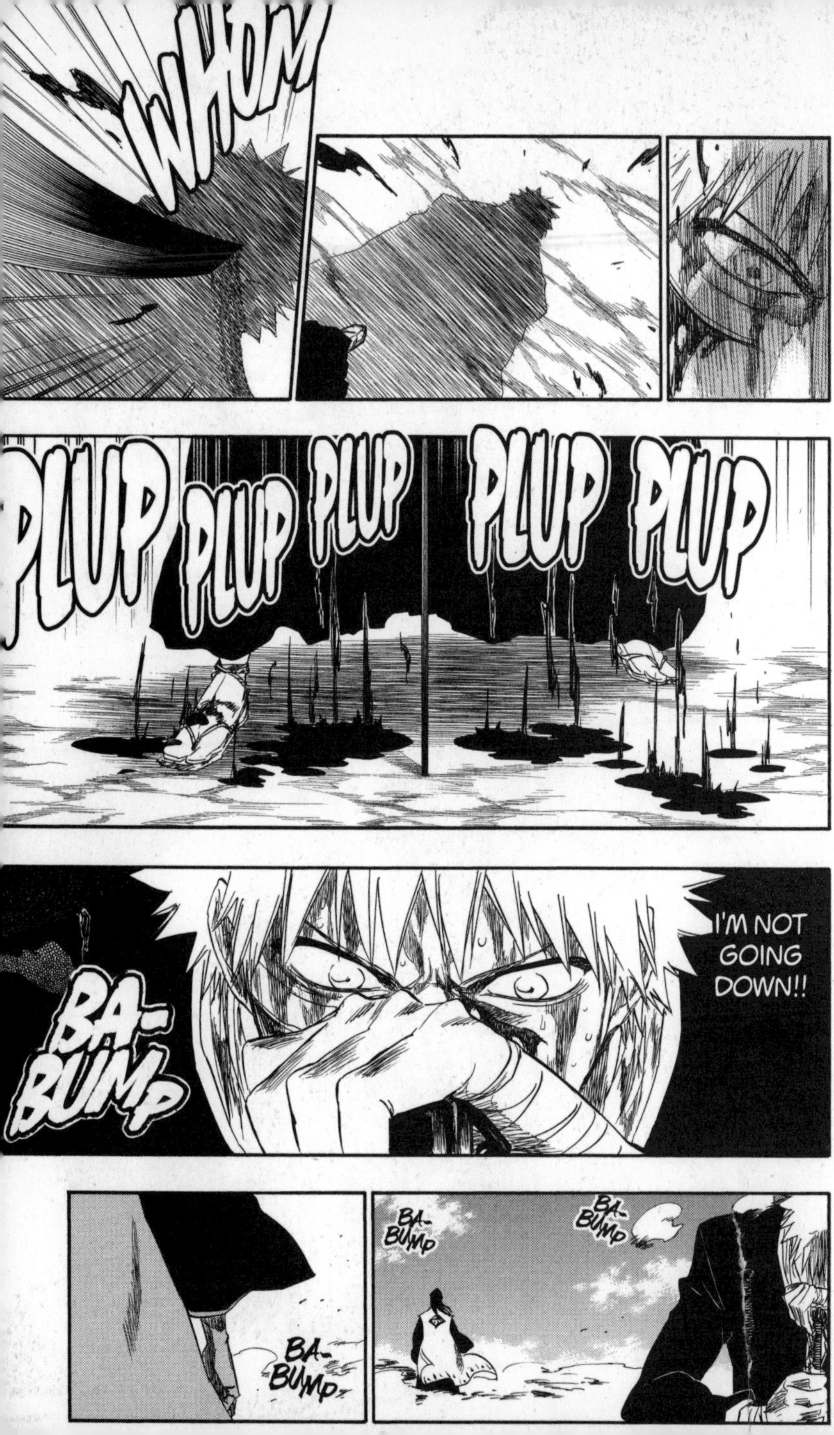
WHOM
PLUP PLUP
PLUP PLUP PLUP
I'M NOT GOING DOWN!!
BA-BUMP
BA-BUMP
BA-BUMP
BA-BUMP

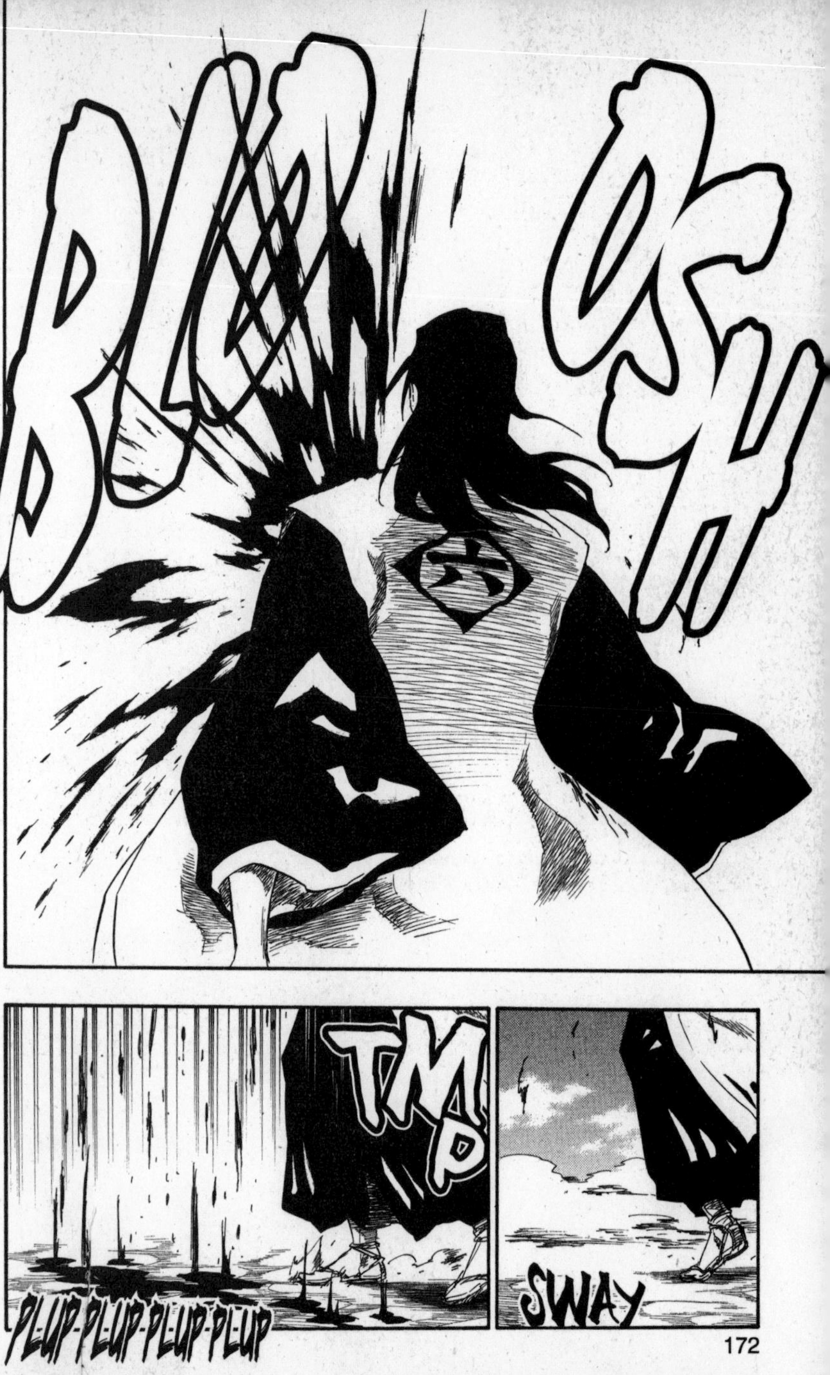
BLOOSH
SWAY
TMP
PLUP-PLUP-PLUP-PLUP

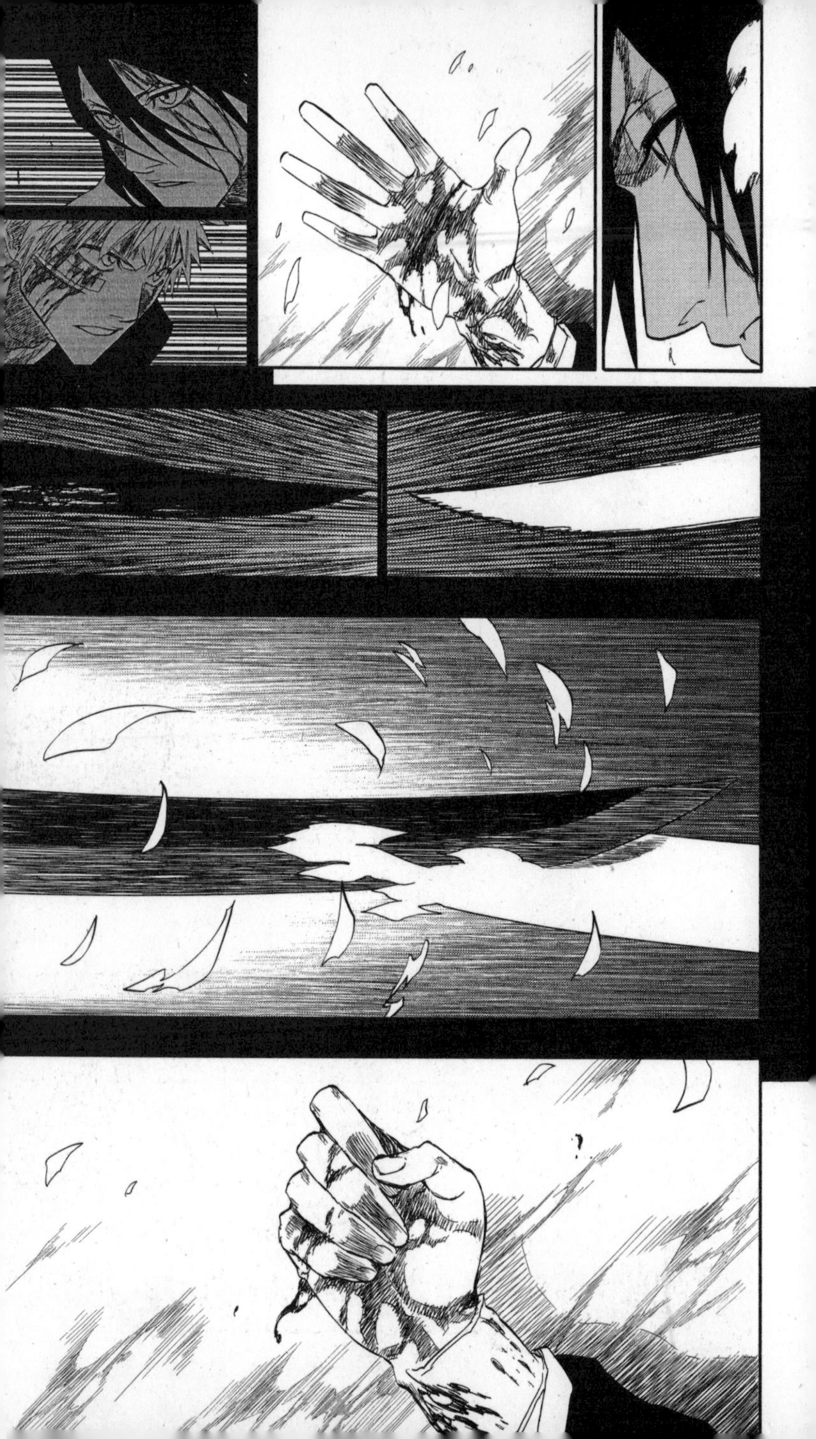

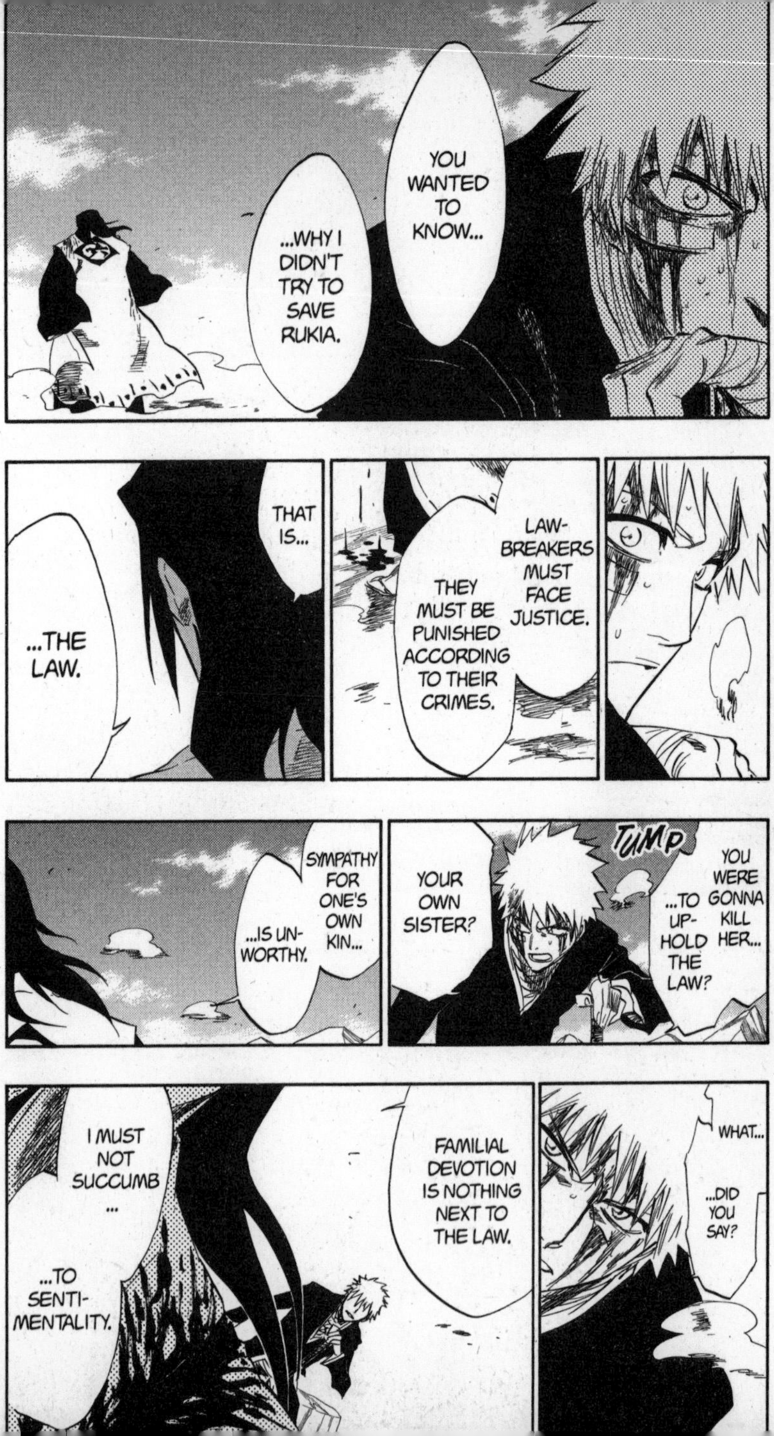
YOU WANTED TO KNOW...
...WHY I DIDN'T TRY TO SAVE RUKIA.
LAW-BREAKERS MUST FACE JUSTICE.
THEY MUST BE PUNISHED ACCORDING TO THEIR CRIMES.
THAT IS...
...THE LAW.
TUMP
YOU WERE GONNA KILL HER...
...TO UP-HOLD THE LAW?
YOUR OWN SISTER?
SYMPATHY FOR ONE'S OWN KIN...
...IS UN-WORTHY.
WHAT...
...DID YOU SAY?
FAMILIAL DEVOTION IS NOTHING NEXT TO THE LAW.
I MUST NOT SUCCUMB ...
...TO SENTI-MENTALITY.

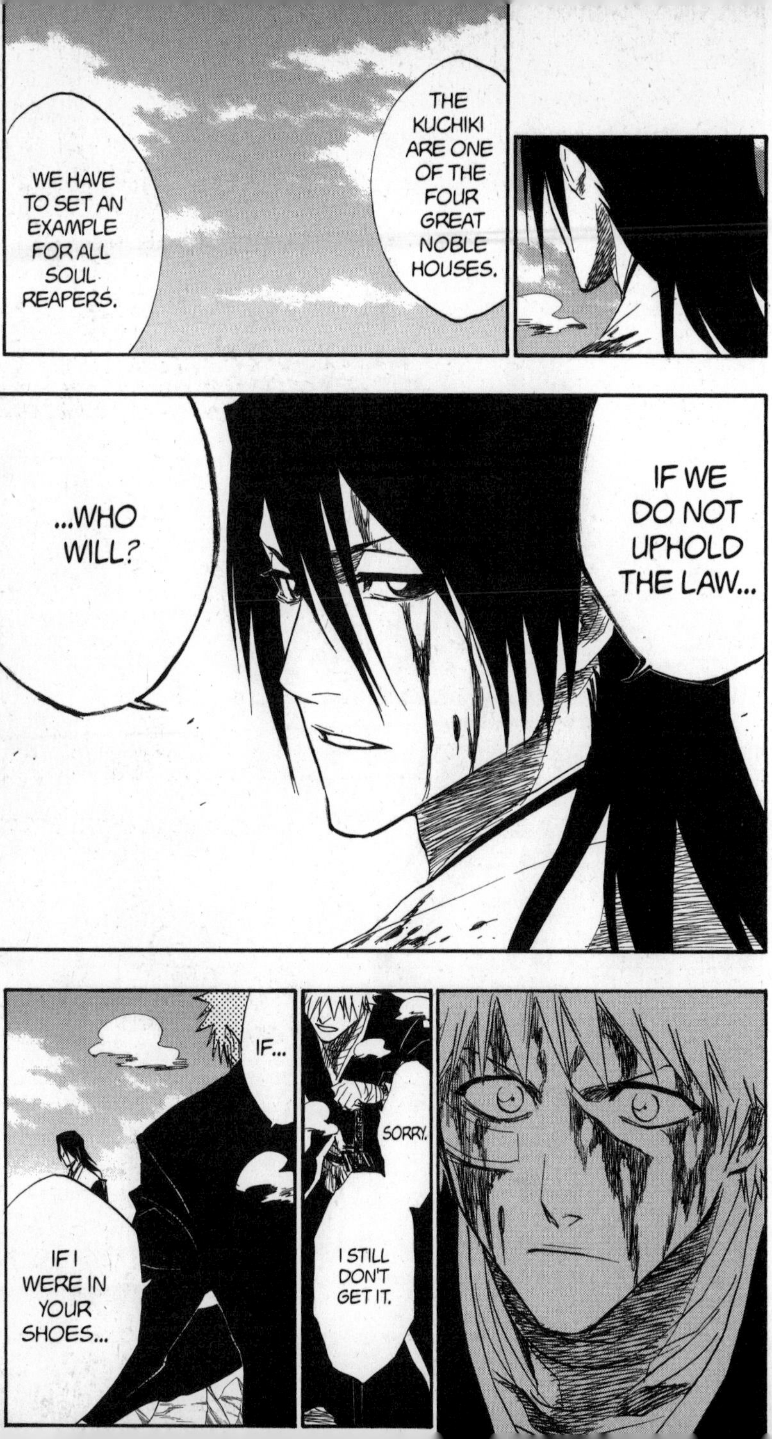
THE KUCHIKI ARE ONE OF THE FOUR GREAT NOBLE HOUSES.
WE HAVE TO SET AN EXAMPLE FOR ALL SOUL REAPERS.
IF WE DO NOT UPHOLD THE LAW...
...WHO WILL?
SORRY.
I STILL DON'T GET IT.
IF...
IF I WERE IN YOUR SHOES...

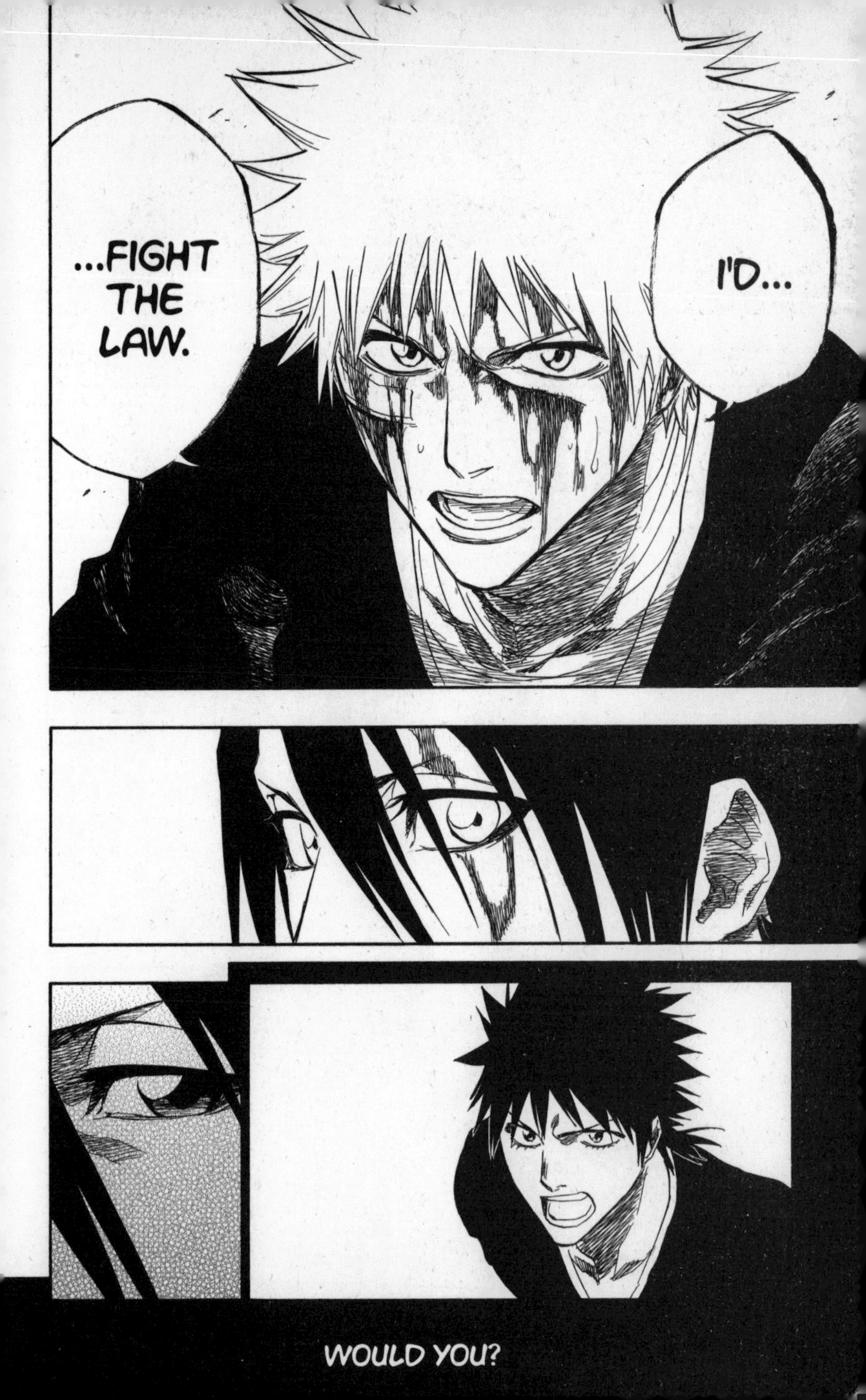
I'D...
...FIGHT THE LAW.
WOULD YOU?

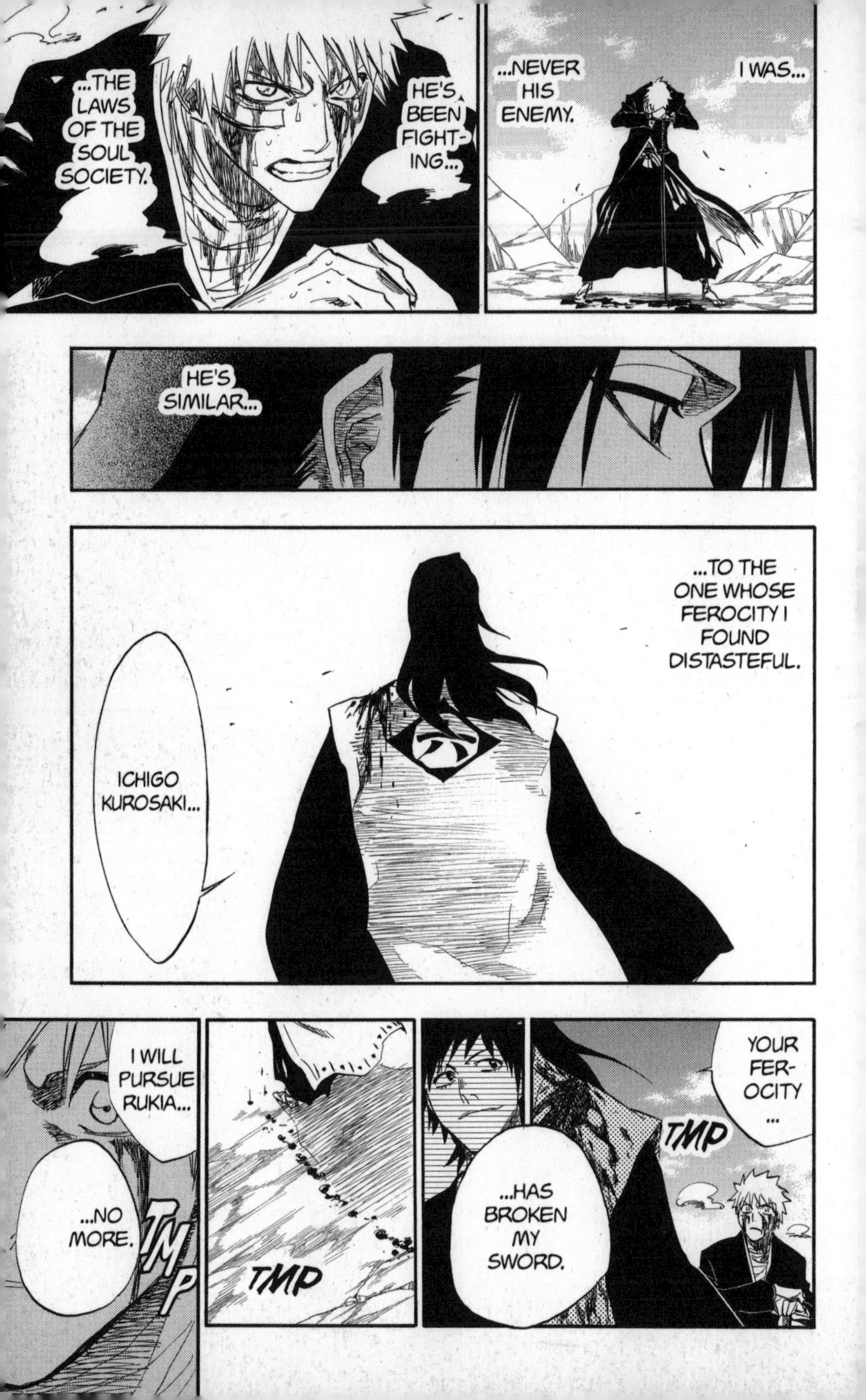
I WAS...
...NEVER HIS ENEMY.
HE'S BEEN FIGHTING...
...THE LAWS OF THE SOUL SOCIETY.
HE'S SIMILAR...
...TO THE ONE WHOSE FEROCITY I FOUND DISTASTEFUL.
ICHIGO KUROSAKI...
YOUR FEROCITY...
TMP
...HAS BROKEN MY SWORD.
TMP
I WILL PURSUE RUKIA...
...NO MORE.
TMP

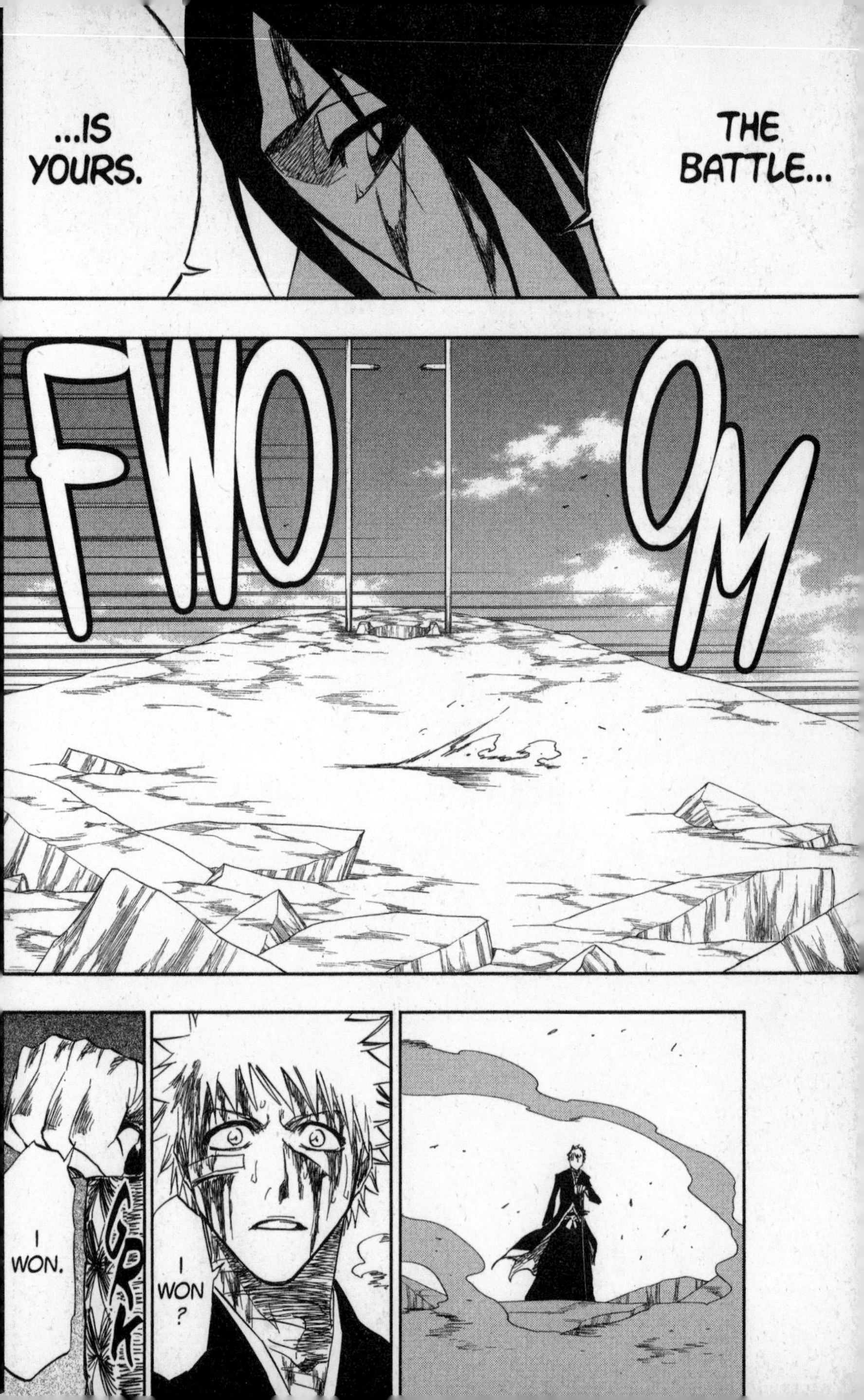
THE BATTLE...
...IS YOURS.
FWOOM
I WON?
GRK
I WON.

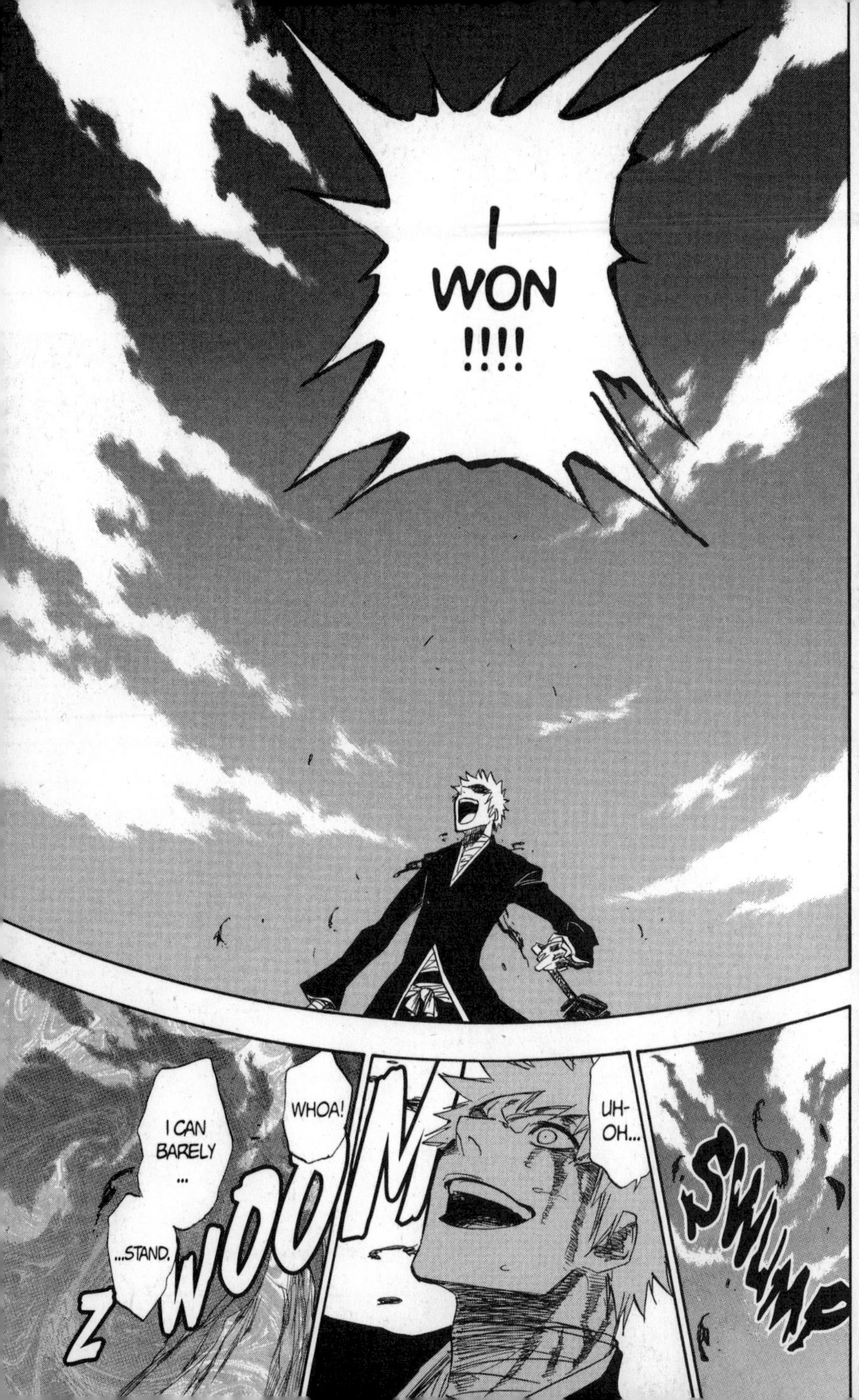
I WON!!!!
SWUMP
UH-OH...
WHOA!
ZWOOOM
I CAN BARELY ...
...STAND.

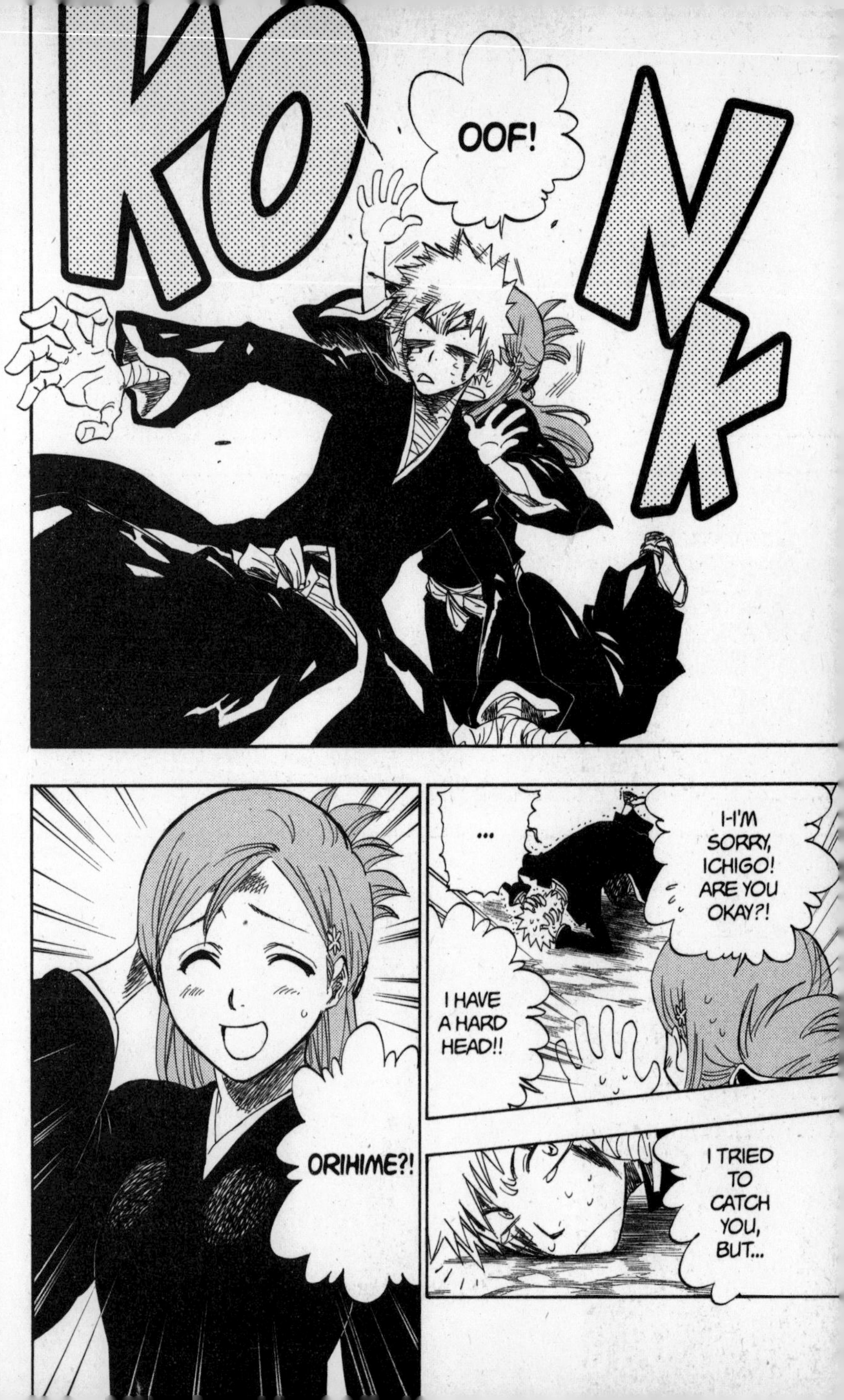
KONK
OOF!
I-I'M SORRY, ICHIGO! ARE YOU OKAY?!
...
I HAVE A HARD HEAD!!
I TRIED TO CATCH YOU, BUT...
ORIHIME?!

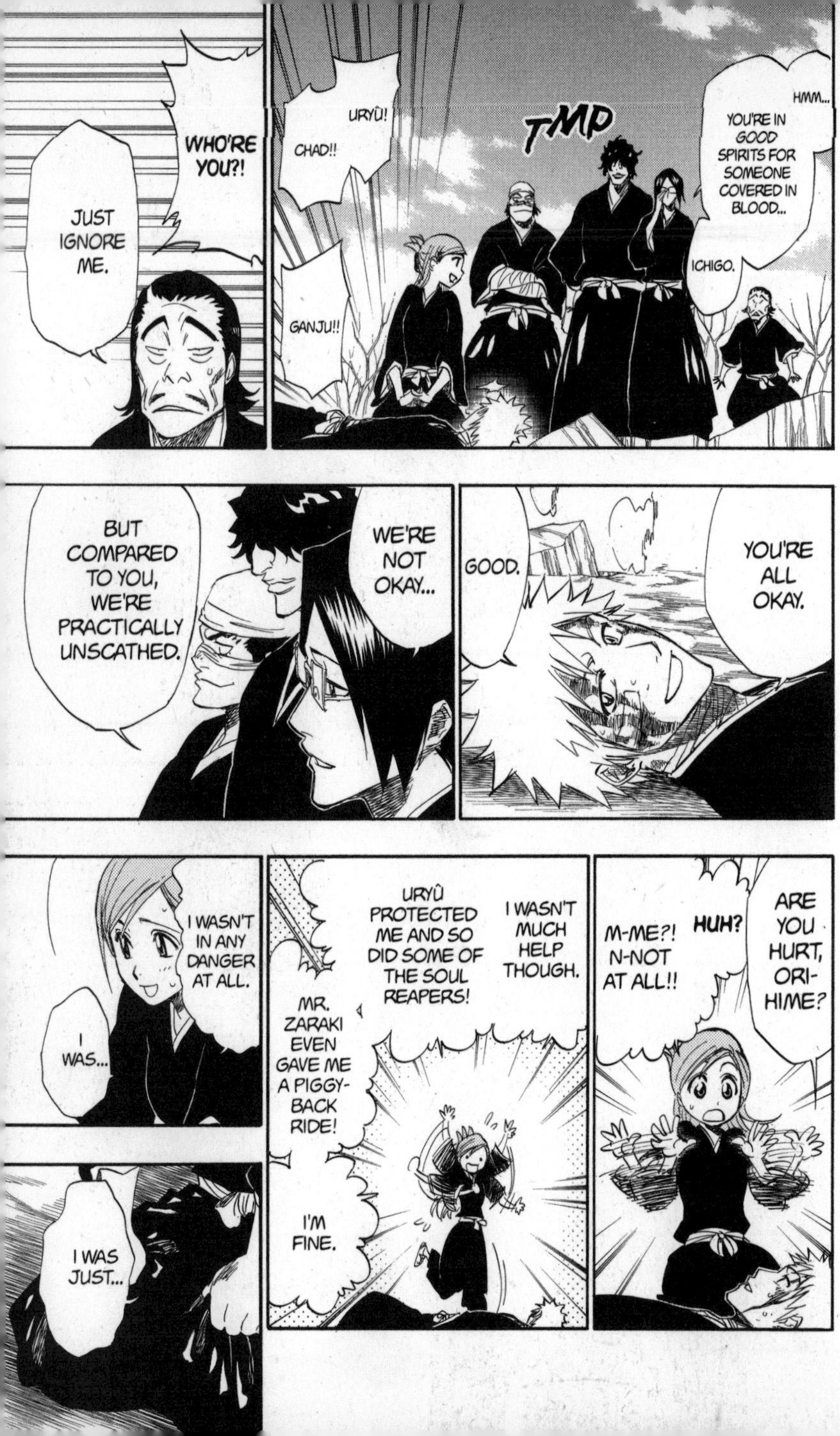
HMM...
YOU'RE IN GOOD SPIRITS FOR SOMEONE COVERED IN BLOOD...
TMP
ICHIGO.
URYÛ!
CHAD!!
GANJU!!
WHO'RE YOU?!
JUST IGNORE ME.
YOU'RE ALL OKAY.
GOOD.
WE'RE NOT OKAY...
BUT COMPARED TO YOU, WE'RE PRACTICALLY UNSCATHED.
ARE YOU HURT, ORI-HIME?
HUH?
M-ME?! N-NOT AT ALL!!
I WASN'T MUCH HELP THOUGH.
URYÛ PROTECTED ME AND SO DID SOME OF THE SOUL REAPERS!
MR. ZARAKI EVEN GAVE ME A PIGGY-BACK RIDE!
I'M FINE.
I WASN'T IN ANY DANGER AT ALL.
I WAS...
I WAS JUST...

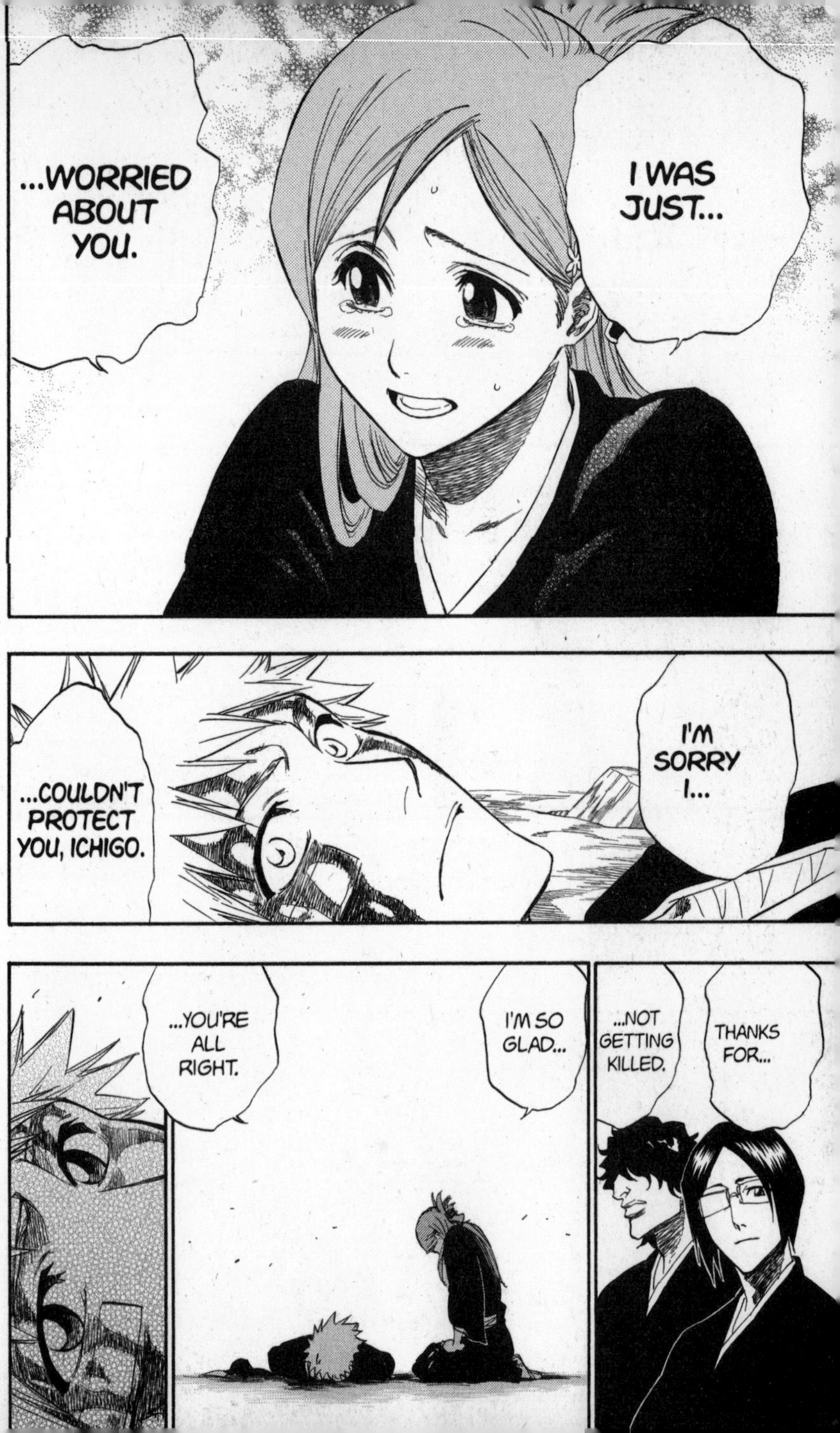
I WAS JUST...
...WORRIED ABOUT YOU.
I'M SORRY I...
...COULDN'T PROTECT YOU, ICHIGO.
THANKS FOR...
...NOT GETTING KILLED.
I'M SO GLAD...
...YOU'RE ALL RIGHT.

THANKS...

...ORI-HIME.

SIGN: CENTRAL 46

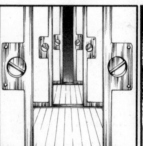

WHAT HAP-PENED?!

WHA...

WHAT IS THIS?

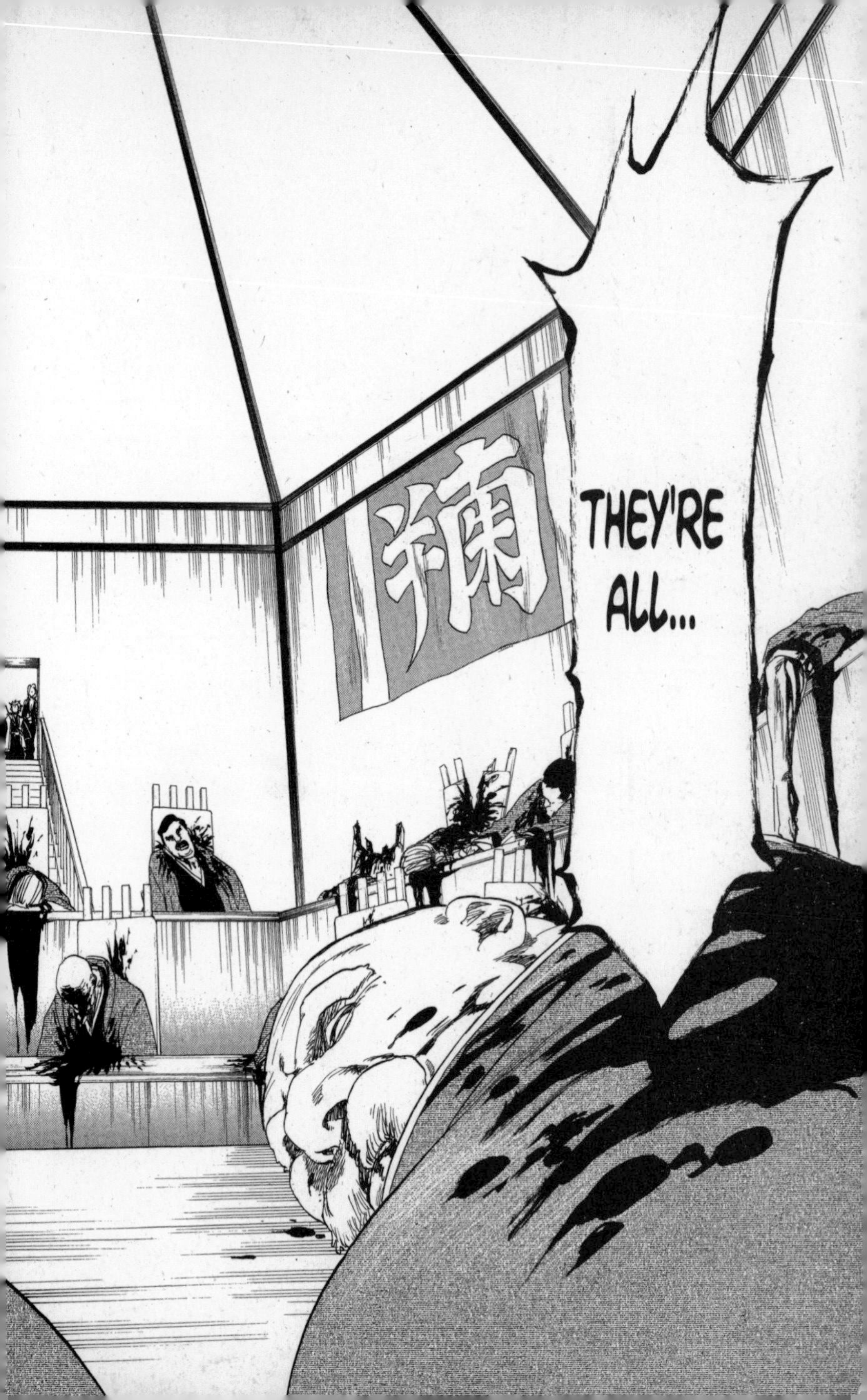
THEY'RE ALL...

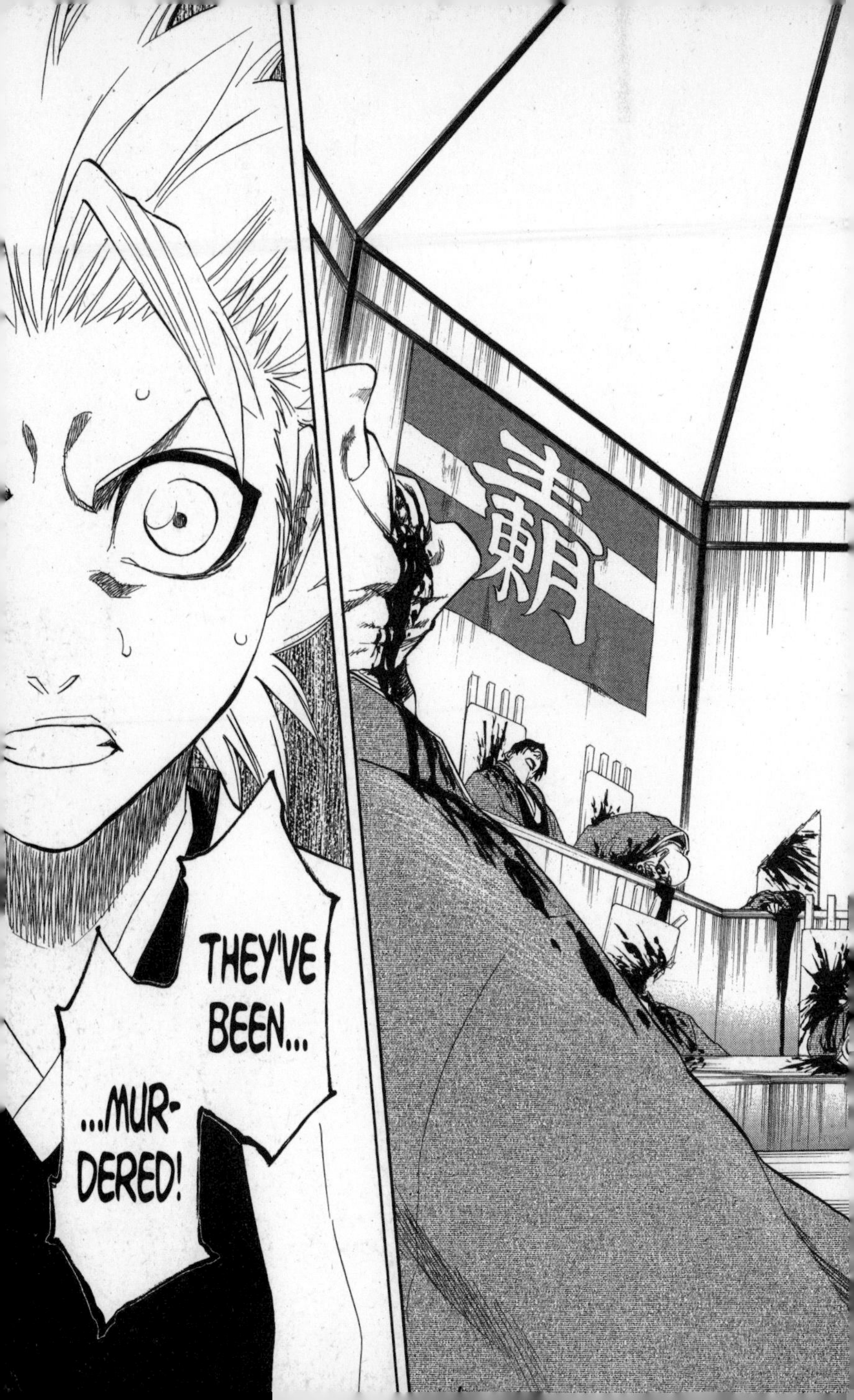
THEY'VE BEEN...
...MURDERED!

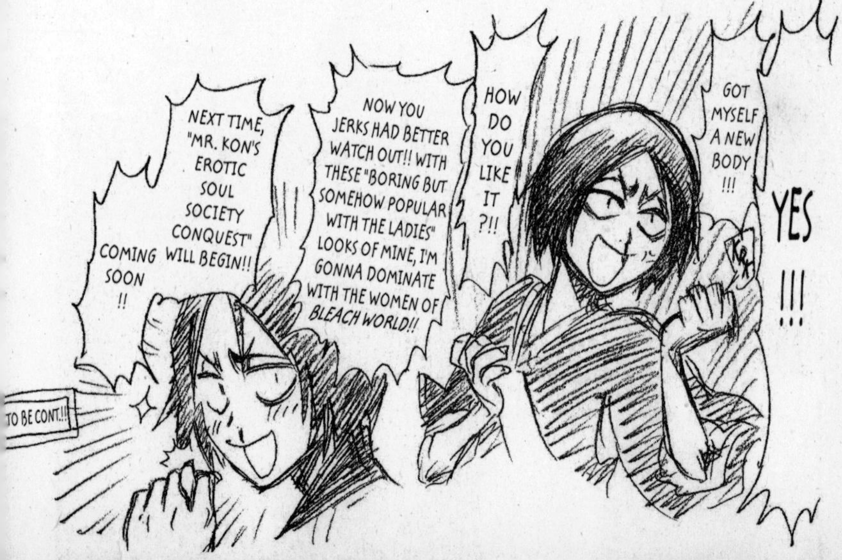
GOT MYSELF A NEW BODY !!!
YES !!!
HOW DO YOU LIKE IT ?!!
NOW YOU JERKS HAD BETTER WATCH OUT!! WITH THESE "BORING BUT SOMEHOW POPULAR WITH THE LADIES" LOOKS OF MINE, I'M GONNA DOMINATE WITH THE WOMEN OF *BLEACH WORLD*!!
NEXT TIME, "MR. KON'S EROTIC SOUL SOCIETY CONQUEST" WILL BEGIN!!
COMING SOON !!
TO BE CONT.!!

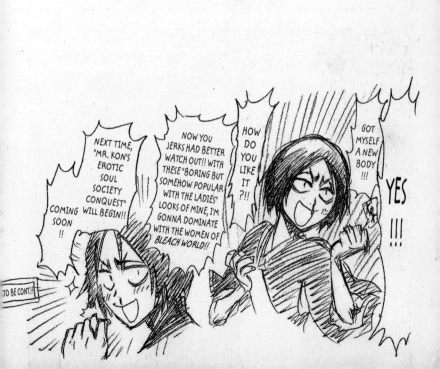

168. Behind Me, Behind You

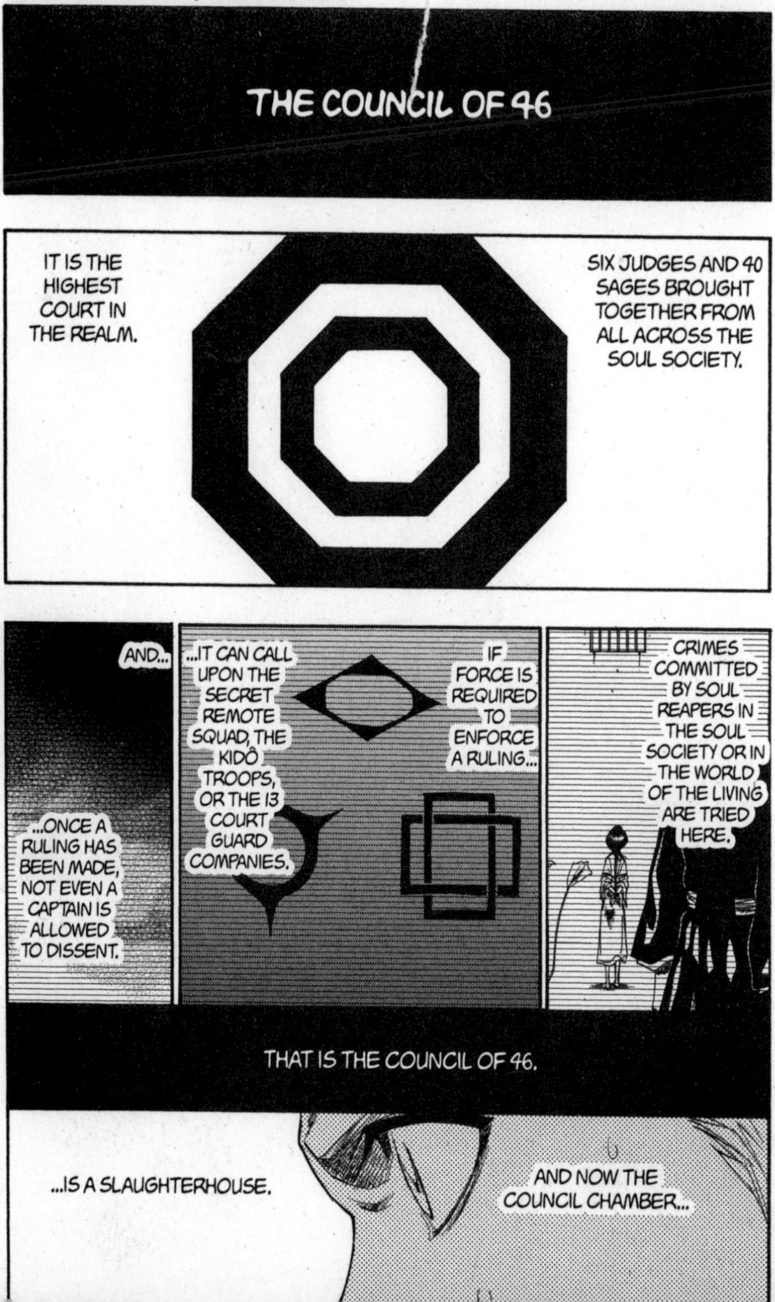
THE COUNCIL OF 46
SIX JUDGES AND 40 SAGES BROUGHT TOGETHER FROM ALL ACROSS THE SOUL SOCIETY.
IT IS THE HIGHEST COURT IN THE REALM.
CRIMES COMMITTED BY SOUL REAPERS IN THE SOUL SOCIETY OR IN THE WORLD OF THE LIVING ARE TRIED HERE.
IF FORCE IS REQUIRED TO ENFORCE A RULING...
...IT CAN CALL UPON THE SECRET REMOTE SQUAD, THE KIDÔ TROOPS, OR THE 13 COURT GUARD COMPANIES.
AND...
...ONCE A RULING HAS BEEN MADE, NOT EVEN A CAPTAIN IS ALLOWED TO DISSENT.
THAT IS THE COUNCIL OF 46.
AND NOW THE COUNCIL CHAMBER...
...IS A SLAUGHTERHOUSE.

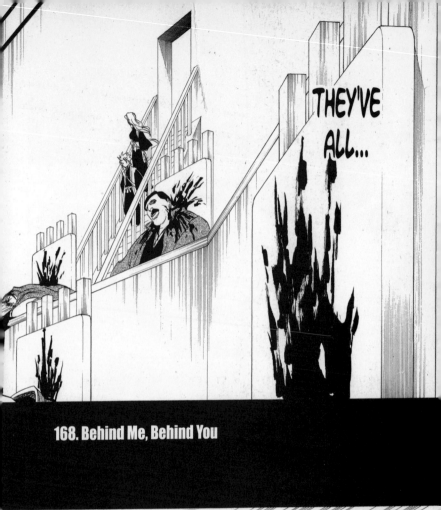

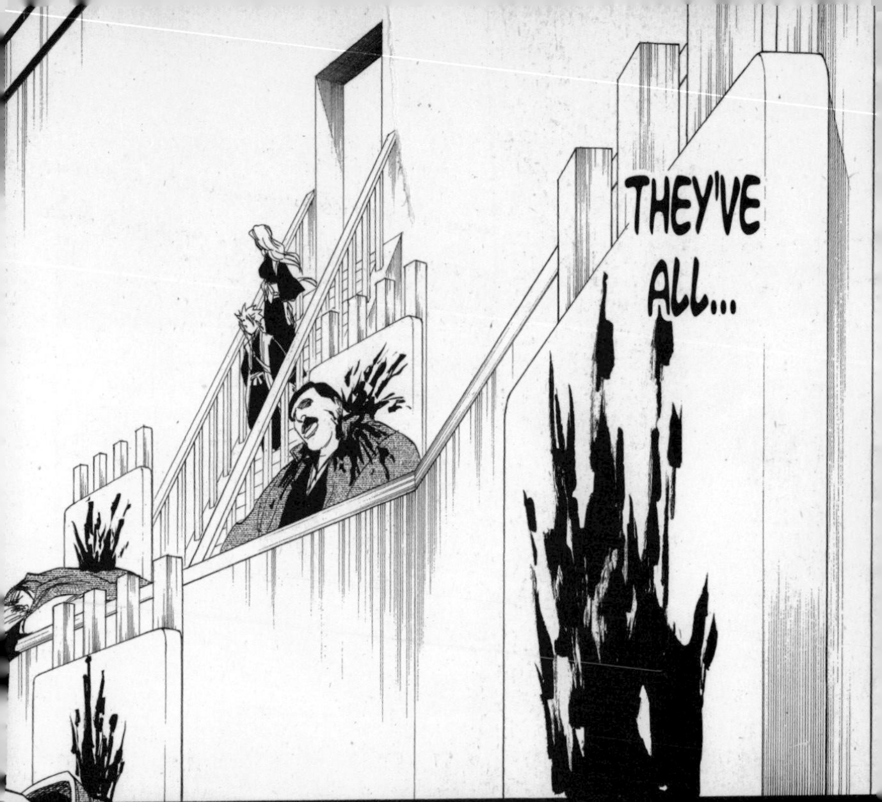
THEY'VE ALL...

168. Behind Me, Behind You

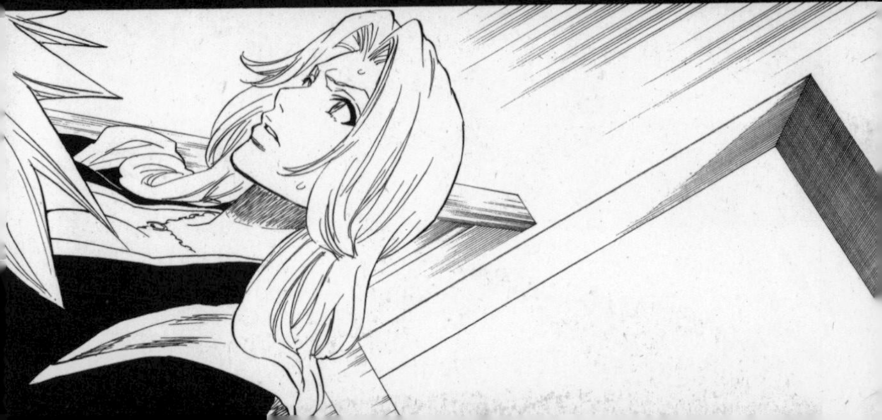

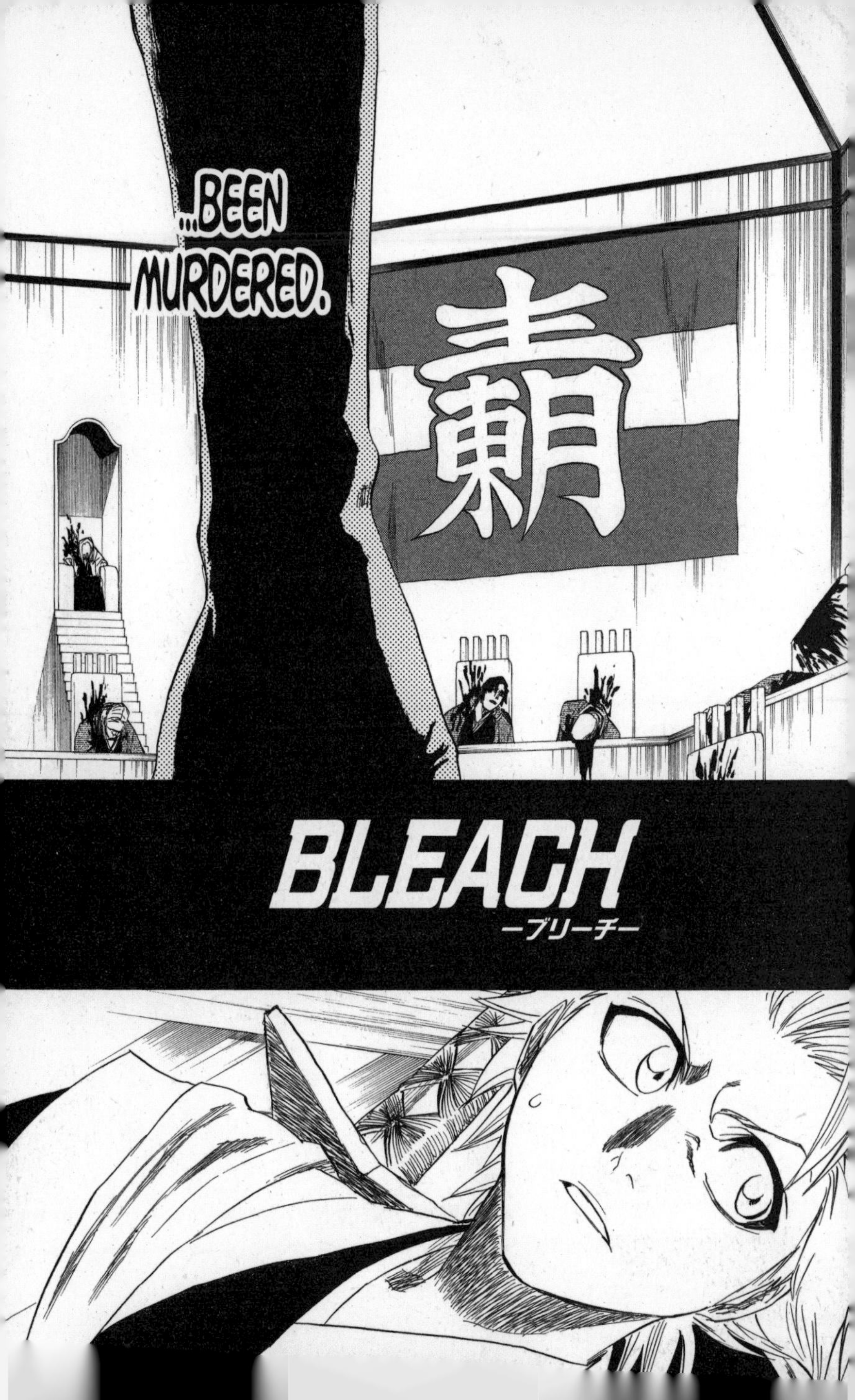
...BEEN MURDERED.
BLEACH
—ブリーチ—

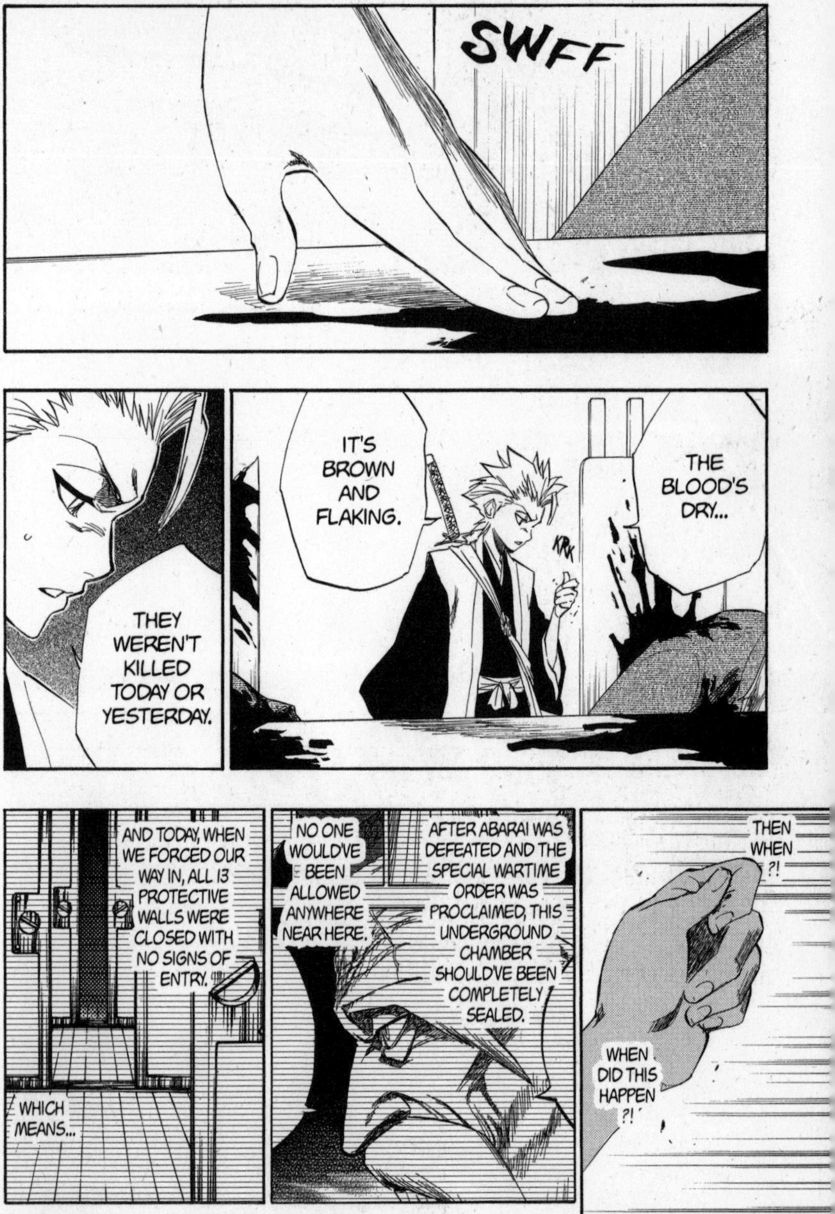
SWFF
THE BLOOD'S DRY...
KRK
IT'S BROWN AND FLAKING.
THEY WEREN'T KILLED TODAY OR YESTERDAY.
THEN WHEN ?!
WHEN DID THIS HAPPEN ?!
AFTER ABARAI WAS DEFEATED AND THE SPECIAL WARTIME ORDER WAS PROCLAIMED, THIS UNDERGROUND CHAMBER SHOULD'VE BEEN COMPLETELY SEALED.
NO ONE WOULD'VE BEEN ALLOWED ANYWHERE NEAR HERE.
AND TODAY, WHEN WE FORCED OUR WAY IN, ALL 13 PROTECTIVE WALLS WERE CLOSED WITH NO SIGNS OF ENTRY.
WHICH MEANS...

READ THIS WAY

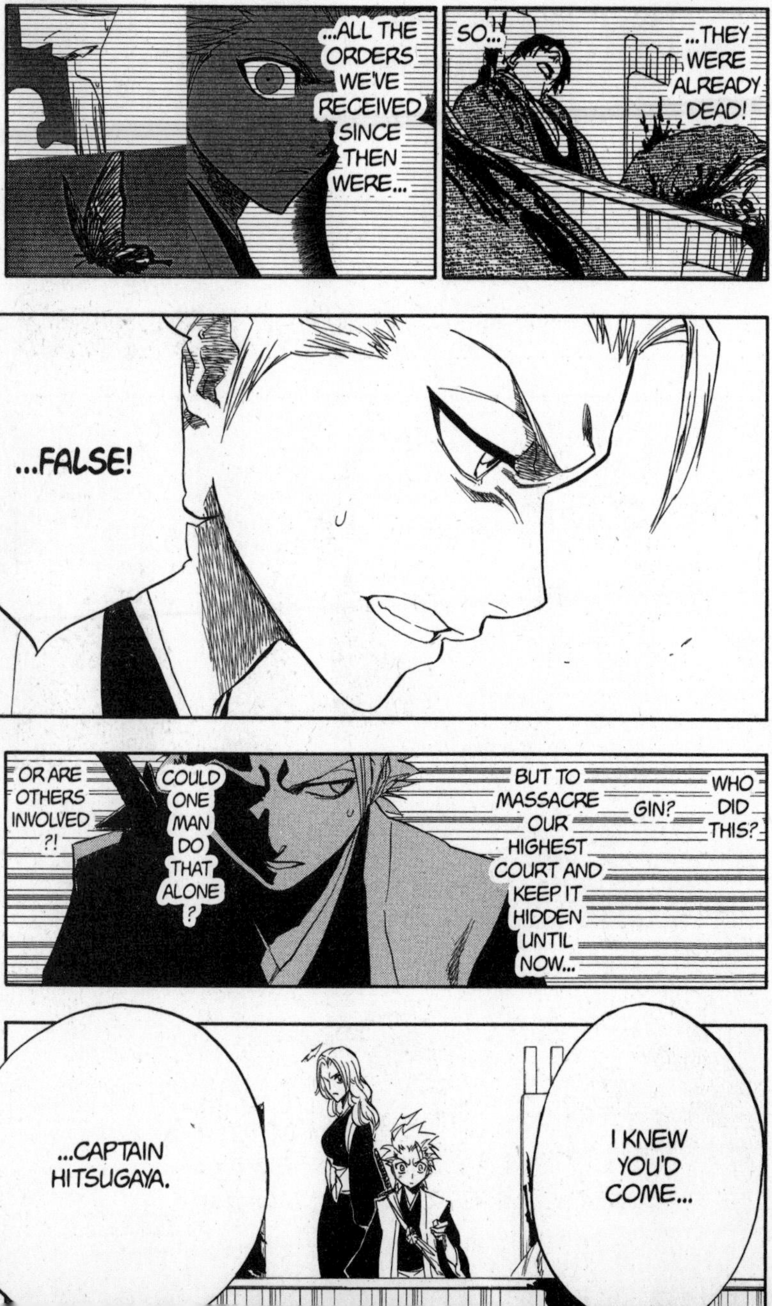
SO...
...THEY WERE ALREADY DEAD!
...ALL THE ORDERS WE'VE RECEIVED SINCE THEN WERE...
...FALSE!
WHO DID THIS?
GIN?
BUT TO MASSACRE OUR HIGHEST COURT AND KEEP IT HIDDEN UNTIL NOW...
COULD ONE MAN DO THAT ALONE?
OR ARE OTHERS INVOLVED?!
I KNEW YOU'D COME...
...CAPTAIN HITSUGAYA.

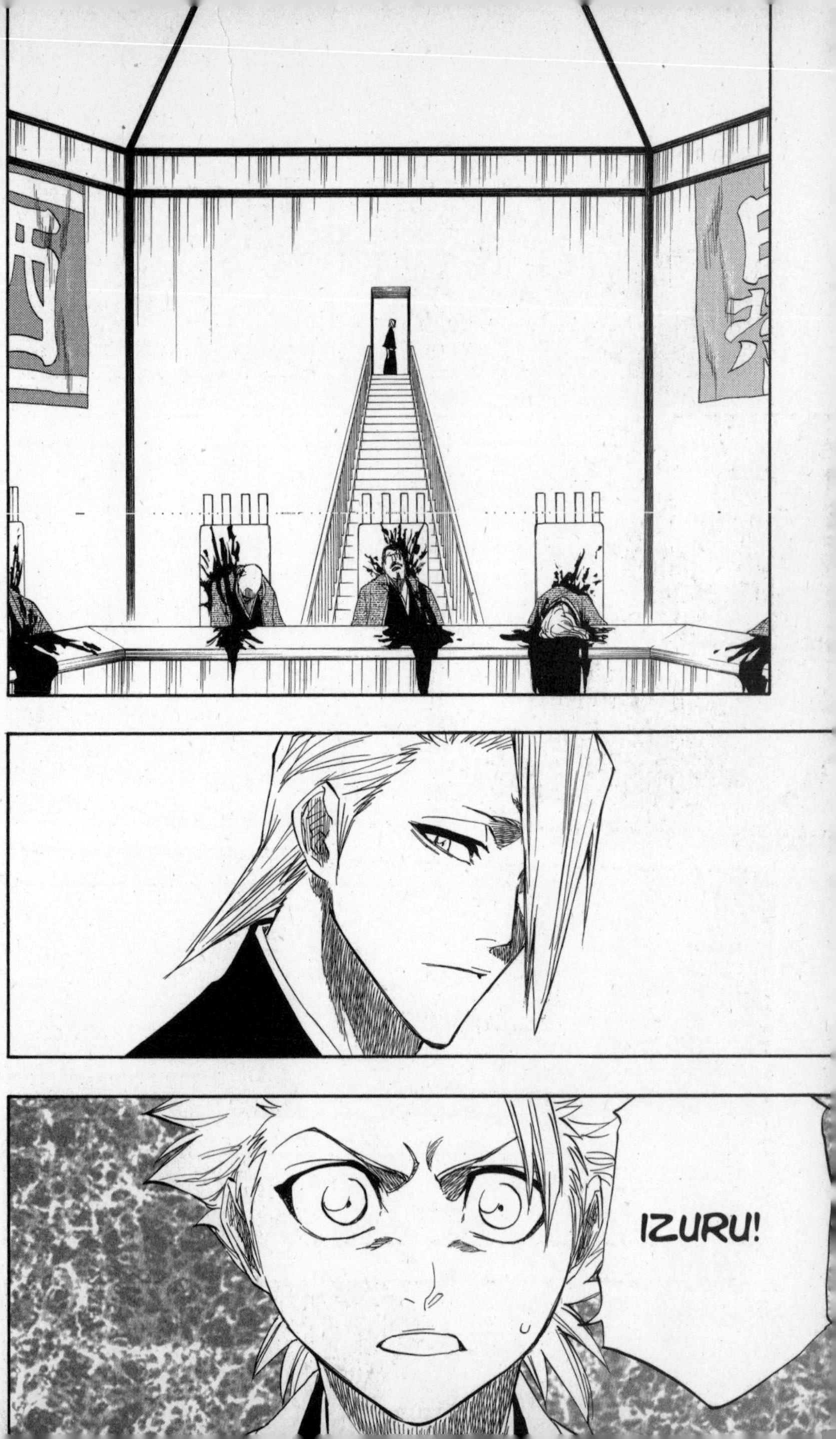
IZURU!

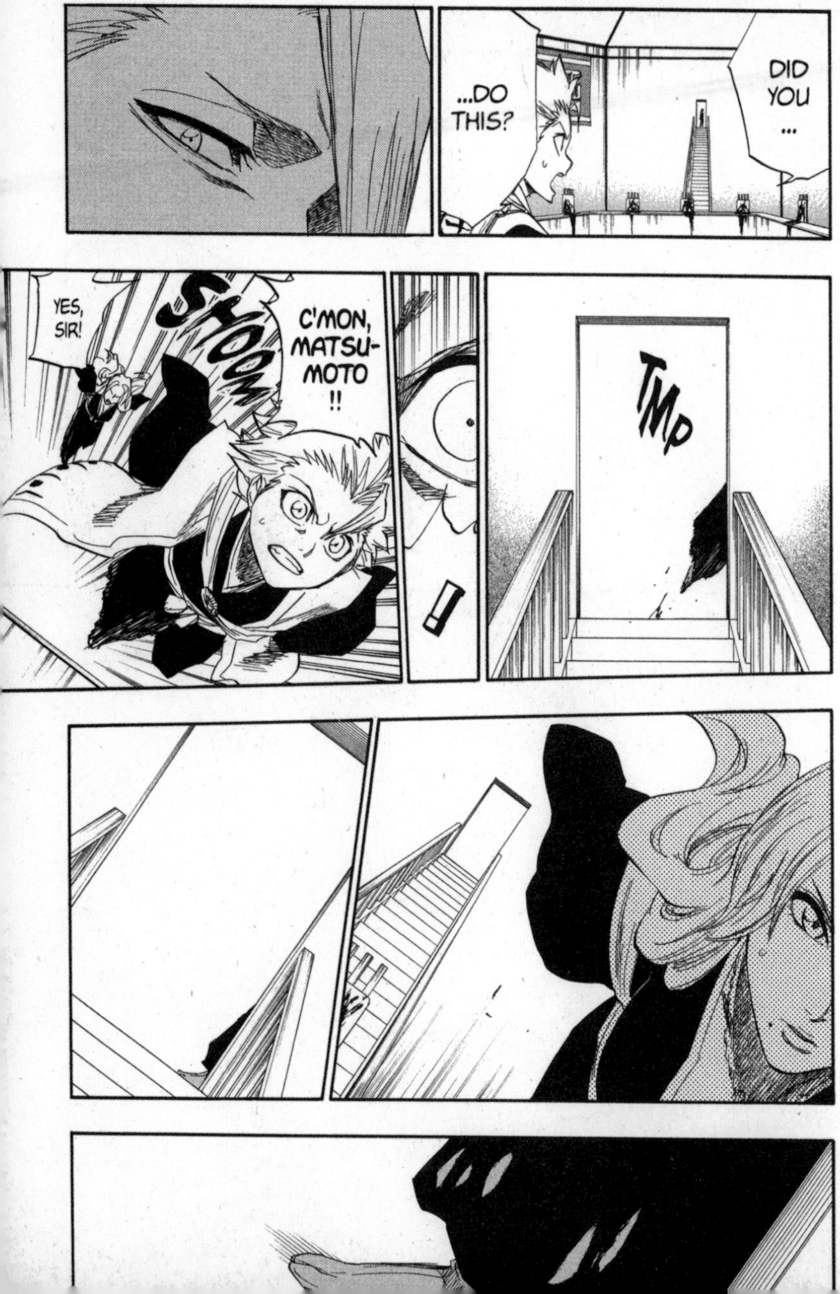
DID YOU ...
...DO THIS?
TMP
!
C'MON, MATSU-MOTO !!
SHOOM
YES, SIR!

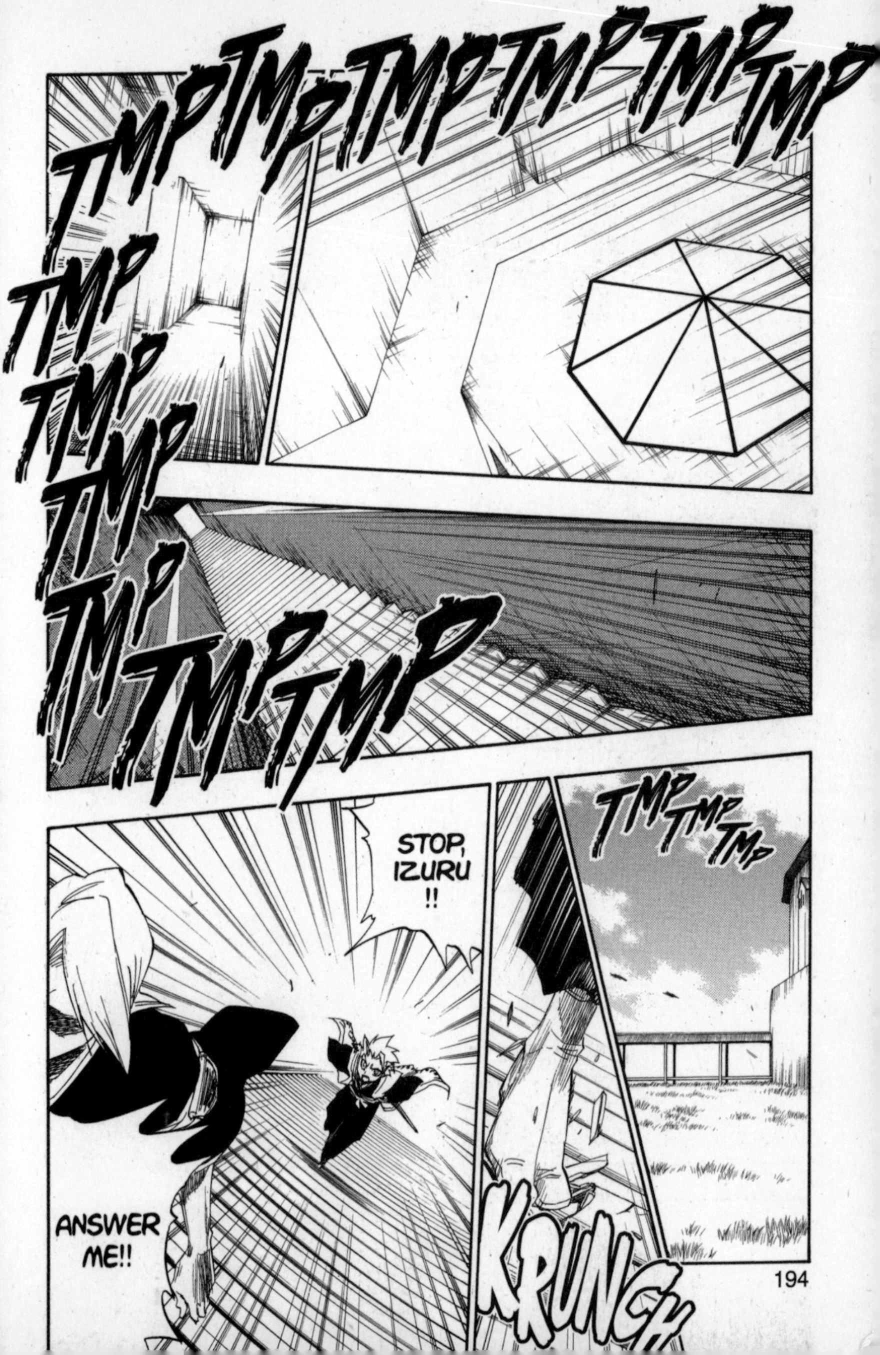
TMP TMP TMP TMP TMP TMP
TMP
TMP
TMP
TMP
TMP TMP
TMP TMP TMP
STOP, IZURU!!
KRUNCH
ANSWER ME!!

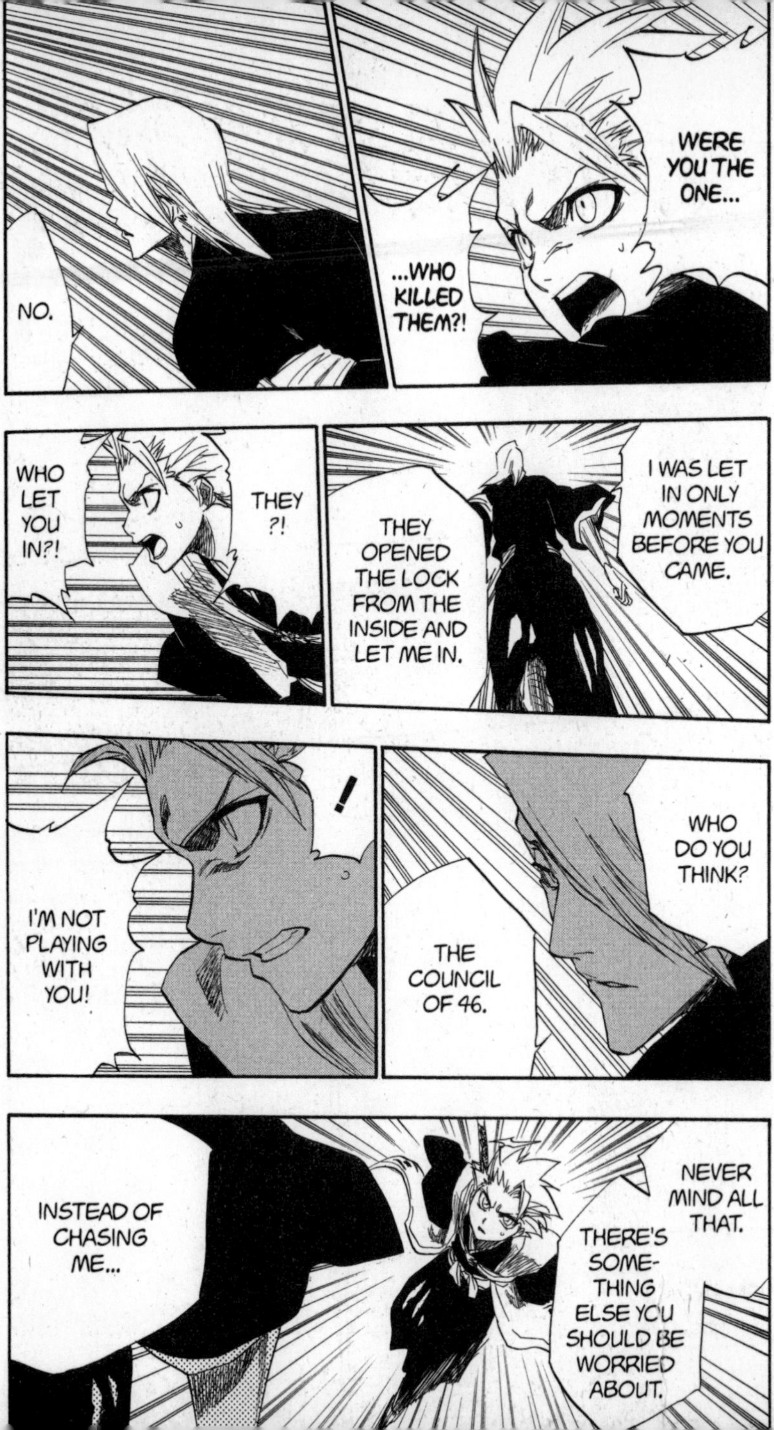
WERE YOU THE ONE...
...WHO KILLED THEM?!
NO.
I WAS LET IN ONLY MOMENTS BEFORE YOU CAME.
THEY OPENED THE LOCK FROM THE INSIDE AND LET ME IN.
THEY ?!
WHO LET YOU IN?!
WHO DO YOU THINK?
THE COUNCIL OF 46.
!
I'M NOT PLAYING WITH YOU!
NEVER MIND ALL THAT.
THERE'S SOME-THING ELSE YOU SHOULD BE WORRIED ABOUT.
INSTEAD OF CHASING ME...

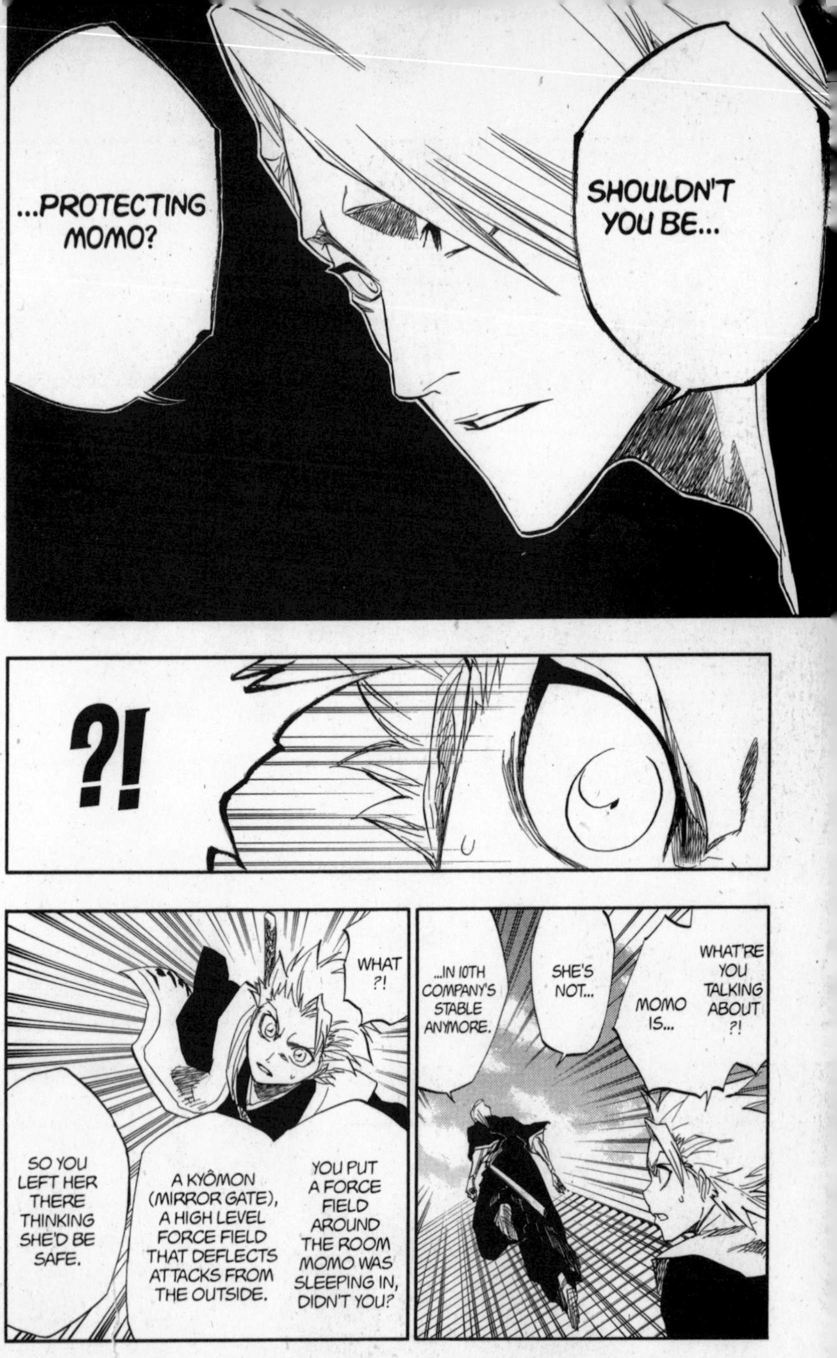
SHOULDN'T YOU BE...
...PROTECTING MOMO?
?!
WHAT'RE YOU TALKING ABOUT ?!
MOMO IS...
SHE'S NOT...
...IN 10TH COMPANY'S STABLE ANYMORE.
WHAT ?!
YOU PUT A FORCE FIELD AROUND THE ROOM MOMO WAS SLEEPING IN, DIDN'T YOU?
A KYÔMON (MIRROR GATE), A HIGH LEVEL FORCE FIELD THAT DEFLECTS ATTACKS FROM THE OUTSIDE.
SO YOU LEFT HER THERE THINKING SHE'D BE SAFE.

READ THIS WAY

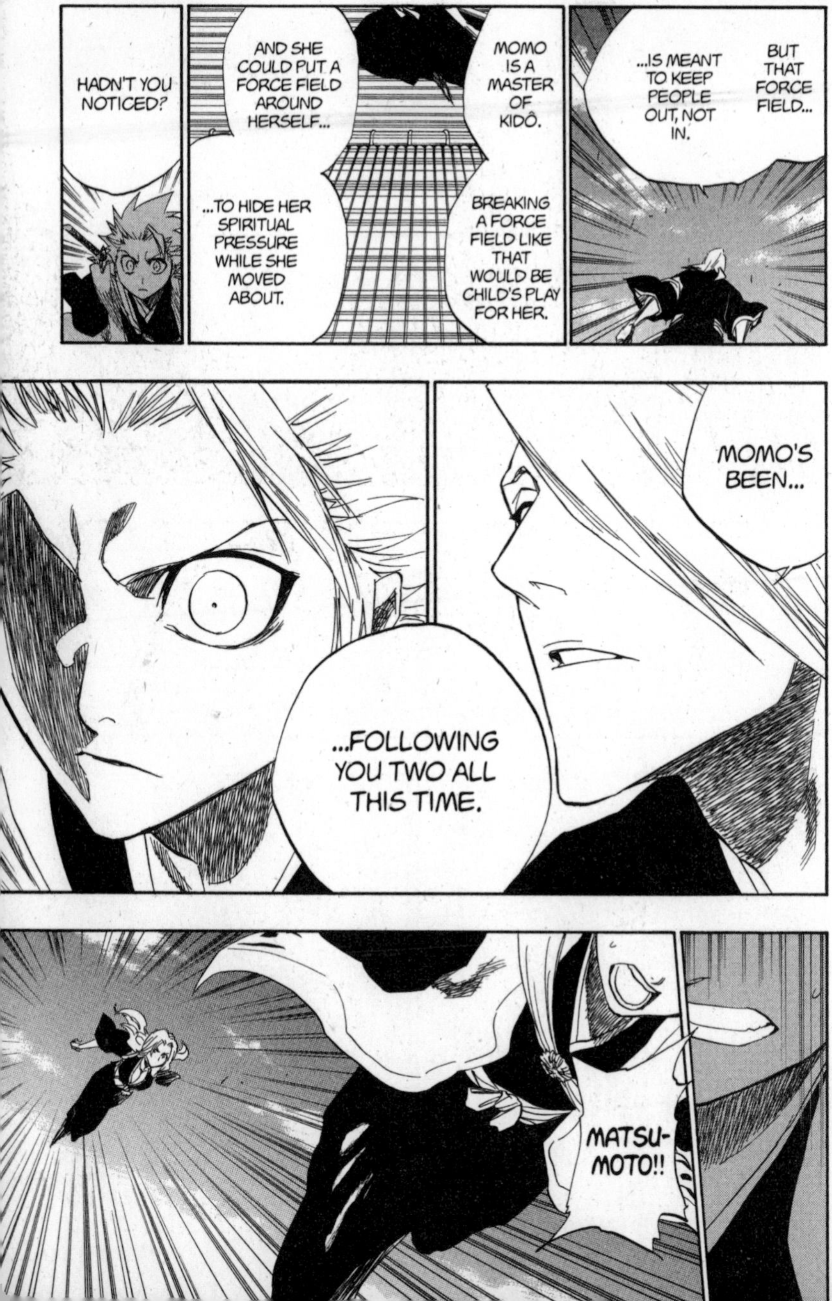
BUT THAT FORCE FIELD...
...IS MEANT TO KEEP PEOPLE OUT, NOT IN.
MOMO IS A MASTER OF KIDÔ.
BREAKING A FORCE FIELD LIKE THAT WOULD BE CHILD'S PLAY FOR HER.
AND SHE COULD PUT A FORCE FIELD AROUND HERSELF...
...TO HIDE HER SPIRITUAL PRESSURE WHILE SHE MOVED ABOUT.
HADN'T YOU NOTICED?
MOMO'S BEEN...
...FOLLOWING YOU TWO ALL THIS TIME.
MATSU-MOTO!!

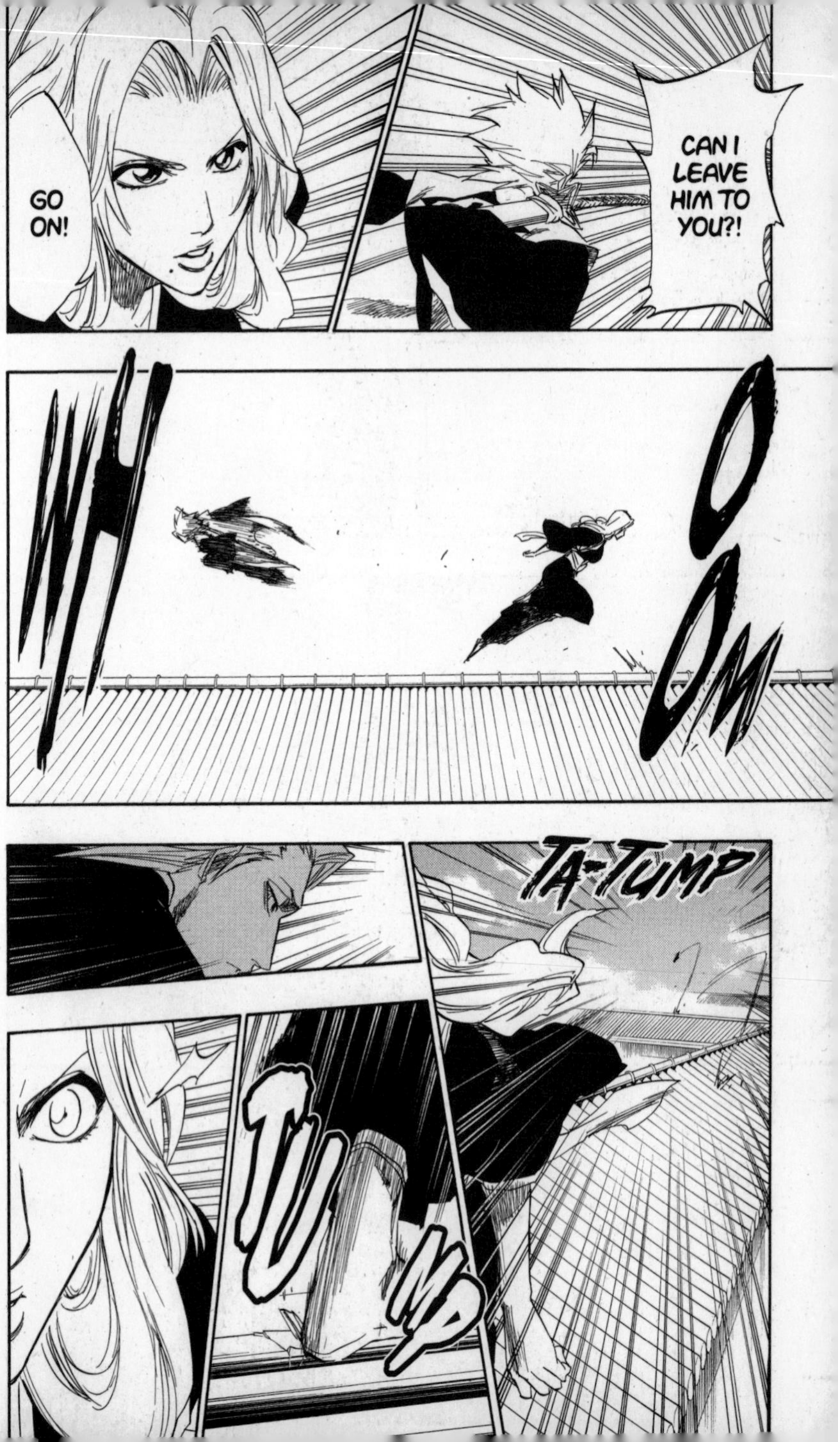
CAN I LEAVE HIM TO YOU?!
GO ON!
WHOOM
TA-TUMP
TUMP

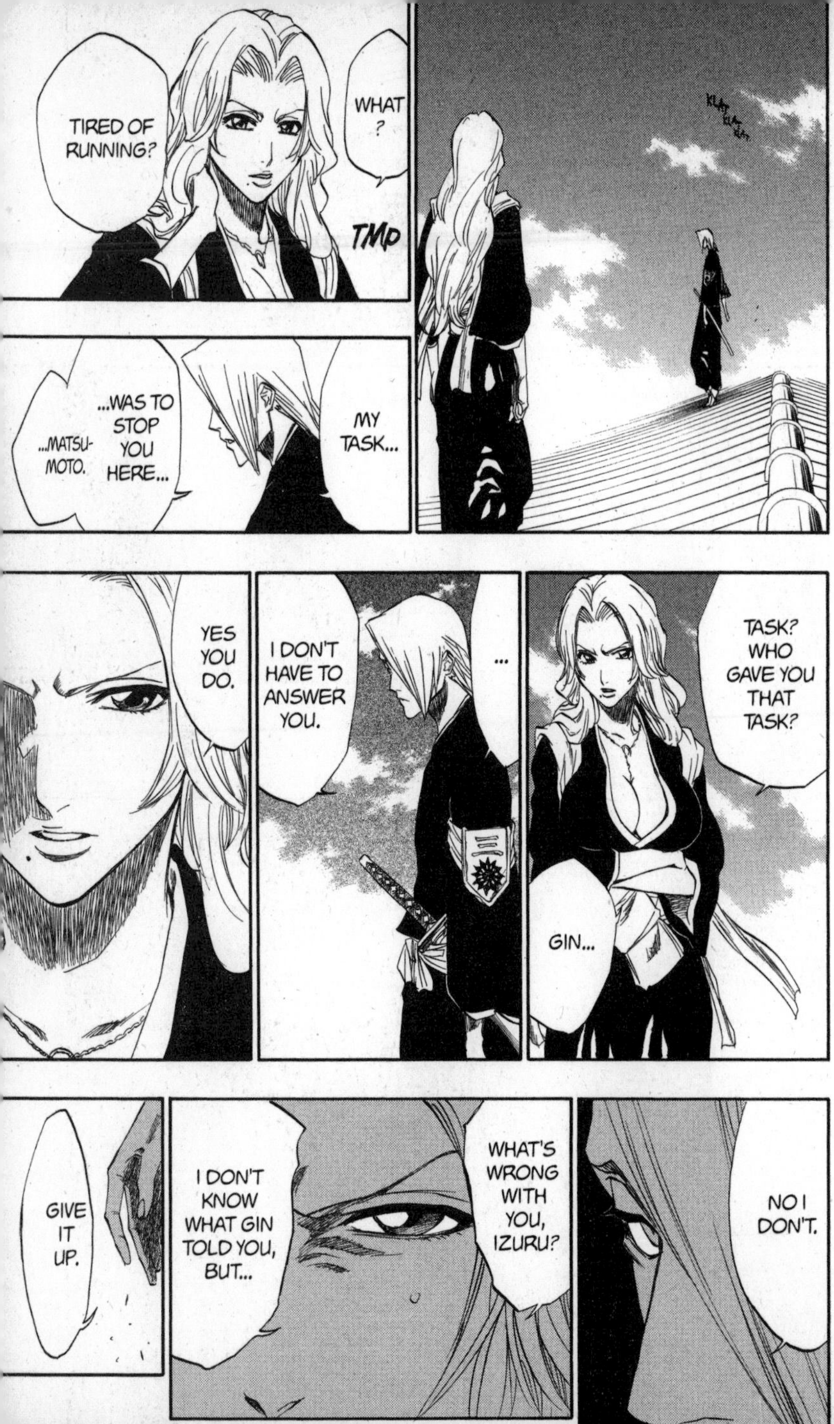
WHAT ?
TMP
TIRED OF RUNNING?
MY TASK...
...WAS TO STOP YOU HERE...
...MATSU-MOTO.
TASK? WHO GAVE YOU THAT TASK?
GIN...
...
I DON'T HAVE TO ANSWER YOU.
YES YOU DO.
NO I DON'T.
WHAT'S WRONG WITH YOU, IZURU?
I DON'T KNOW WHAT GIN TOLD YOU, BUT...
GIVE IT UP.

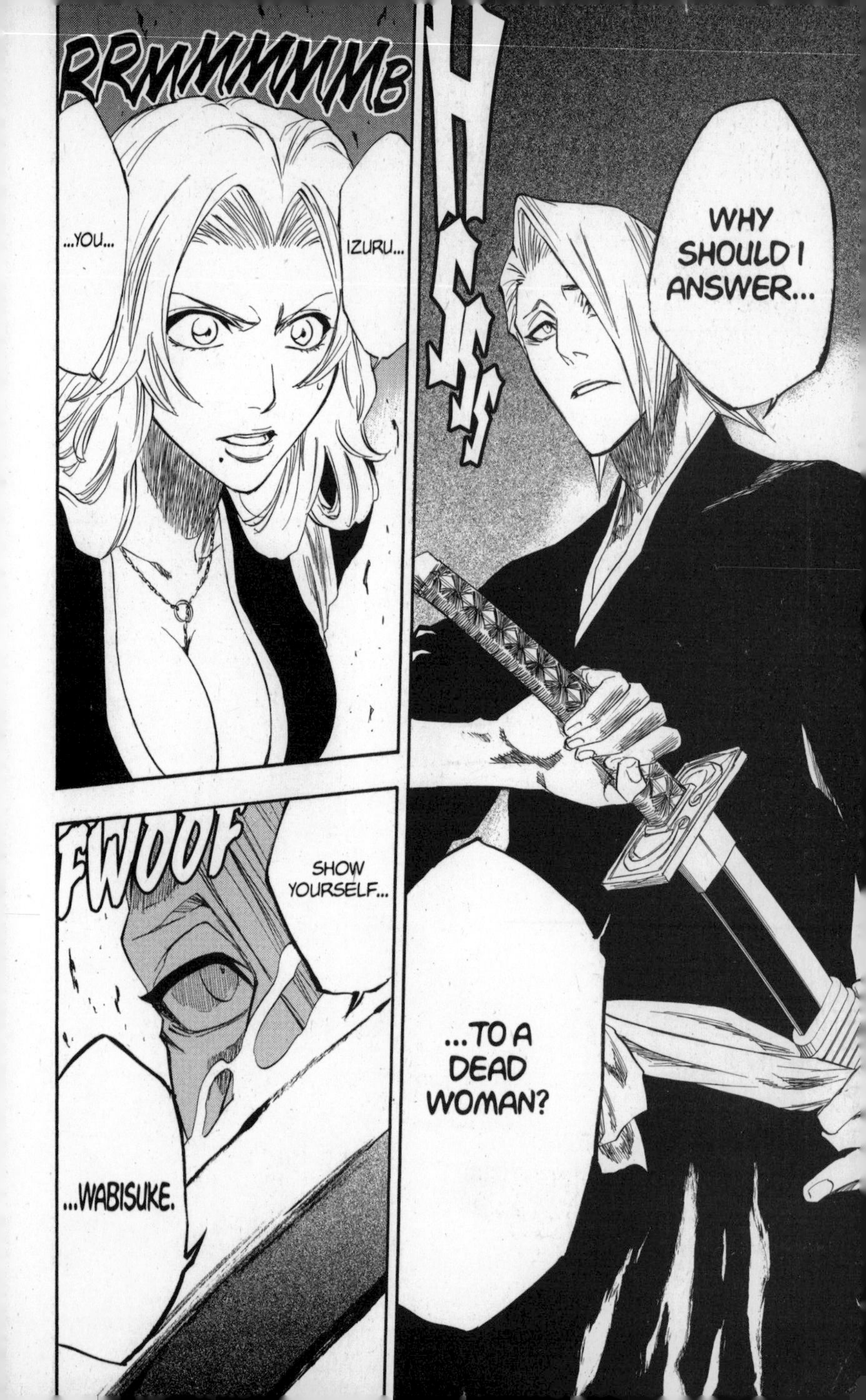
WHY SHOULD I ANSWER...
...TO A DEAD WOMAN?
RRMMMMMMB
IZURU...
...YOU...
FWOOF
SHOW YOURSELF...
...WABISUKE.

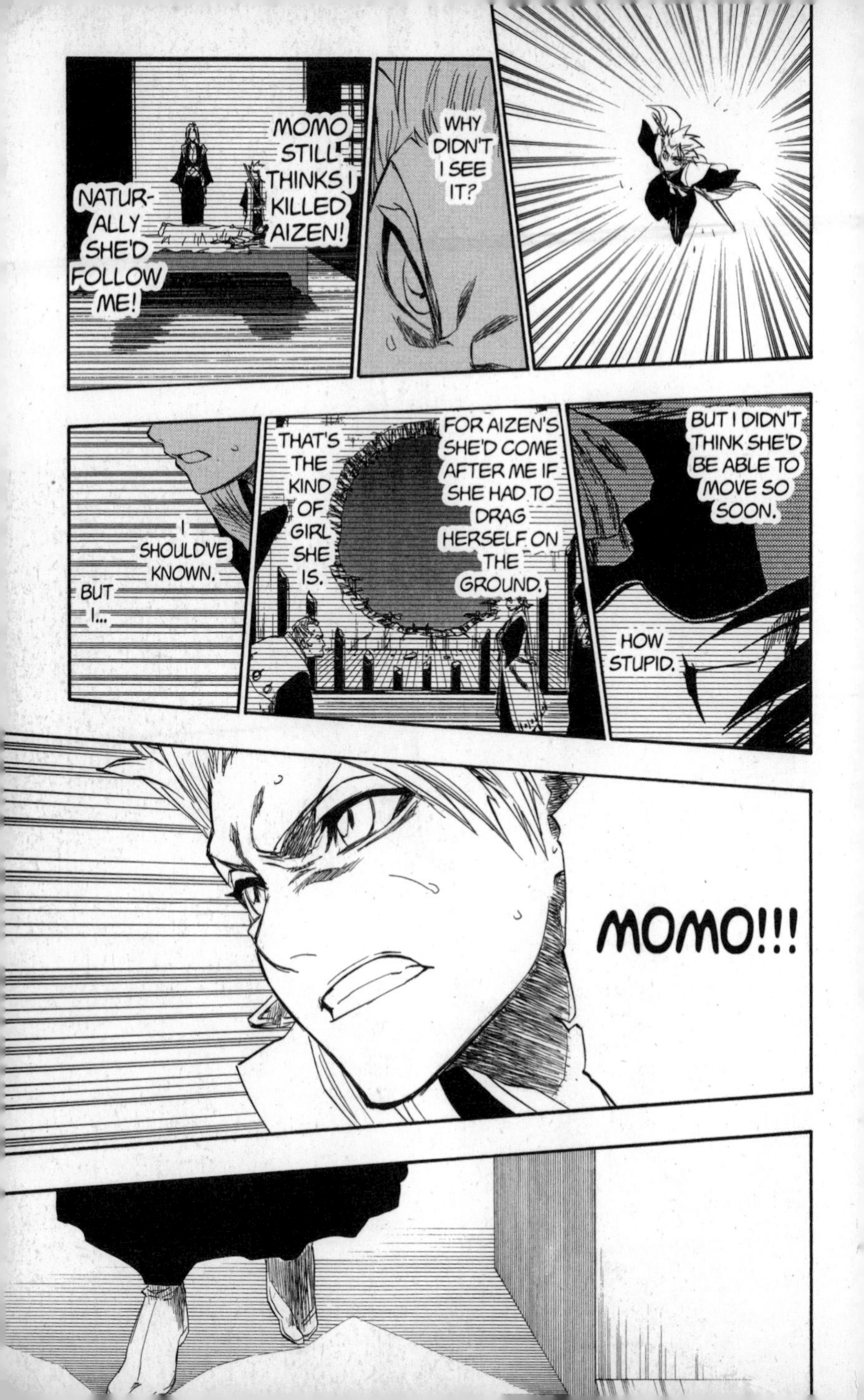
WHY DIDN'T I SEE IT?
MOMO STILL THINKS I KILLED AIZEN!
NATURALLY SHE'D FOLLOW ME!
BUT I DIDN'T THINK SHE'D BE ABLE TO MOVE SO SOON.
HOW STUPID.
FOR AIZEN'S SHE'D COME AFTER ME IF SHE HAD TO DRAG HERSELF ON THE GROUND.
THAT'S THE KIND OF GIRL SHE IS.
I SHOULD'VE KNOWN.
BUT I...
MOMO!!!

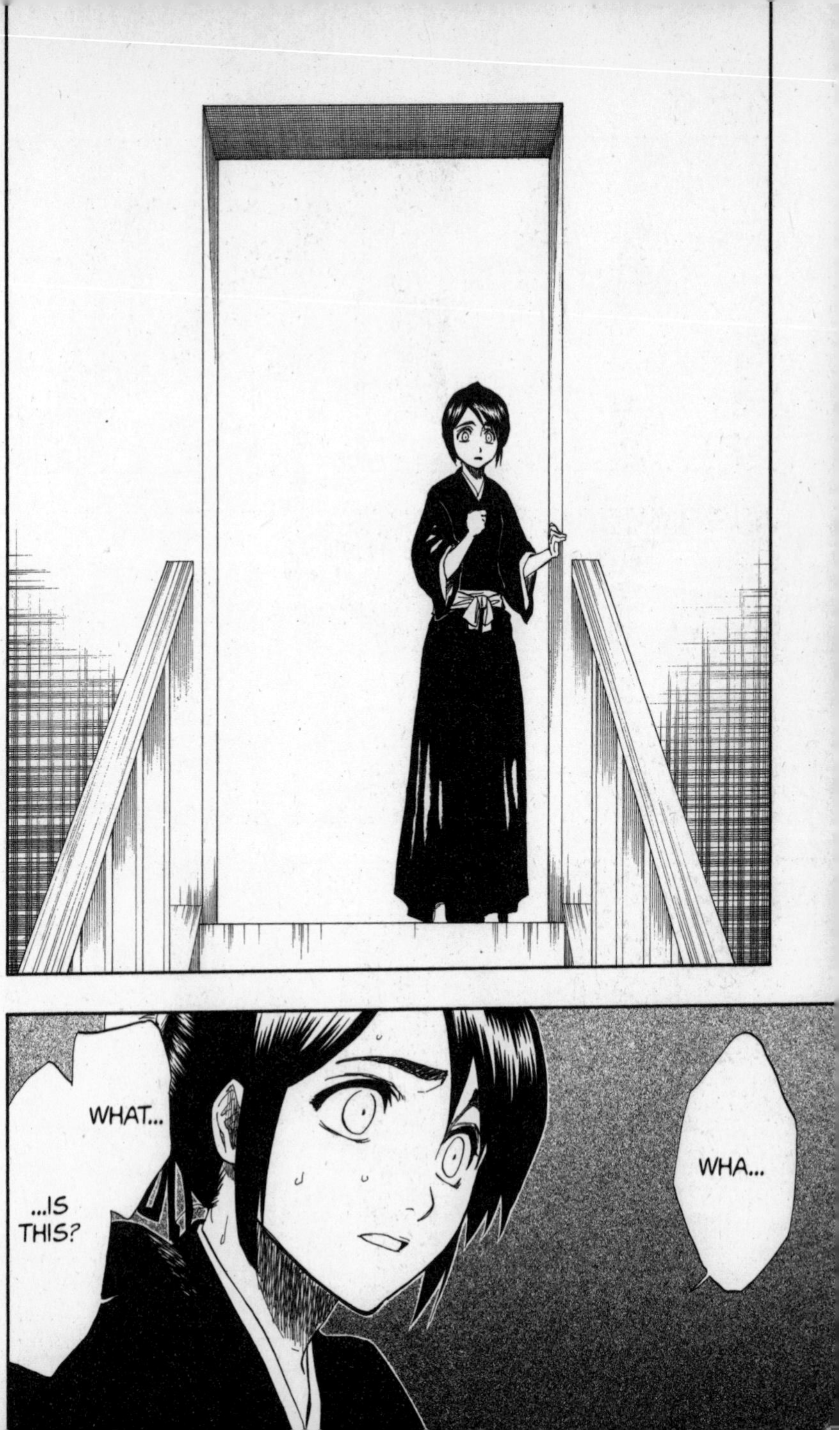
WHA...
WHAT...
...IS THIS?

READ THIS WAY

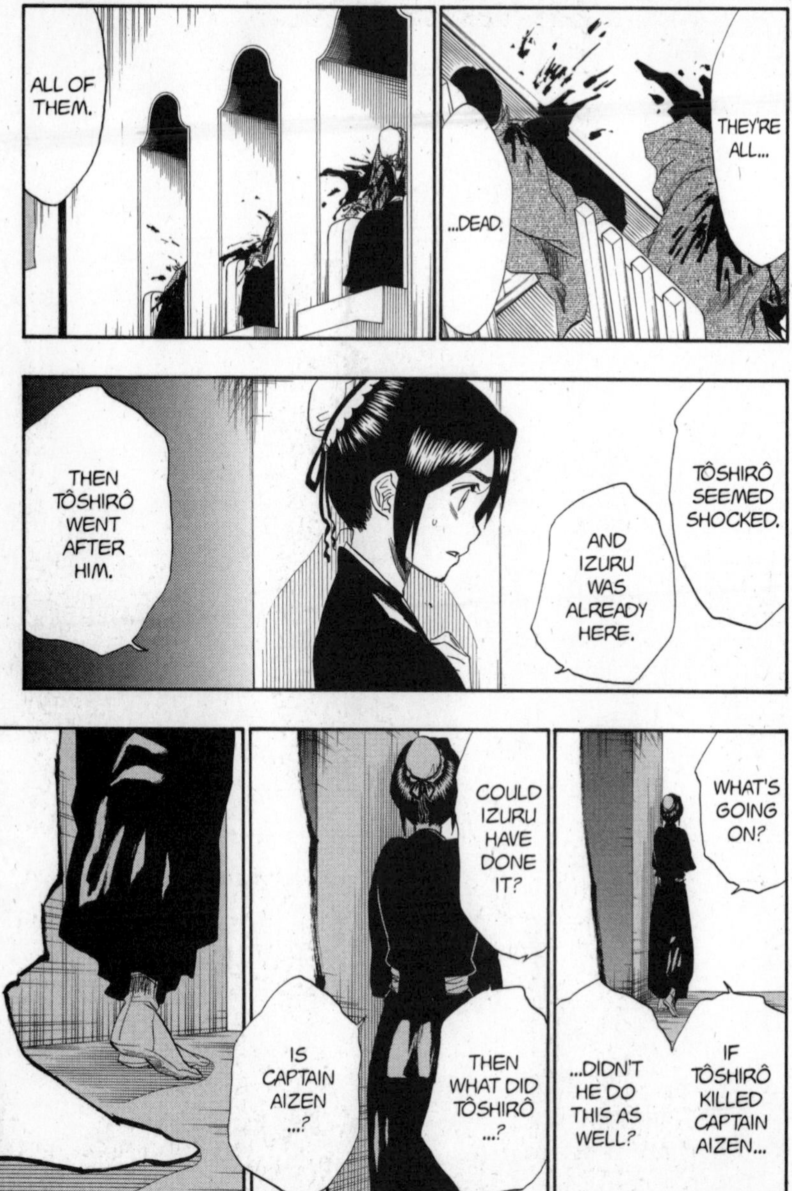
THEY'RE ALL...
...DEAD.
ALL OF THEM.
TÔSHIRÔ SEEMED SHOCKED.
AND IZURU WAS ALREADY HERE.
THEN TÔSHIRÔ WENT AFTER HIM.
WHAT'S GOING ON?
IF TÔSHIRÔ KILLED CAPTAIN AIZEN...
...DIDN'T HE DO THIS AS WELL?
COULD IZURU HAVE DONE IT?
THEN WHAT DID TÔSHIRÔ ...?
IS CAPTAIN AIZEN ...?

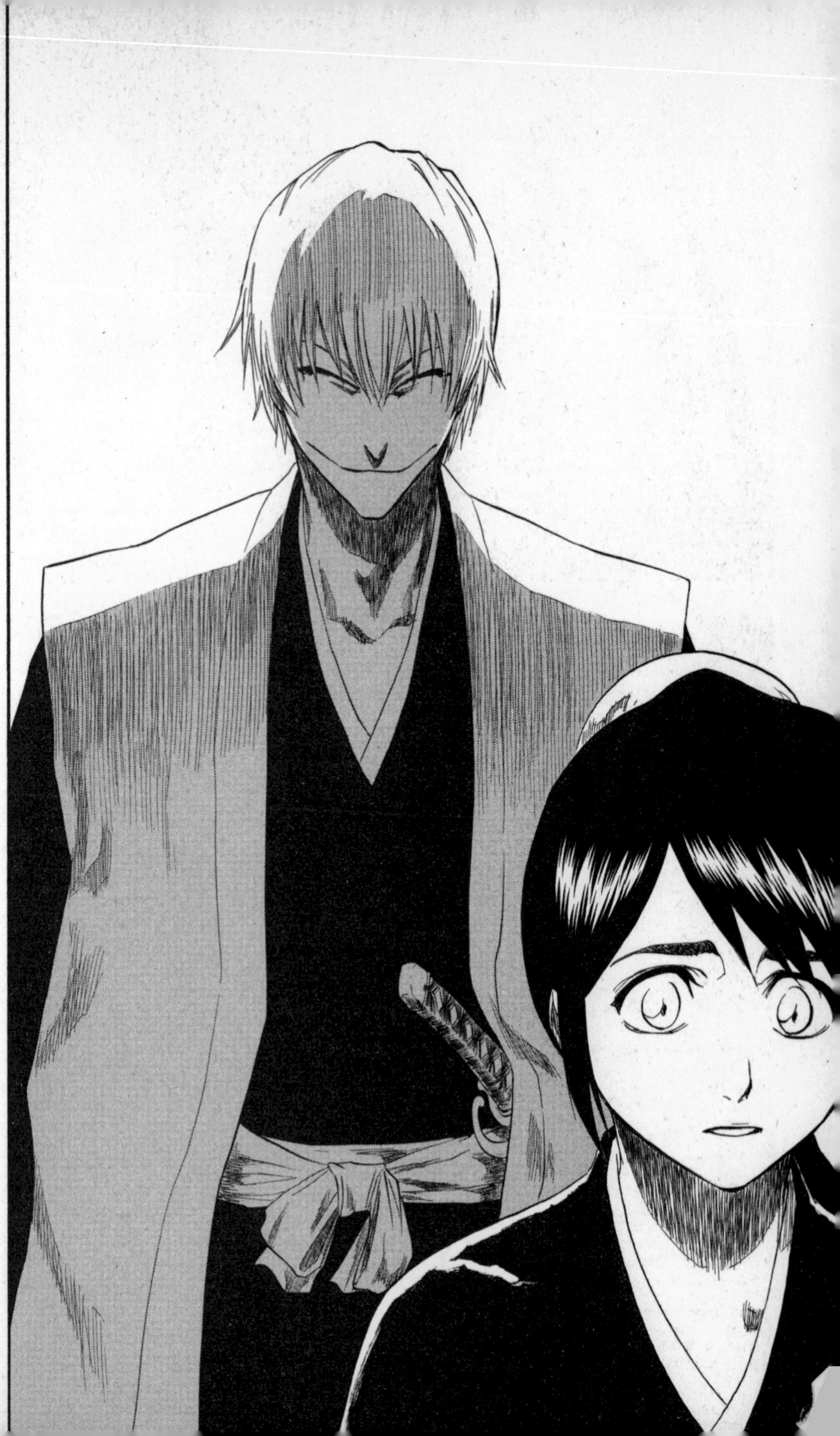

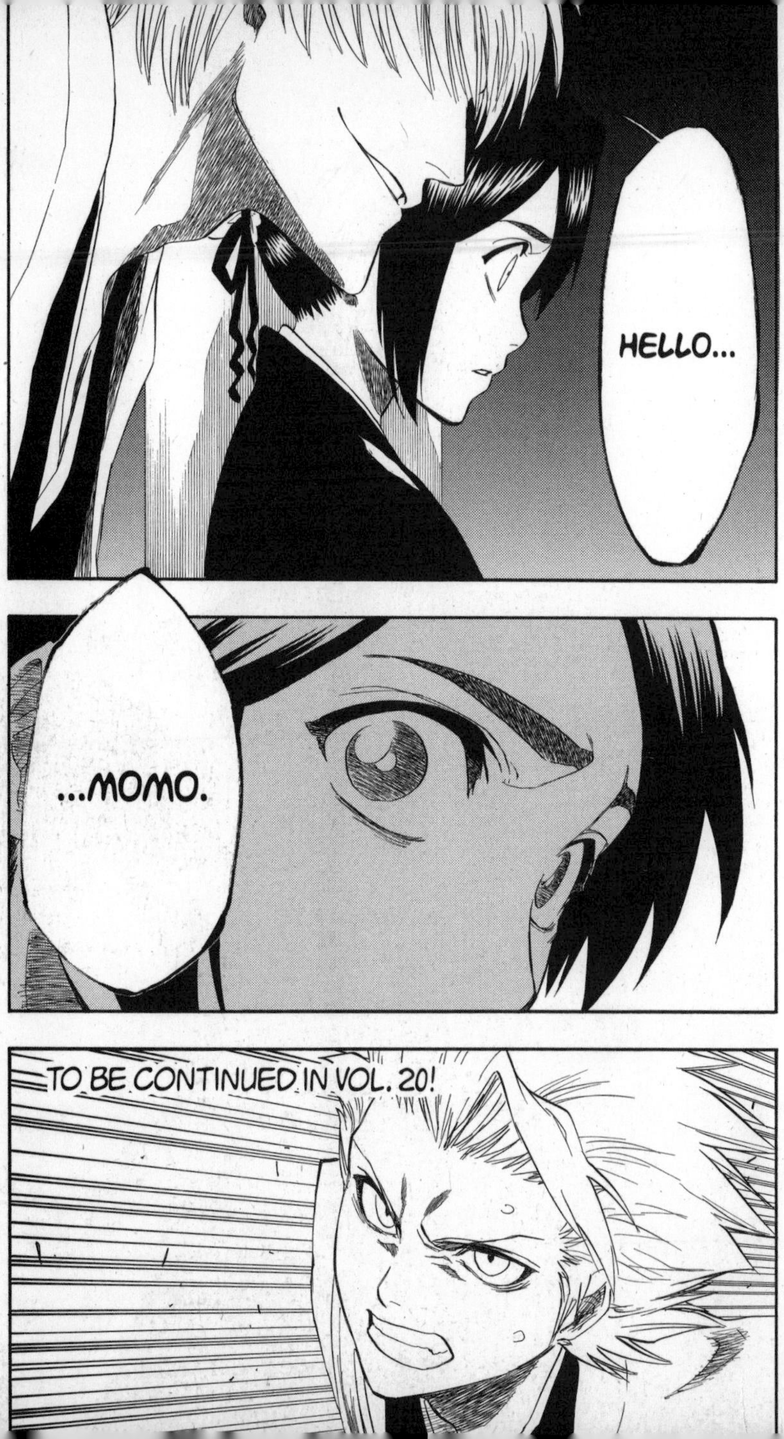
HELLO...
...MOMO.
TO BE CONTINUED IN VOL. 20!

Next Volume Preview

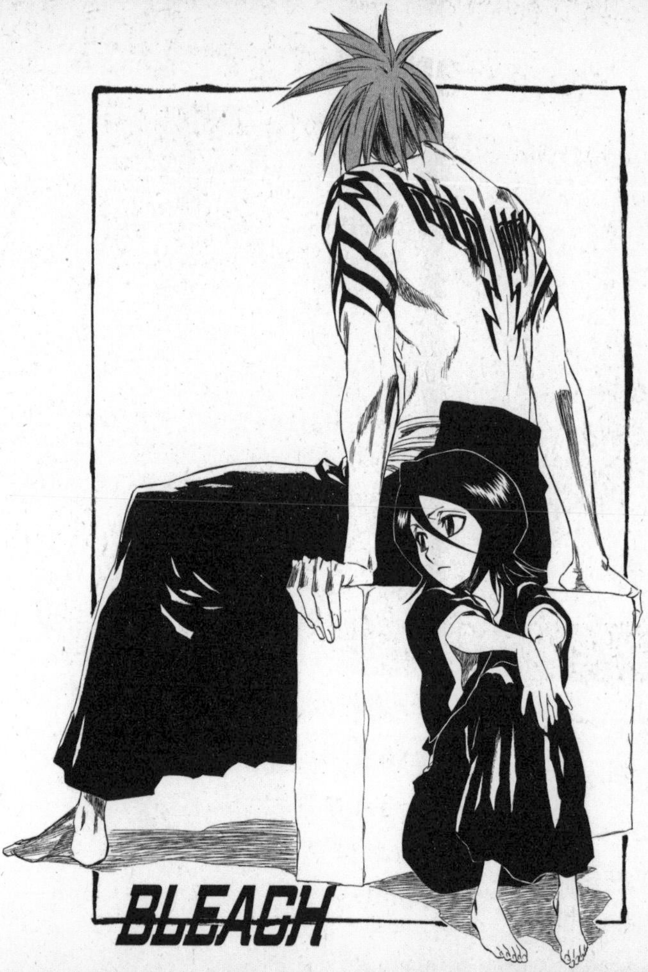
BLEACH

Gin leads Momo to the last person she expects to see—someone who will finally reveal to her the identity of the mastermind behind the Central 46 massacre and the plot against the Soul Society!

Available Now

Read where
the ninja action
began in the
manga

Fiction based
on your favorite
characters'
adventures

JOURNEY INTO THE
WORLD OF NARUTO BOOKS!

Hardcover art
book with full-
color images,
a Masashi
Kishimoto
interview and
a double-sided
poster

 RATED T FOR TEEN ratings.viz.com

 VIZ media www.viz.com

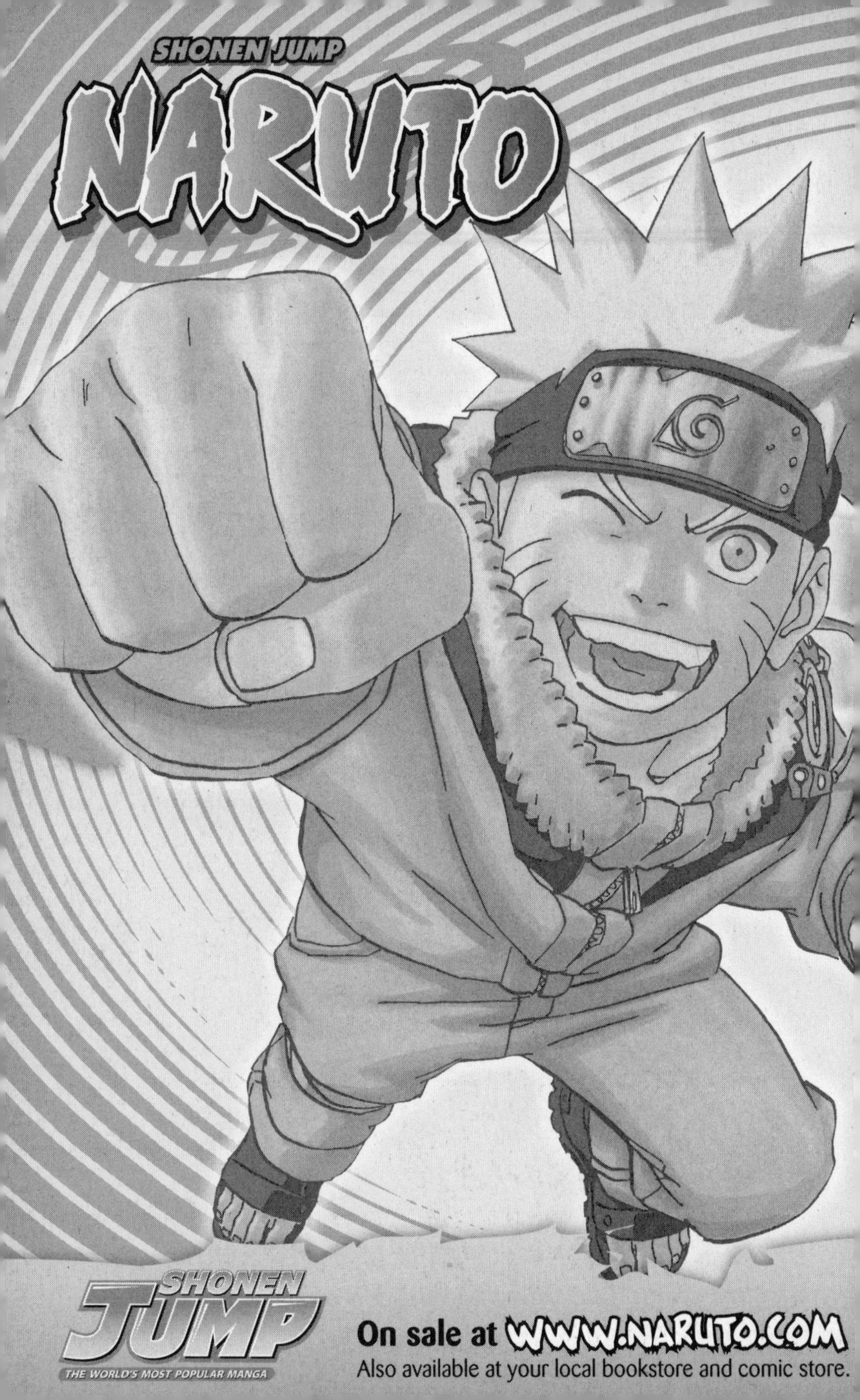
SHONEN JUMP
NARUTO
SHONEN JUMP
THE WORLD'S MOST POPULAR MANGA
On sale at WWW.NARUTO.COM
Also available at your local bookstore and comic store.

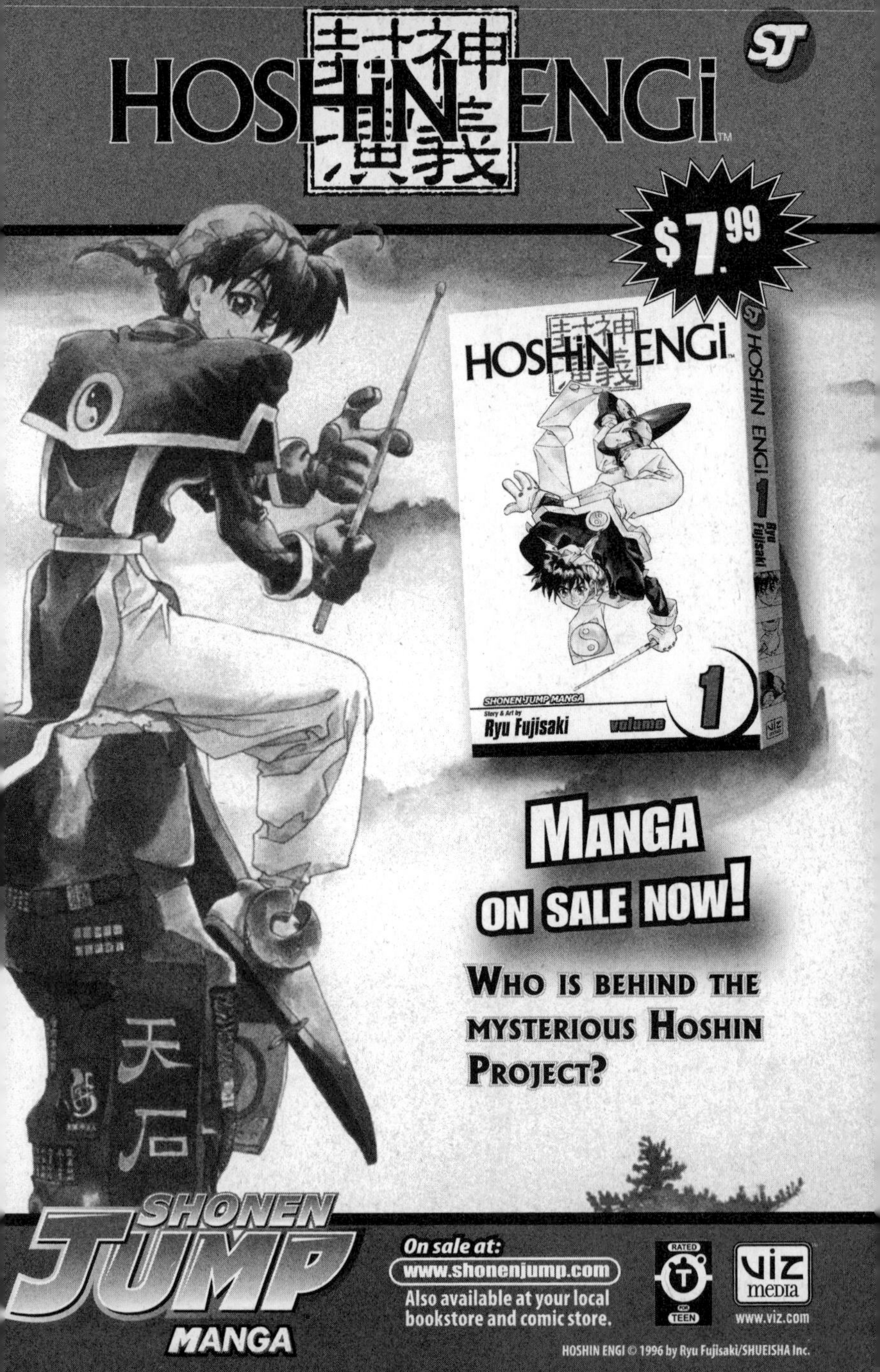
HOSHIN ENGI™
SJ
$7.99
HOSHIN ENGI
SHONEN JUMP MANGA
Story & Art by
Ryu Fujisaki
volume 1
MANGA
ON SALE NOW!
WHO IS BEHIND THE MYSTERIOUS HOSHIN PROJECT?
SHONEN JUMP MANGA
On sale at:
www.shonenjump.com
Also available at your local bookstore and comic store.
RATED T FOR TEEN
viz media
www.viz.com
HOSHIN ENGI © 1996 by Ryu Fujisaki/SHUEISHA Inc.

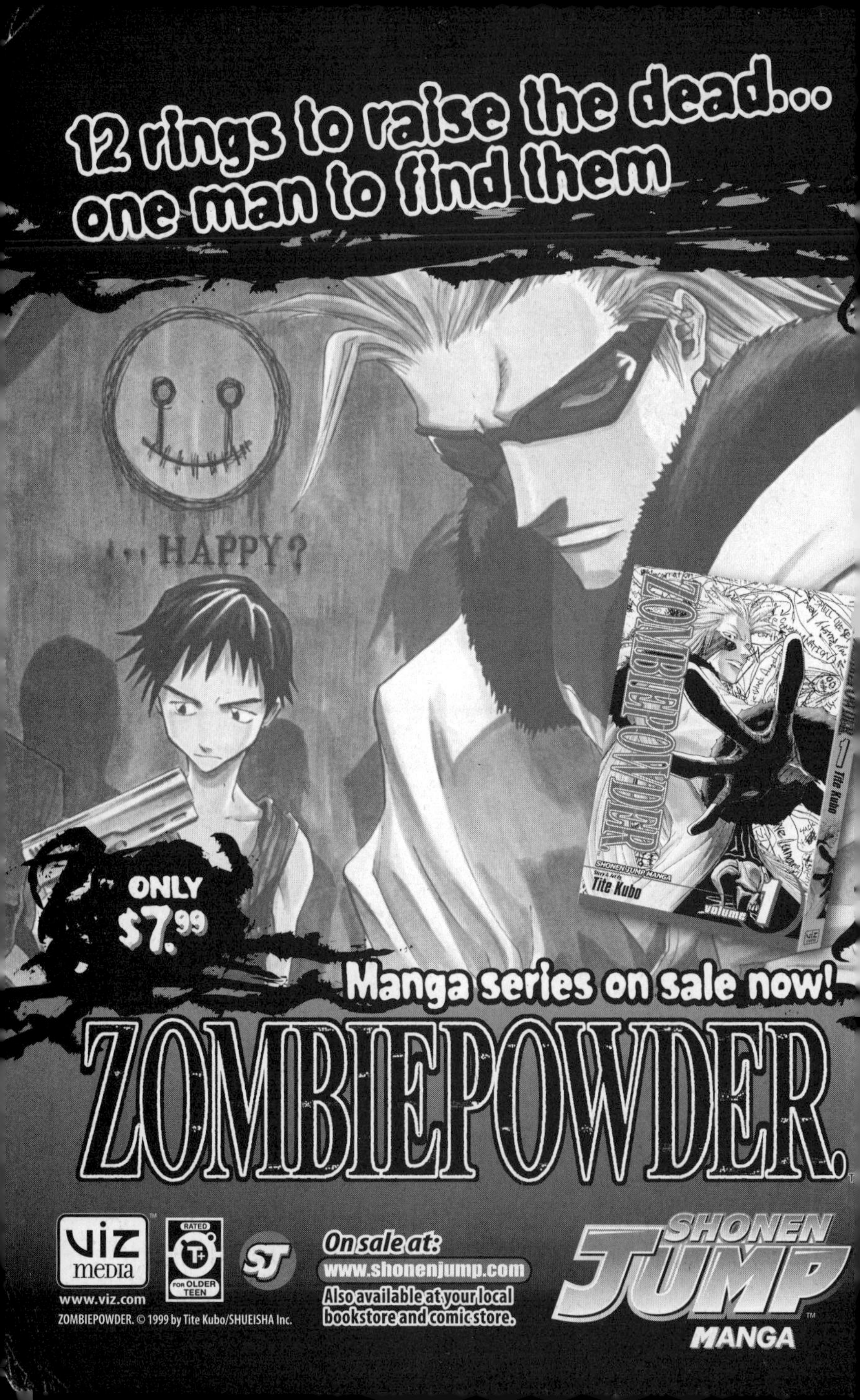

12 rings to raise the dead...
one man to find them
...HAPPY?
ONLY $7.99
ZOMBIEPOWDER.
SHONEN JUMP MANGA
Story & Art by Tite Kubo
volume 1
Manga series on sale now!
ZOMBIEPOWDER.
viz media
www.viz.com
RATED T+ FOR OLDER TEEN
SJ
On sale at:
www.shonenjump.com
Also available at your local bookstore and comic store.
SHONEN JUMP MANGA
ZOMBIEPOWDER. © 1999 by Tite Kubo/SHUEISHA Inc.

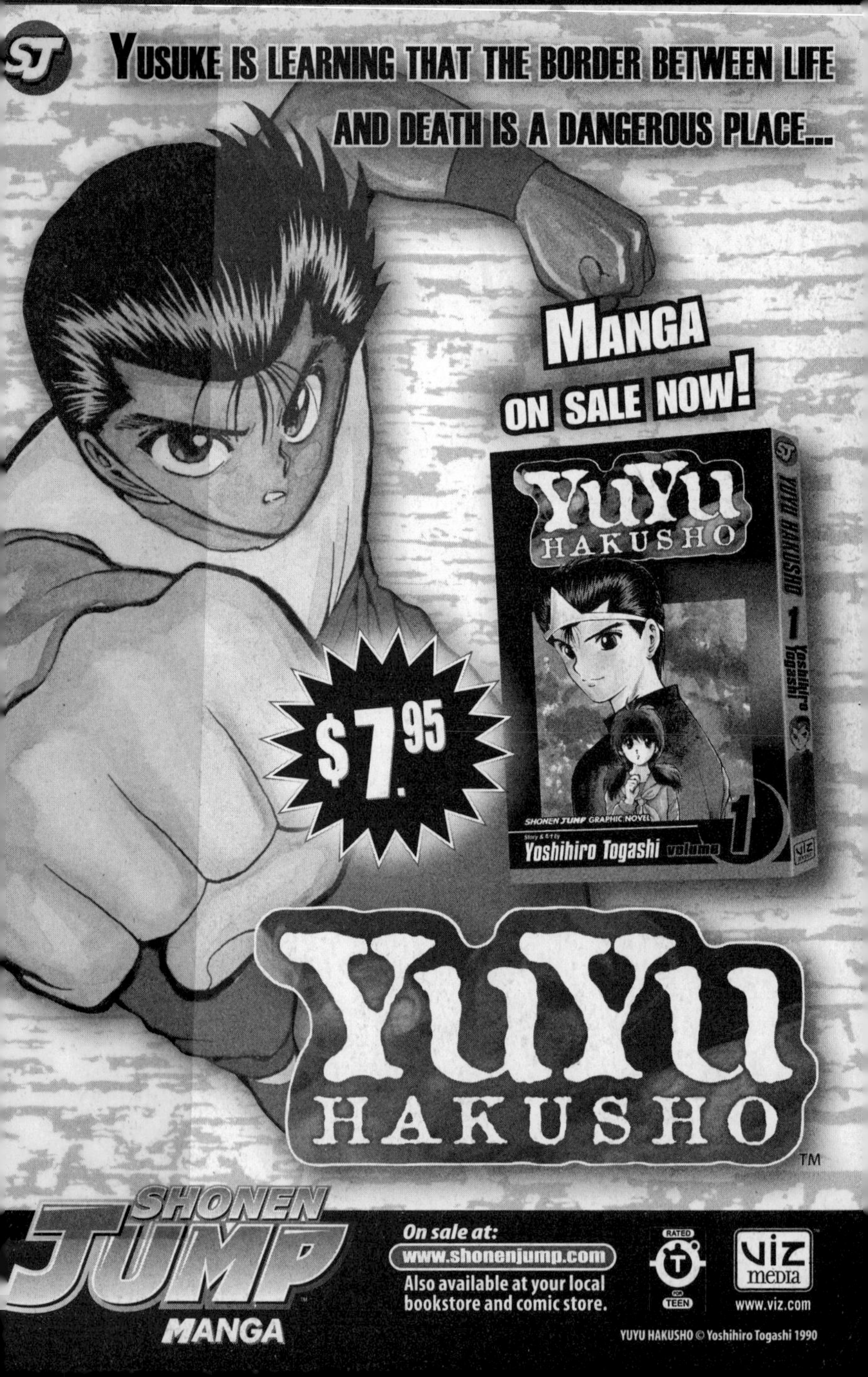
SJ
YUSUKE IS LEARNING THAT THE BORDER BETWEEN LIFE
AND DEATH IS A DANGEROUS PLACE...
MANGA
ON SALE NOW!
YuYu HAKUSHO
YUYU HAKUSHO 1 Yoshihiro Togashi
SHONEN JUMP GRAPHIC NOVEL
Yoshihiro Togashi volume 1
$7.95
YuYu HAKUSHO
TM
SHONEN JUMP MANGA
On sale at:
www.shonenjump.com
Also available at your local
bookstore and comic store.
RATED T FOR TEEN
viz media
www.viz.com
YUYU HAKUSHO © Yoshihiro Togashi 1990

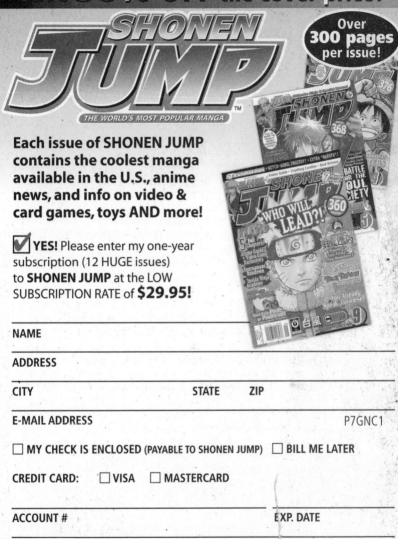